STEFAN SOELL

VOLCANIC GIRLS

Third Edition revised and enlarged

EDITION Skylight

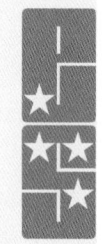

3rd Edition in Paperback
revised and enlarged
2025

Copyright © 2011
by Edition Skylight

EDITION SKYLIGHT
Rosengartenstr. 13B
CH-8608 Bubikon / Zürich
Switzerland
info@edition-skylight.com
www.edition-skylight.com

ISBN 978-3-03766-709-5

Please also visit: www.stefansoell.de

Design: Weiß-Freiburg GmbH – Graphik & Buchgestaltung
Übersetzung: Eugene Edwards

Printed in Bosnia and Herzegovina

VOLCANIC GIRLS is the title of this book by the renowned German photographer Stefan Soell. It is a collection of some of the finest modern nude photography. Stefan Soell's works are characterised by their striking quality, and ability to offer a glimpse into the personalities of his models. He captures their beauty at some awe-inspiring natural locations, where he combines art with the glory of nature. The location selected for this unique collection is Lanzarote, a small but beautiful island off the coast of north-east Africa.

It is beauty that tickles our fancy, arouses our moral sensibilities and lets us become who we truly are through revealing to us our identity and true potential, and by freeing us from the shackles that were instilled into our minds by a lifetime of negative forces. Beauty is nature's most powerful tool. It can be as violent as a hurricane, and yet as gentle as a summer breeze. The unique effect it has on each of us is what makes beauty a profound and highly personal experience.

Responding to beauty is an exercise of the mind, a wholesome meditation that is both revealing and powerful. Beauty has the power to heal the life's scars, which is why it is so fascinating.

This book is unique in being composed of hand-picked images from more than five years of work; it represents a glimpse of the beauty that Stefan Soell sees. There is an unrivalled attention to detail. Each nude photograph is accompanied by a still-life that both complements it, and also reveals something hidden in the main photograph. Going through this book is a journey of personal discovery. The images clearly represent a sincere journey by beautiful women who are brave enough to share their beauty and their connection with nature with the world. We can learn a lot by listening to nature's whispers and by learning from her greatest work of art, the human form, patiently represented here to create the most inspiring lesson of all.

David Roland

VOLCANIC GIRLS, das neue Buch des renommierten Fotografen Stefan Soell, präsentiert moderne Aktfotografie vom Feinsten. Stefan Soells Arbeiten zeichnen sich durch ihre bemerkenswerte Qualität aus und gewähren dem Betrachter einen flüchtigen Blick auf die Persönlichkeiten seiner Modelle. Er fängt ihre Schönheit an atemberaubenden Orten ein, wo er Kunst mit der Herrlichkeit der Natur vereint. Die Bilder für diese einmalige Zwusammenstellung entstanden auf Lanzarote, der wunderschönen kleinen Insel vor der nordostafrikanischen Küste. Schönheit beflügelt unsere Fantasie, spricht unser moralisches Feingefühl an; sie läßt uns zu den Menschen werden, die wir wirklich sind, indem sie uns unsere Identität und unser wahres Potential offenbart und uns von den Ketten befreit, mit denen negative Mächte unseren Geist fesseln wollen. Schönheit ist der Natur mächtigstes Werkzeug. Sie kann so gewaltig sein wie ein Orkan, aber auch sanft wie eine sommerliche Brise. Die einzigartige Wirkung, die sie bei jedem Einzelnen von uns entfaltet, macht sie zu einer tiefgreifenden und höchst individuellen Erfahrung. Schönheit bringt unseren Geist auf Trab und läßt ebenso erhellende wie eindrucksvolle Gedanken entstehen. Der Schönheit wohnt die faszinierende Macht inne, die Wunden zu heilen, die uns das Leben zugefügt hat. Dieser einzigartige Band versammelt handverlesene Bilder aus über 5 Jahren fotografischer Arbeit – ein unter die Haut gehender Eindruck der Schönheit, die Stefan Soell sieht, ergänzt durch Stillleben, die einen verborgenen Aspekt der dazugehörigen Fotografie offenlegen. Soells Gespür fürs Detail sucht seinesgleichen. „Volcanic Girls" entführt sie auf eine ganz persönliche Entdeckungsreise. Die Bilder zeigen wunderschöne Frauen, die den Mut haben, ihre Schönheit und ihre Naturverbundenheit mit der ganzen Welt zu teilen.

Wir können viel von der Natur lernen, wenn wir ihrem Flüstern lauschen und ihr großartigstes Kunstwerk betrachten: den menschlichen Körper, das inspirierendste Lehrstück überhaupt.

David Roland

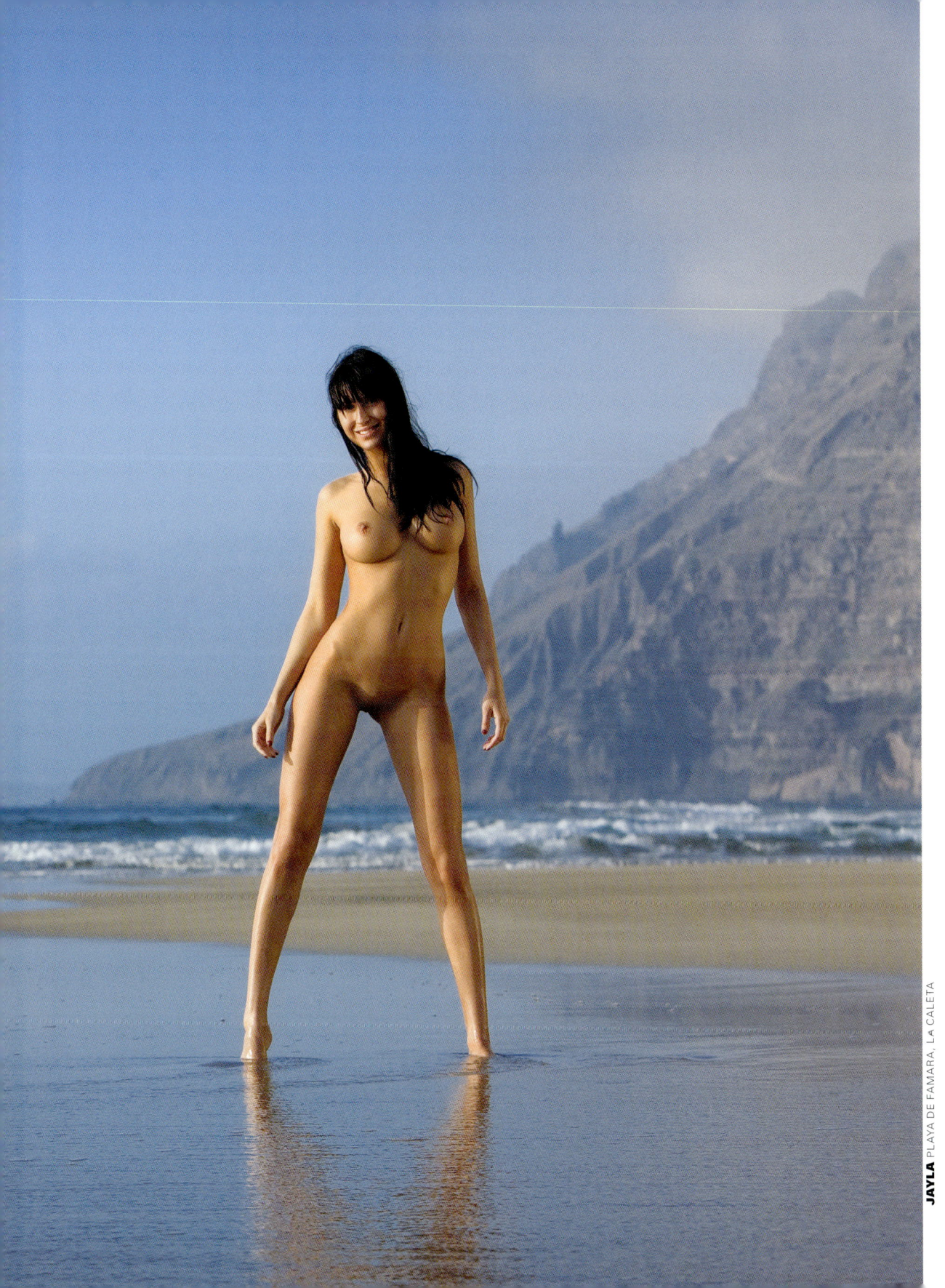

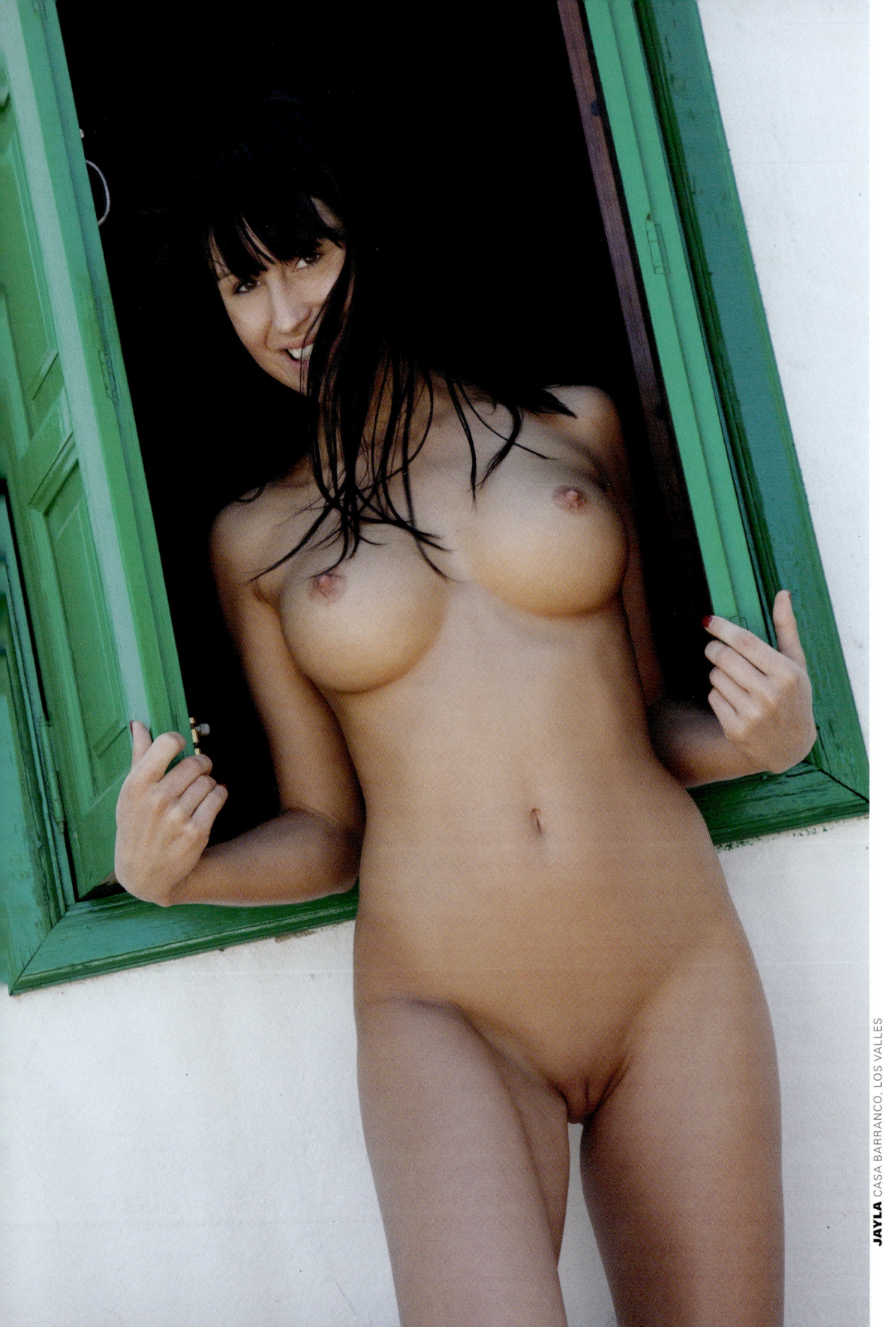

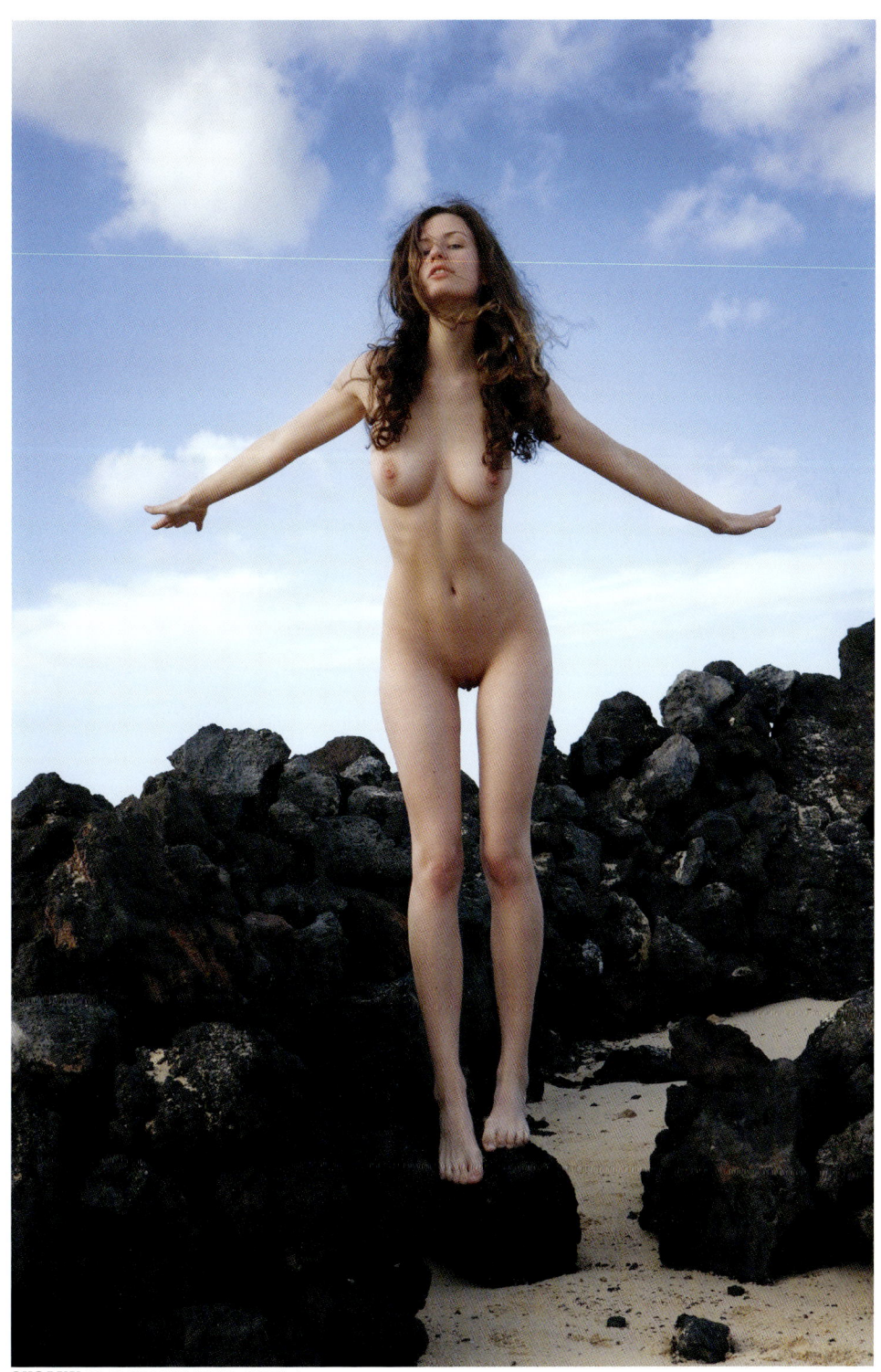

SUSANN BAJO DE LOS SABLES, ORZOLA

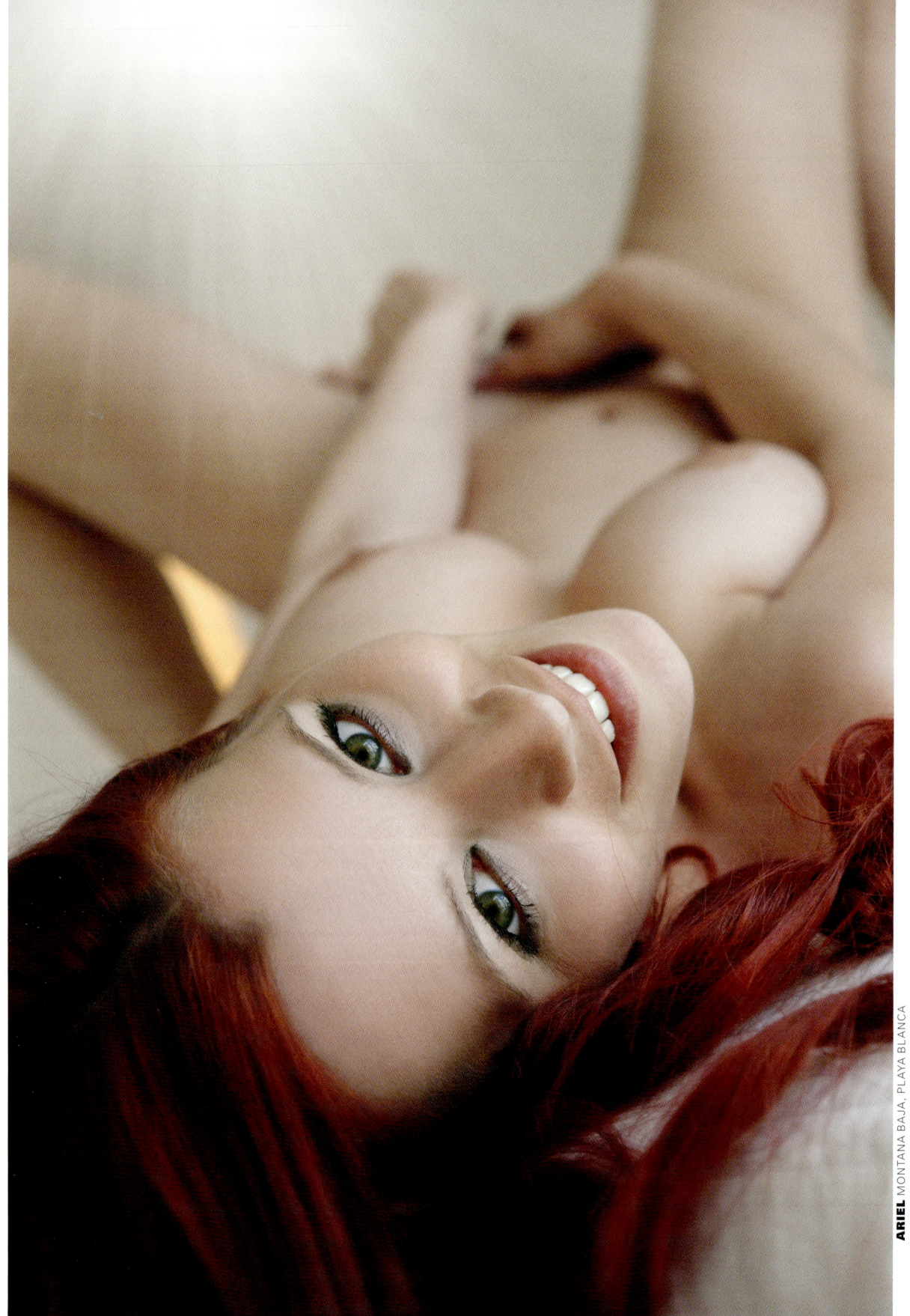

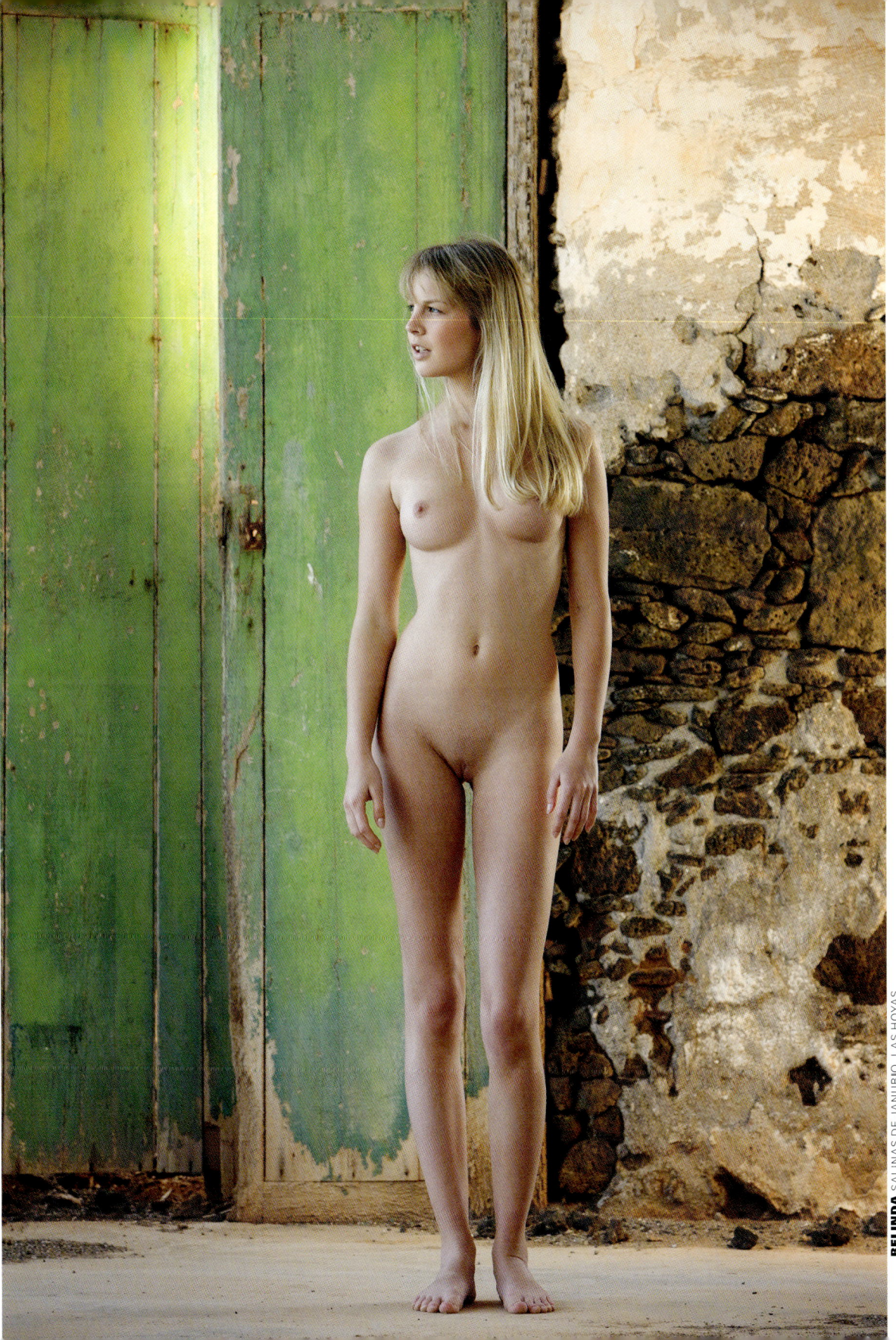

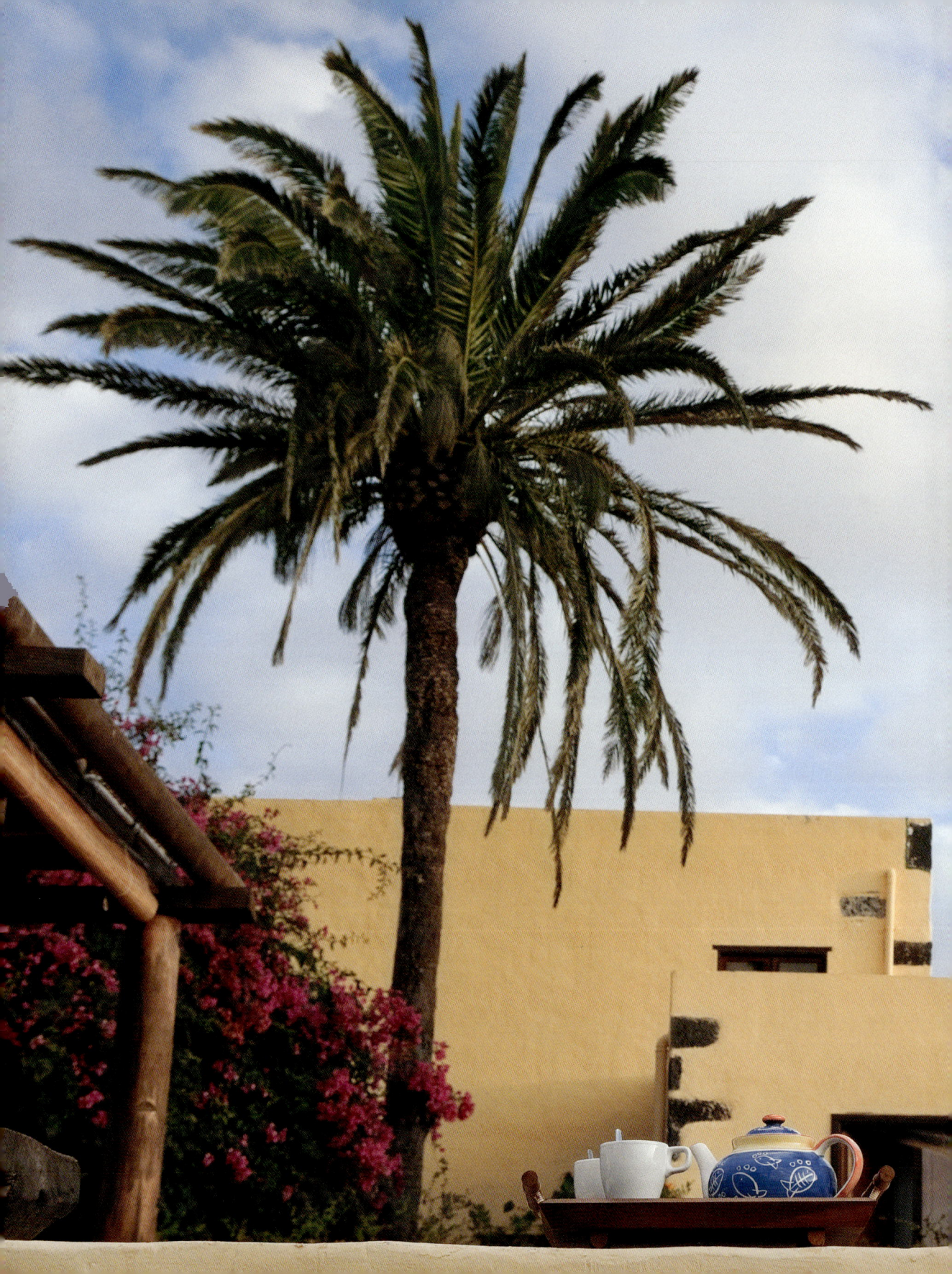

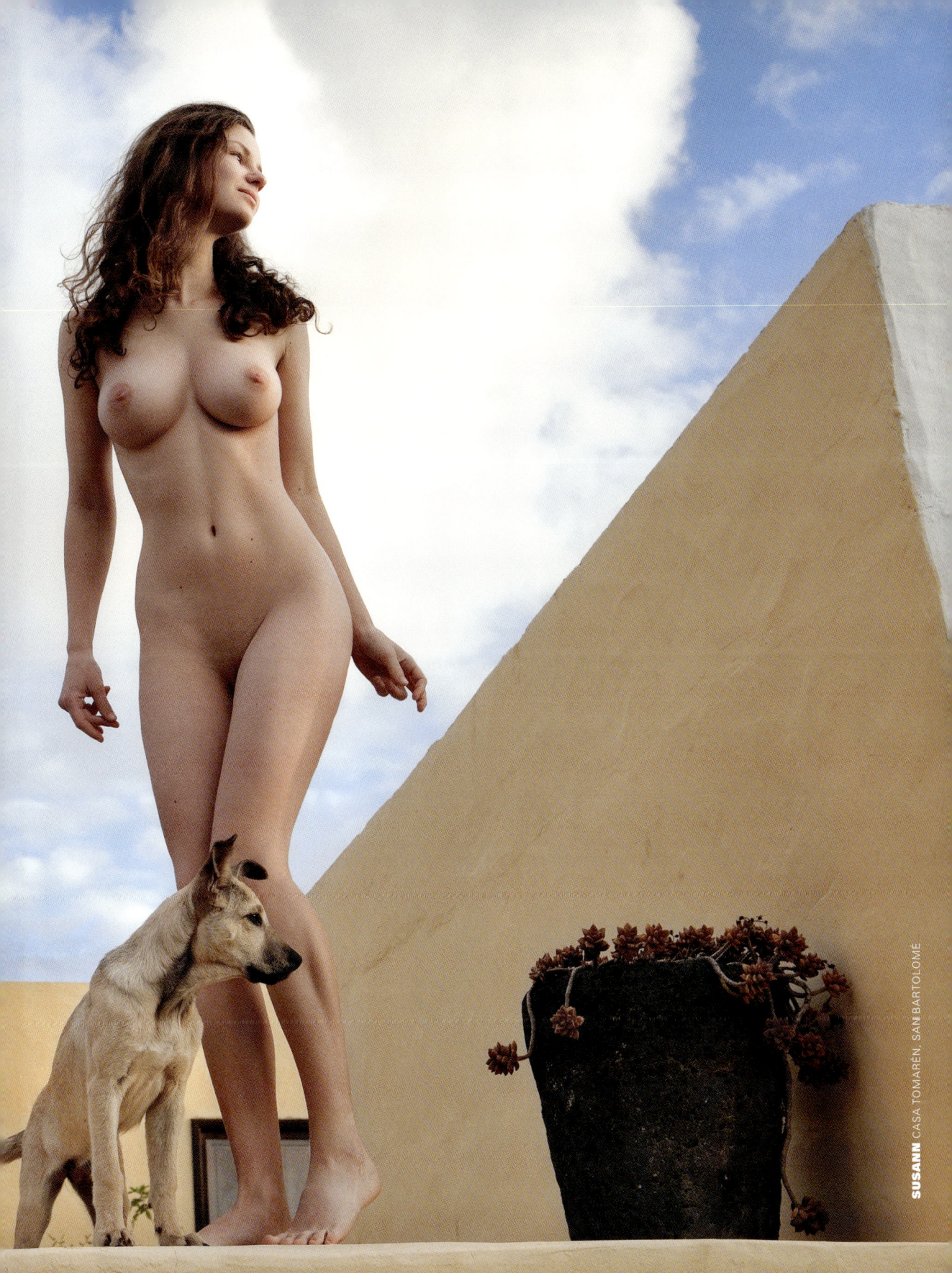

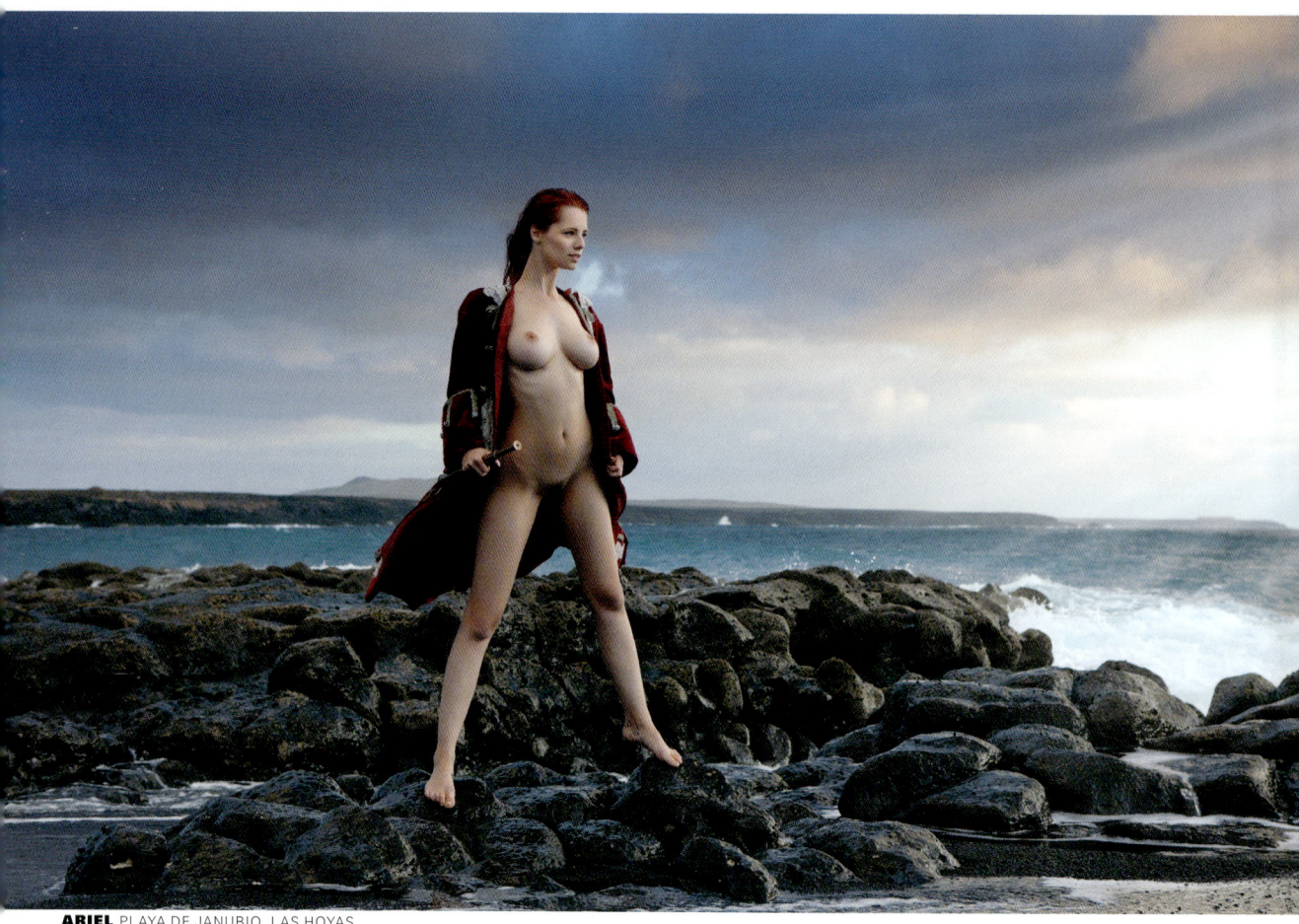

ARIEL PLAYA DE JANUBIO, LAS HOYAS

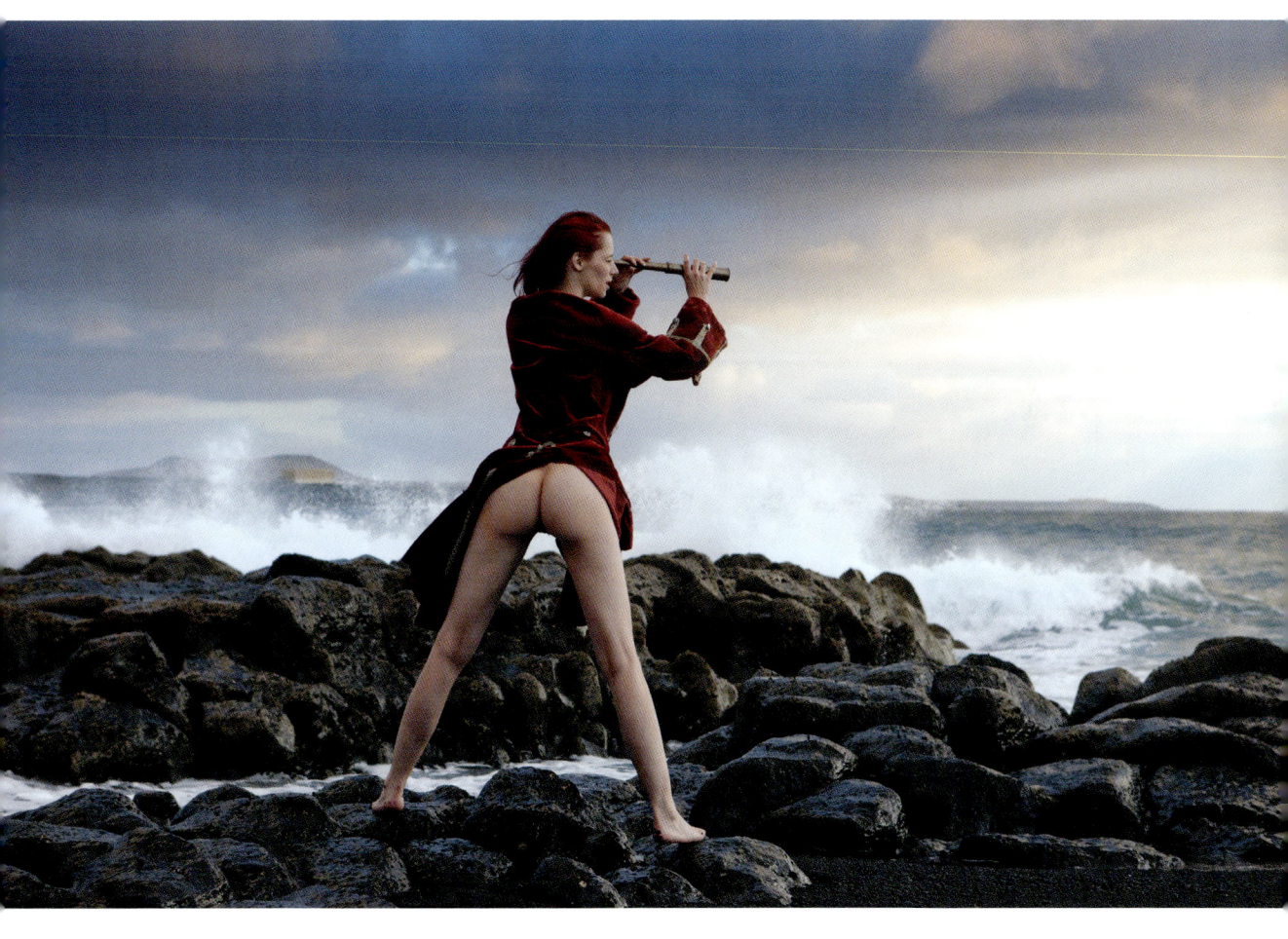

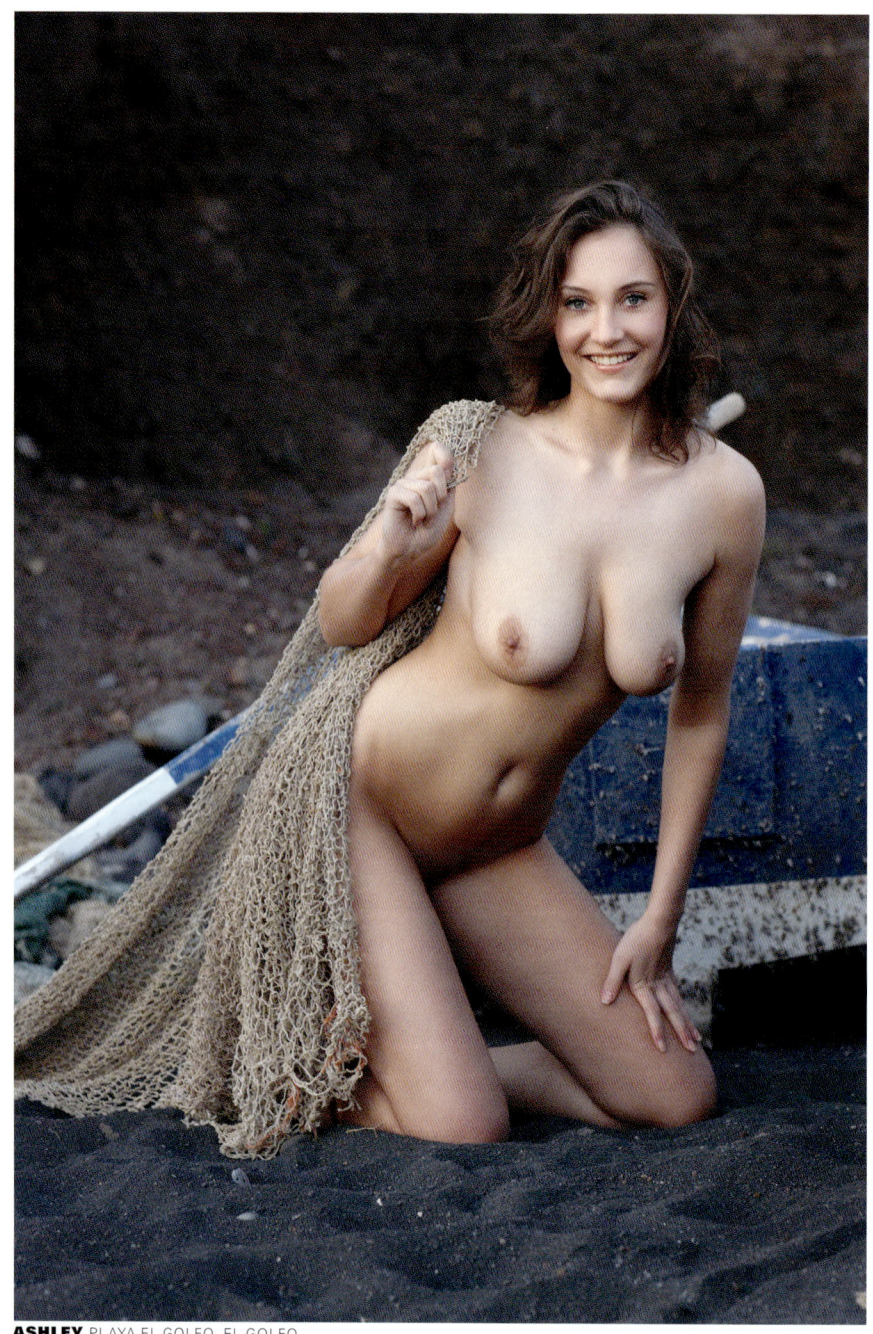

ASHLEY PLAYA EL GOLFO, EL GOLFO

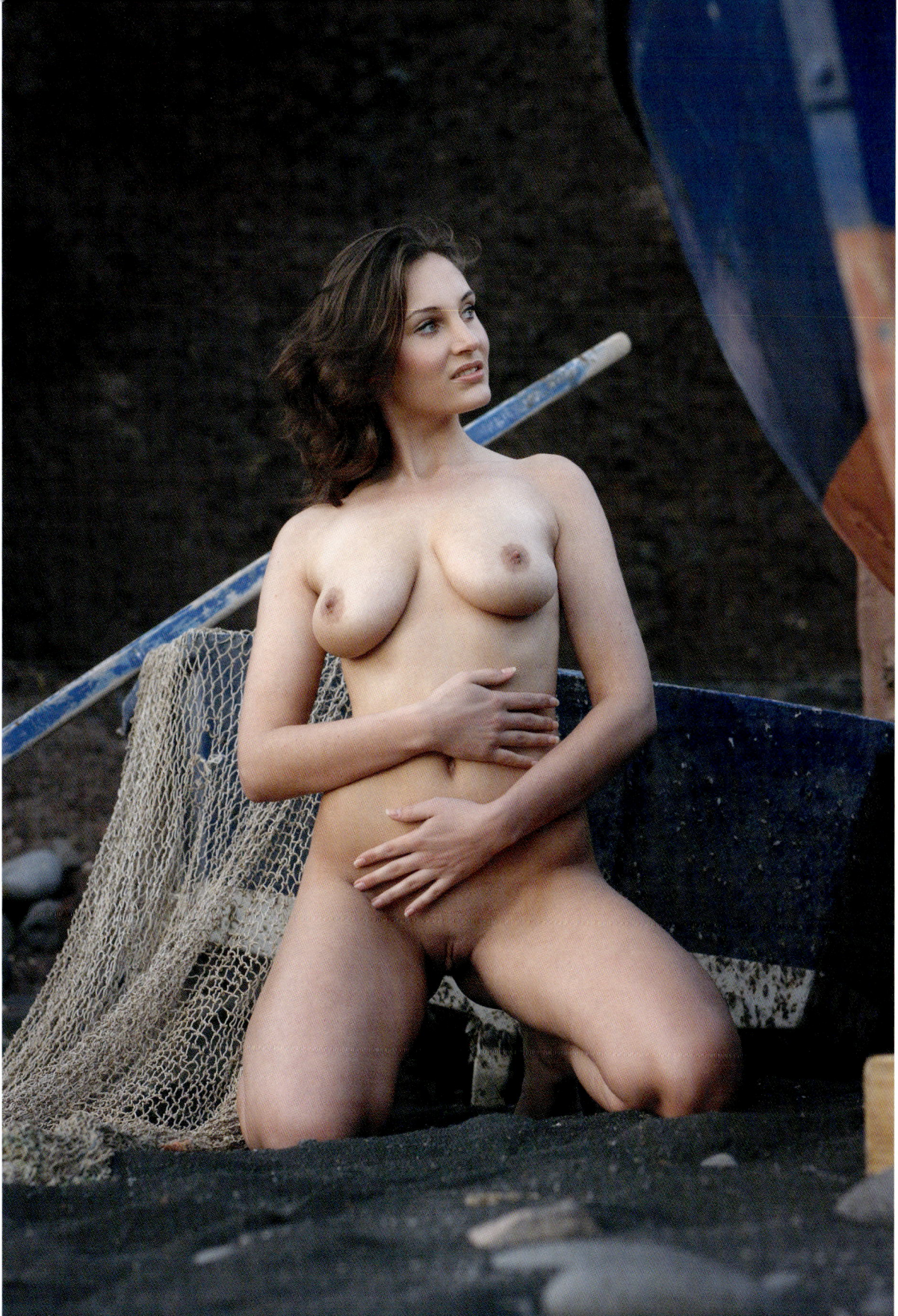

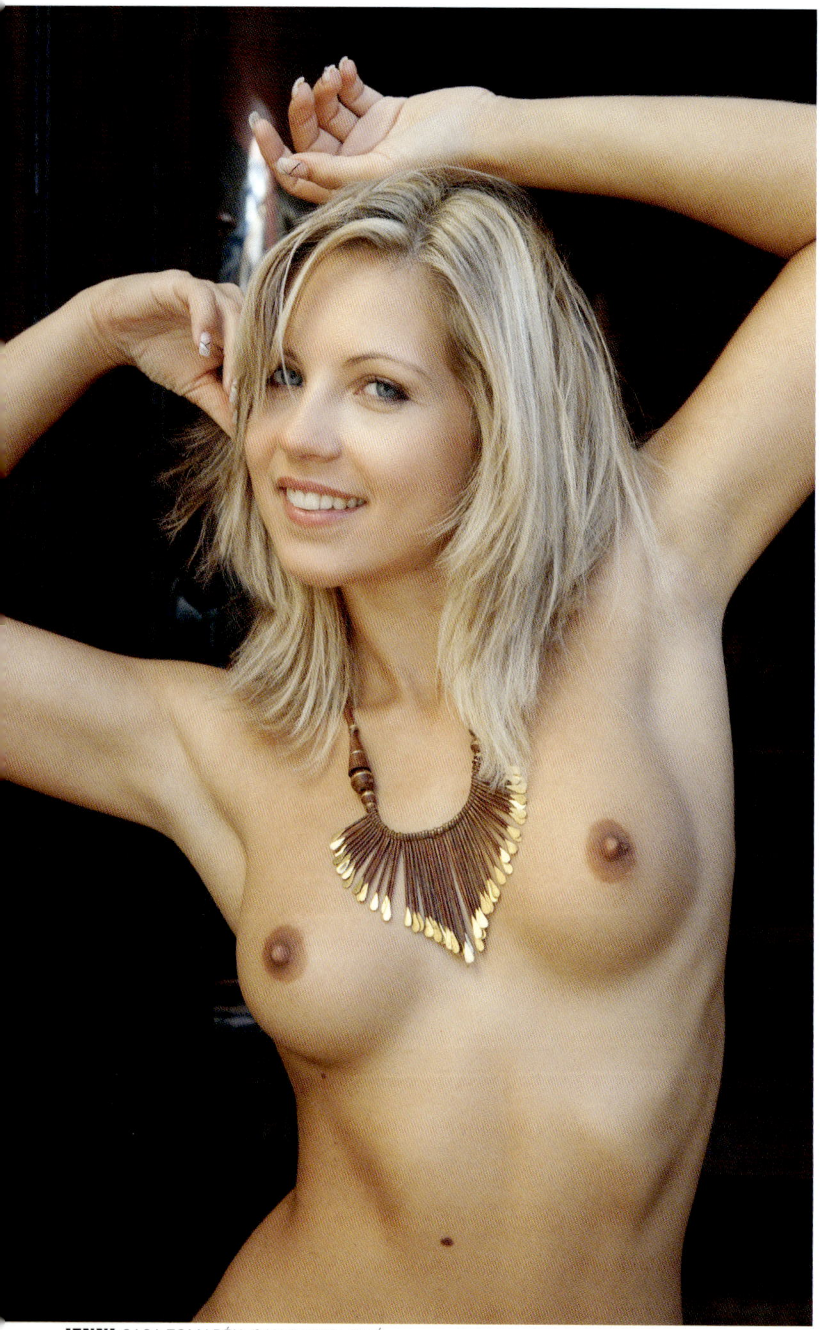

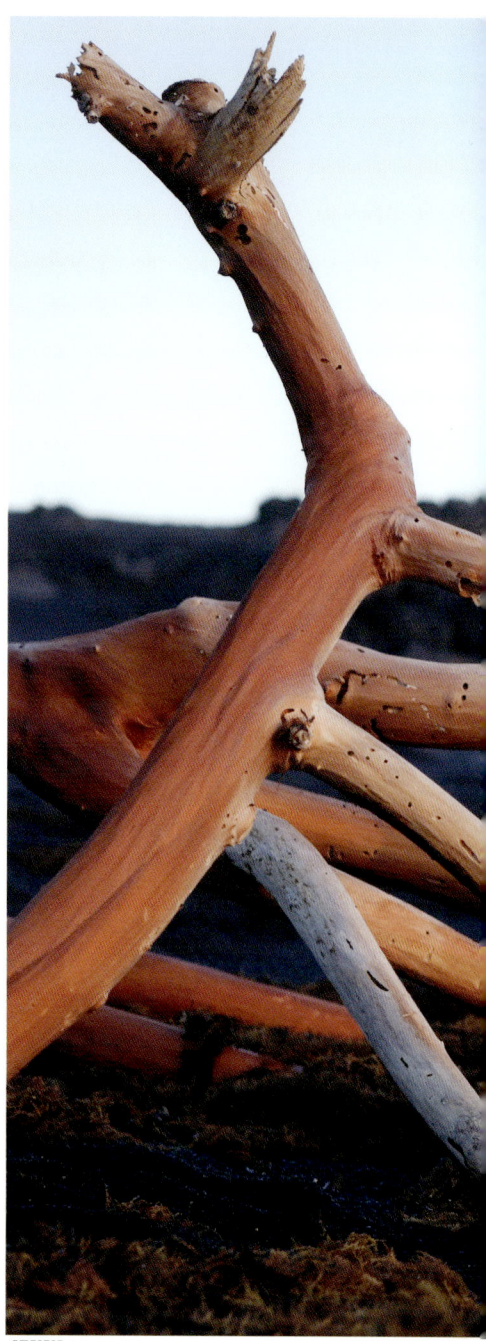

JENNI CASA TOMARÉN, SAN BARTOLOMÉ

JENNI PLAYA DE JANUBIO, LAS HOYAS

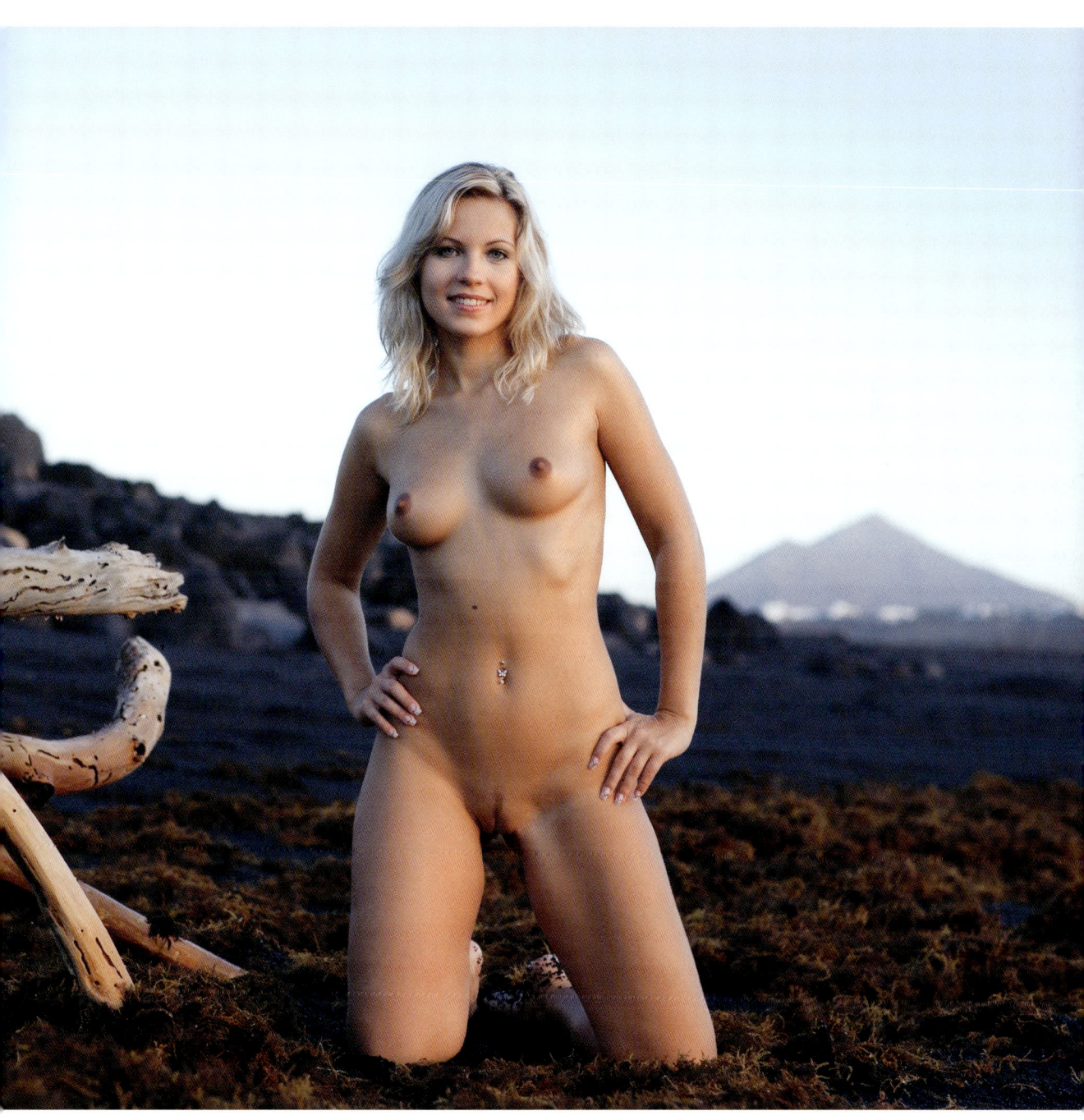

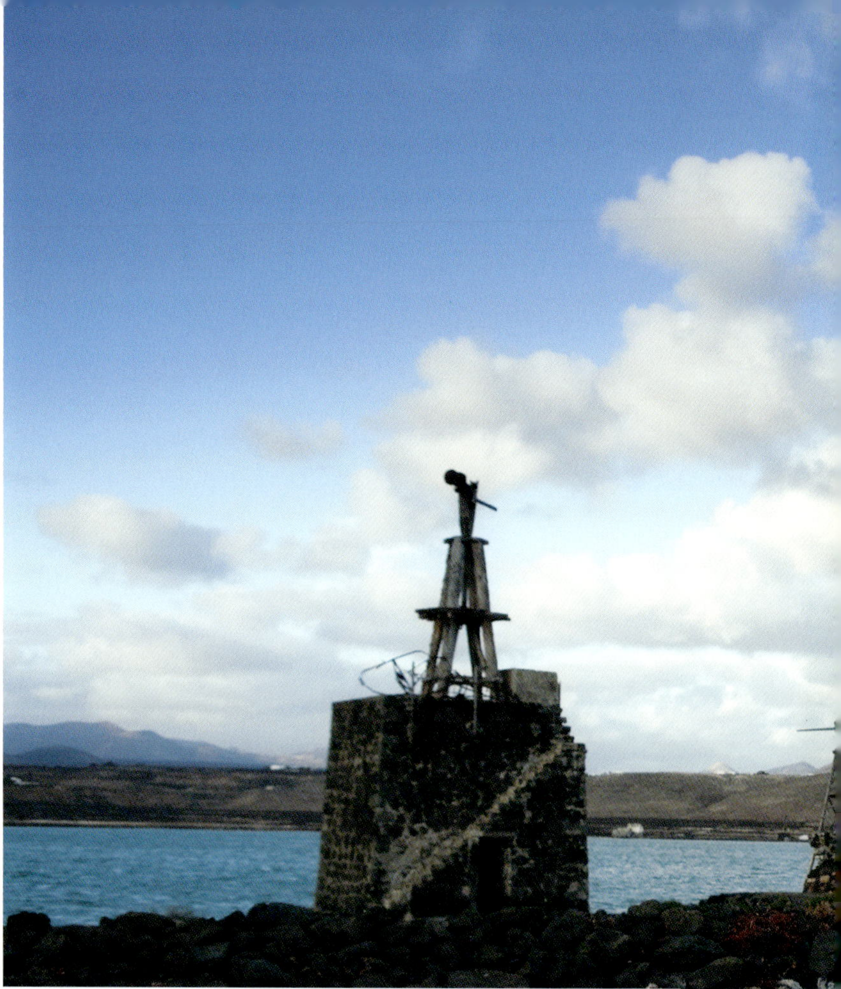
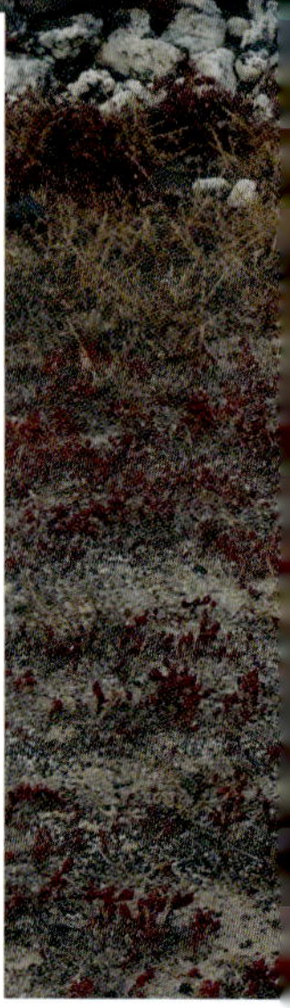
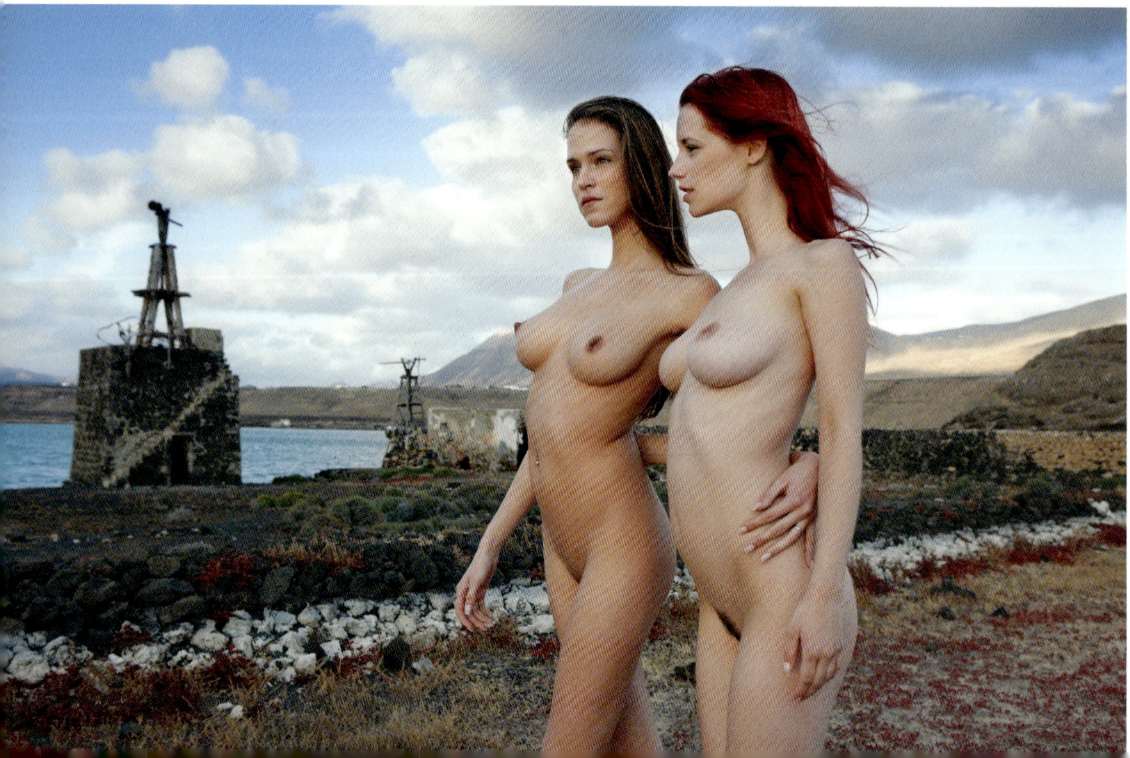

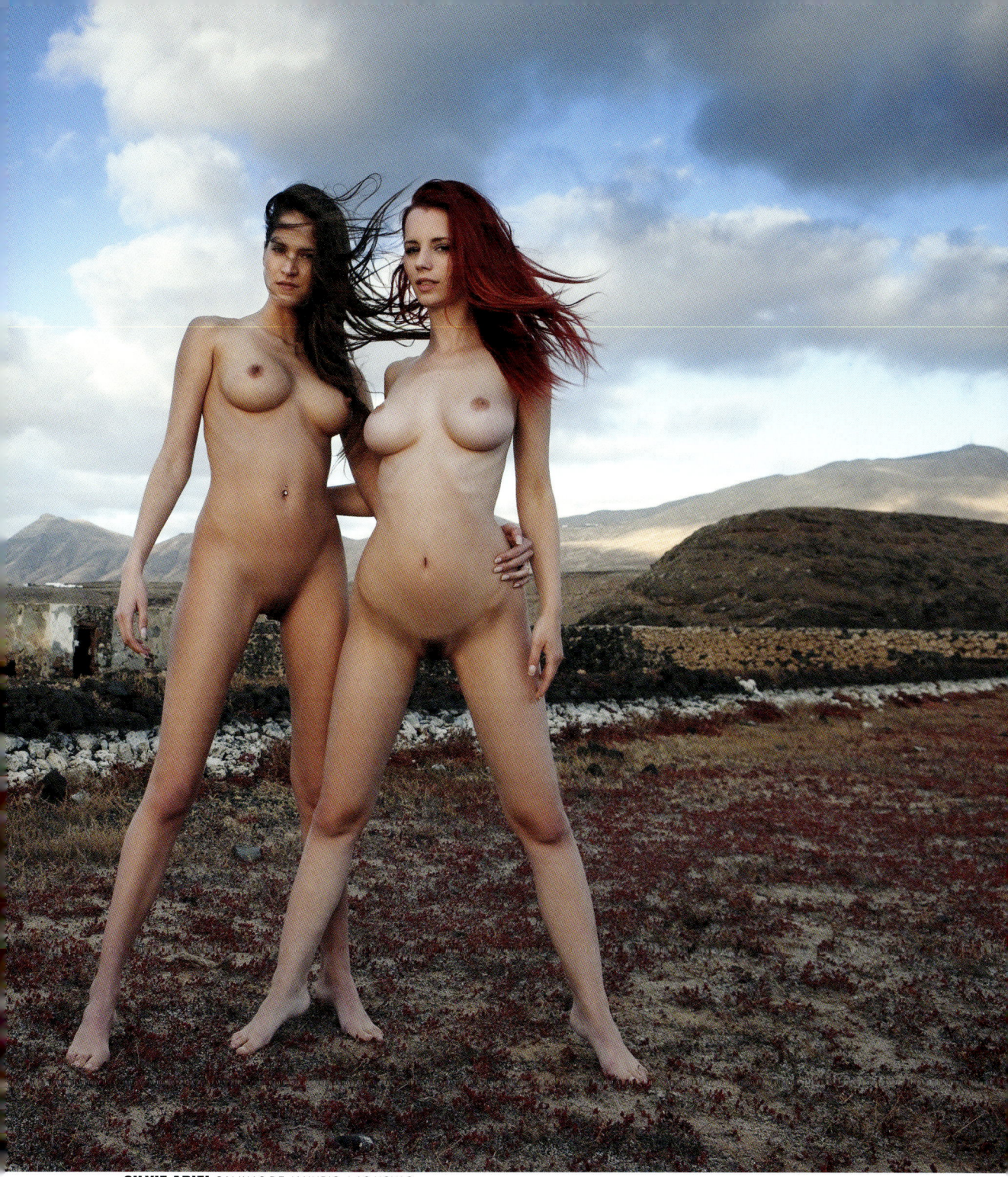

SILVIE ARIEL SALINAS DE JANUBIO, LAS HOYAS

21

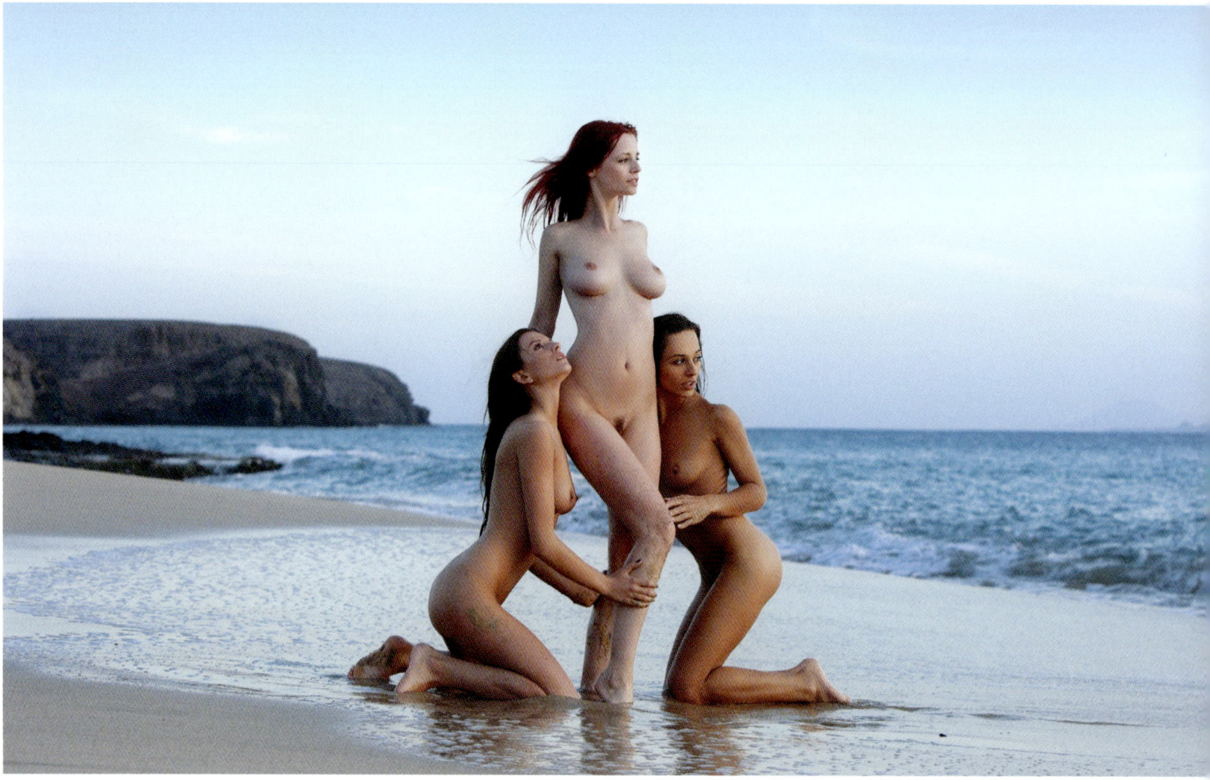

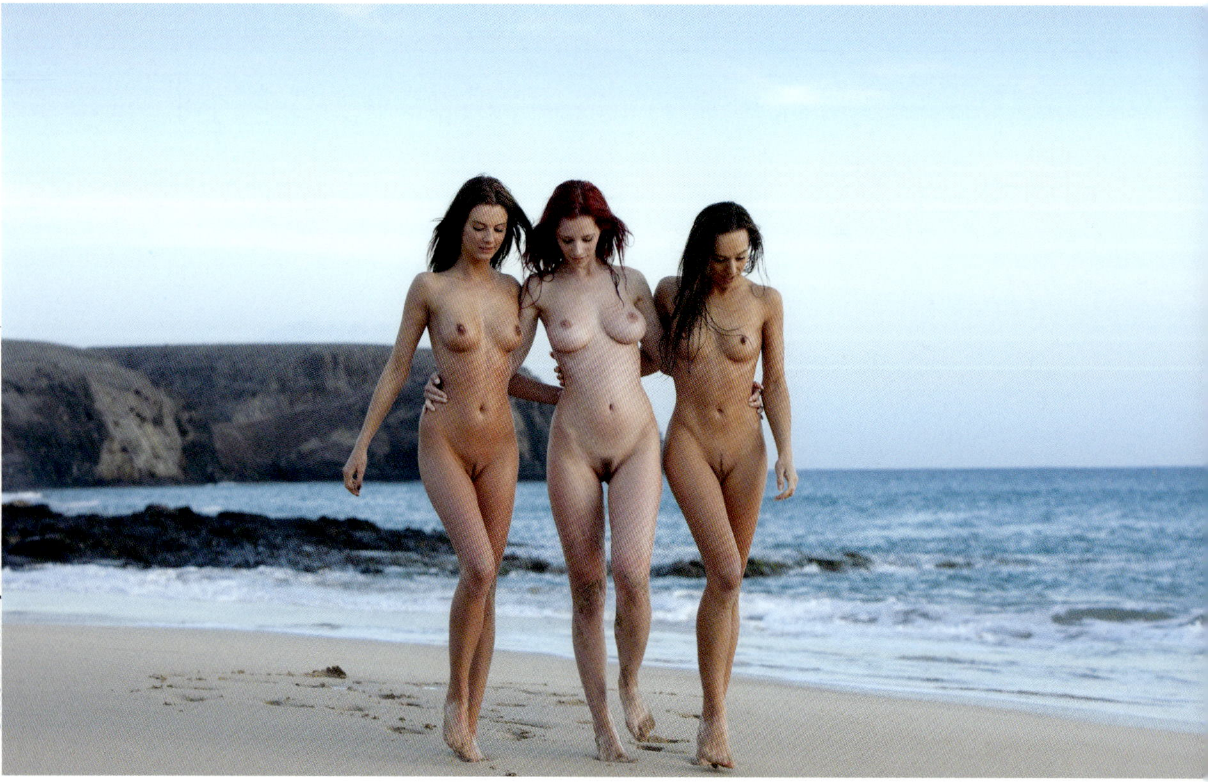

STACEY ARIEL, DOMINIKA PLAYA DE MUJERES, PLAYA BLANCA

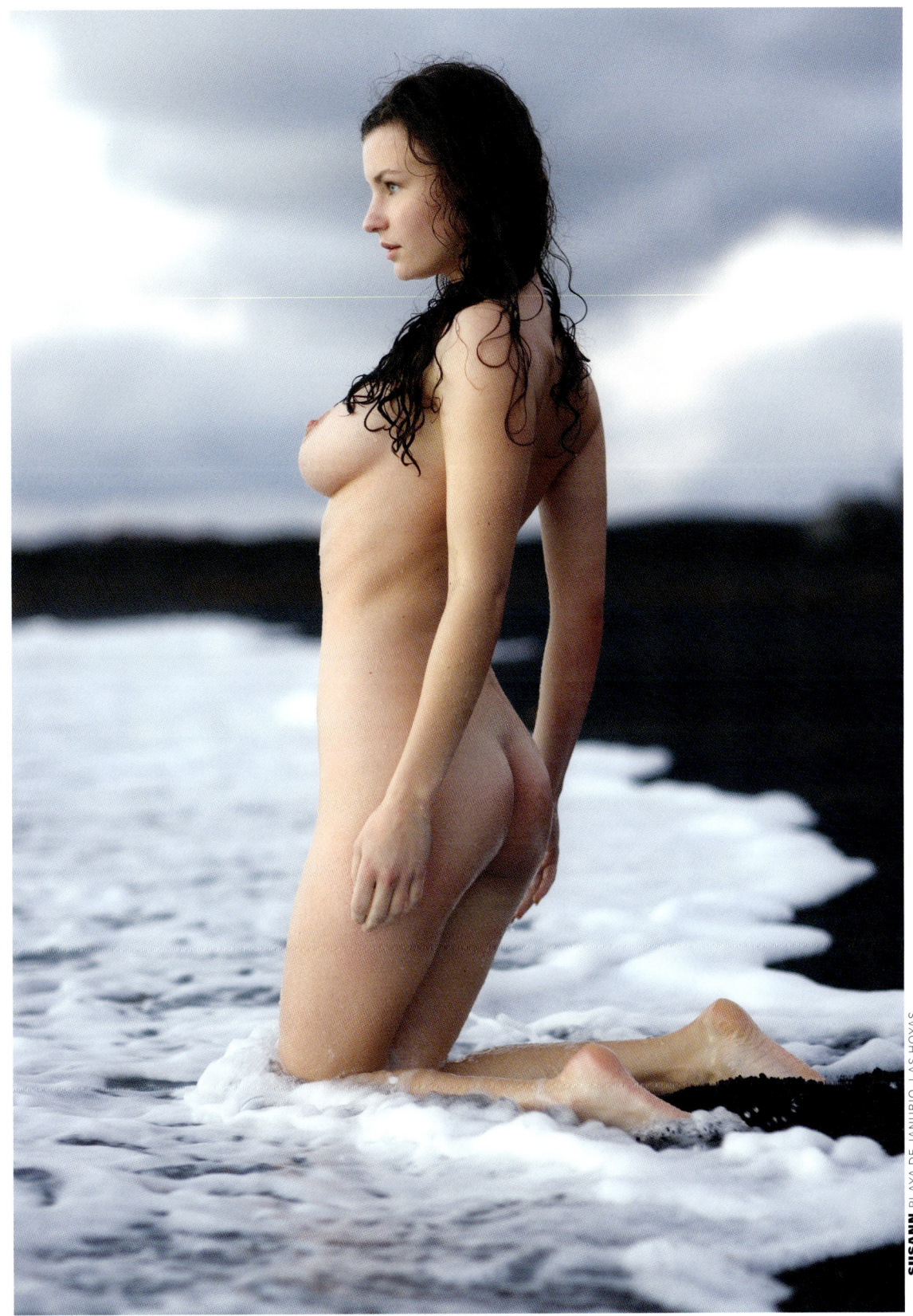

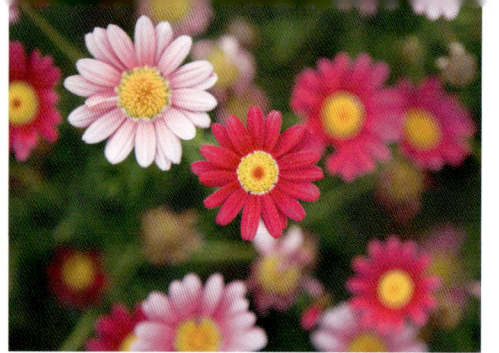

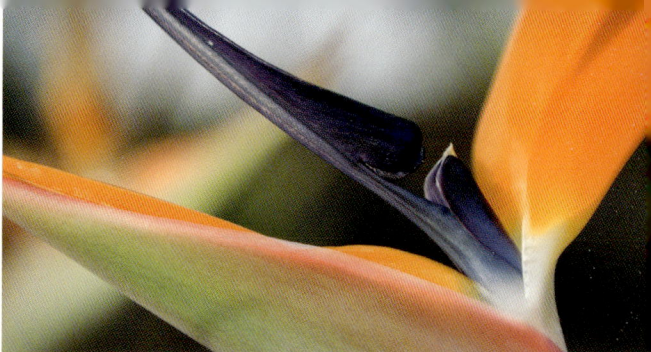

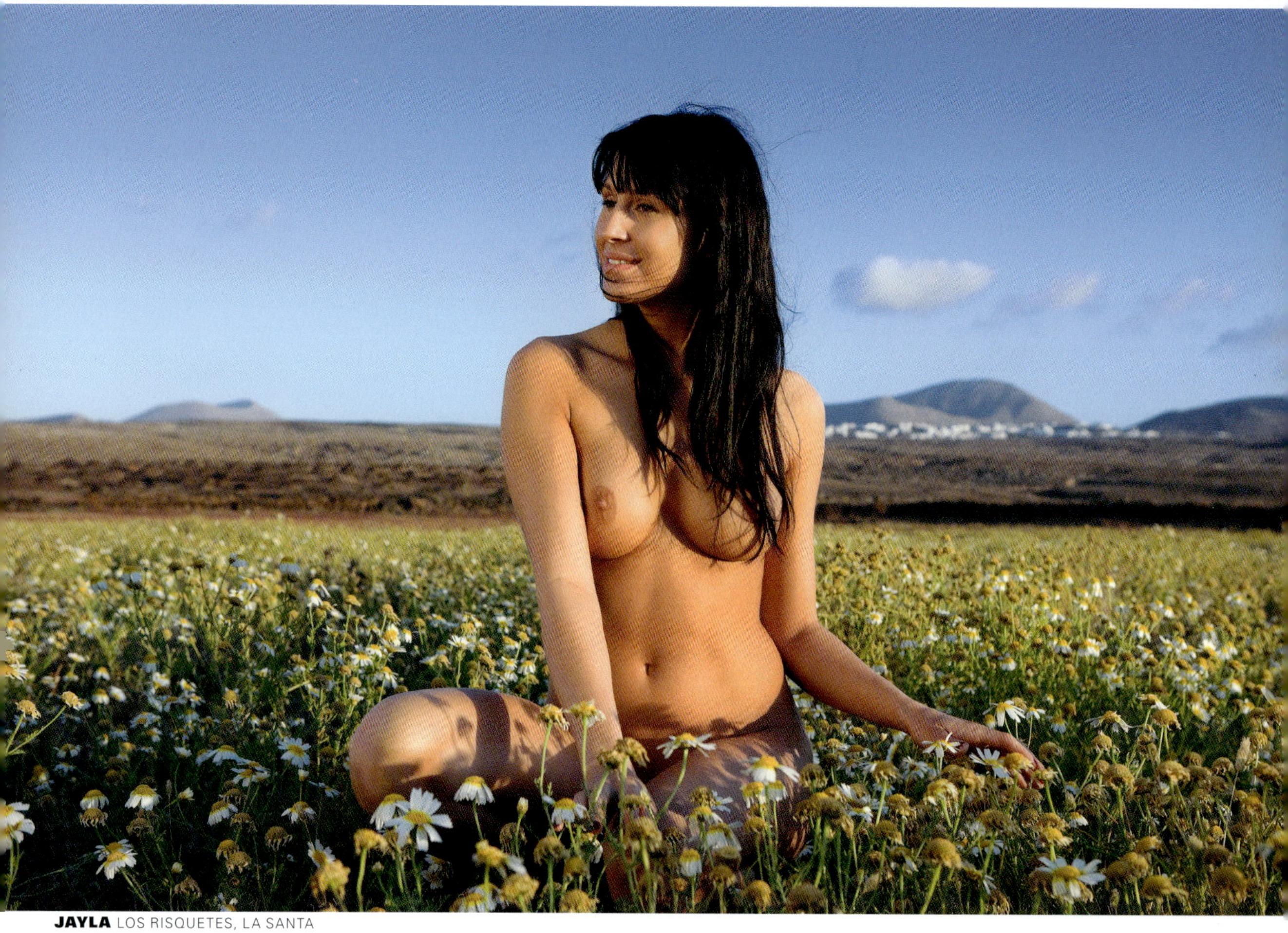

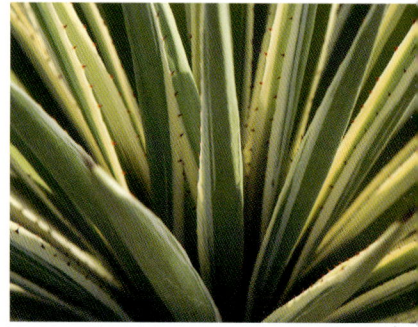

JAYLA LOS RISQUETES, LA SANTA

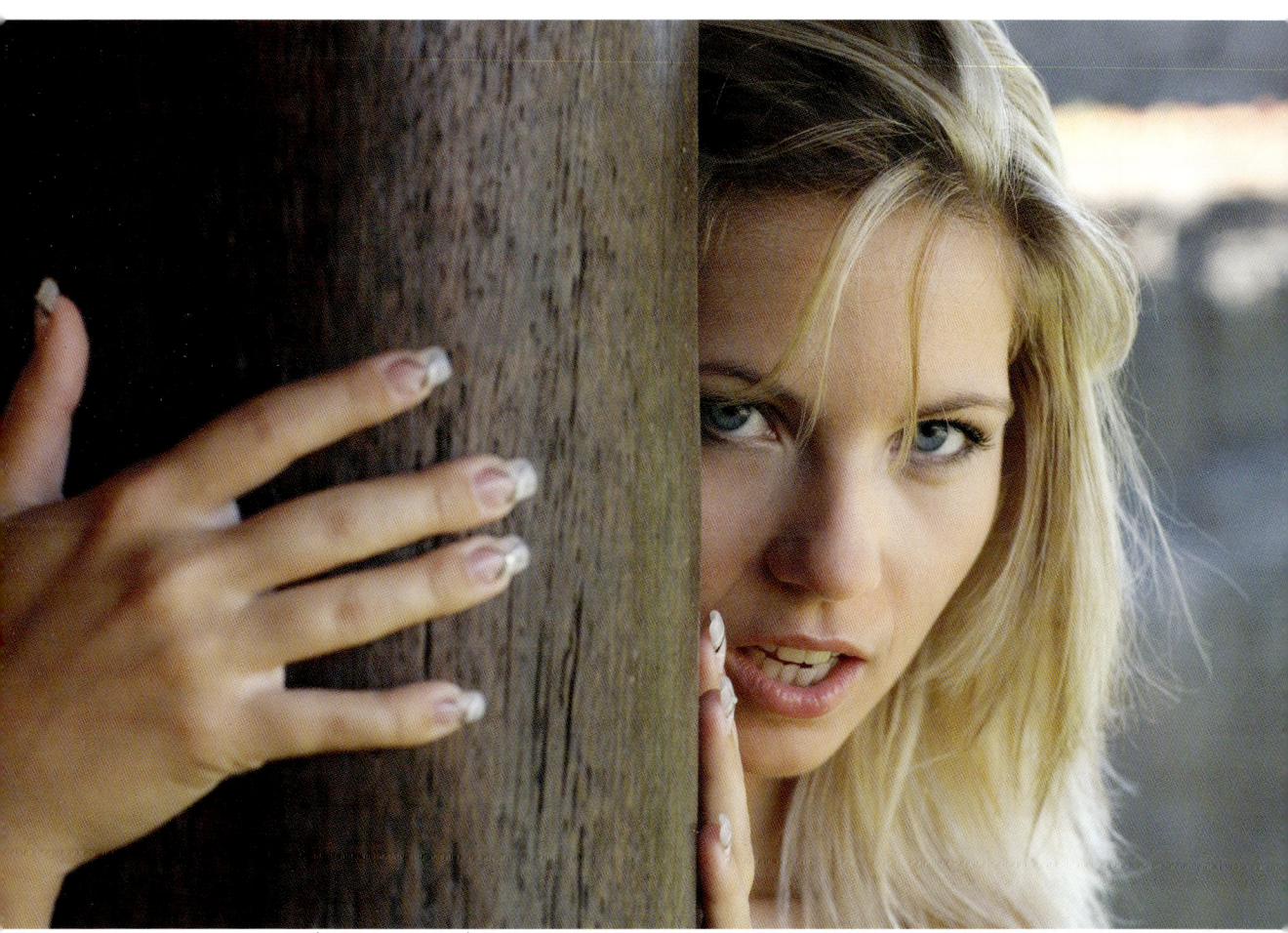

JENNI CASA TOMARÉN, SAN BARTOLOMÉ

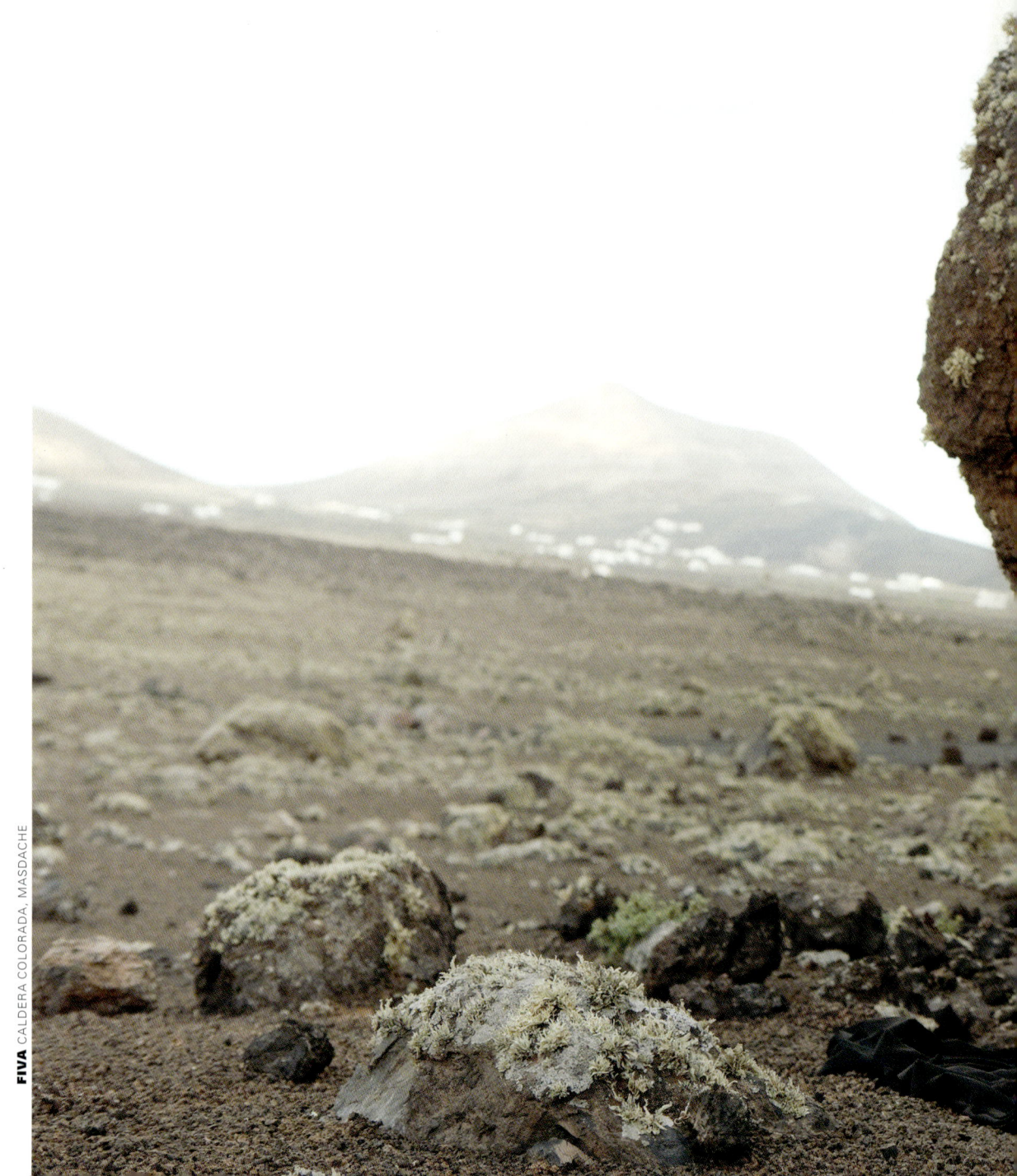

FIVA CALDERA COLORADA, MASDACHE

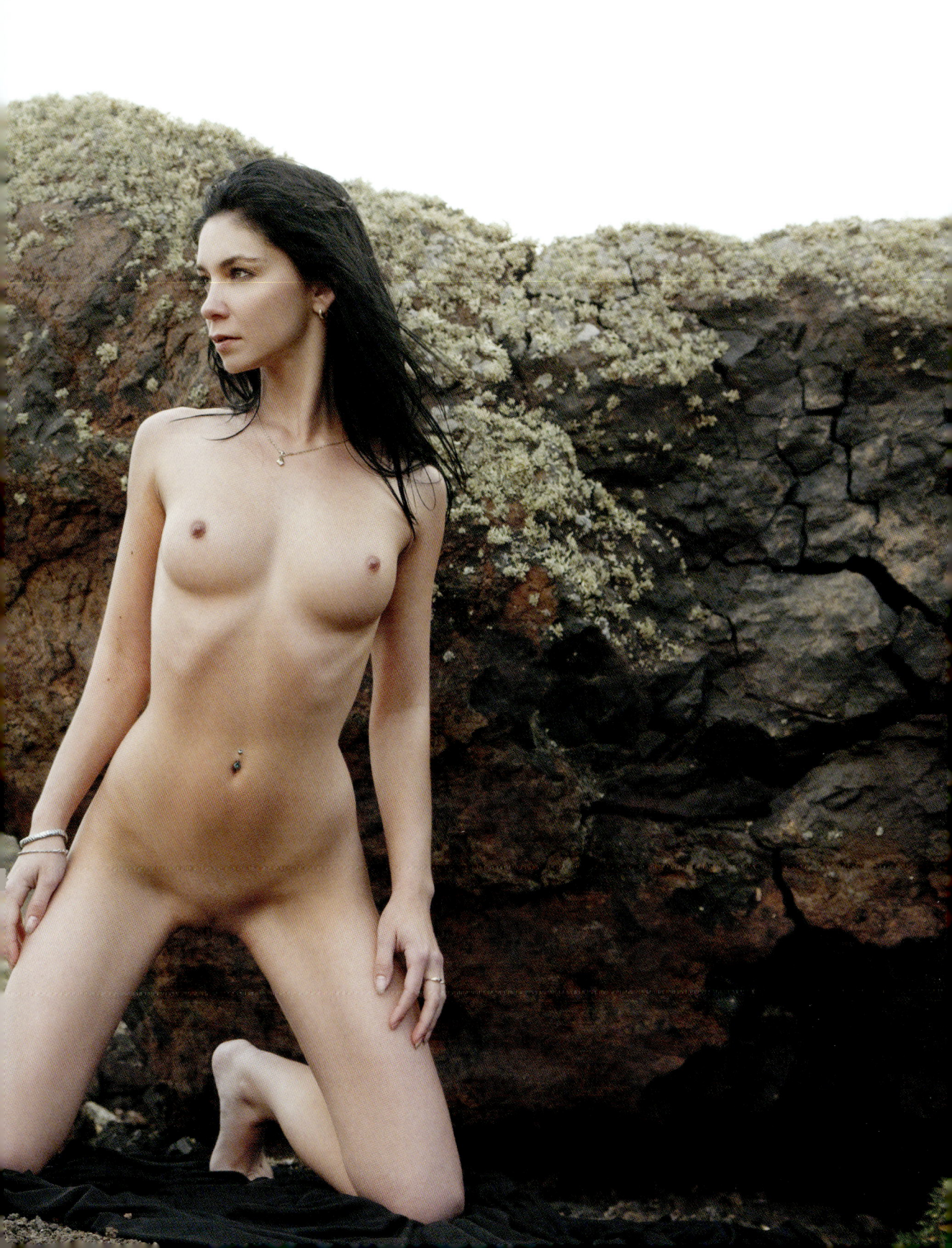

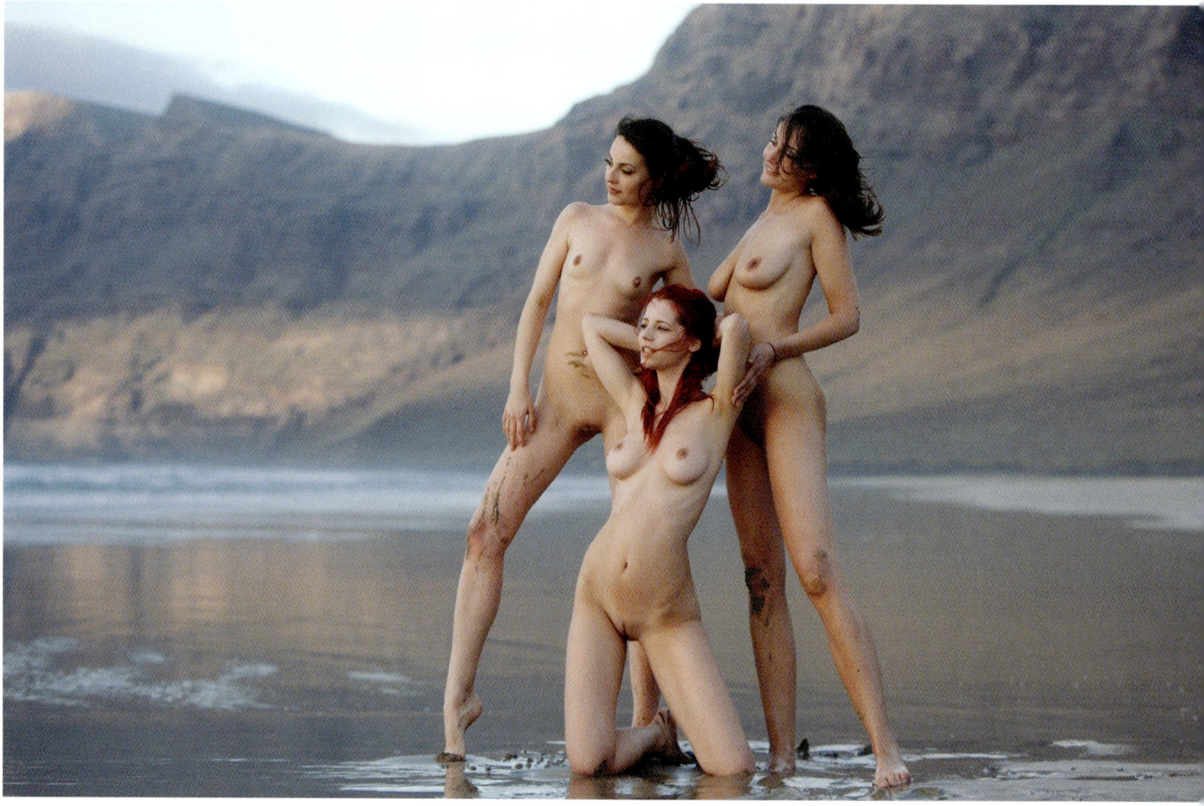

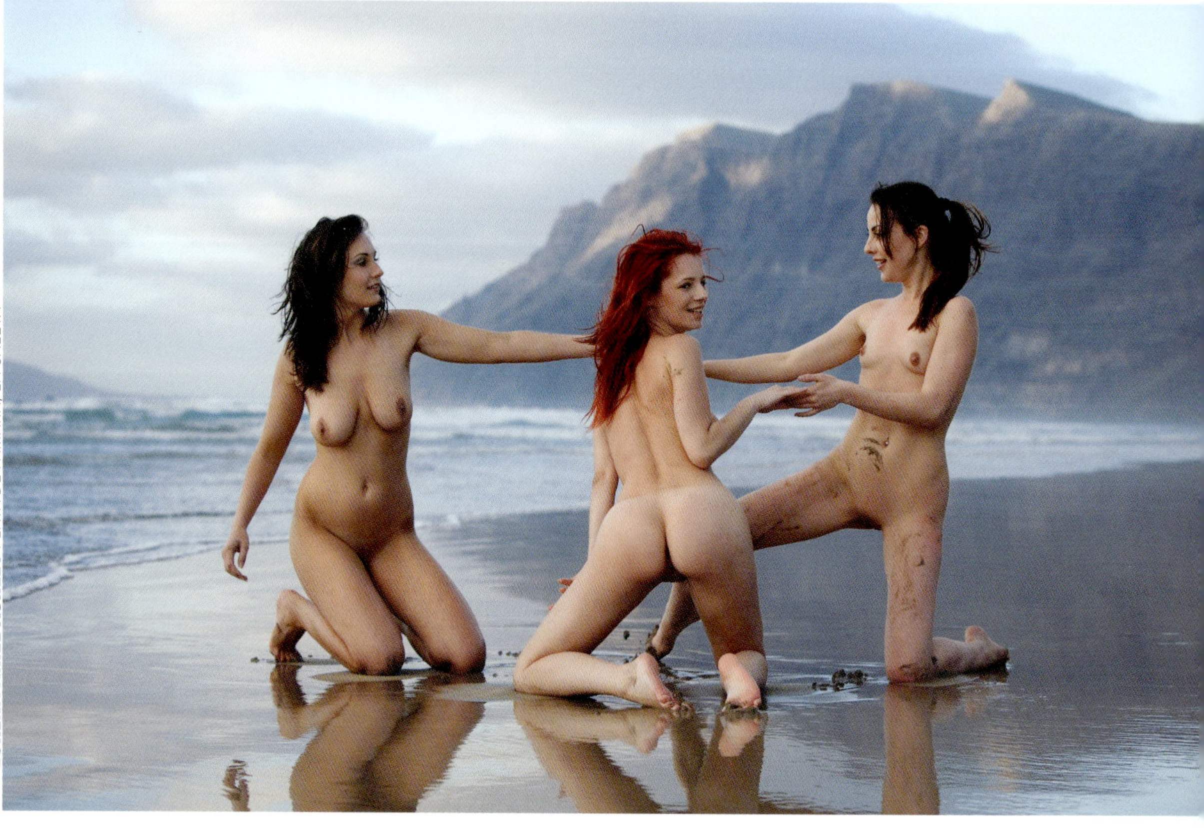

LORENA ARIEL ASHLEY PLAYA DE FAMARA, LA CALETA

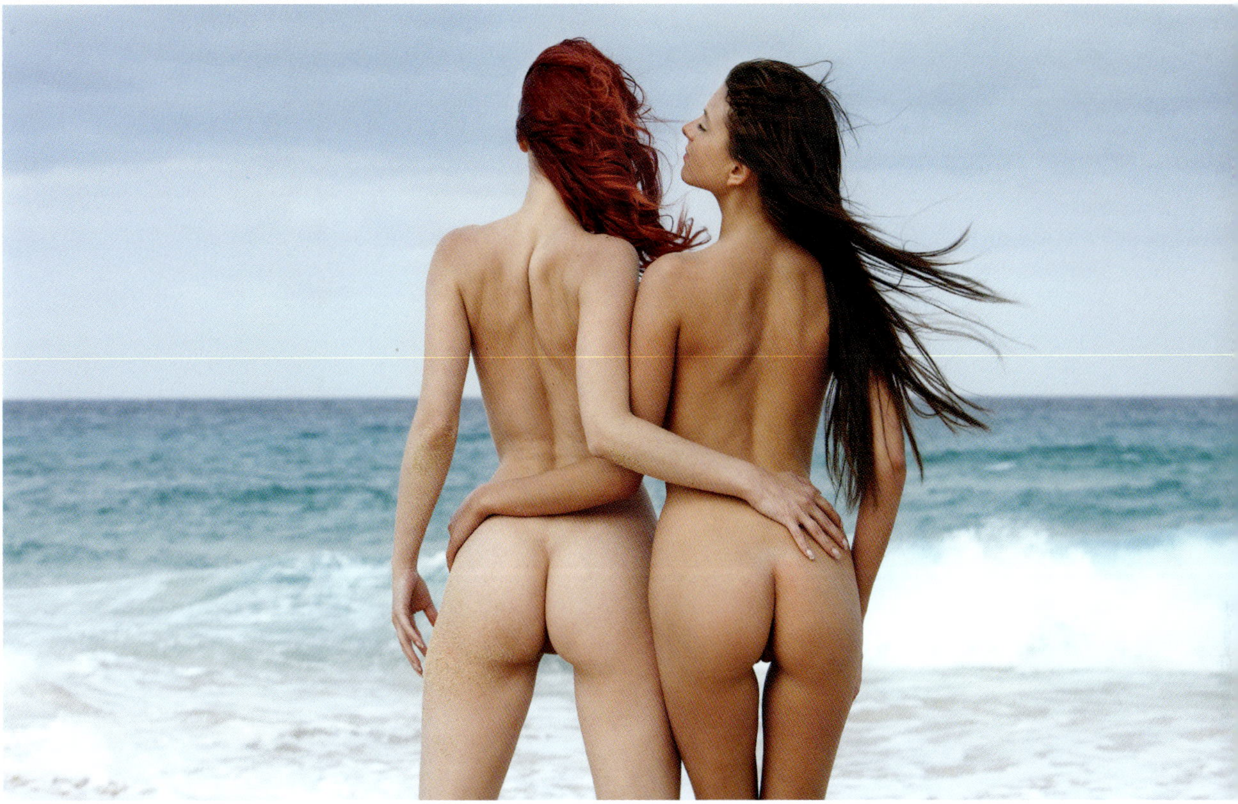

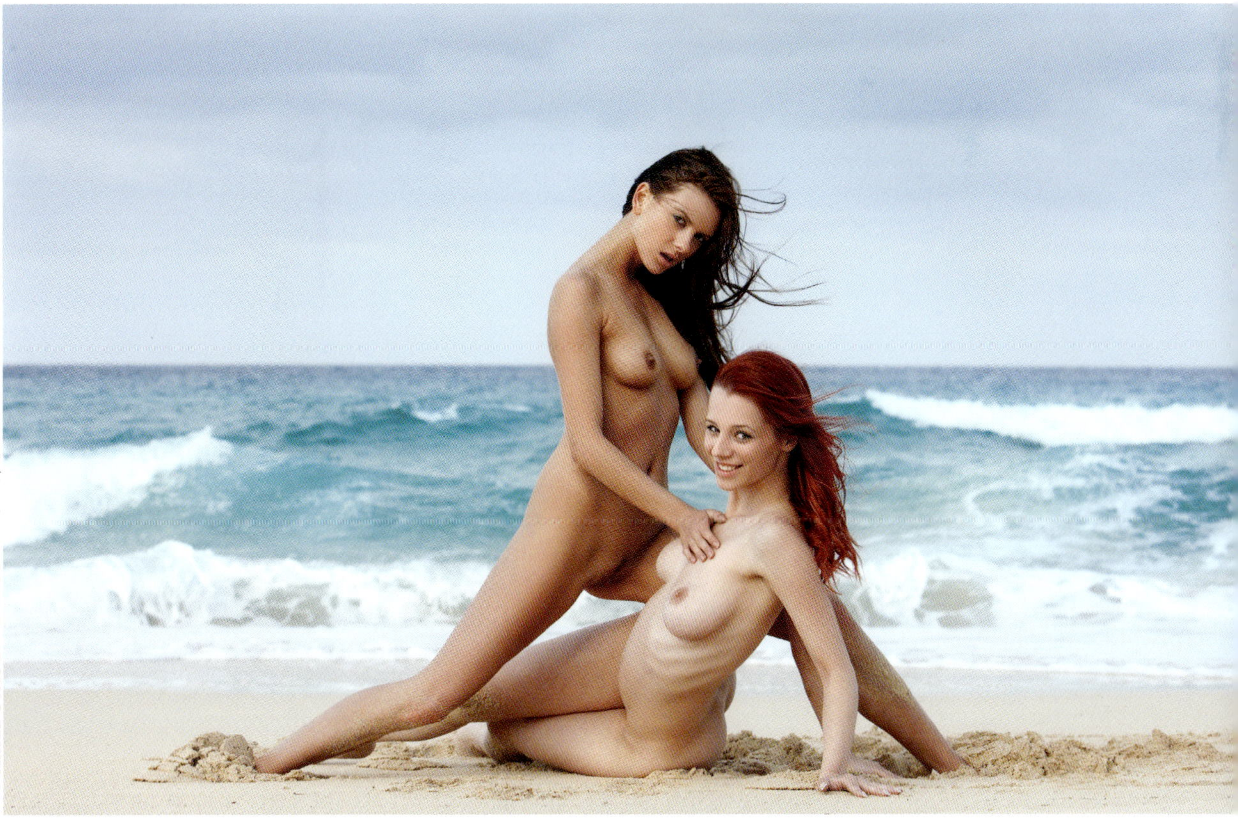

ARIEL STACEY PLAYA DE PAPAGAYO, PLAYA BLANCA

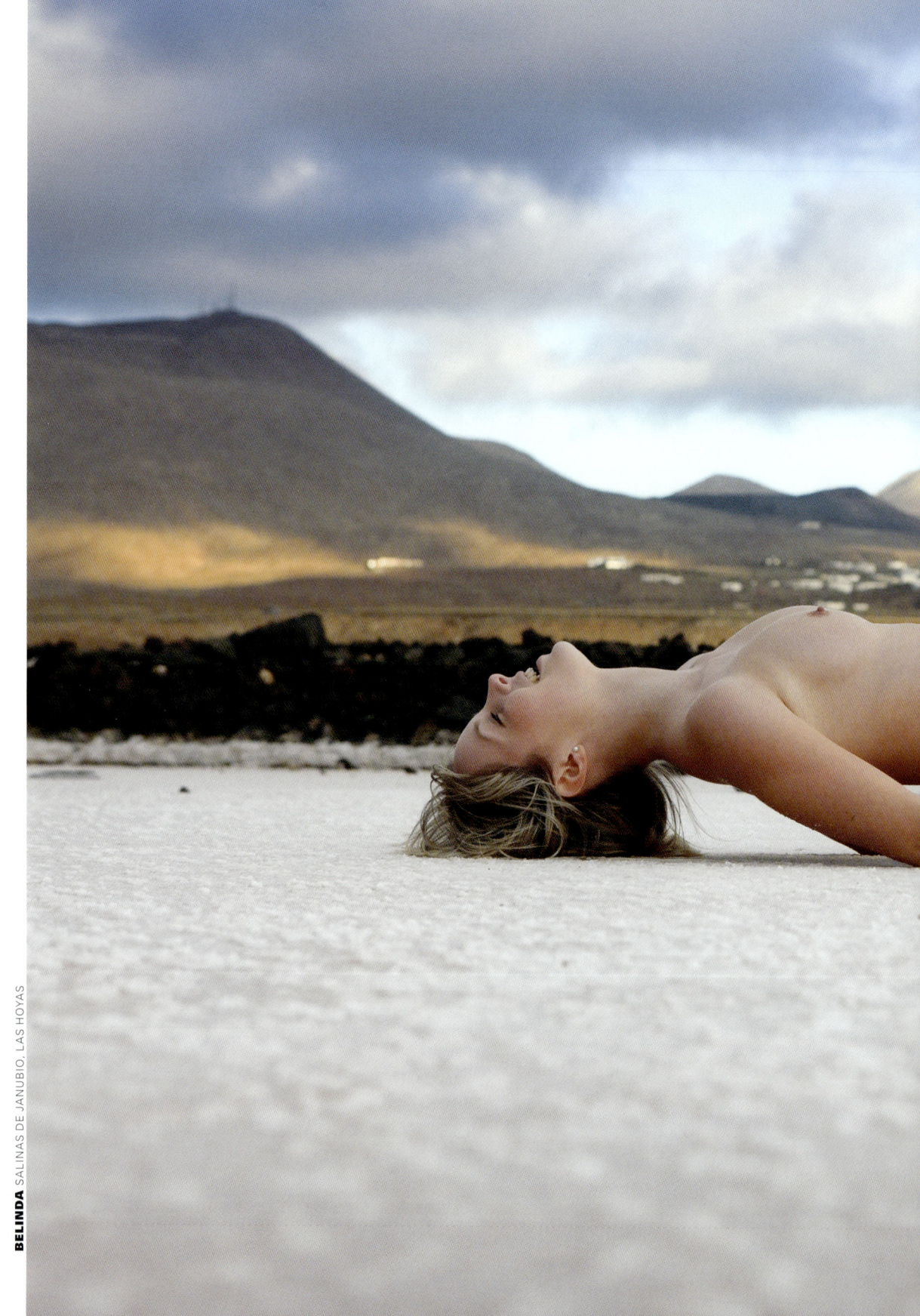

BELINDA SALINAS DE JANUBIO, LAS HOYAS

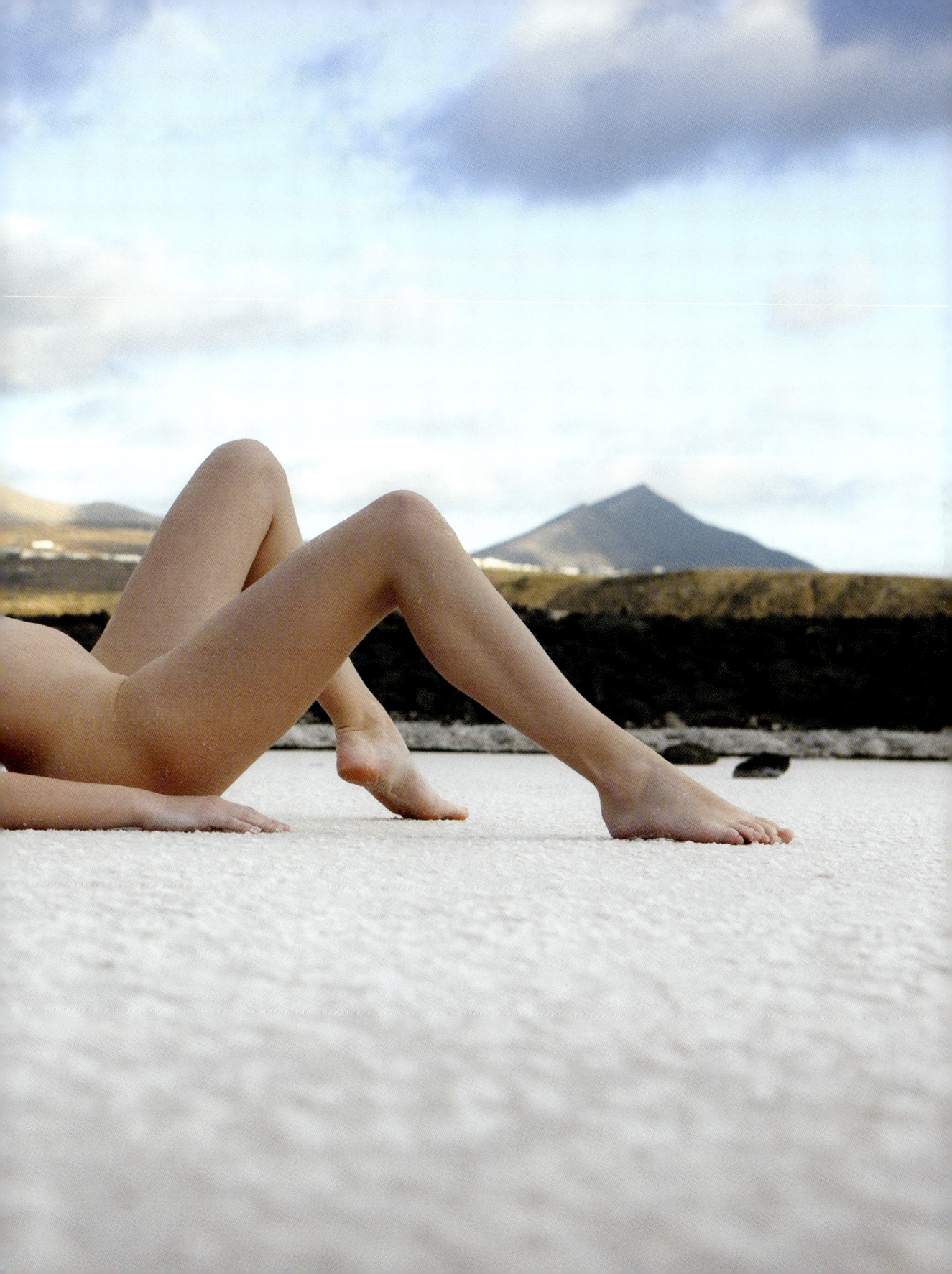

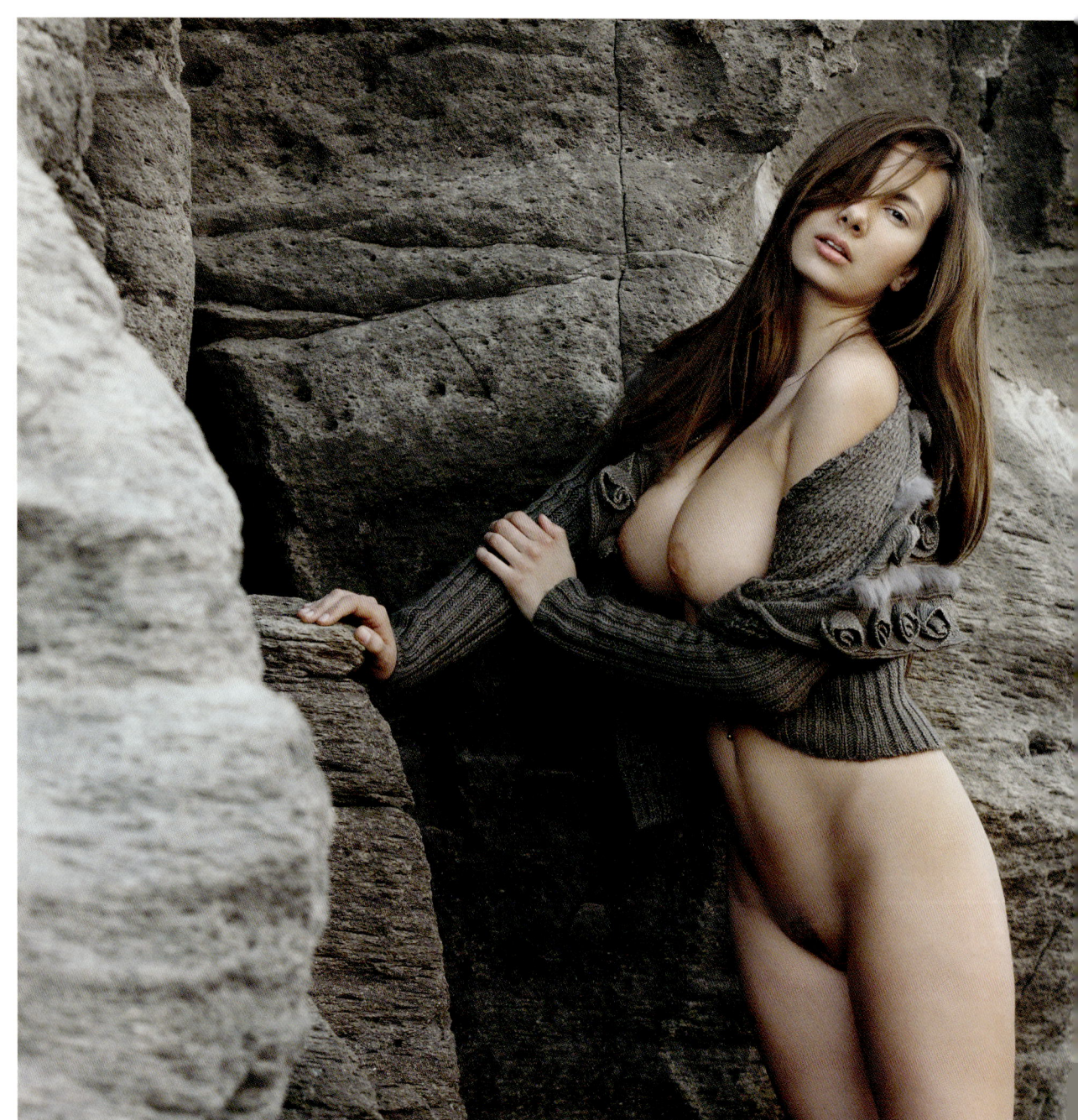

JOSEPHINE PLAYA DE TIRITAÑA

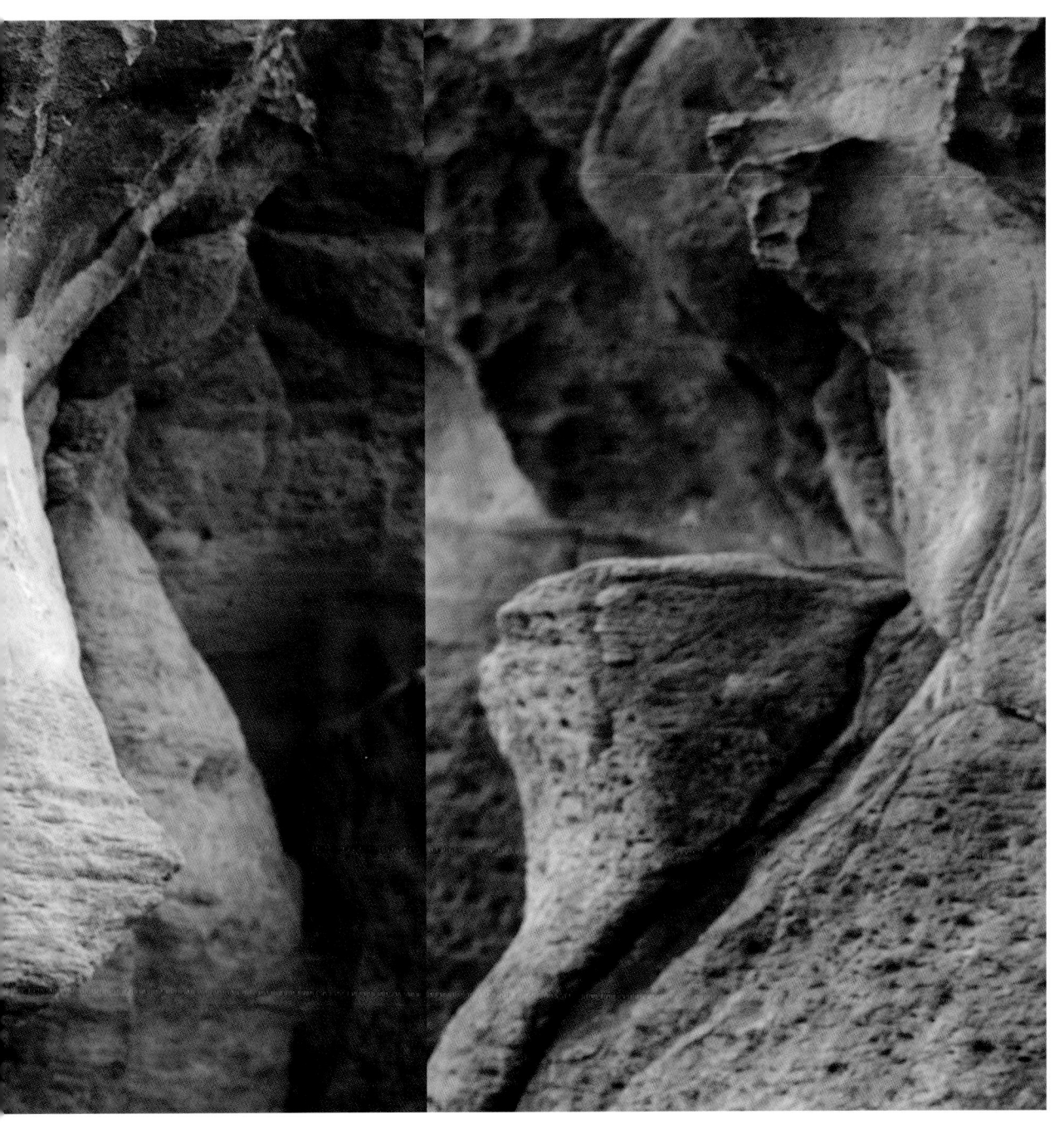

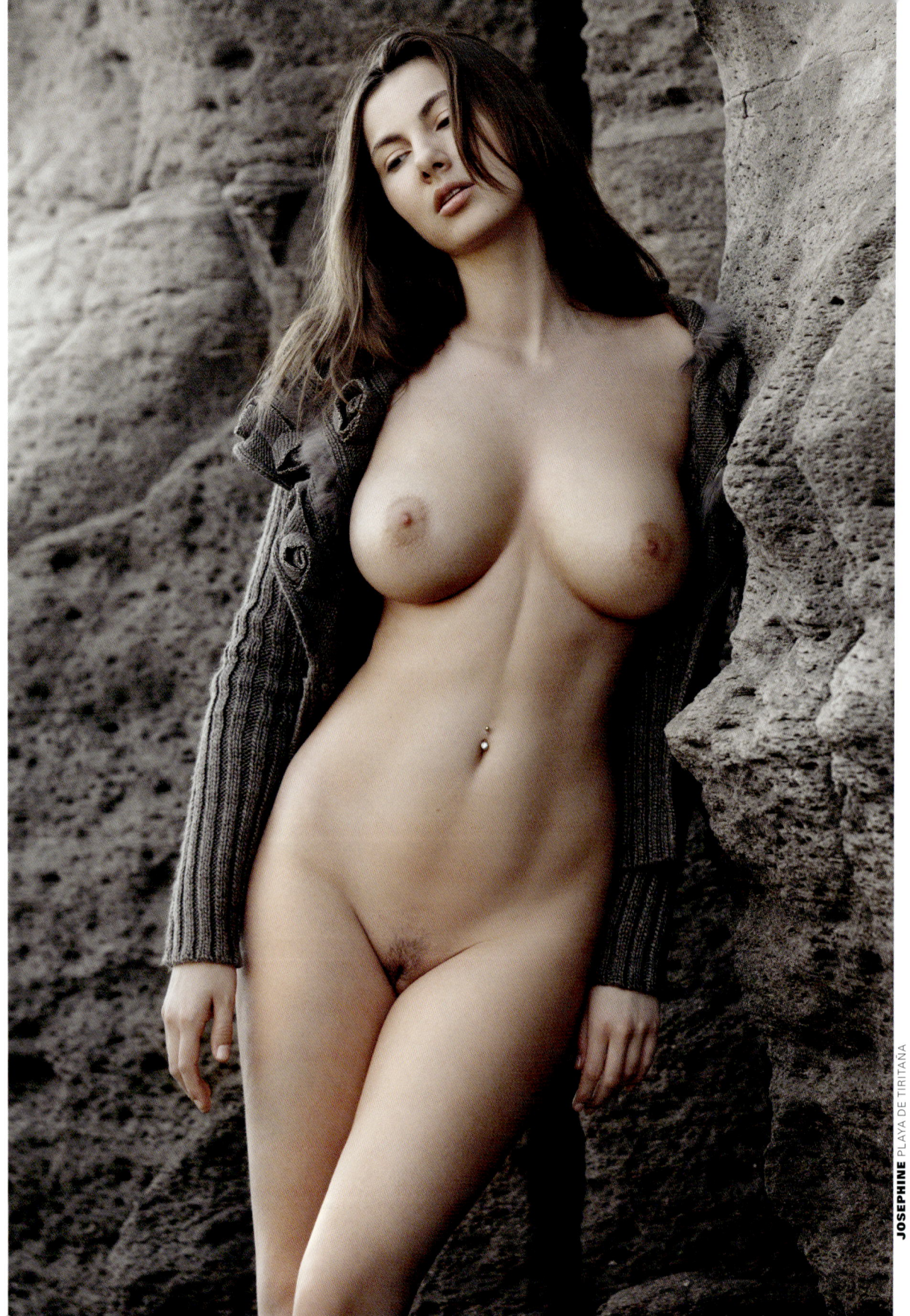

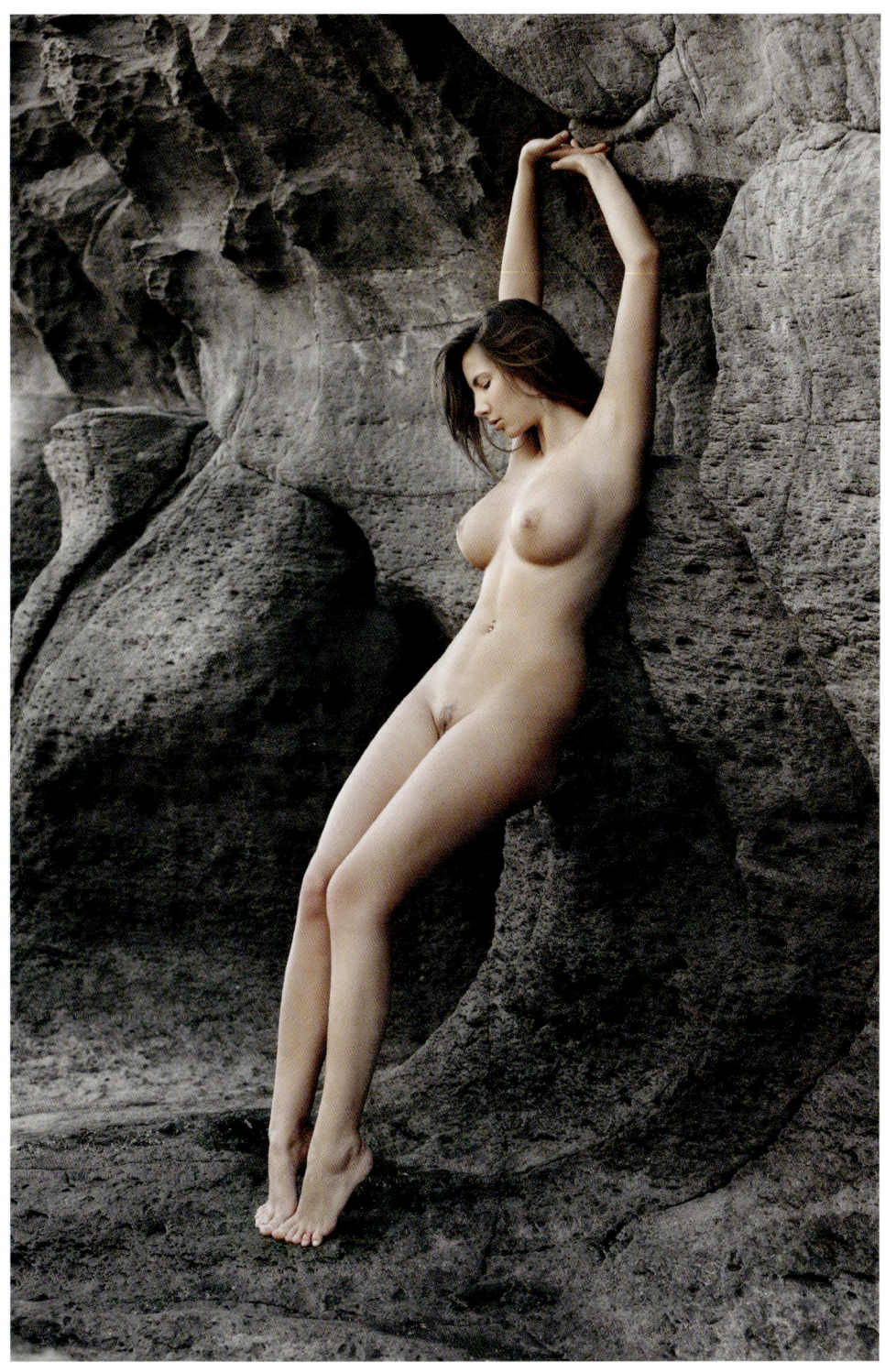

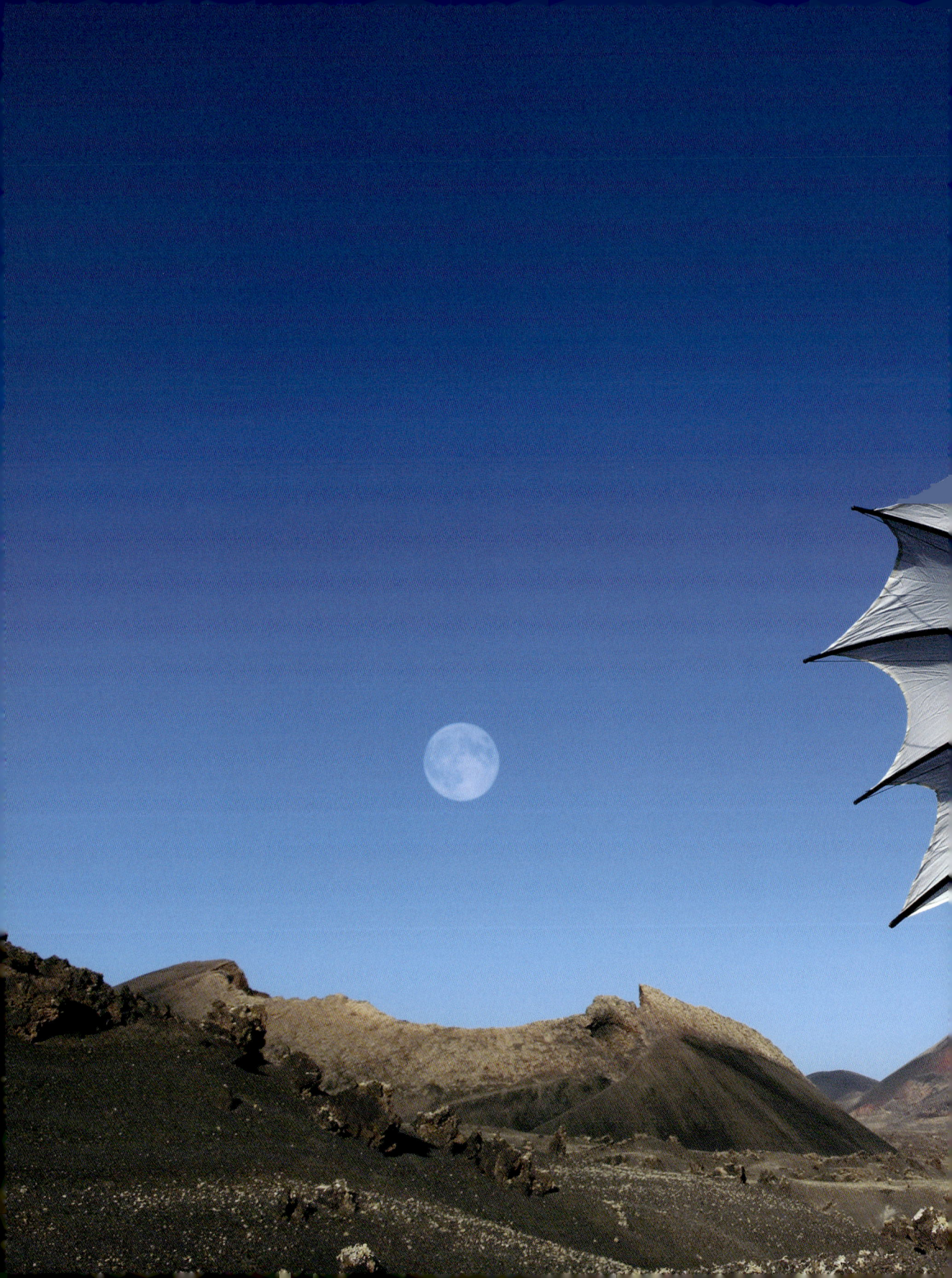

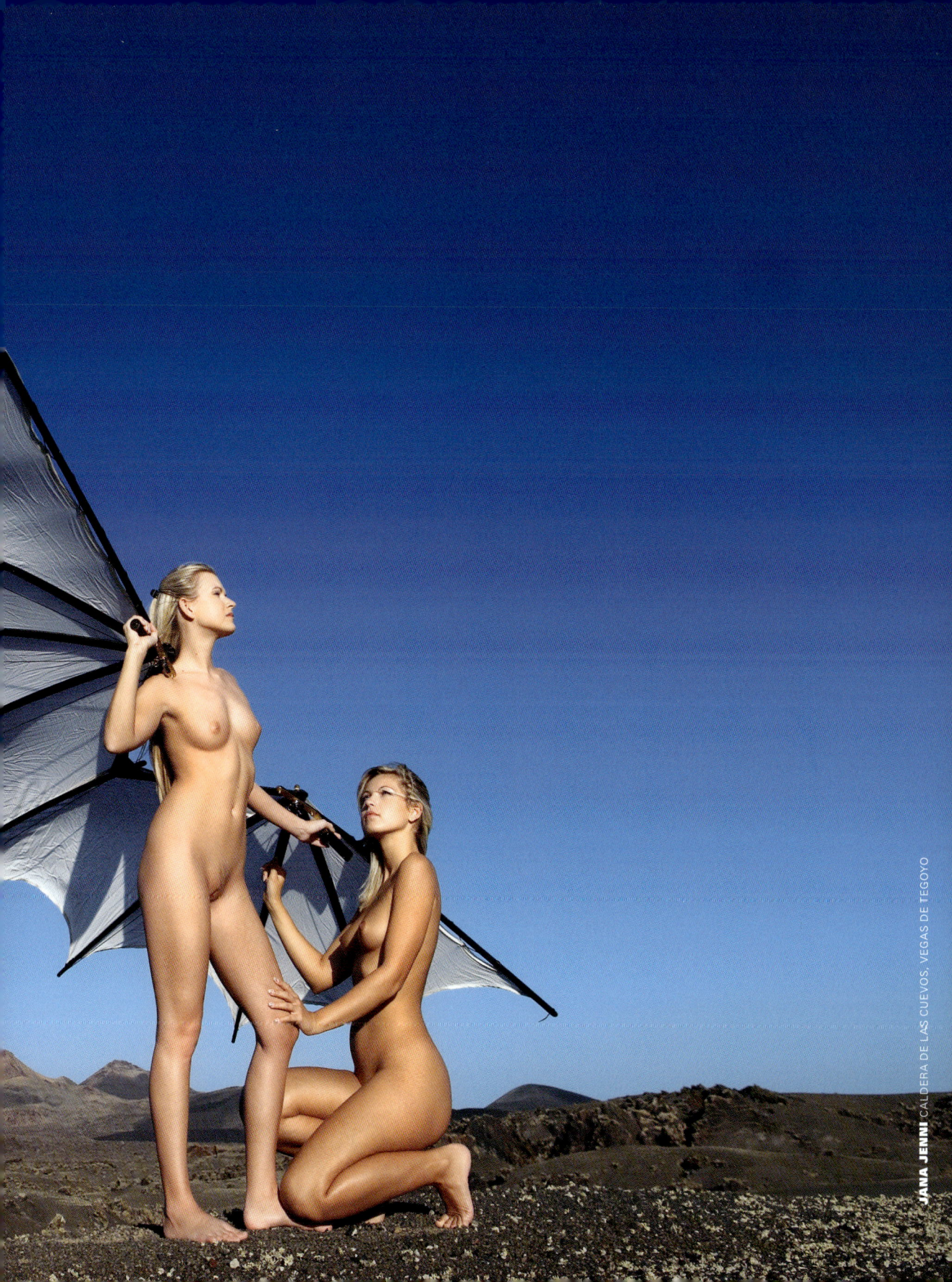

JANA JENNI CALDERA DE LAS CUEVOS. VEGAS DE TEGOYO

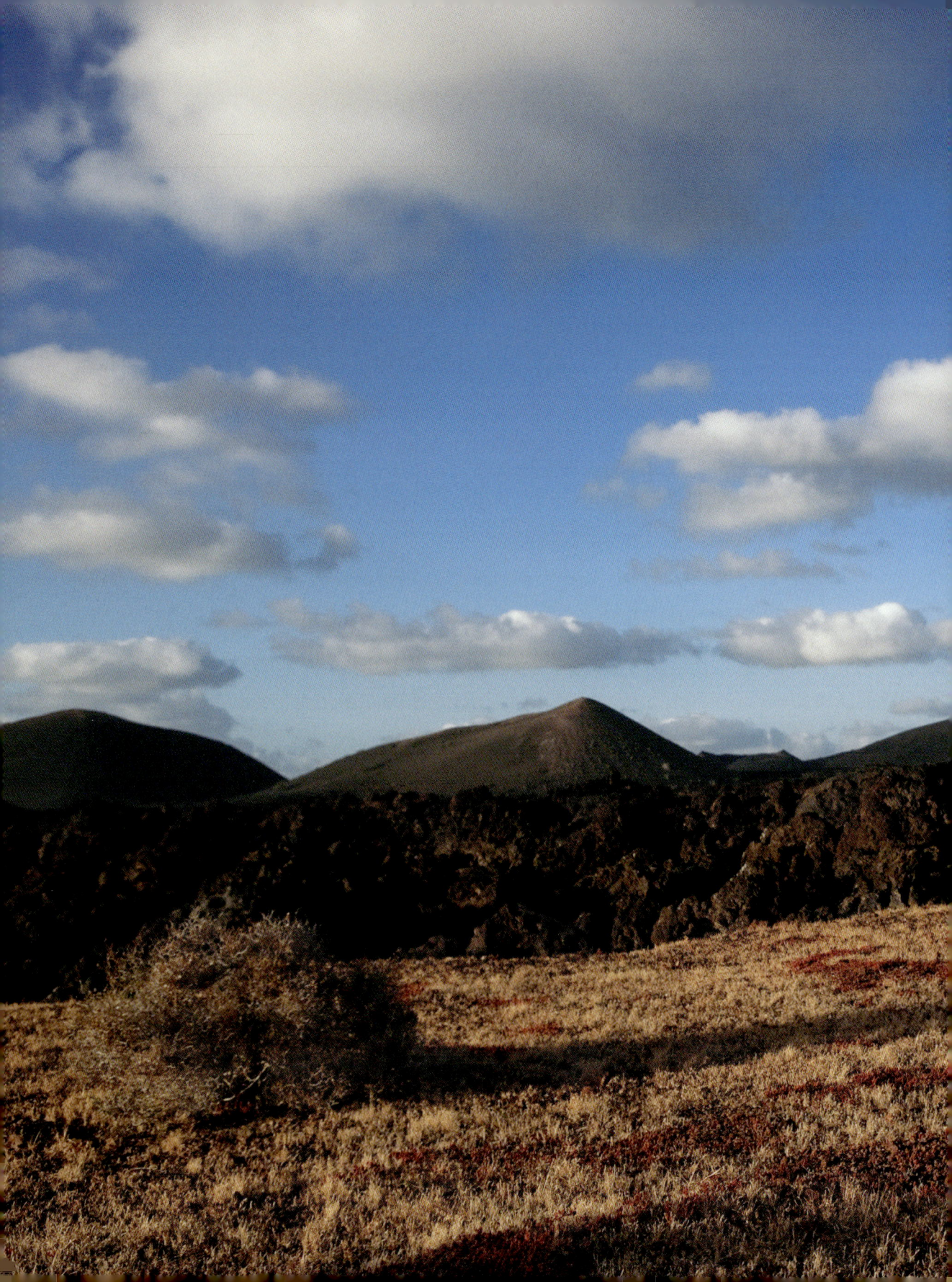

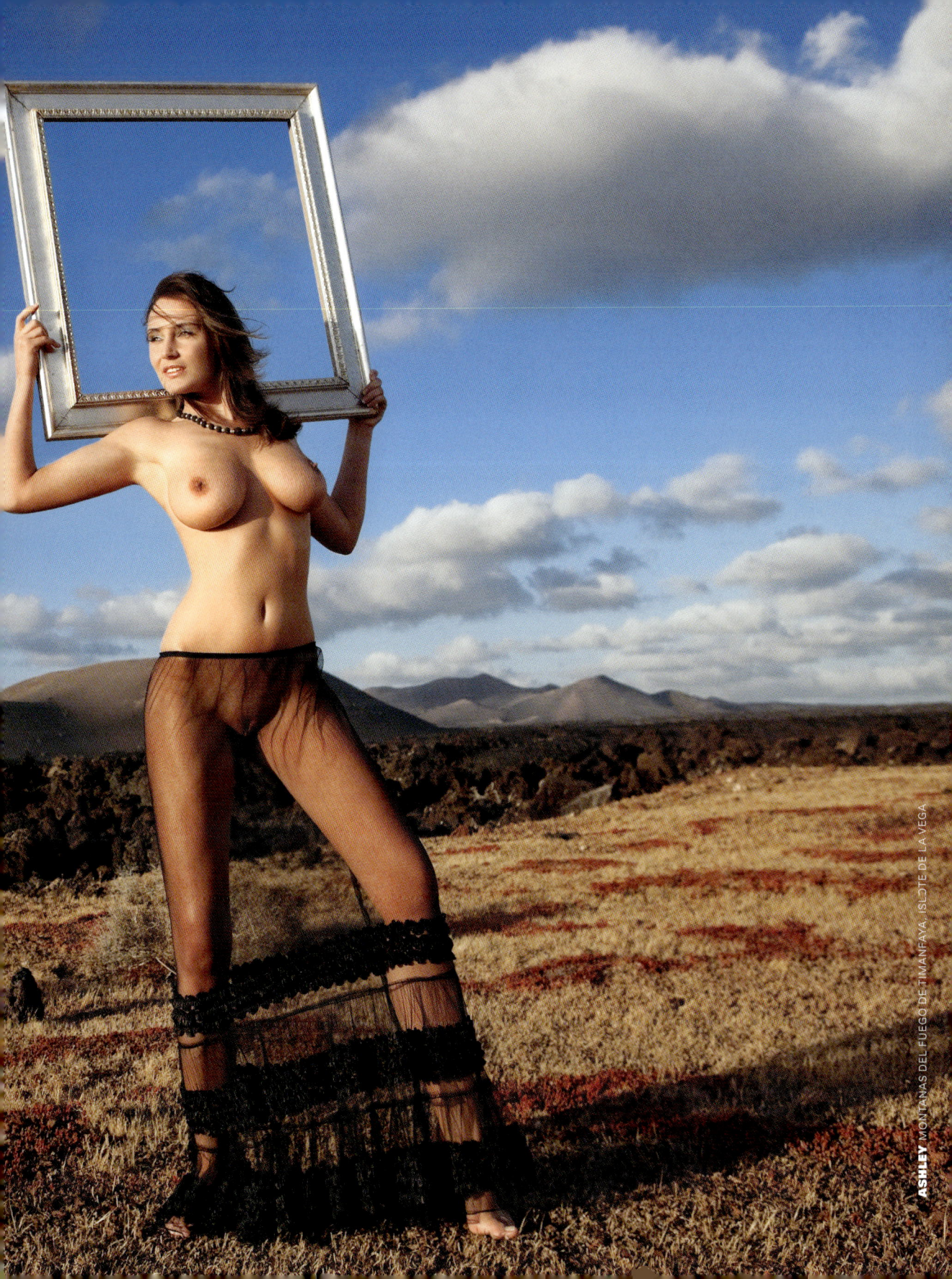

ASHLEY MONTAÑAS DEL FUEGO DE TIMANFAYA, ISLOTE DE LA VEGA

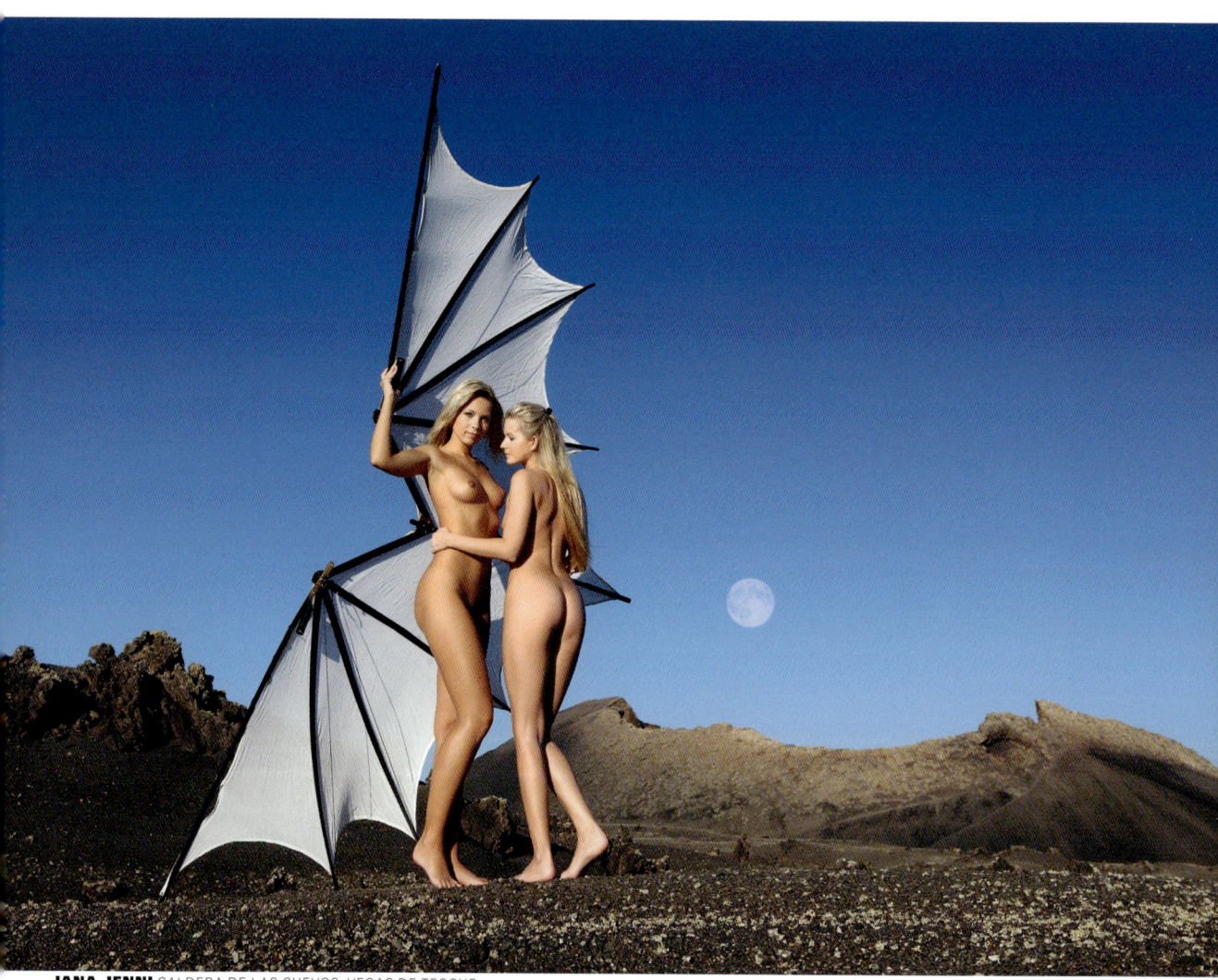

JANA JENNI CALDERA DE LAS CUEVOS, VEGAS DE TEGOYO

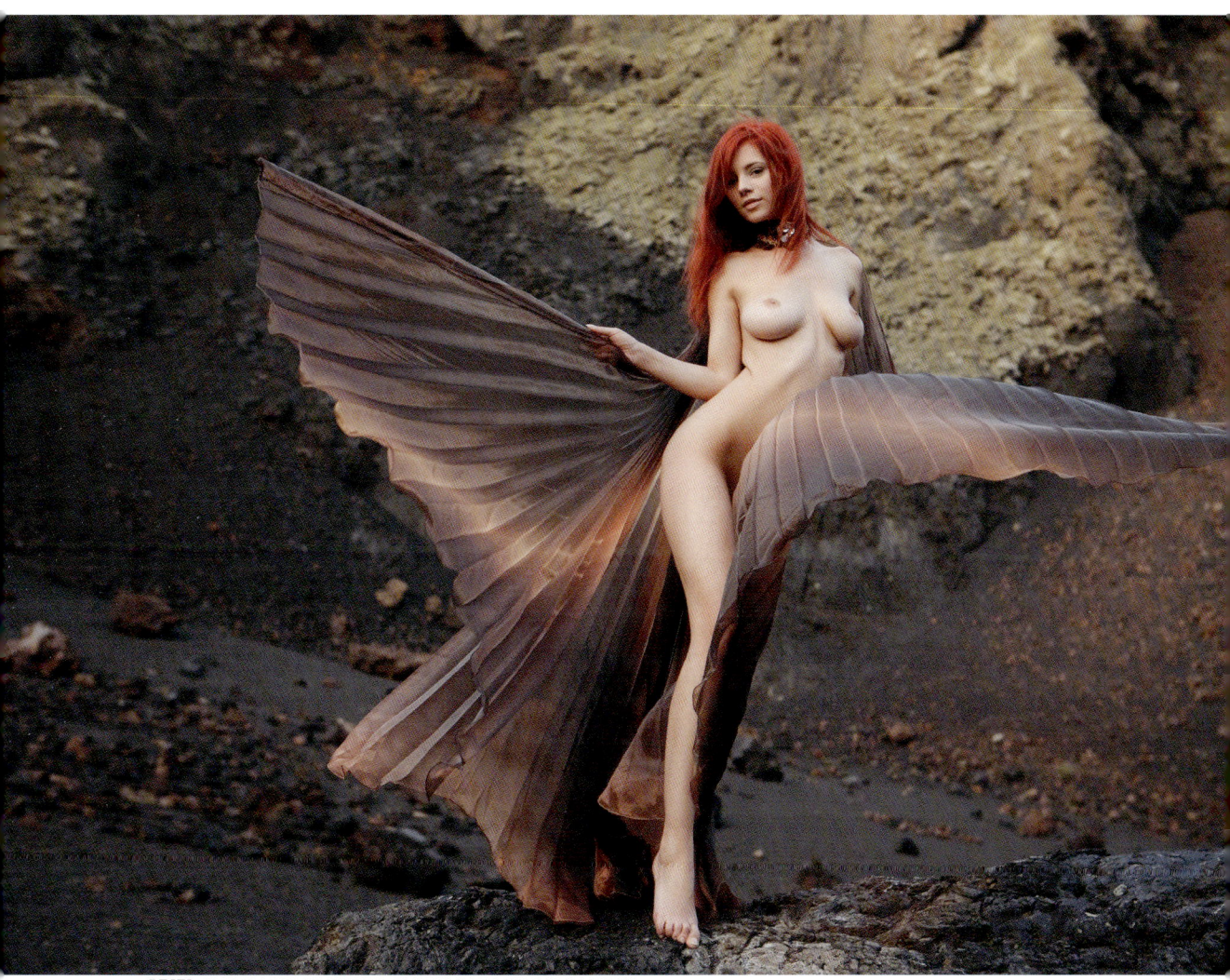

ARIEL CALDERA DE LAS CUEVOS, PARQUE NACIONAL DE TIMANFAYA

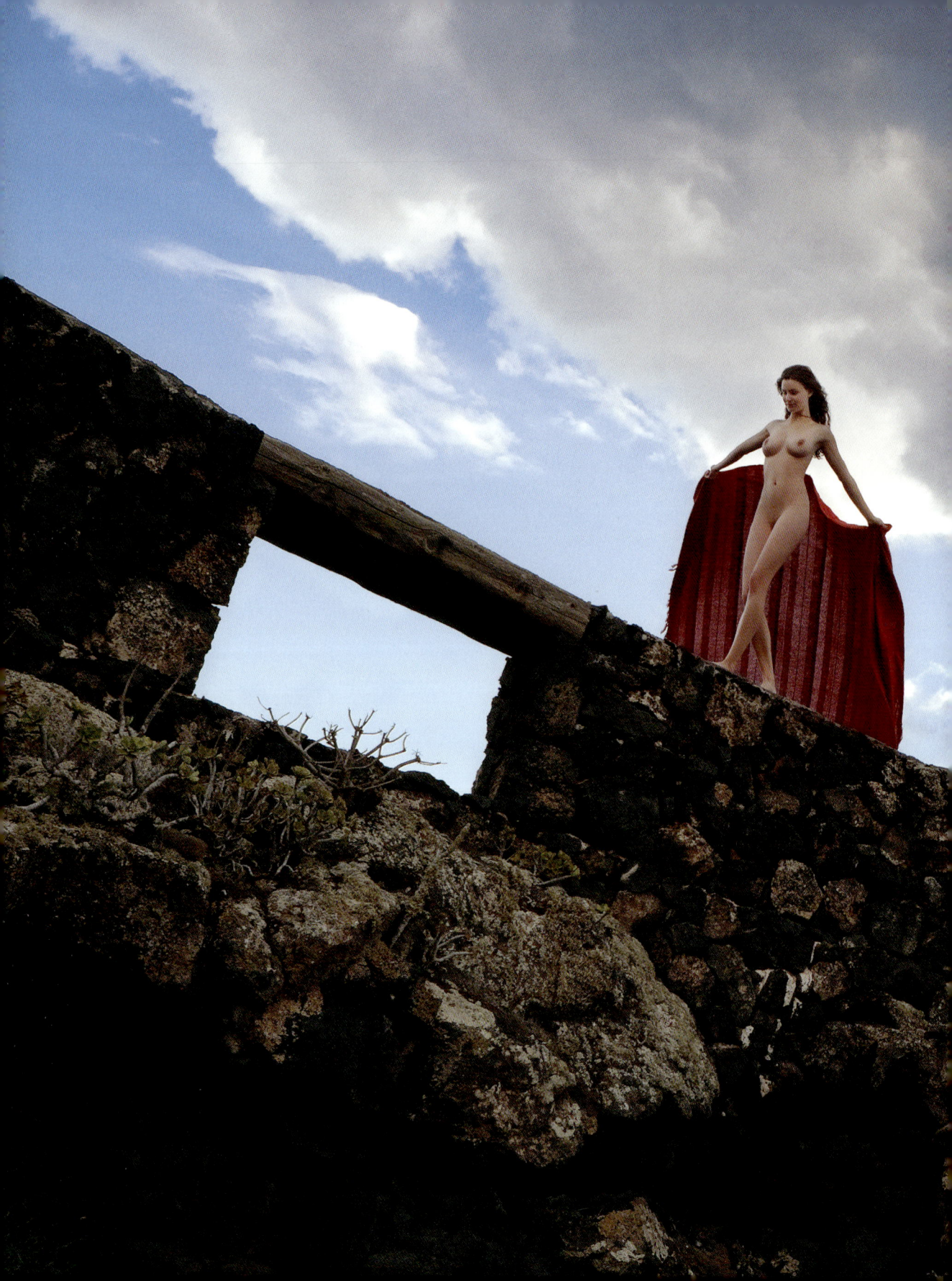

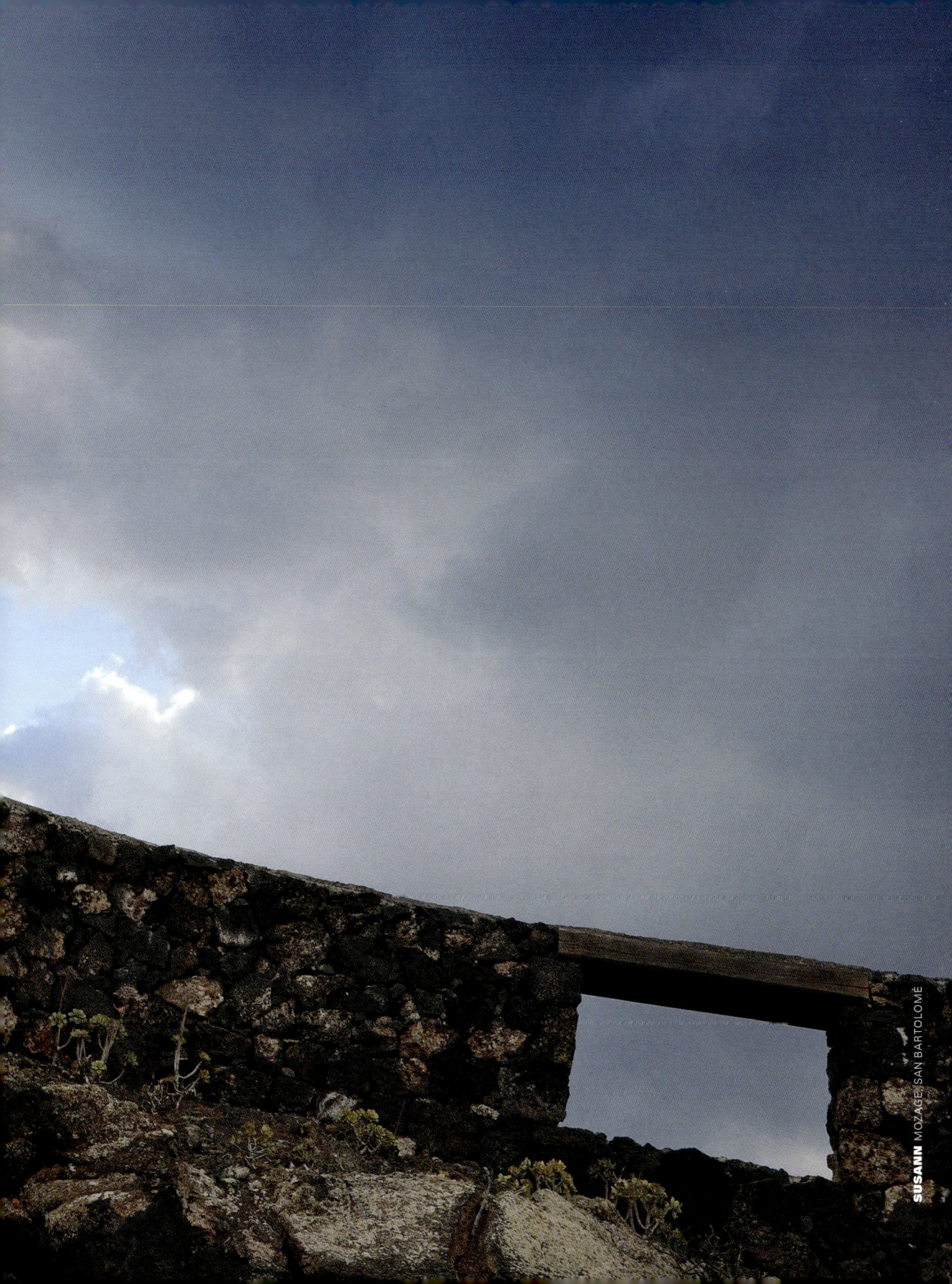

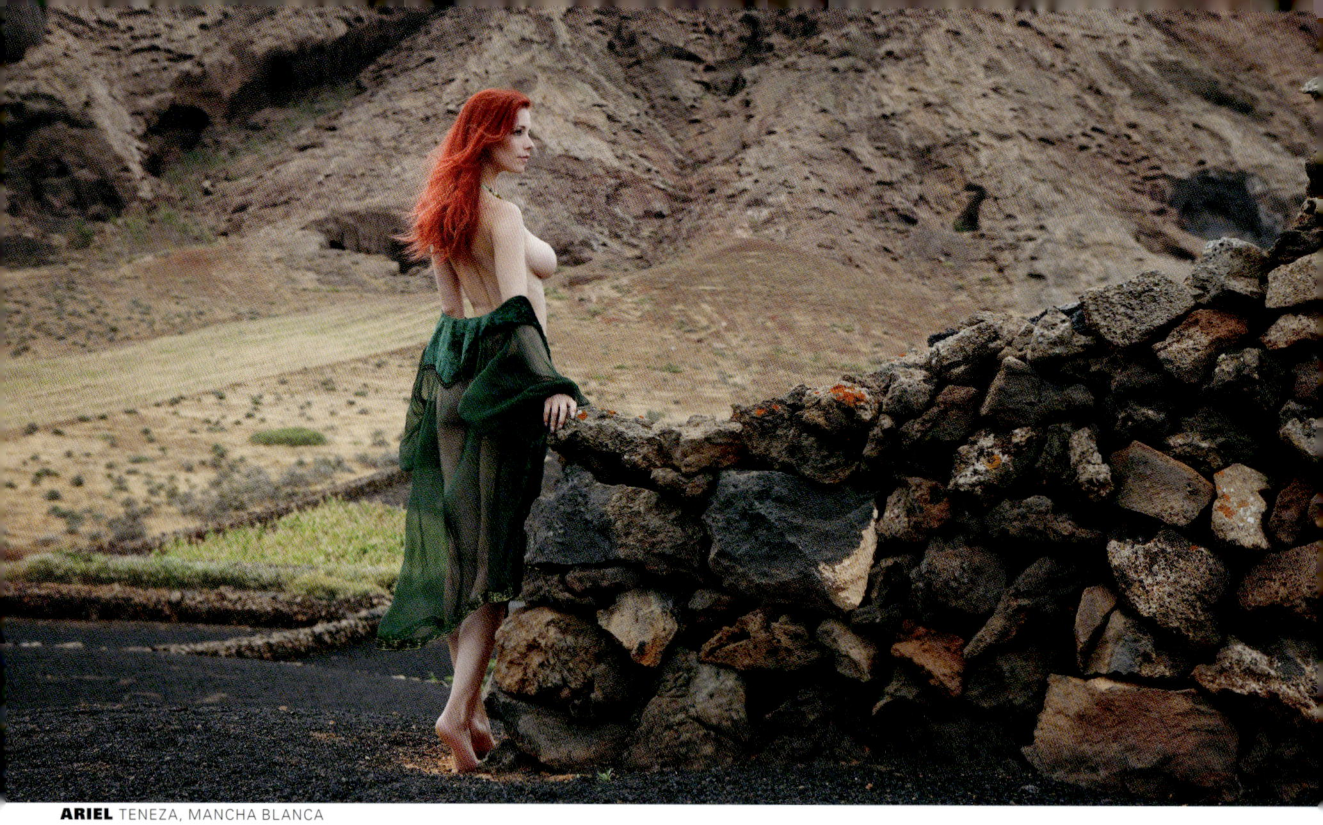

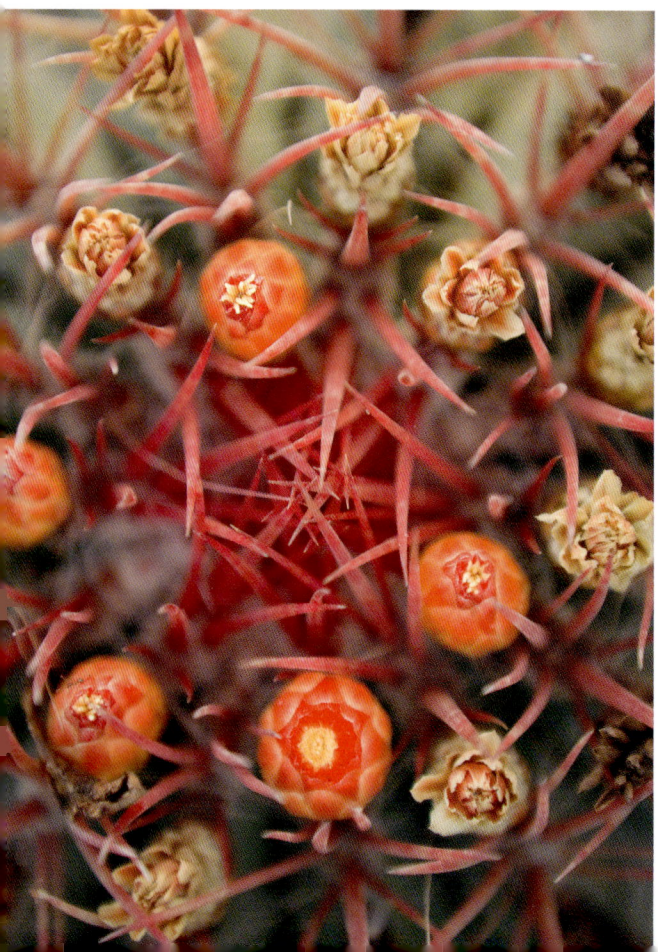

ARIEL TENEZA, MANCHA BLANCA

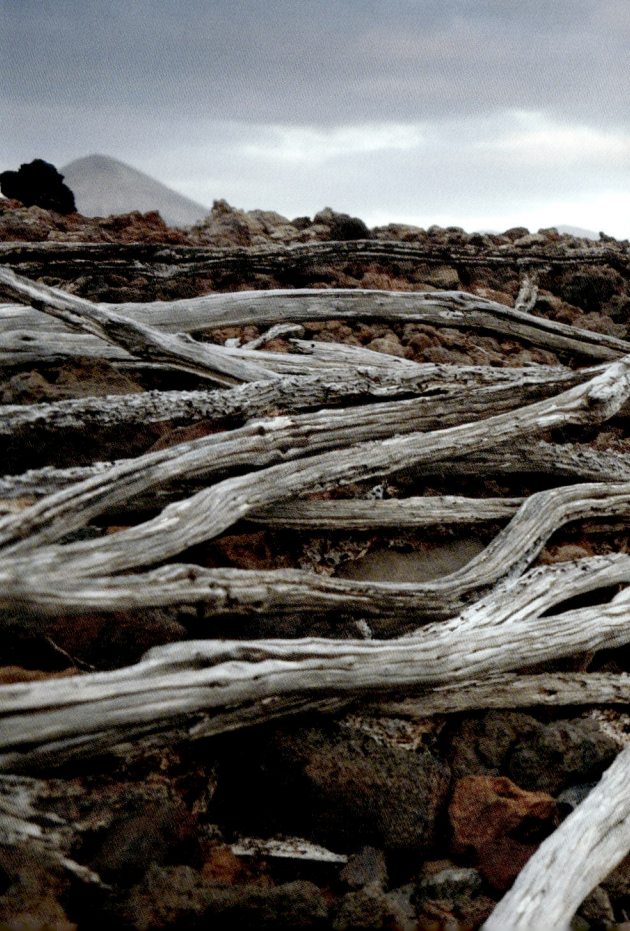

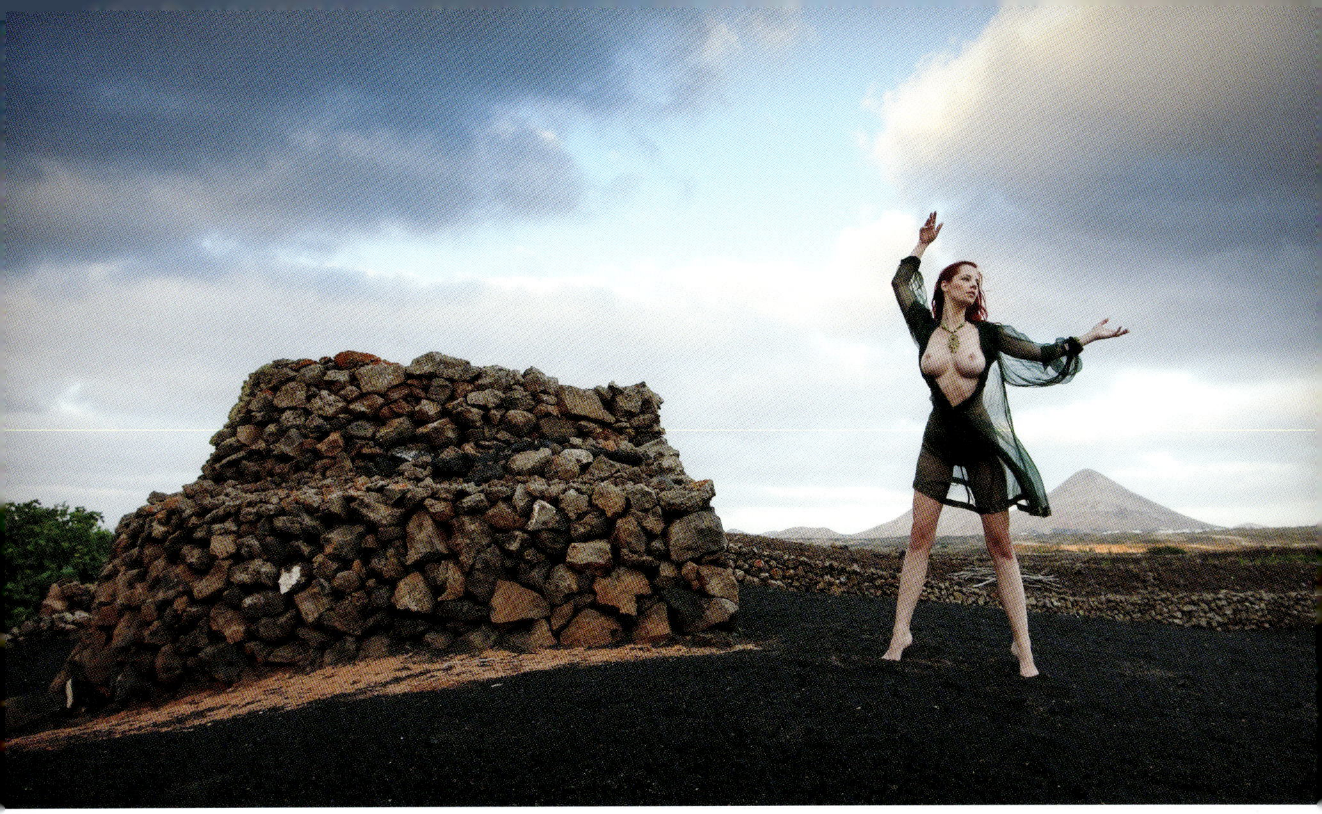

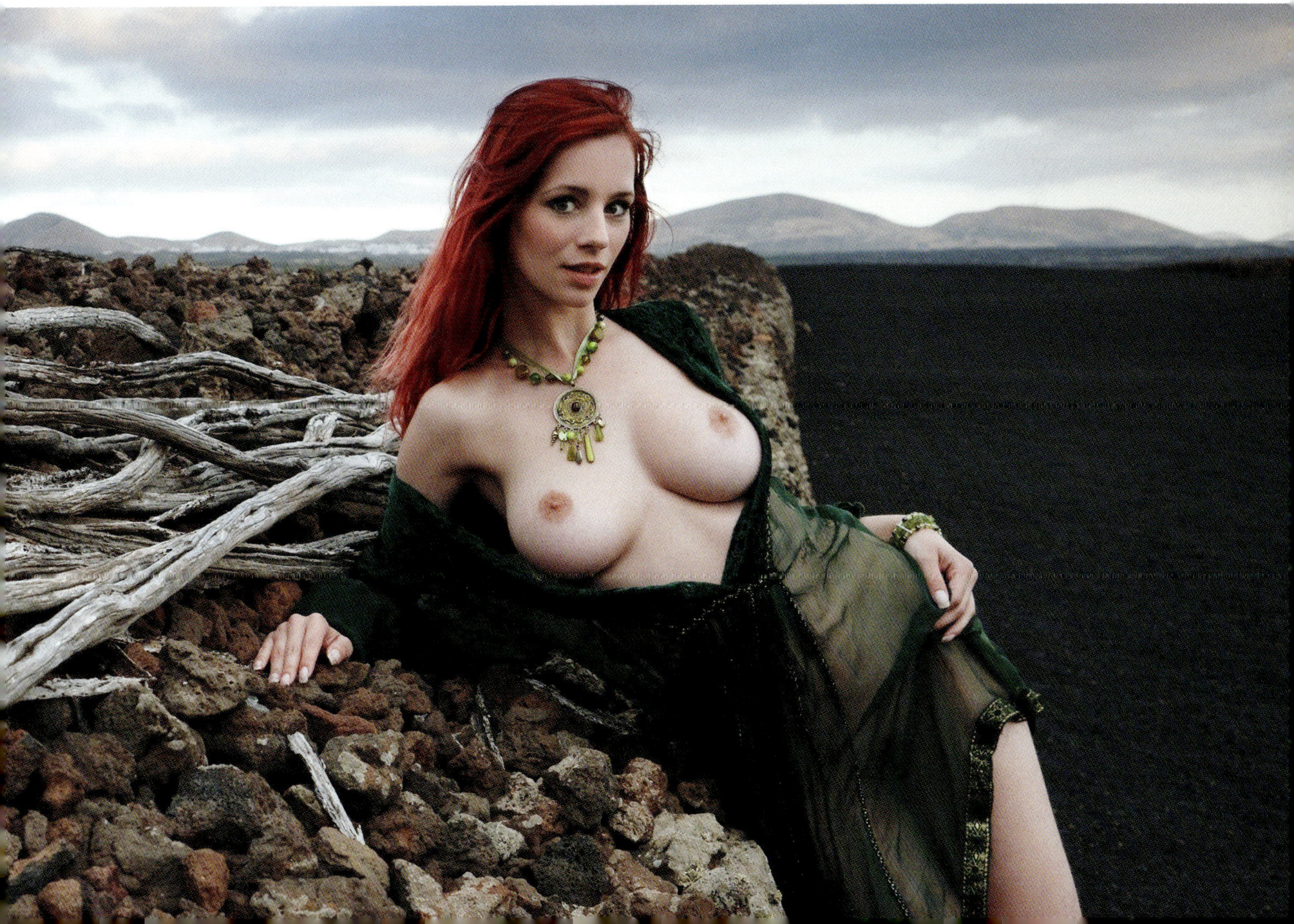

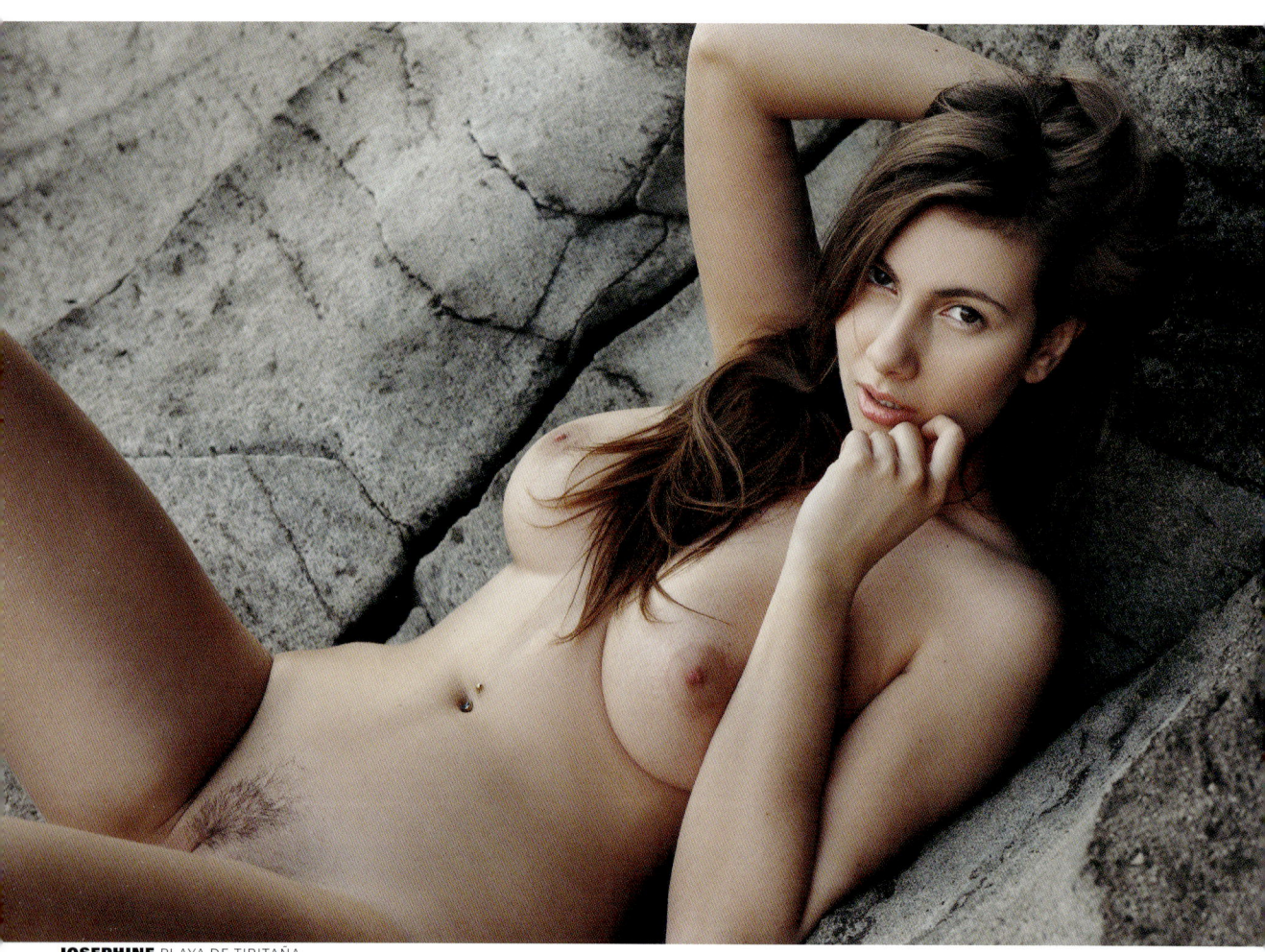
JOSEPHINE PLAYA DE TIRITAÑA

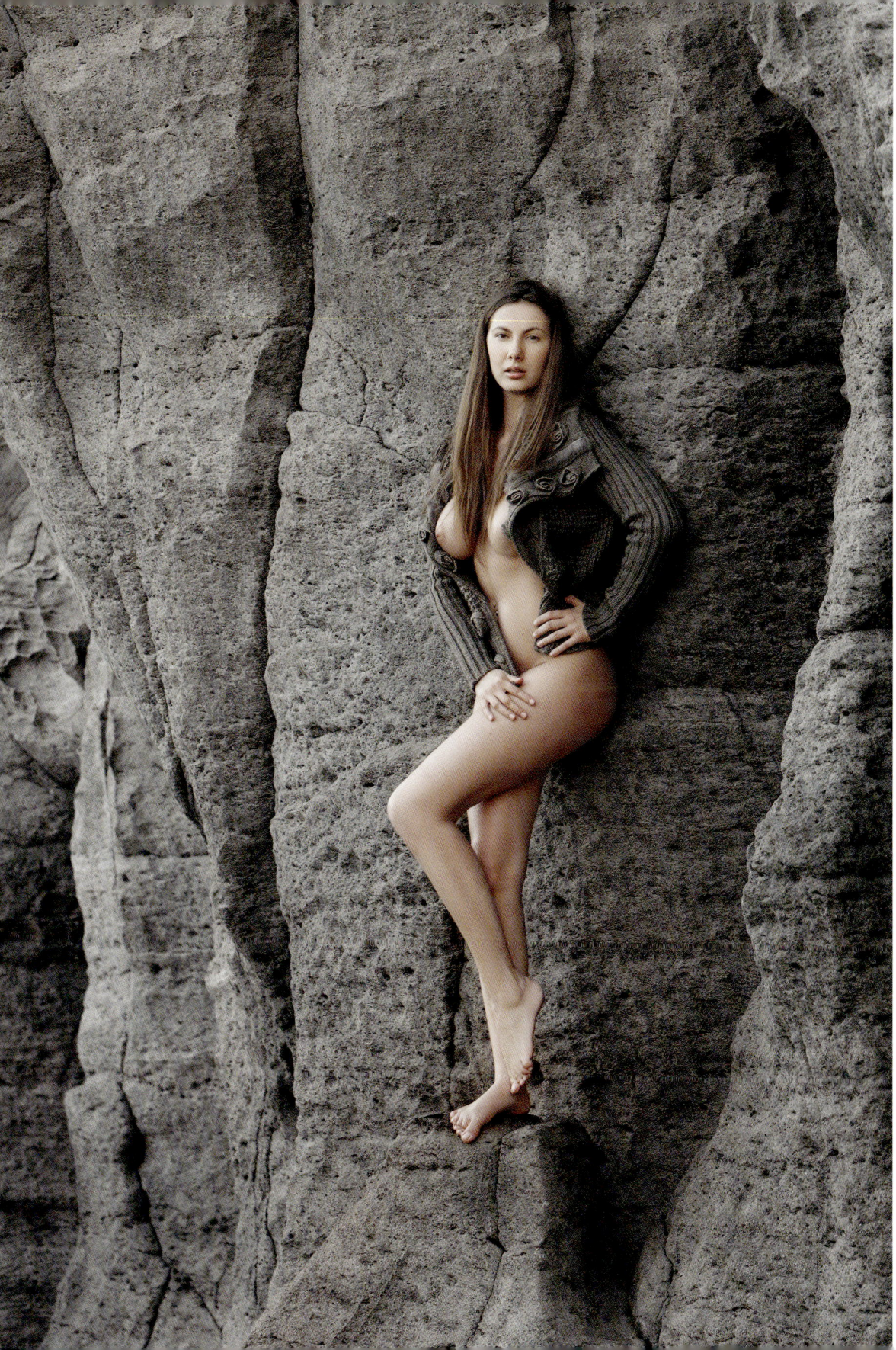

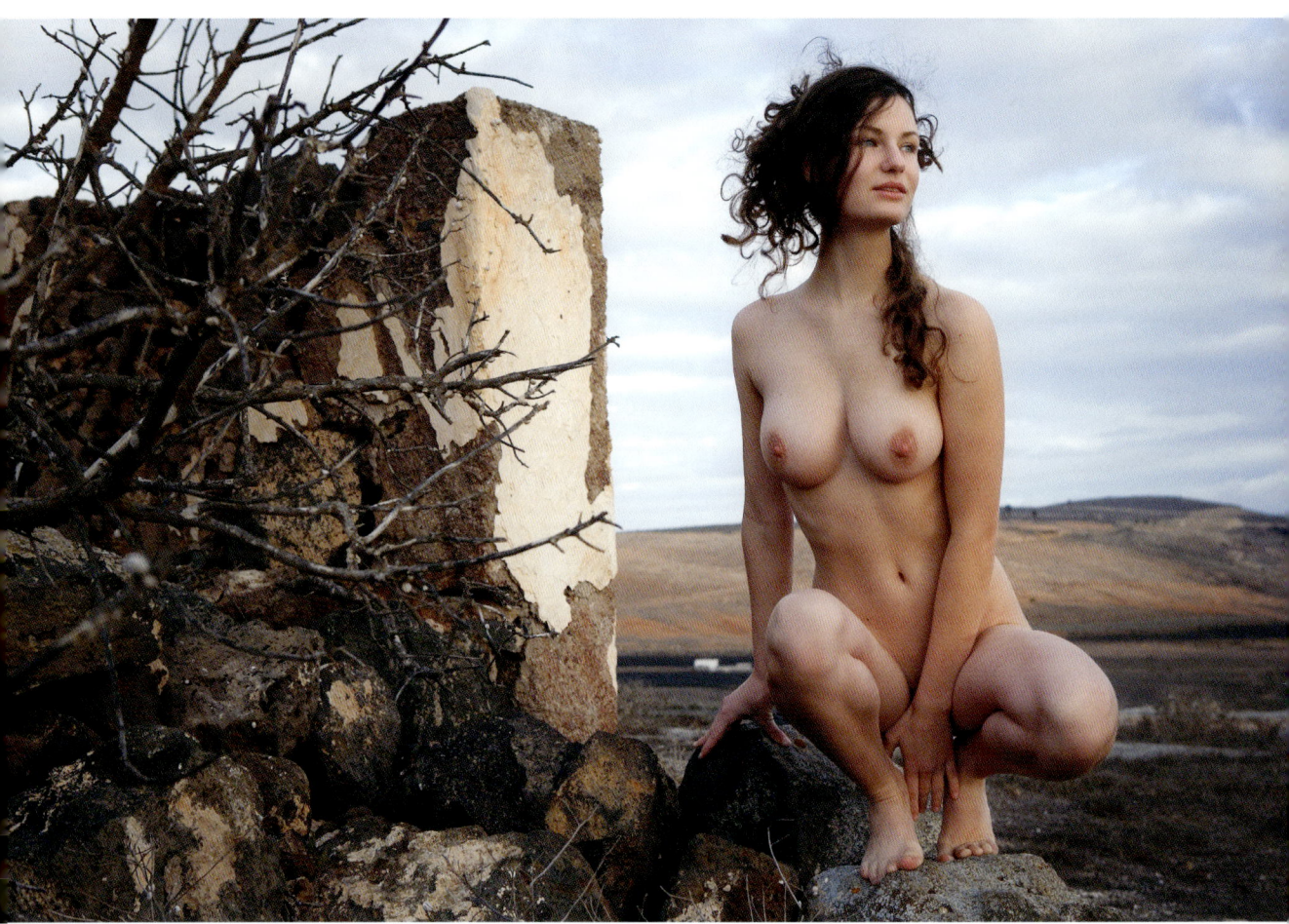

SUSANN GUANAPAY, TEGUISE

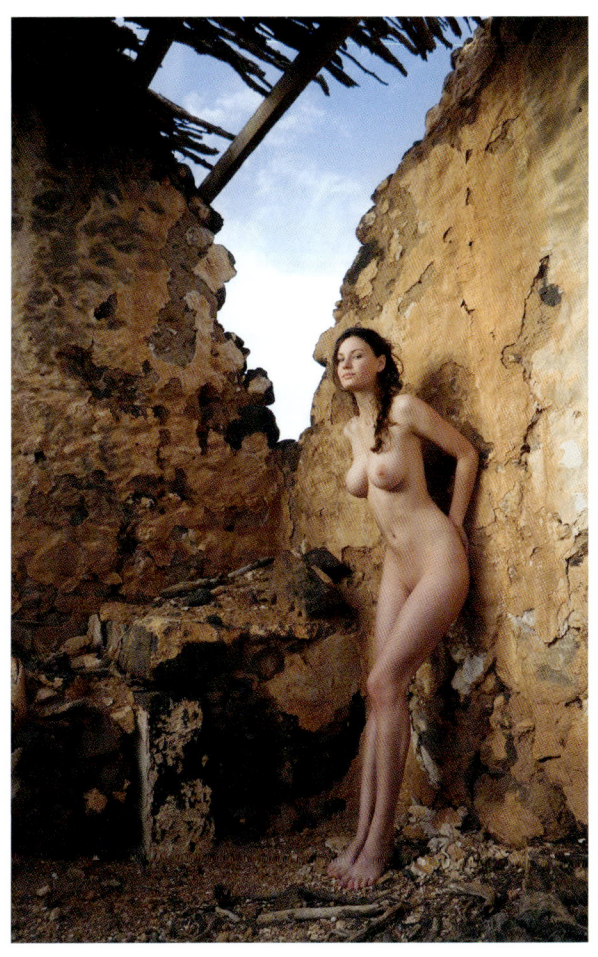
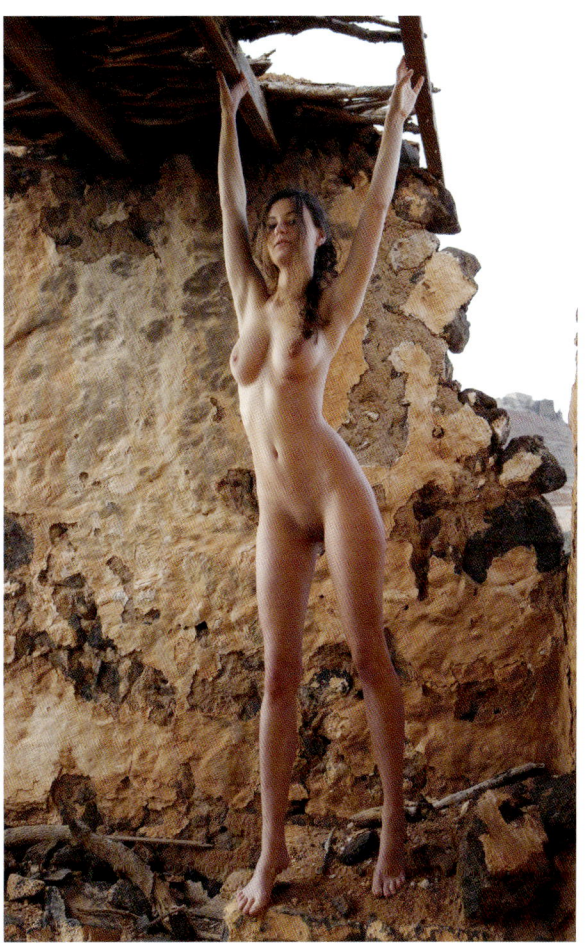

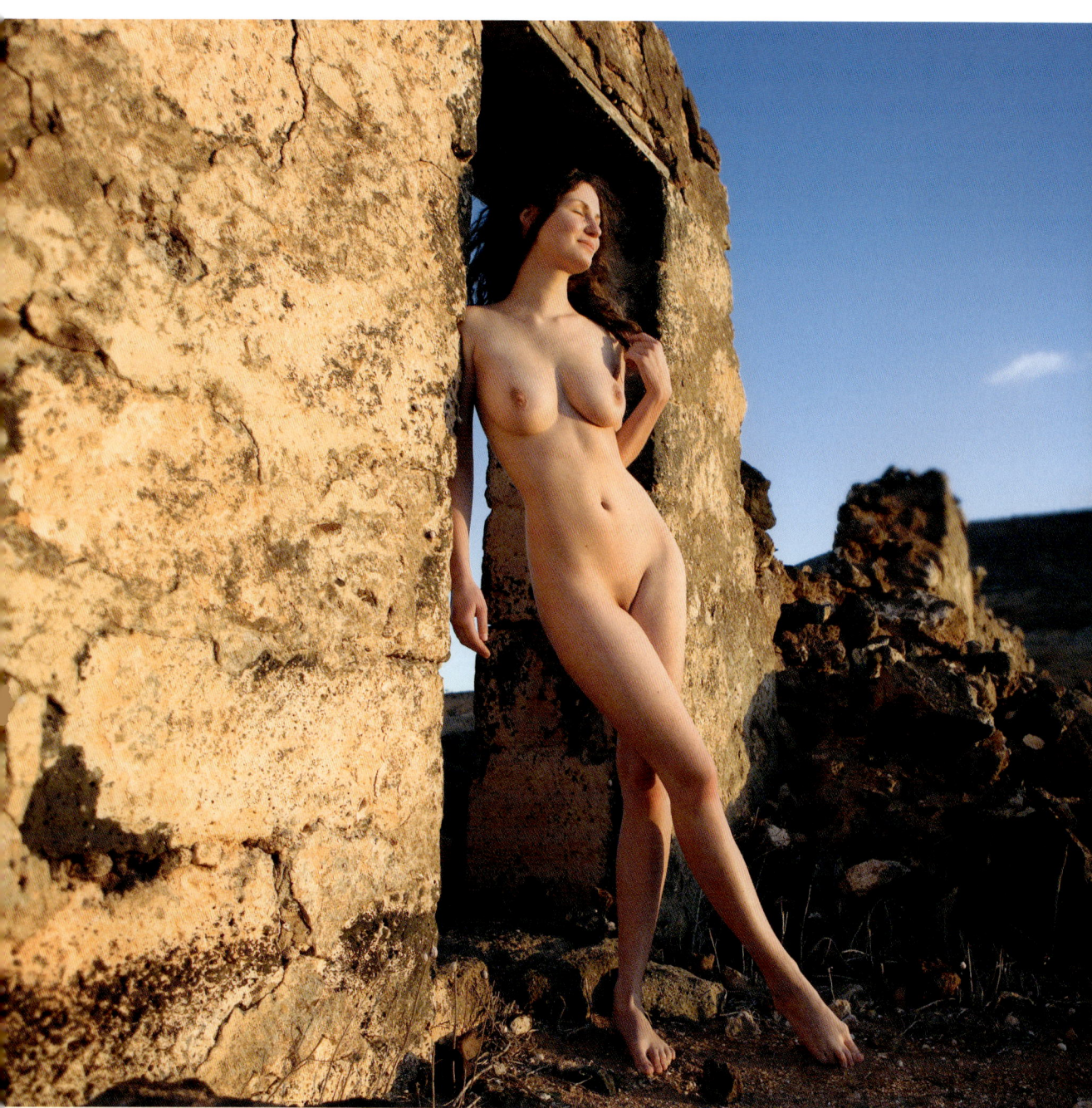

SUSANN GUANAPAY, TEGUISE

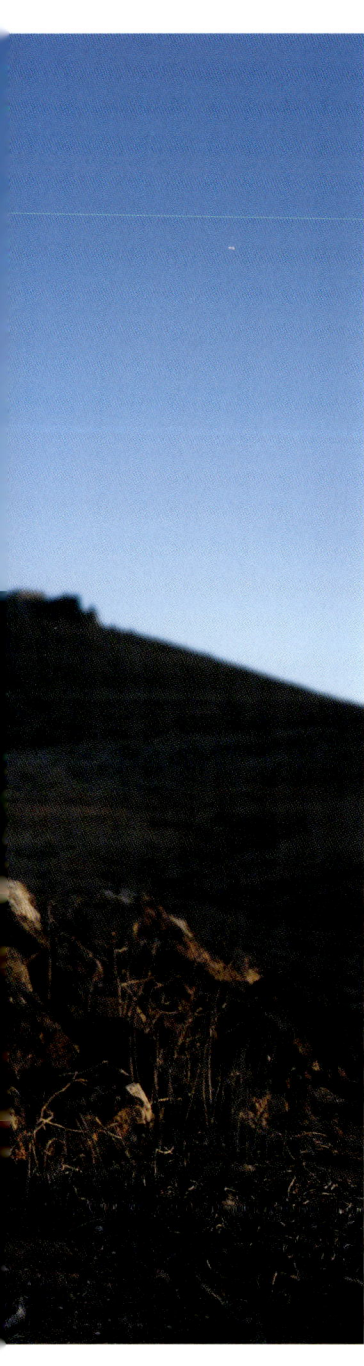

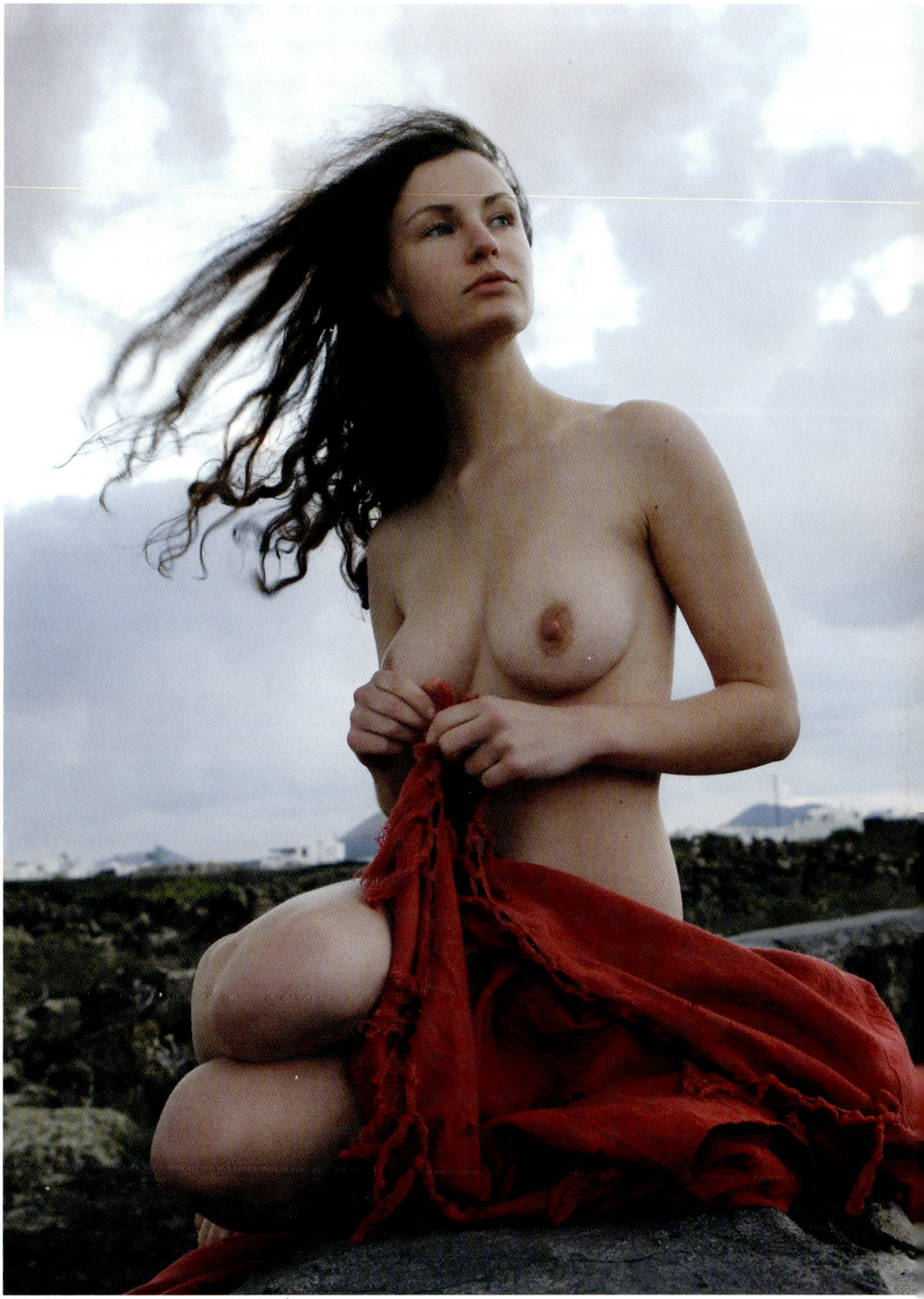

SUSANN MOZAGE, SAN BARTOLOMÉ

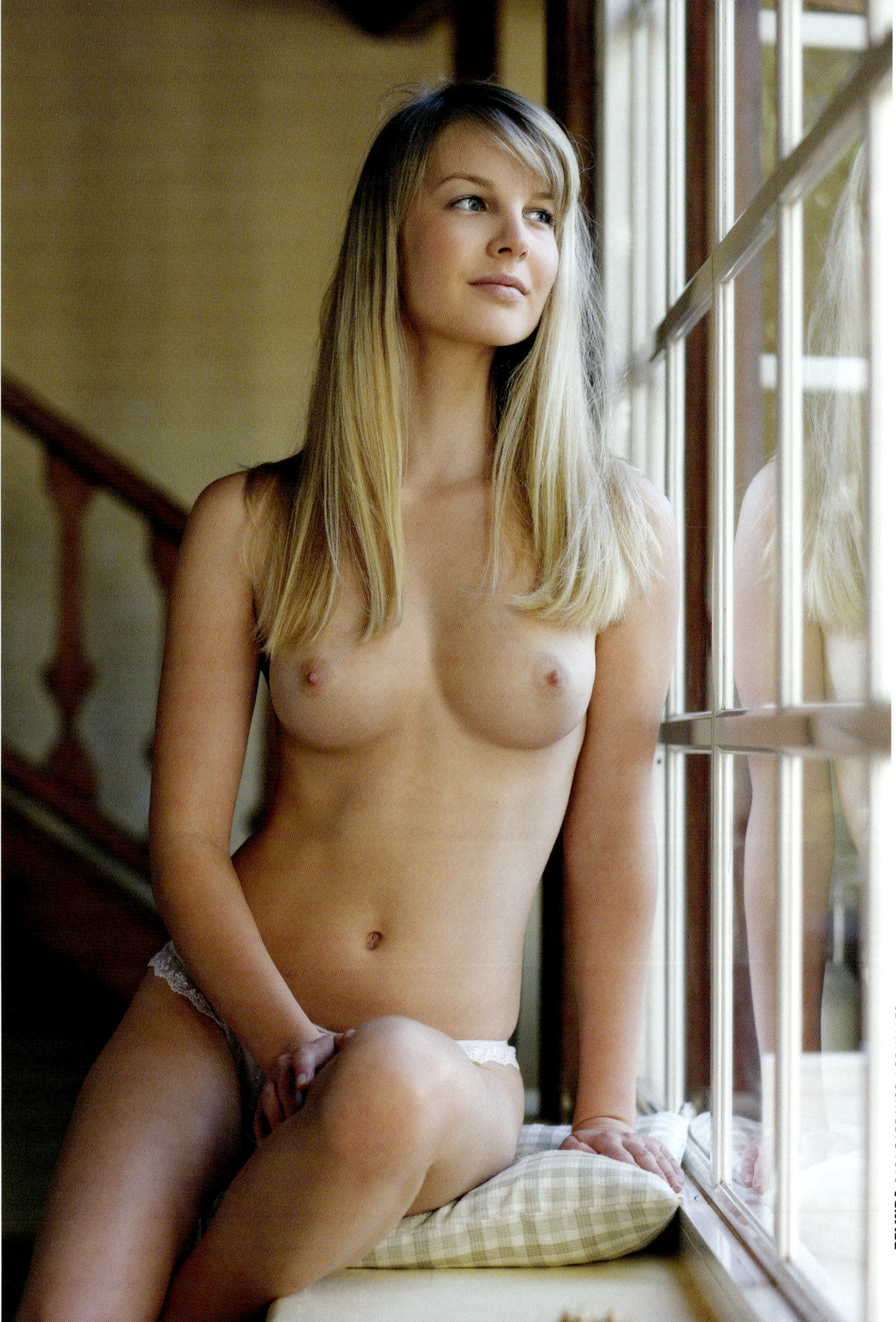

BELINDA CASA BARRANCO, LOS VALLES

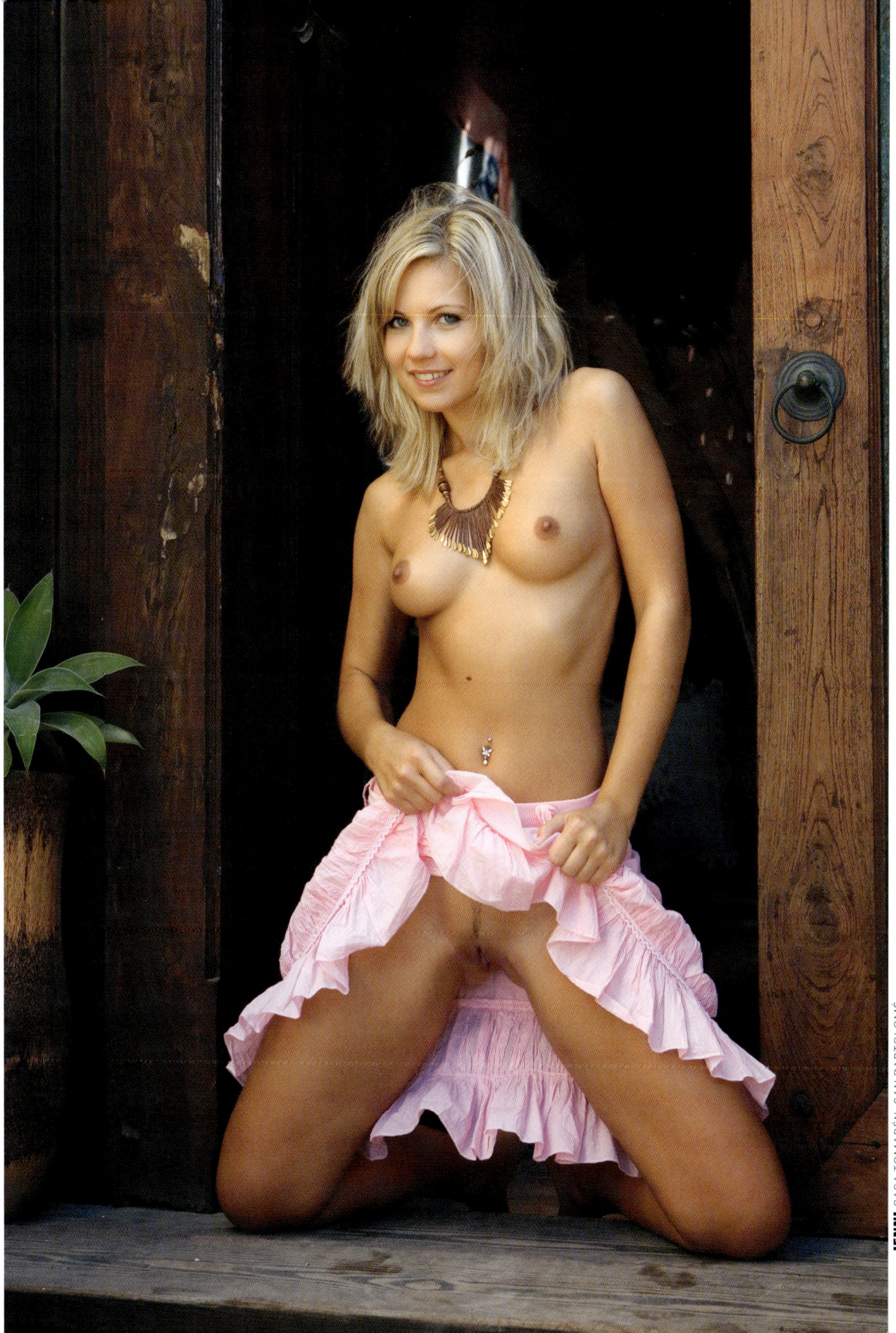

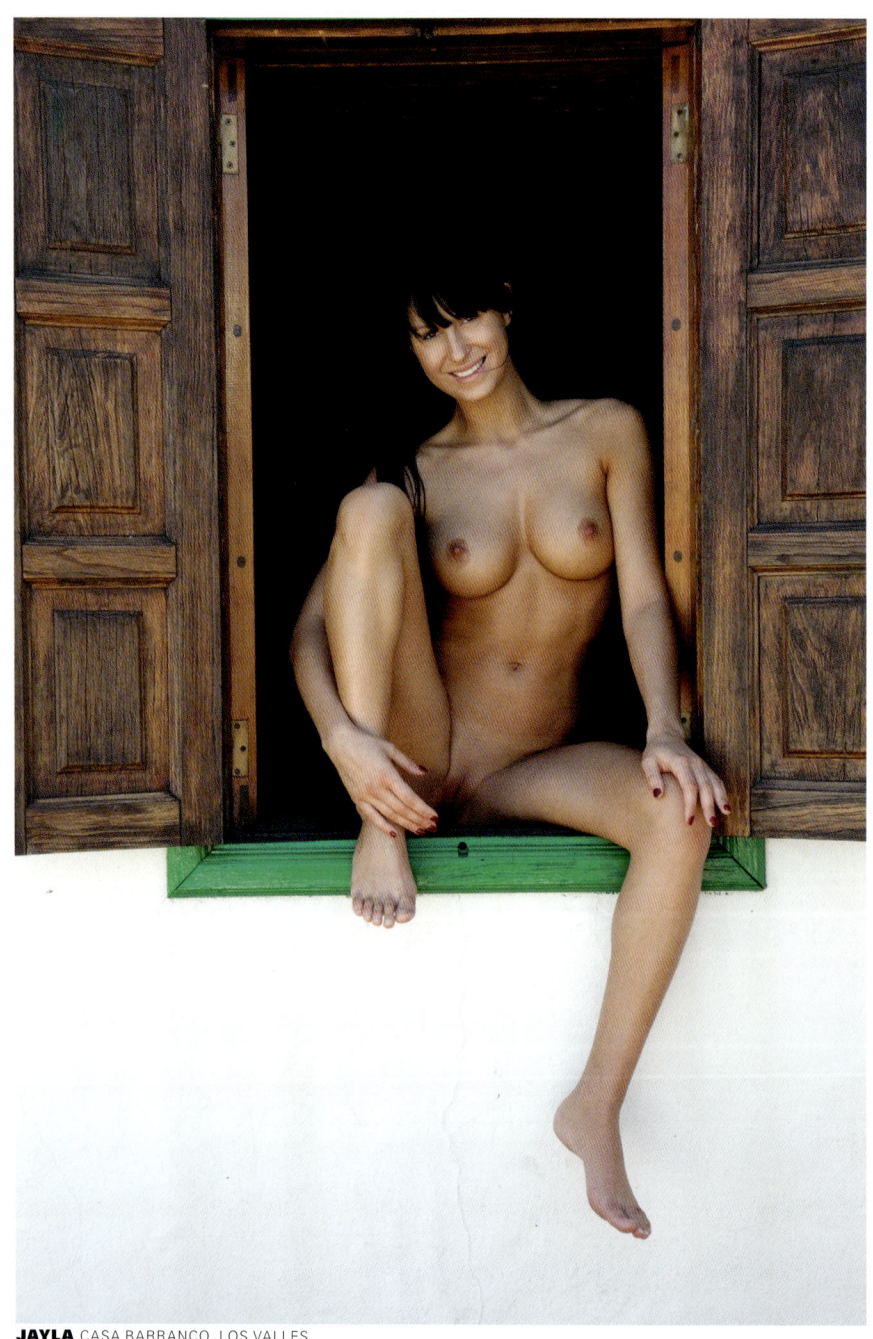

JAYLA CASA BARRANCO, LOS VALLES

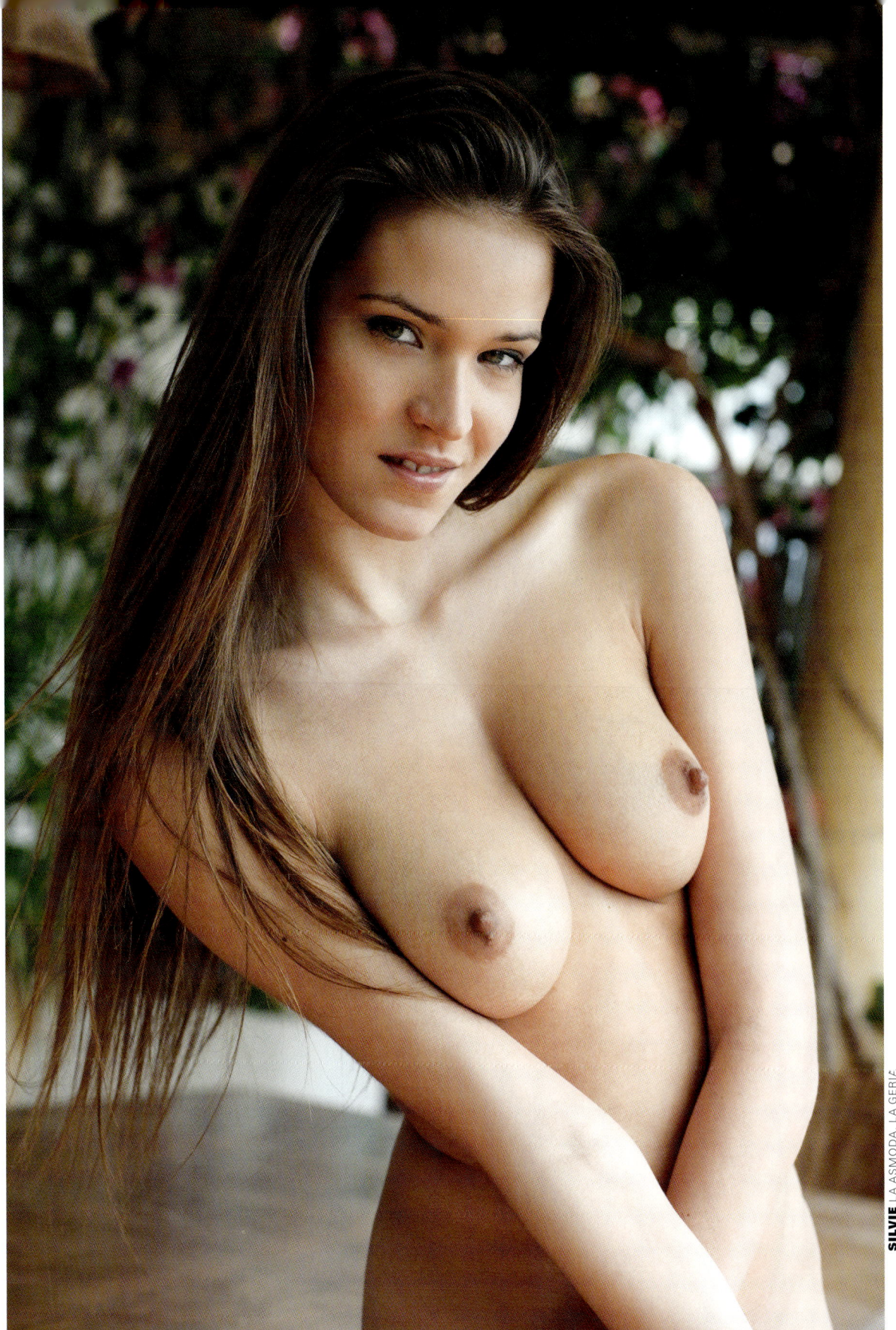

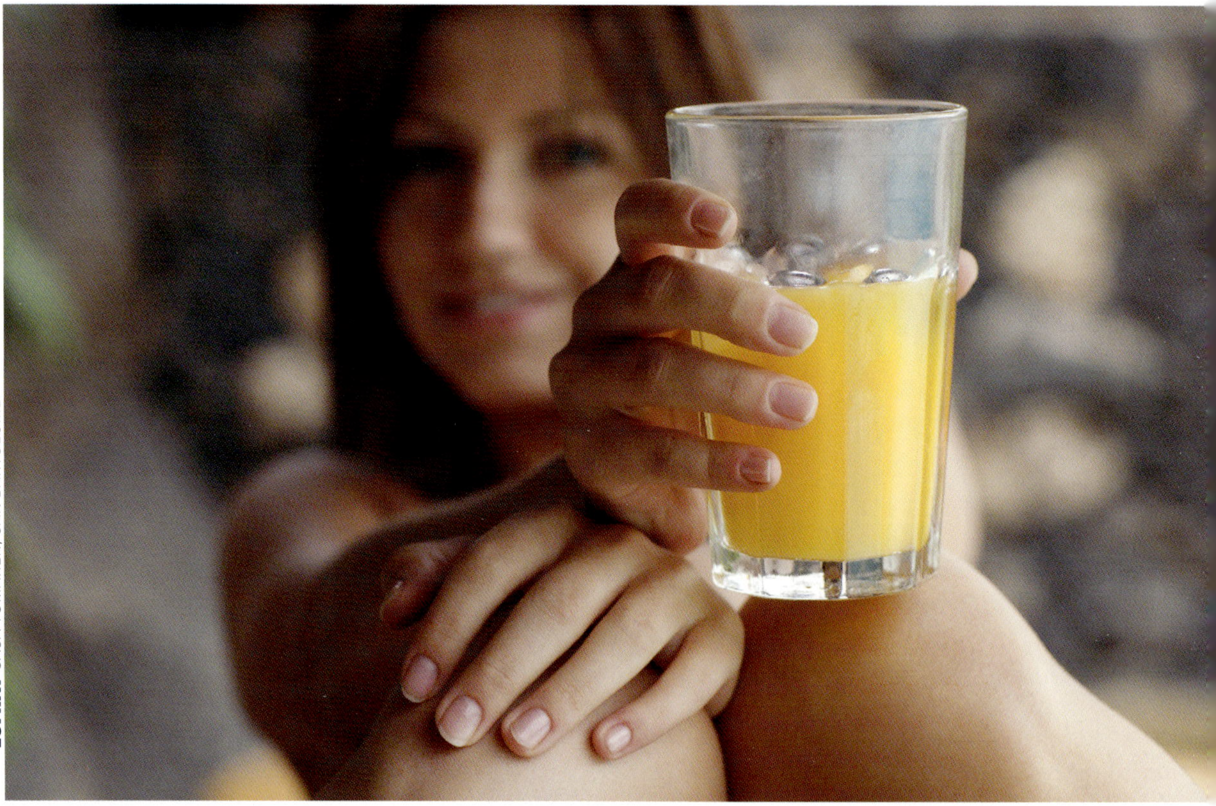

EUFRAT CASA TOMARÉN, SAN BARTOLOMÉ

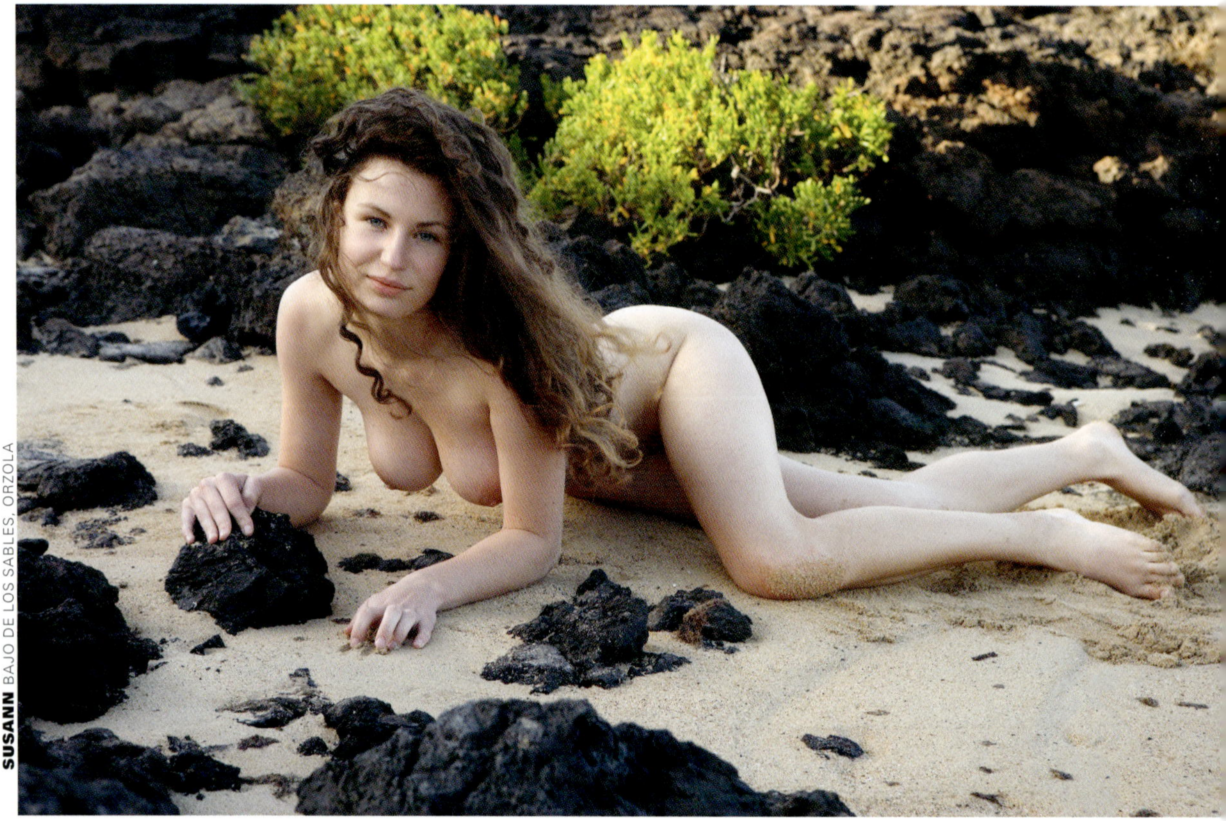

SUSANN BAJO DE LOS SABLES, ORZOLA

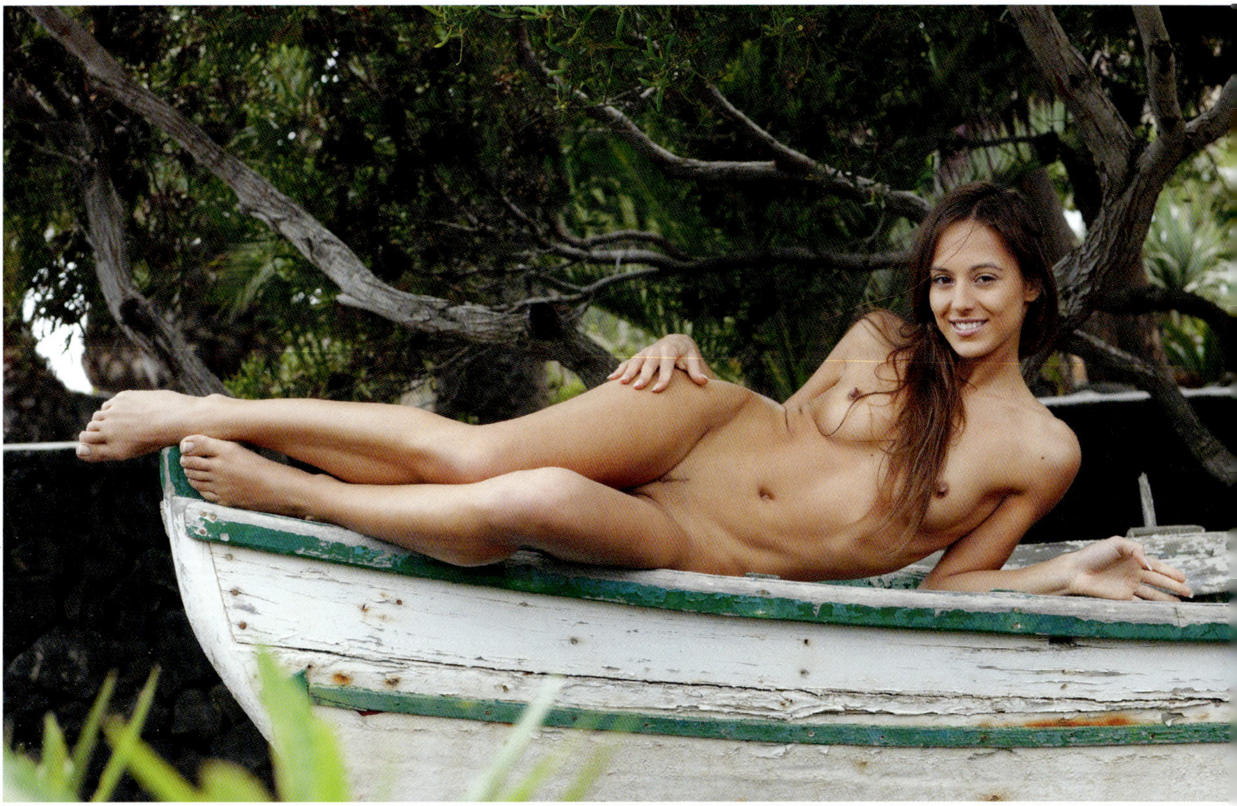

DOMINIKA LA ASMODA, LA GERIA

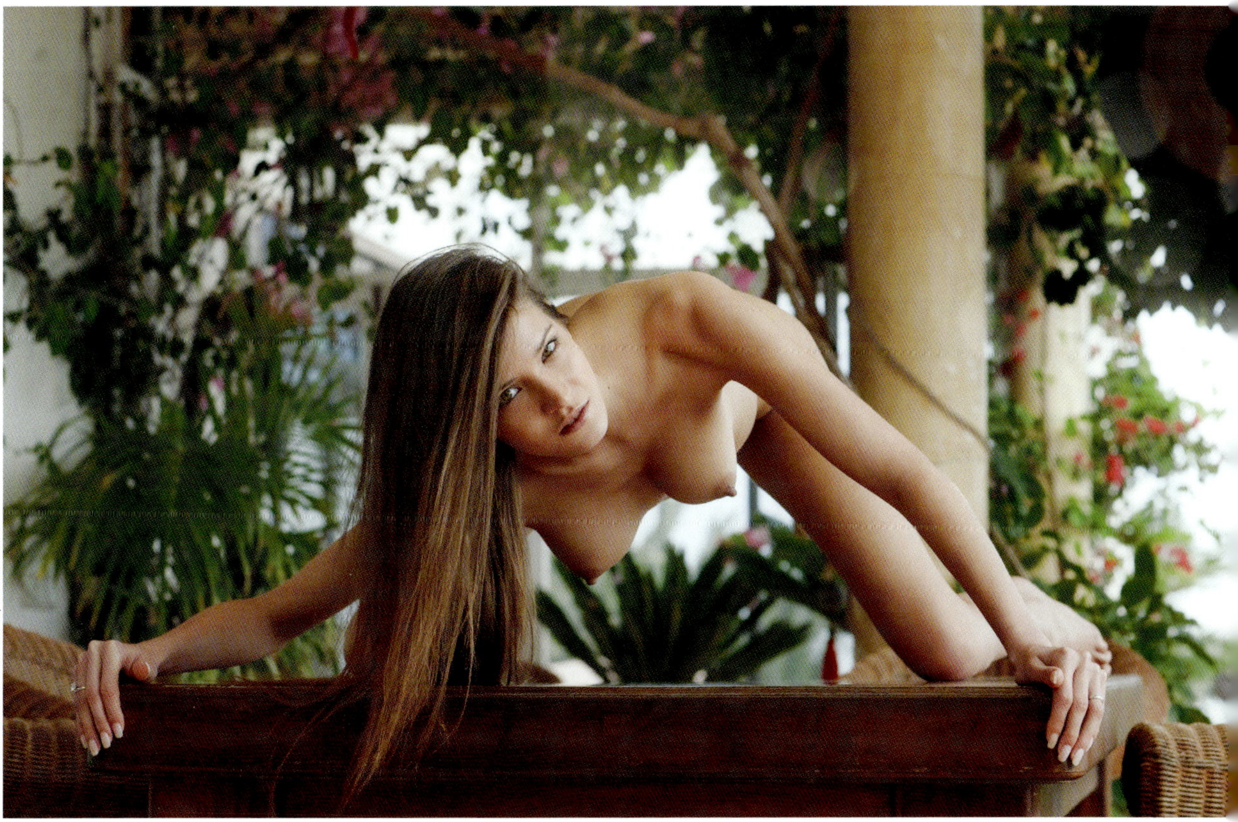

SILVIE LA ASMODA, LA GERIA

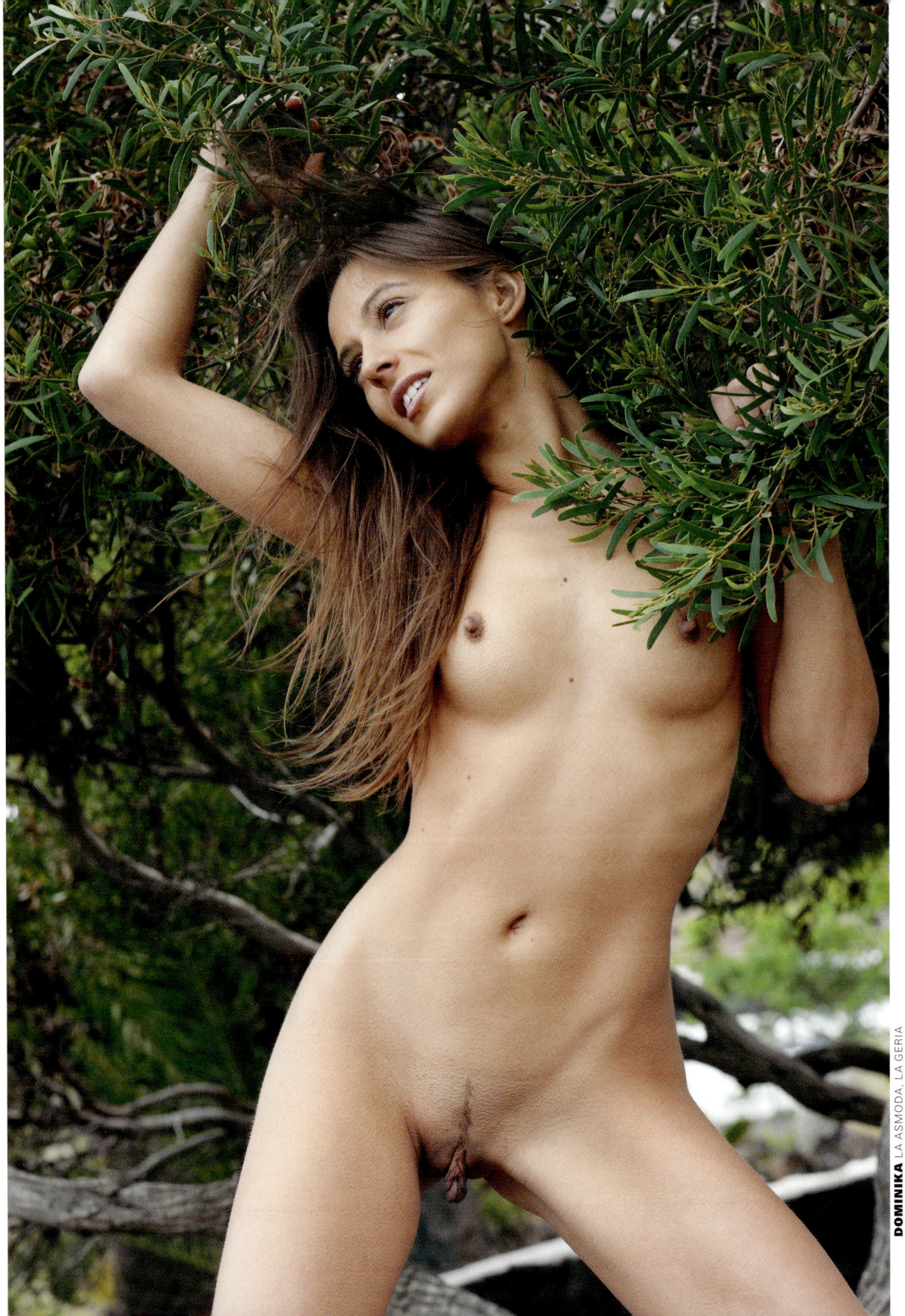

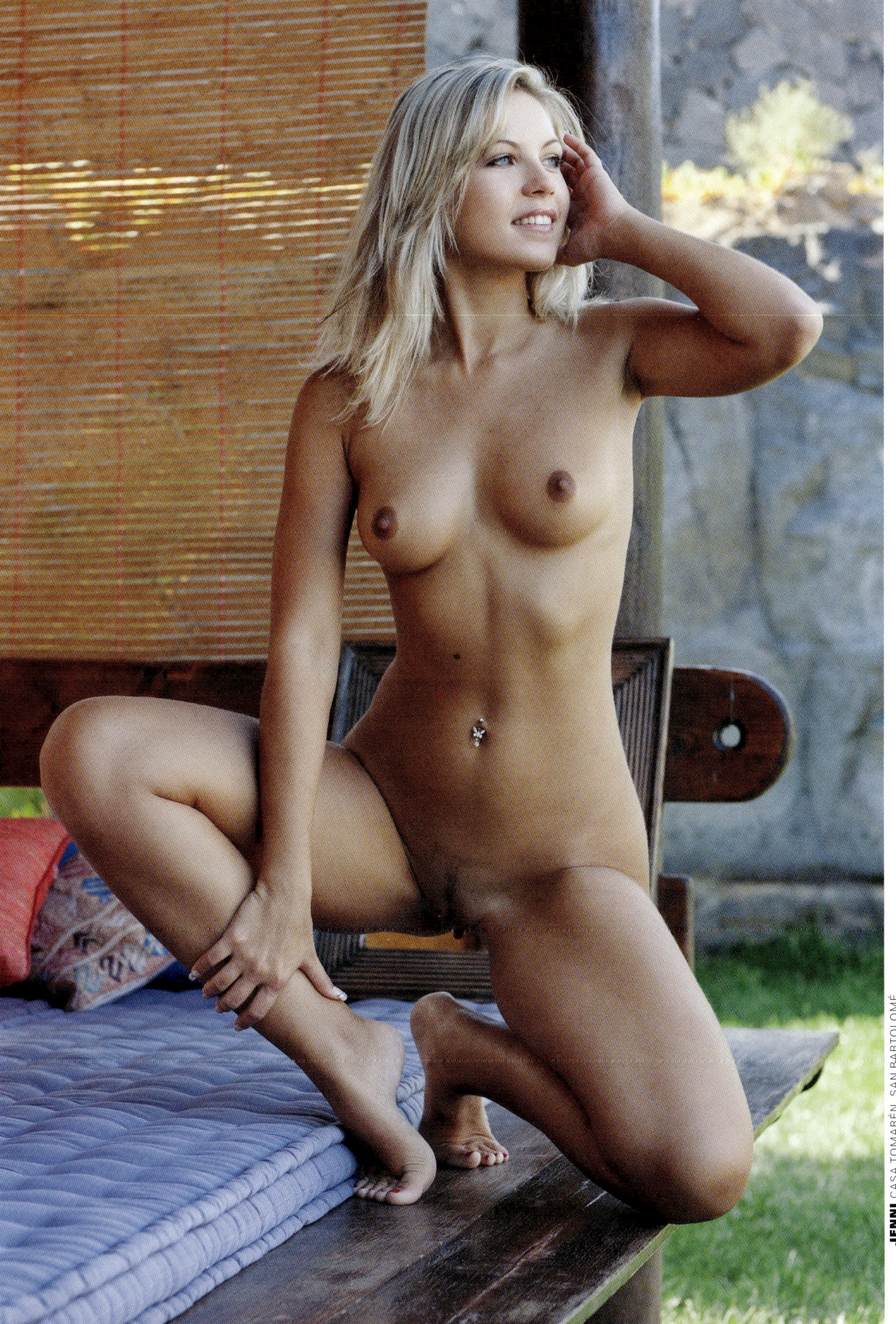

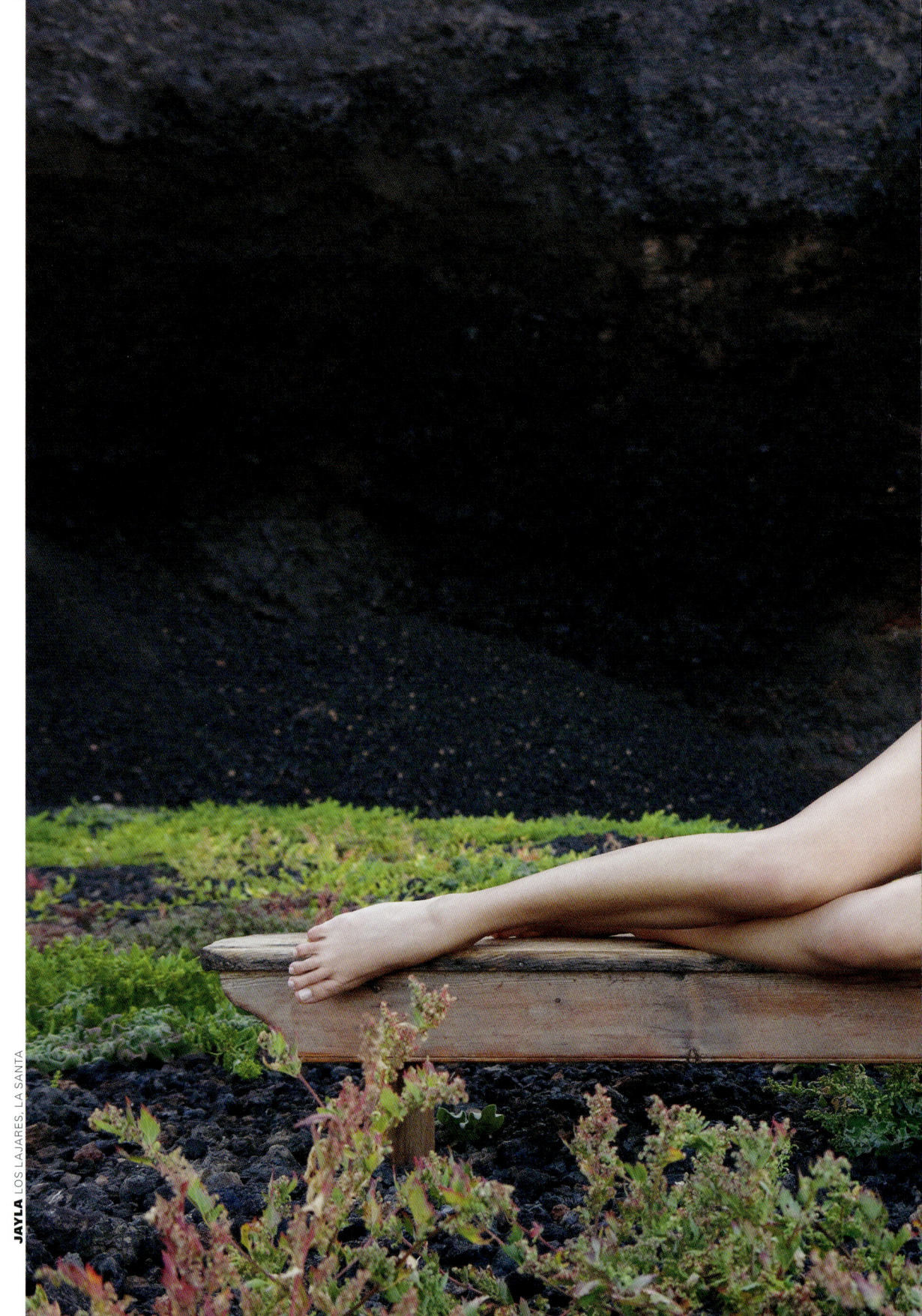

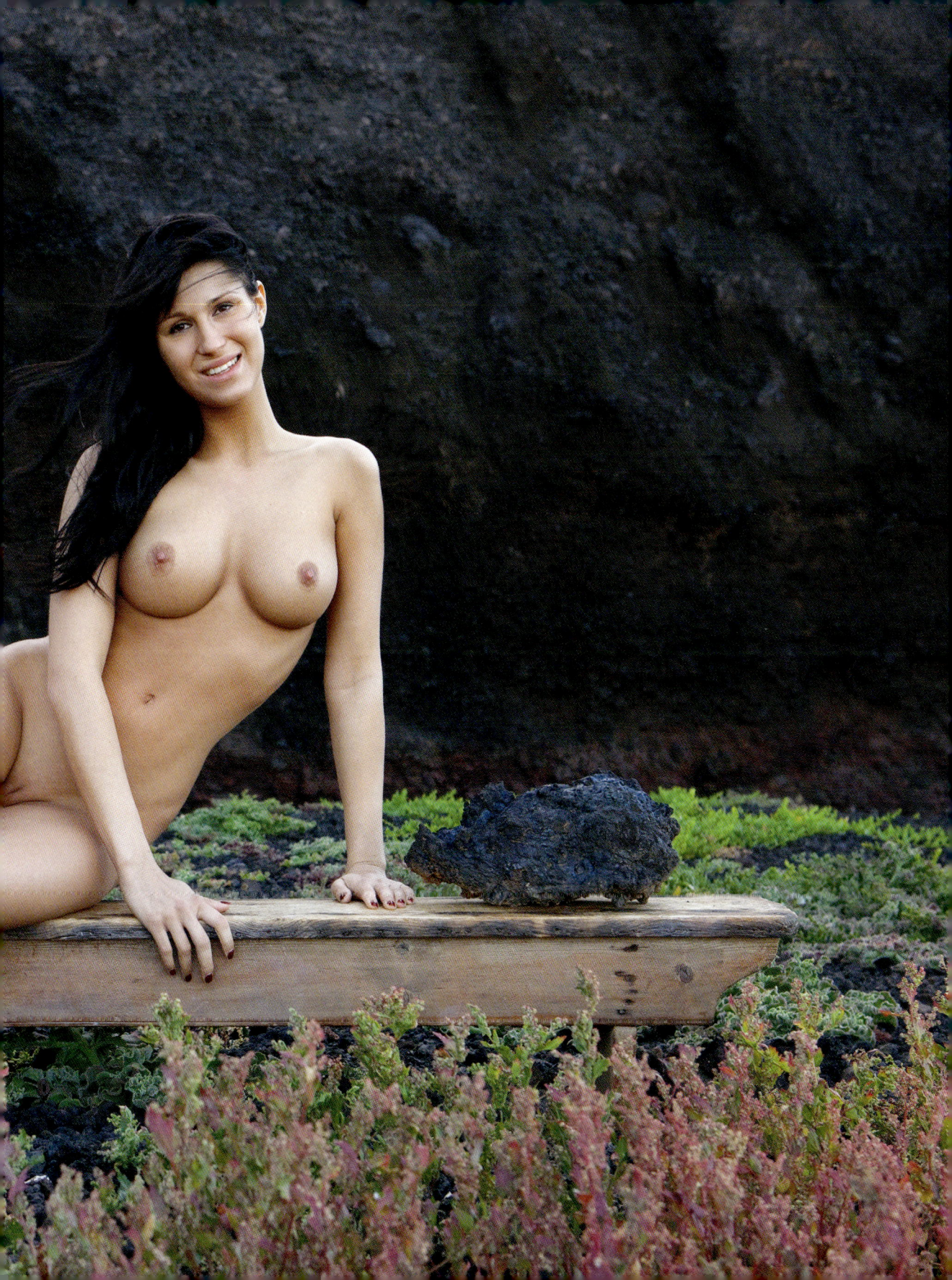

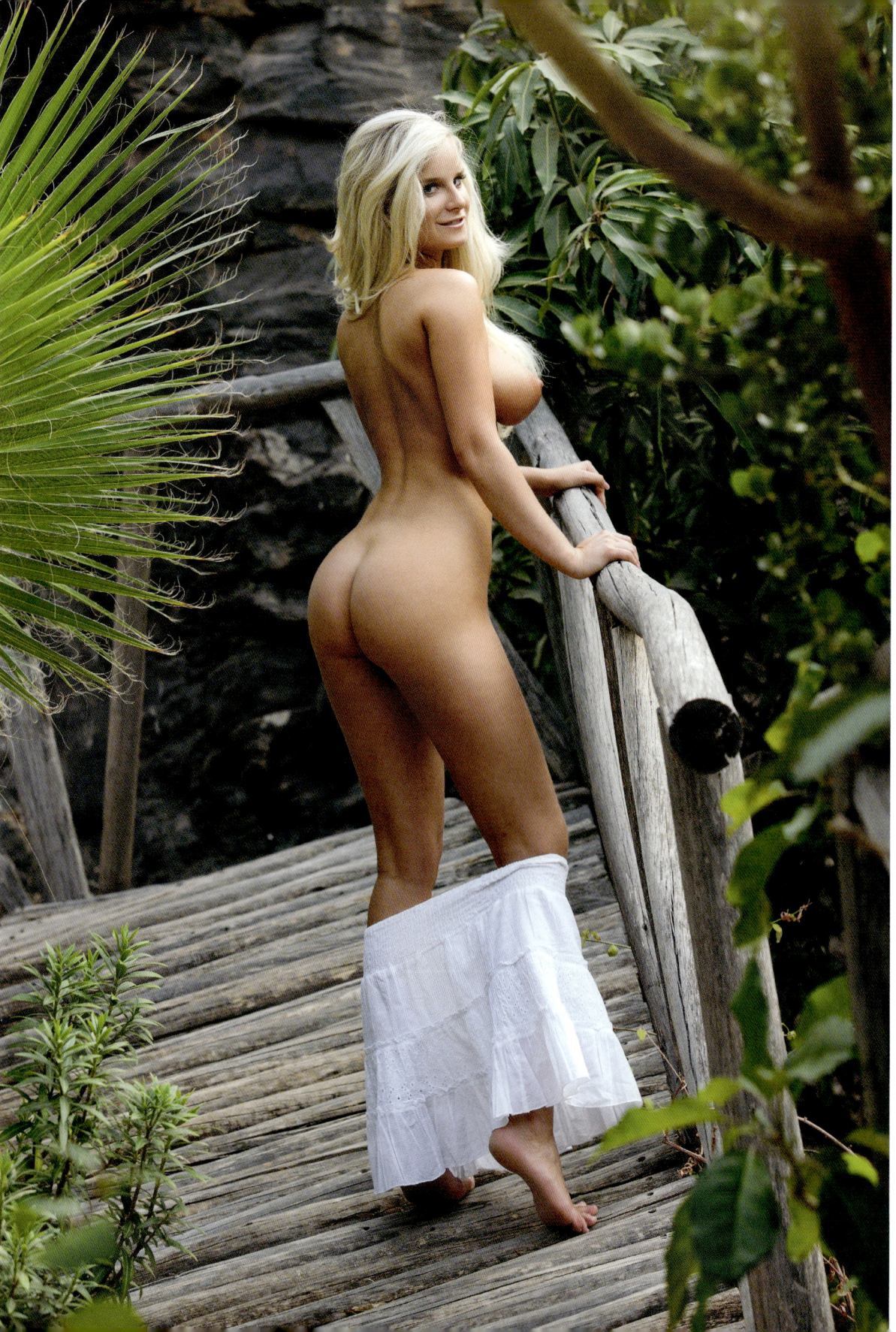

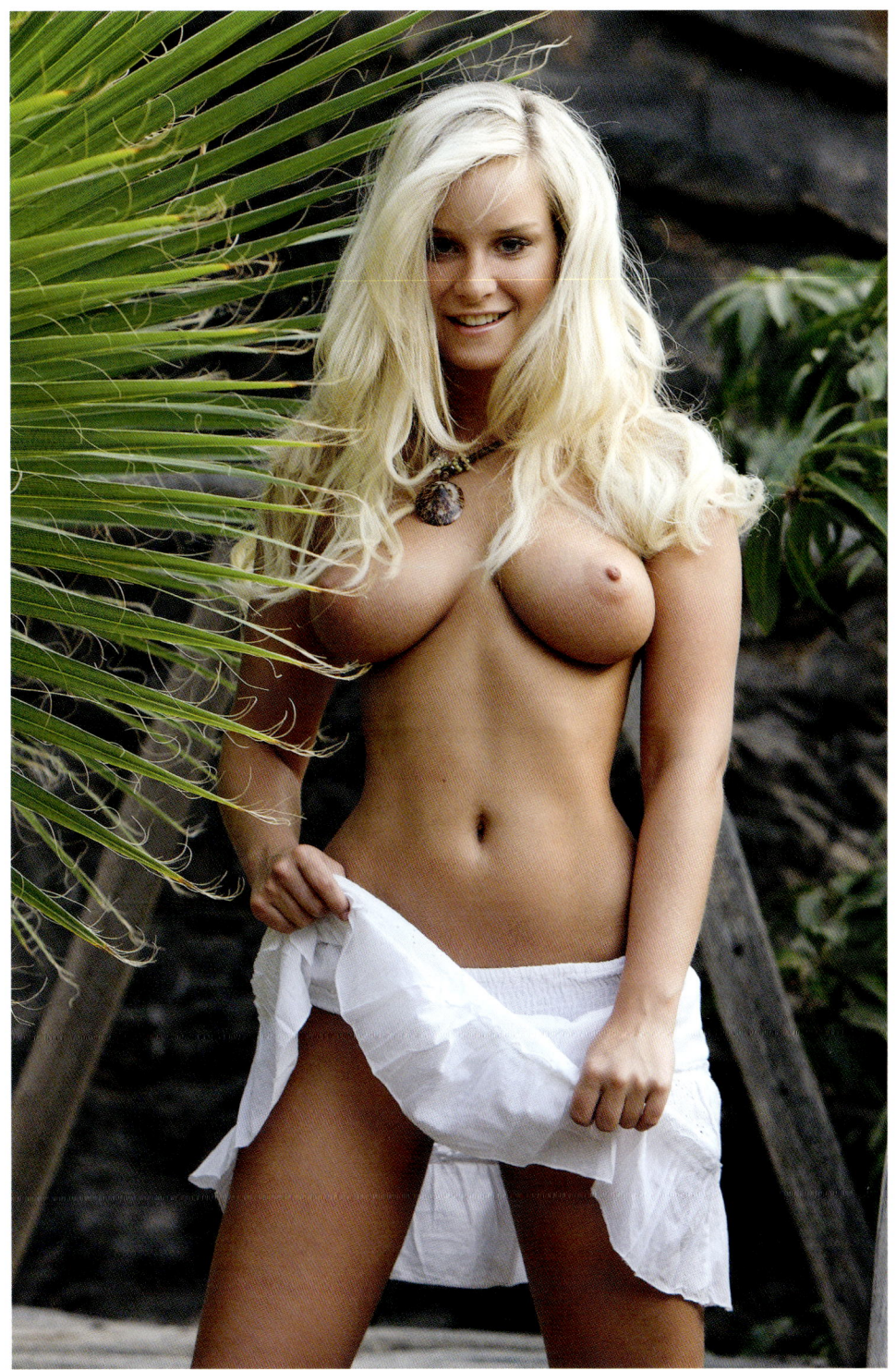

MIELA MONTECRISTO, BARRANCO DE LA DATA

63

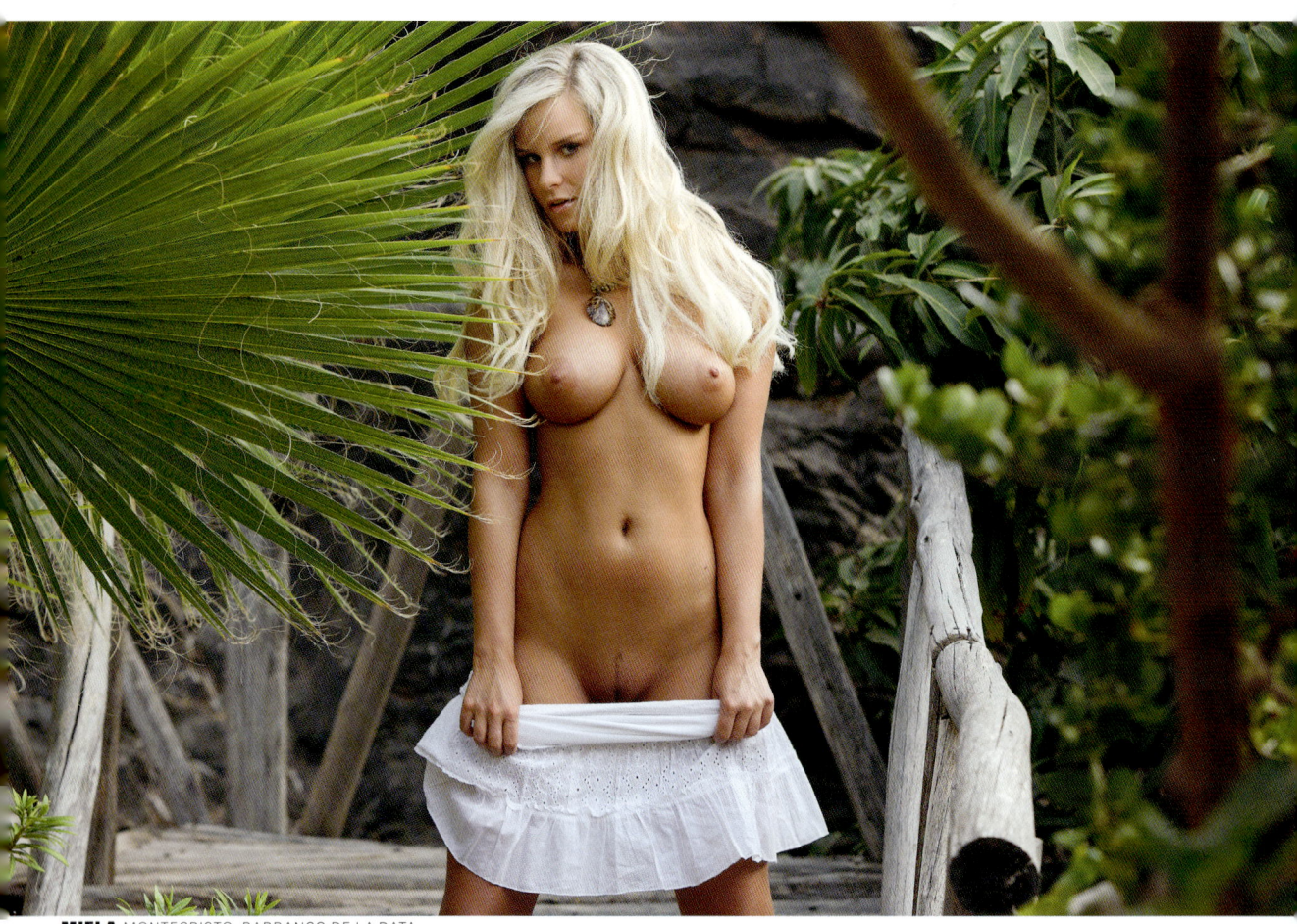

MIELA MONTECRISTO, BARRANCO DE LA DATA

64

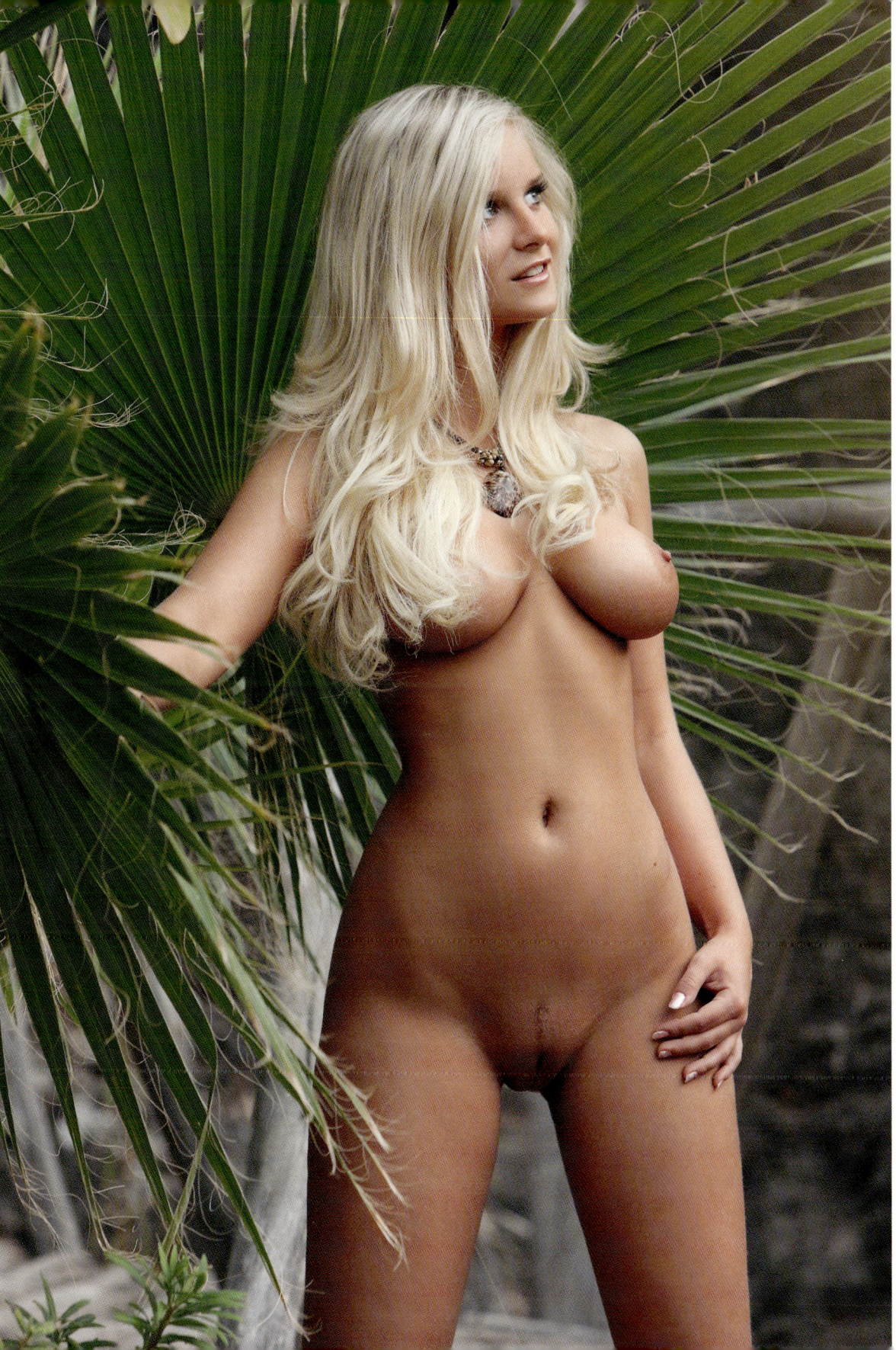

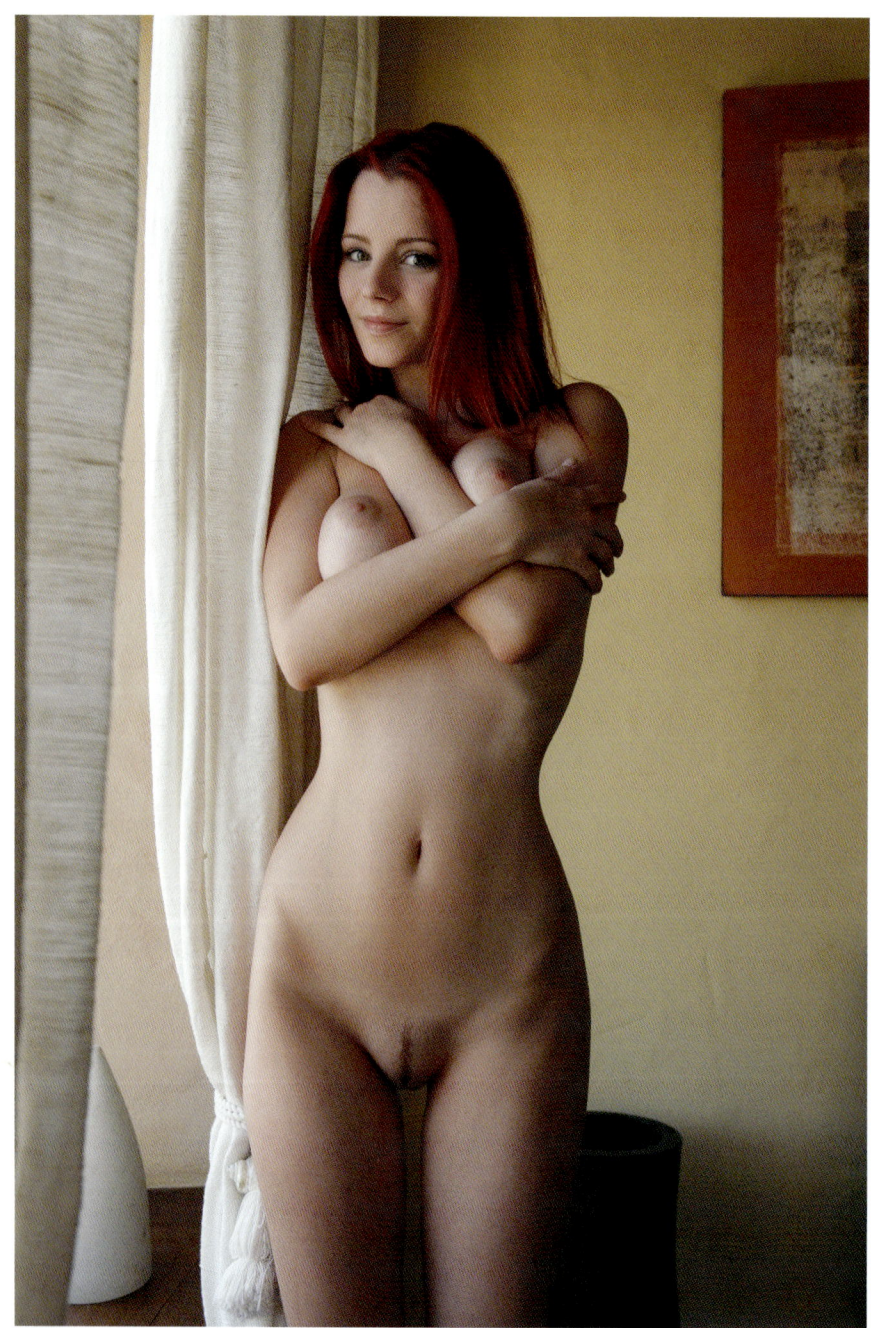

ARIEL AKAR WANGI CASA TOMARÉN, SAN BARTOLOMÉ

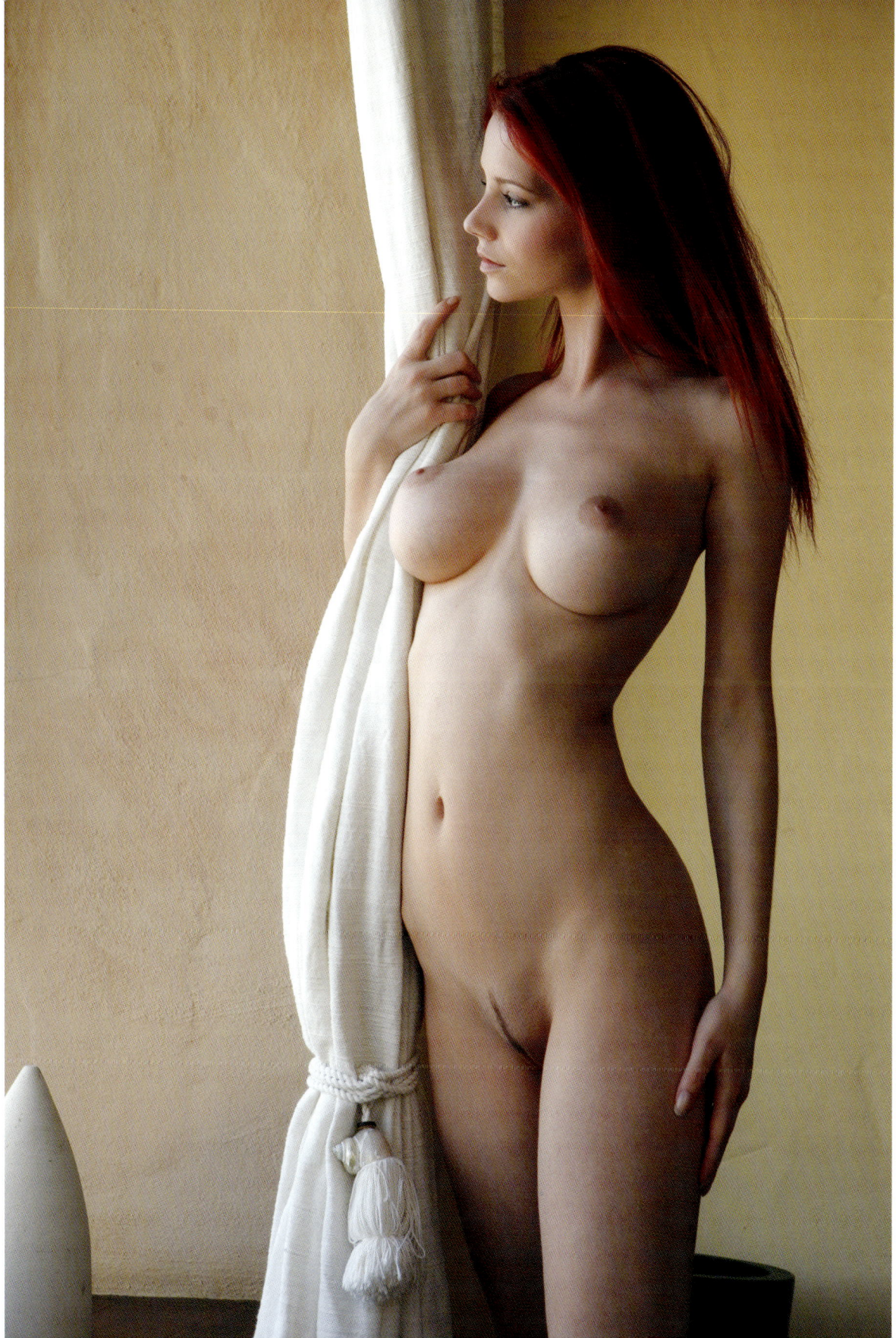

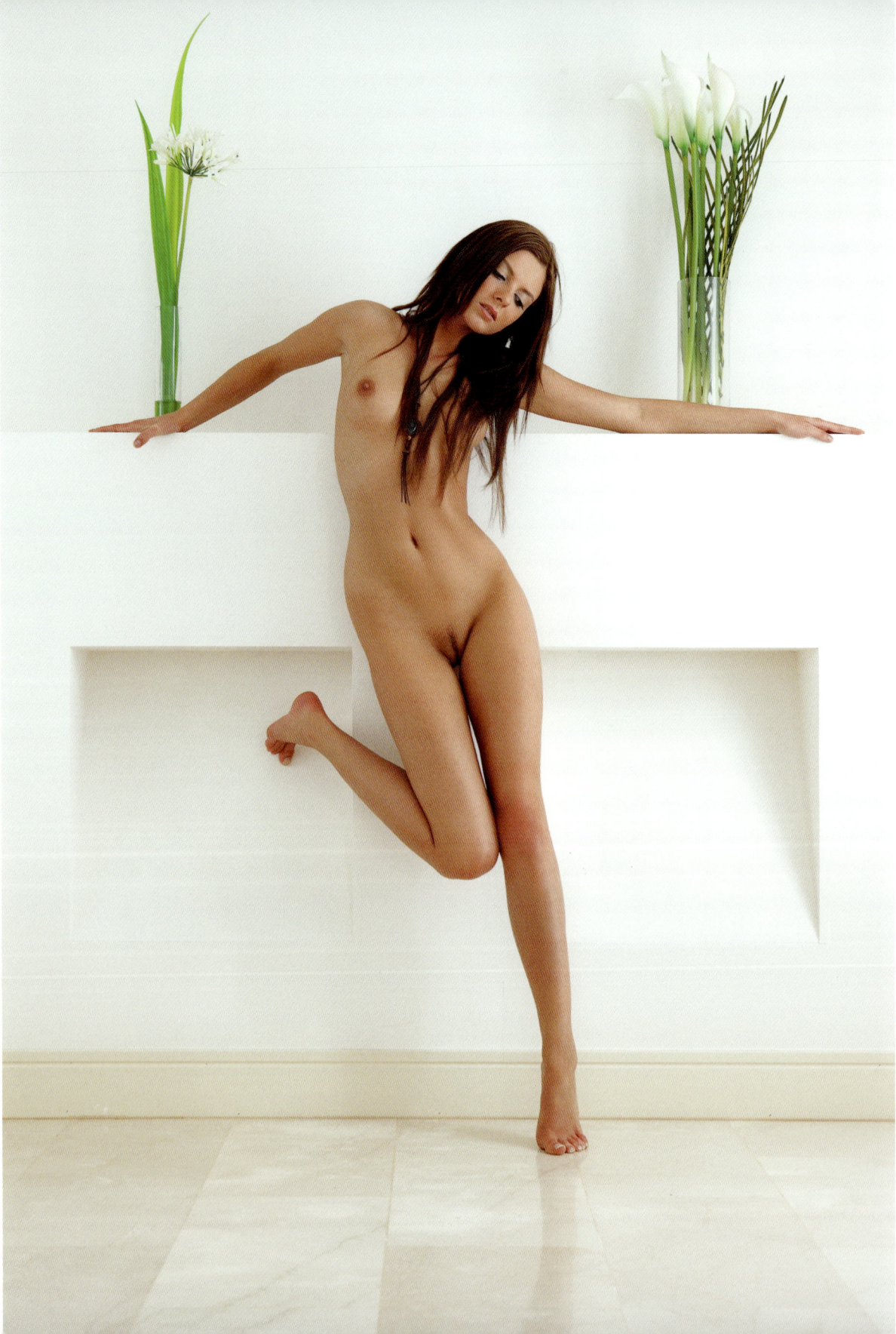

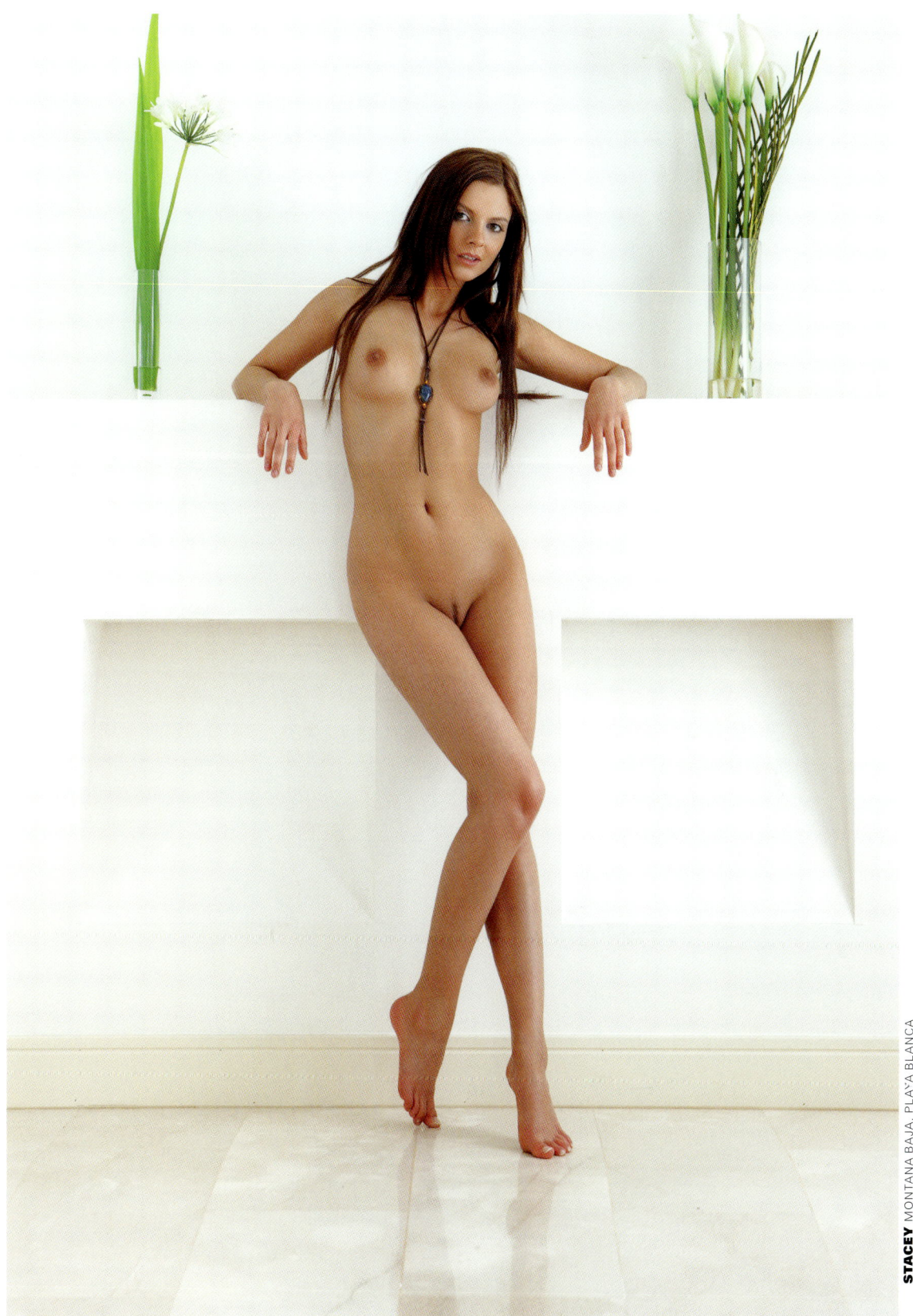

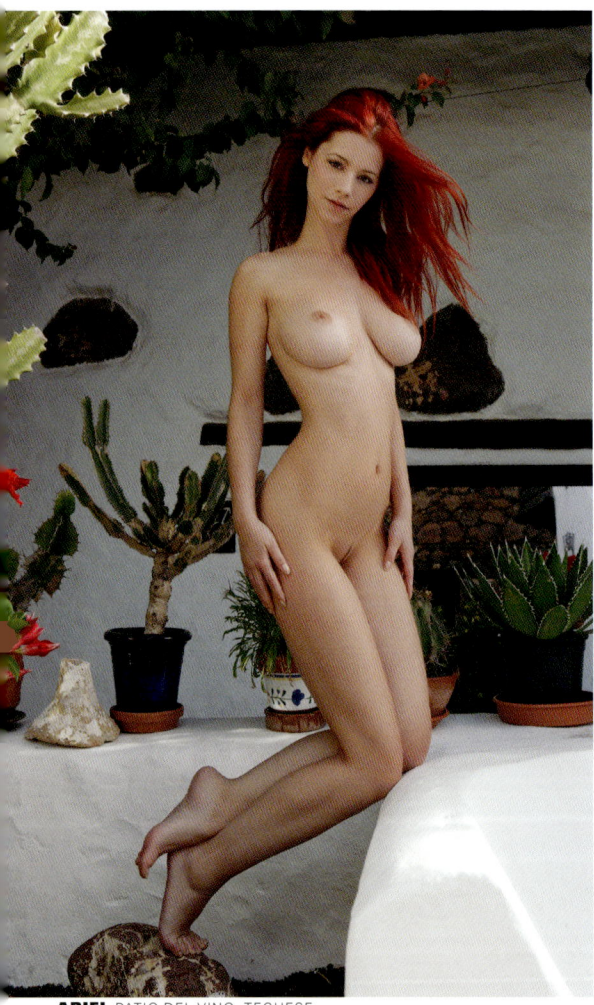
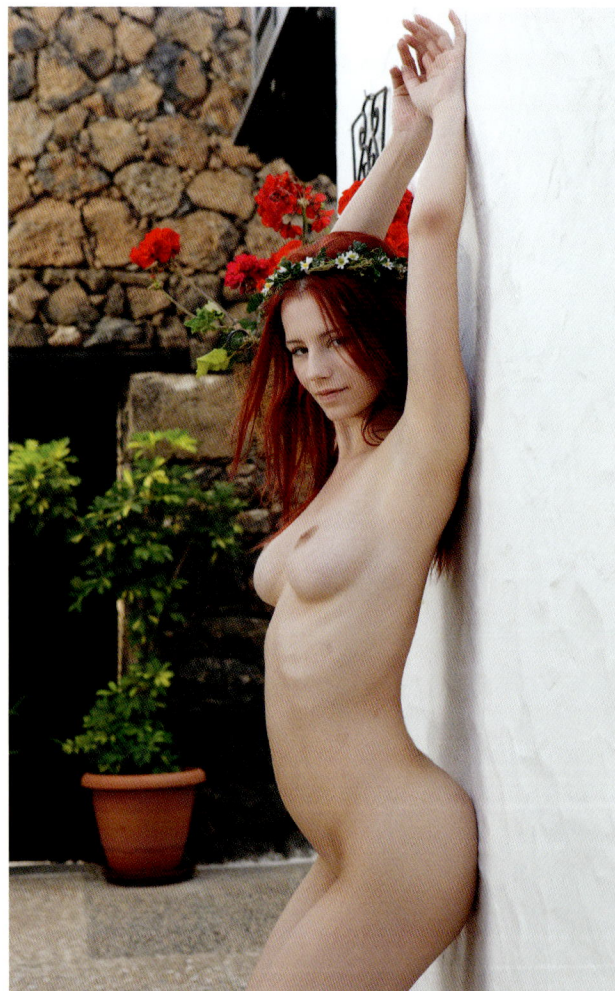

ARIEL PATIO DEL VINO, TEGUESE

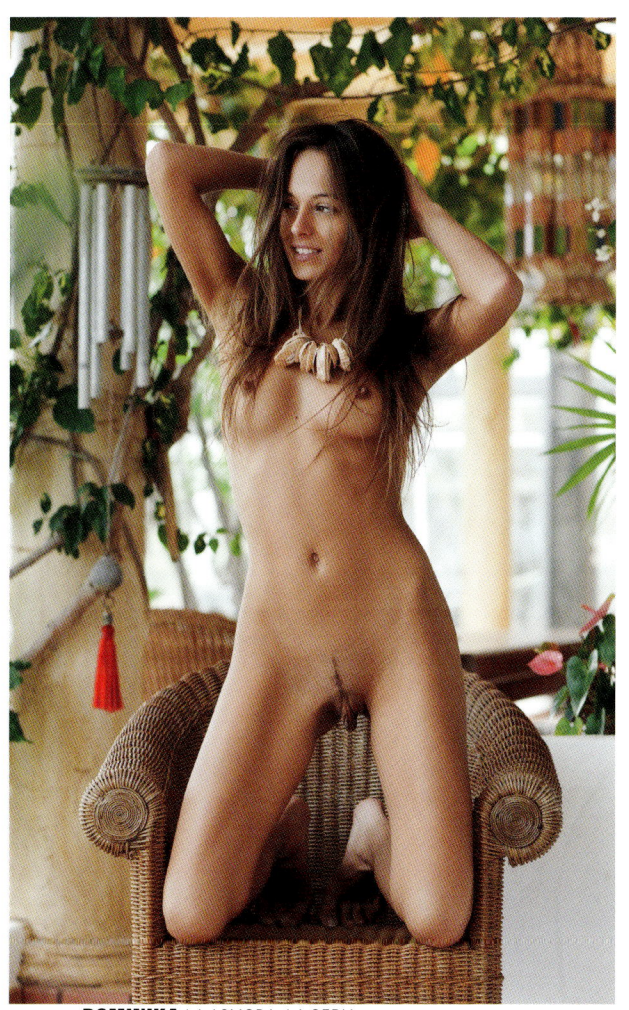

DOMINIKA LA ASMODA, LA GERIA

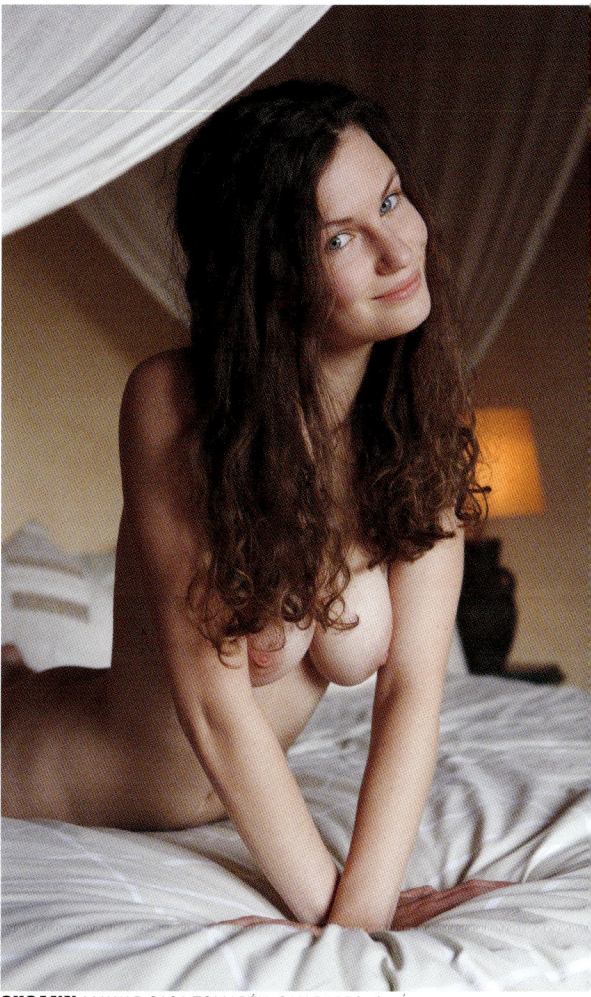

SUSANN MAWAR CASA TOMARÉN, SAN BARTOLOMÉ

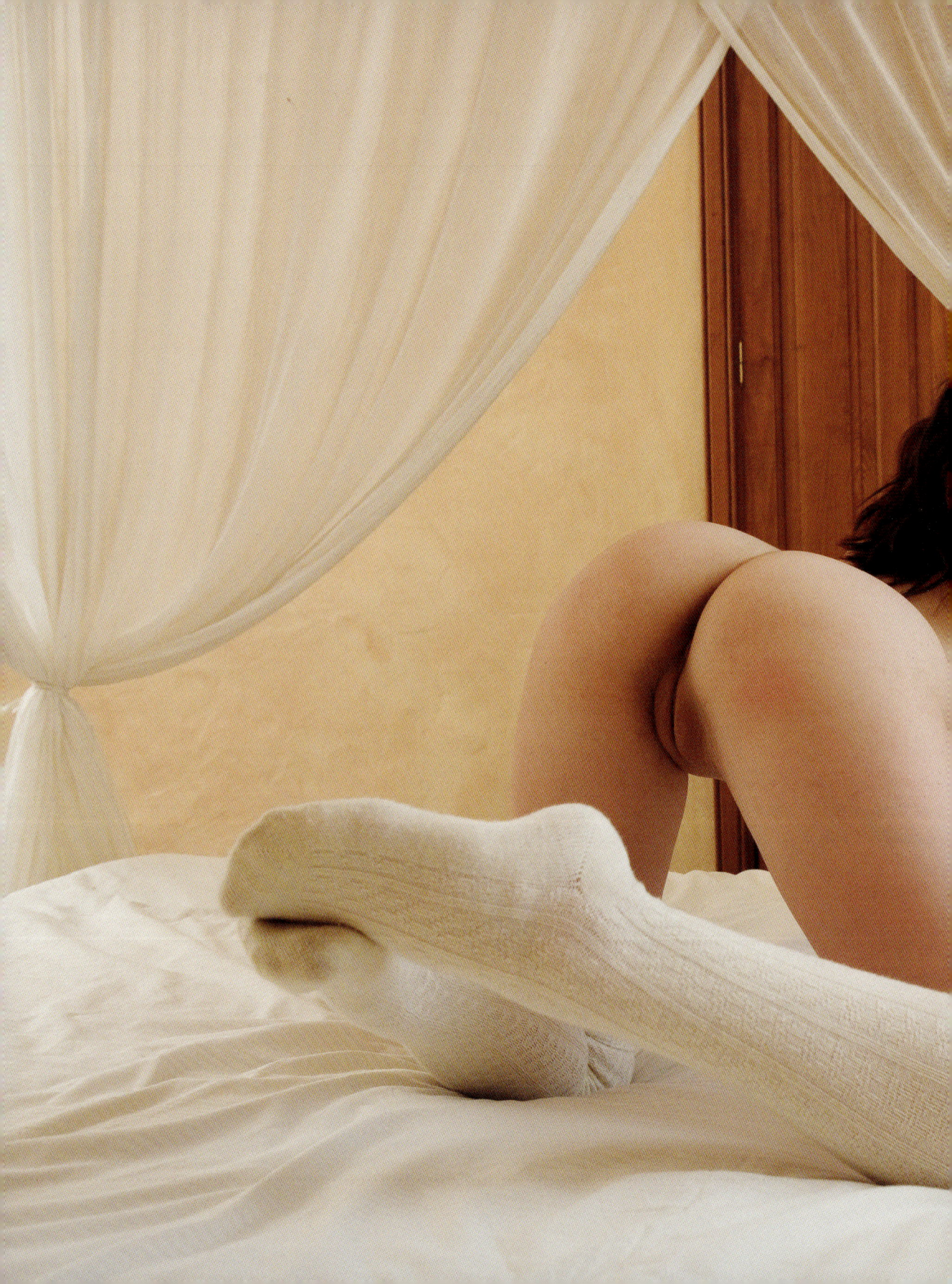

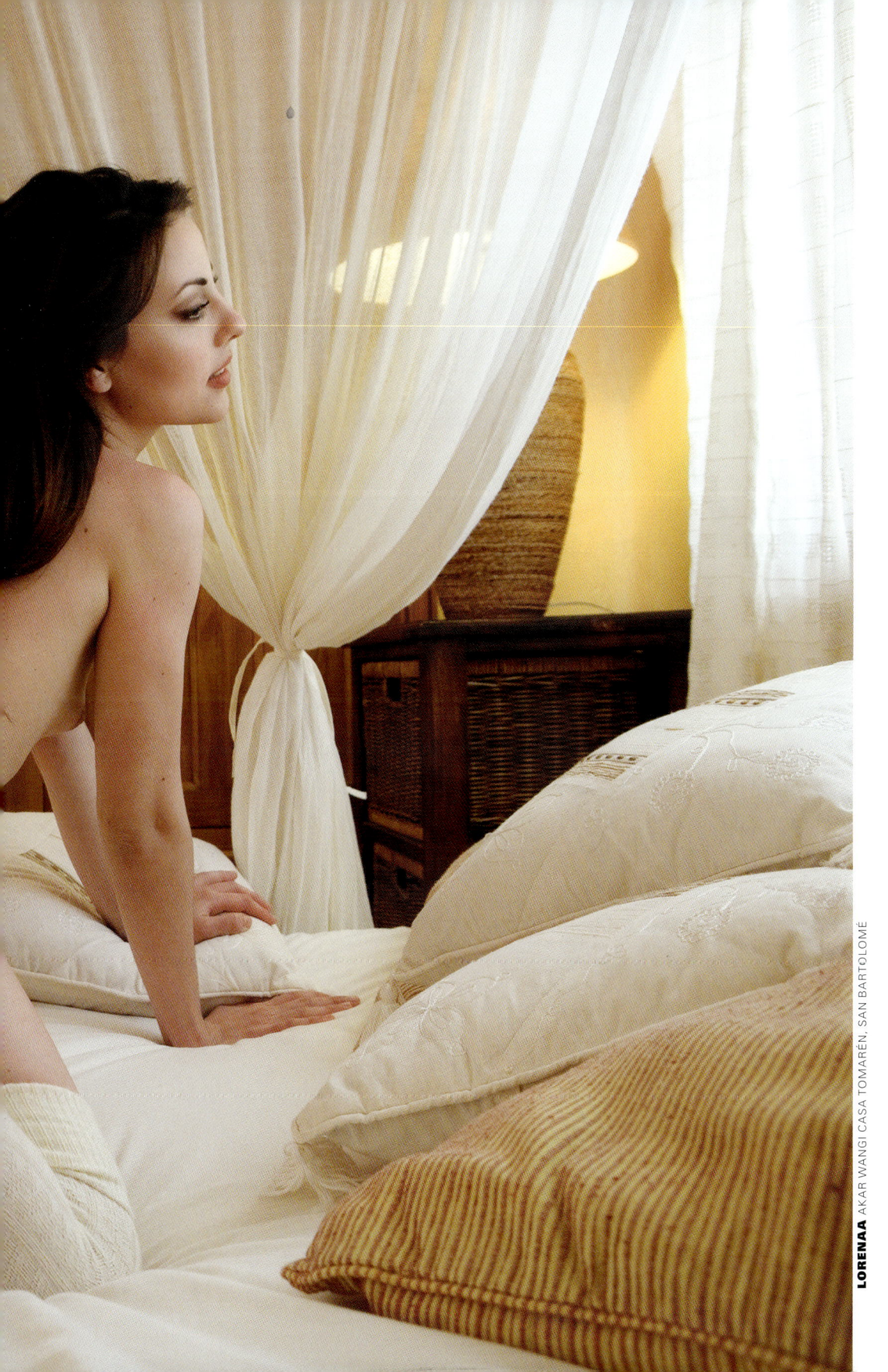

LORENAA AKAR WANGI CASA TOMARÉN, SAN BARTOLOMÉ

73

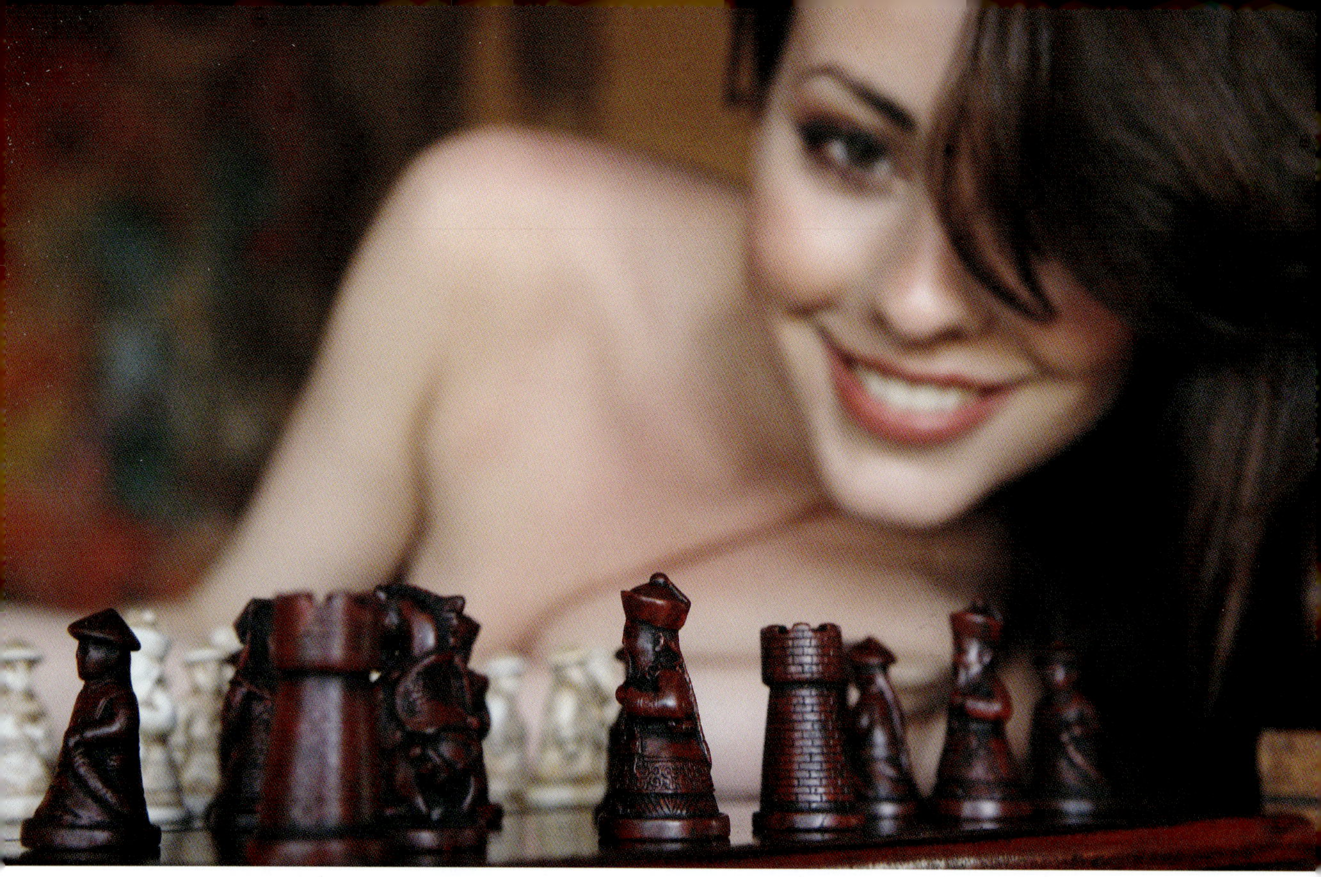

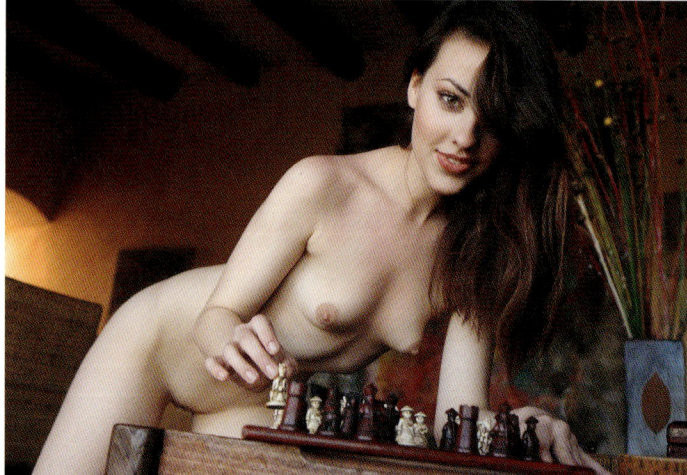

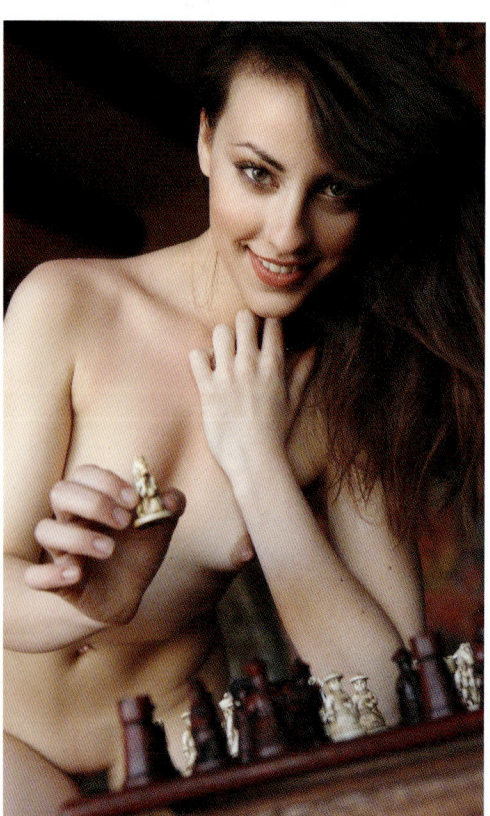

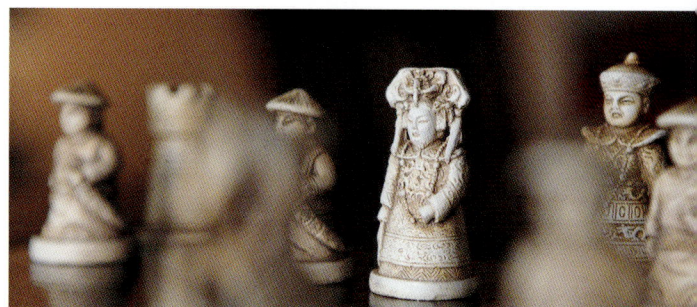

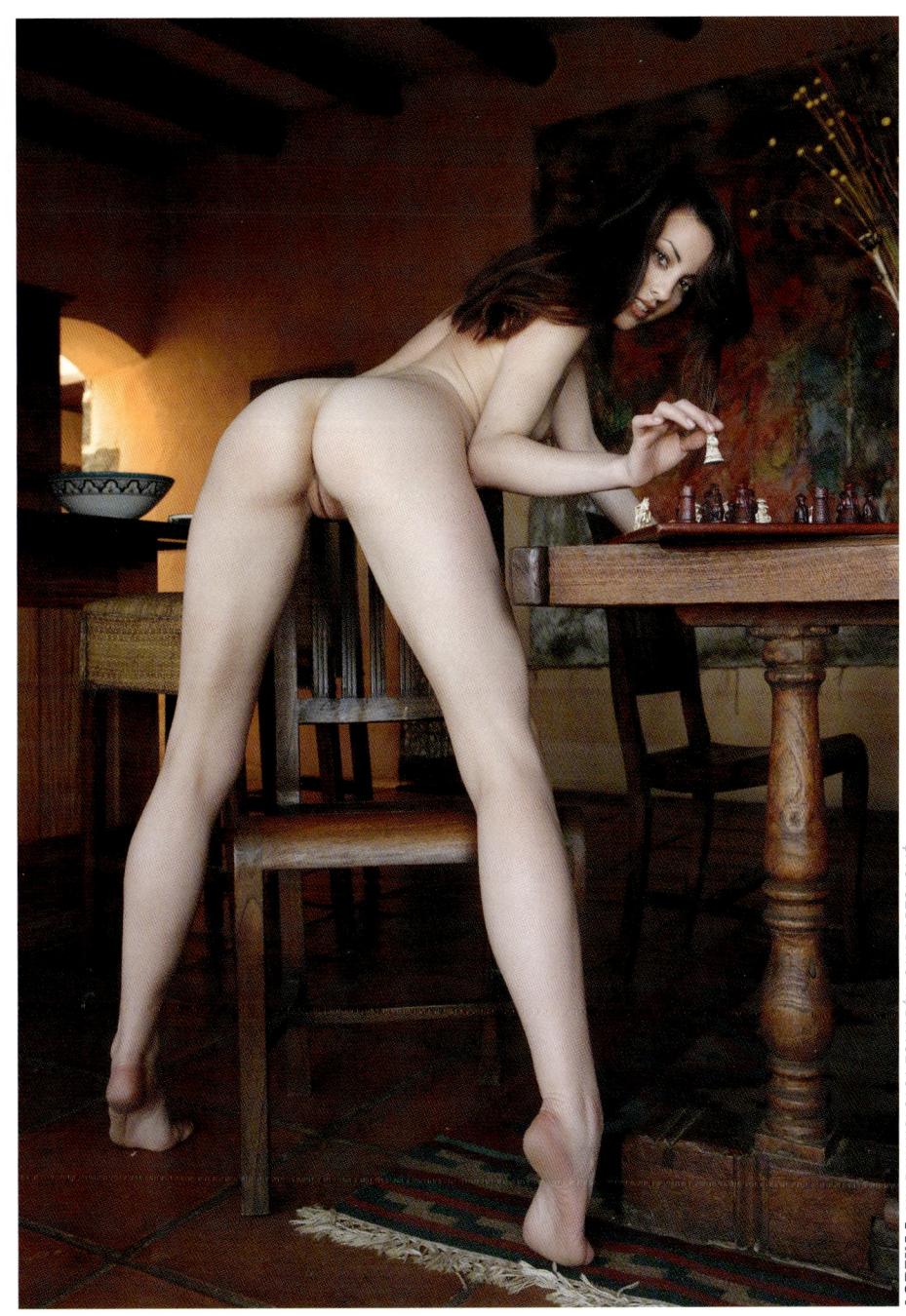

LORENAA AKAR WANGI CASA TOMARÉN, SAN BARTOLOMÉ

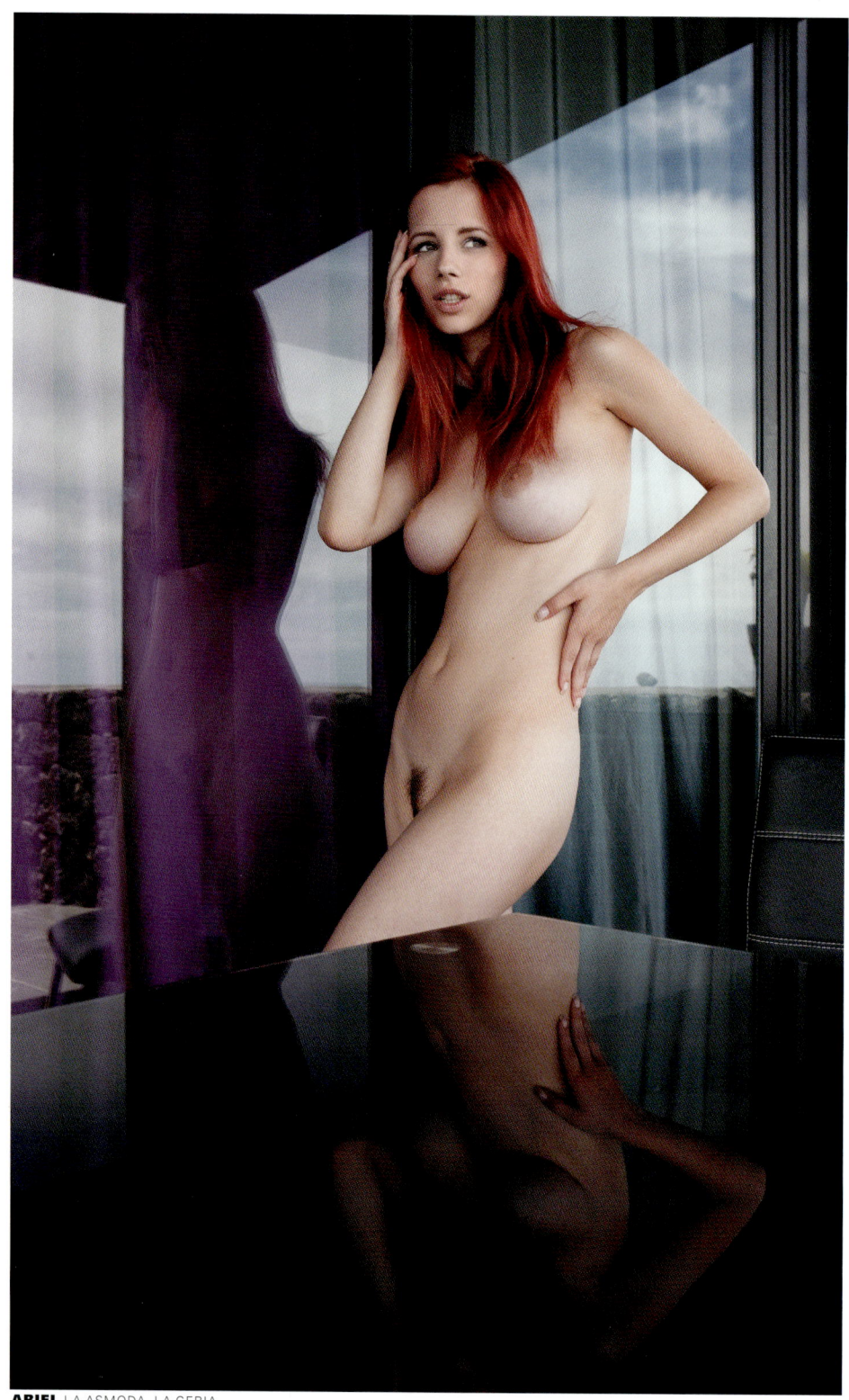

ARIEL LA ASMODA, LA GERIA

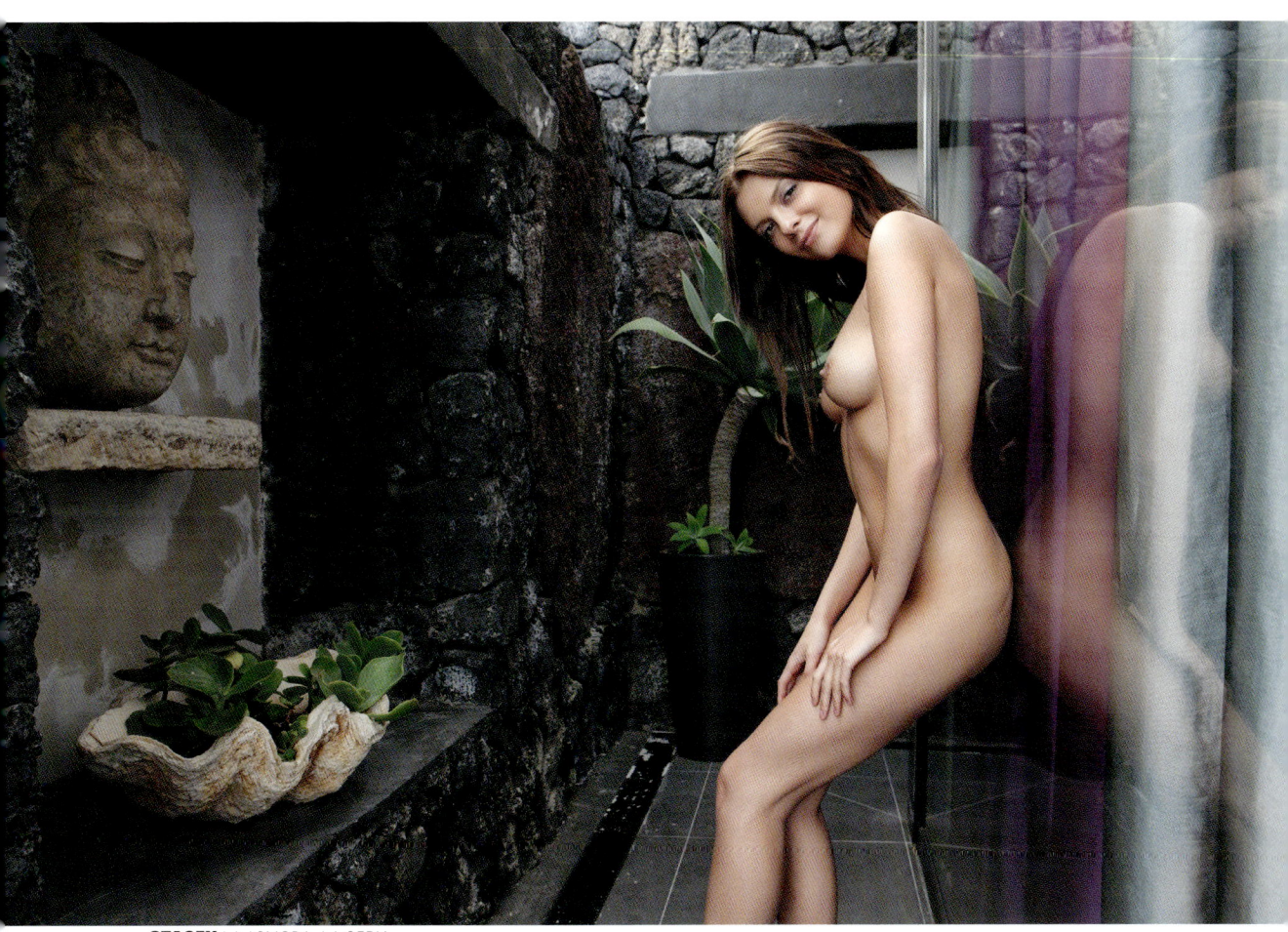

STACEY LA ASMODA, LA GERIA

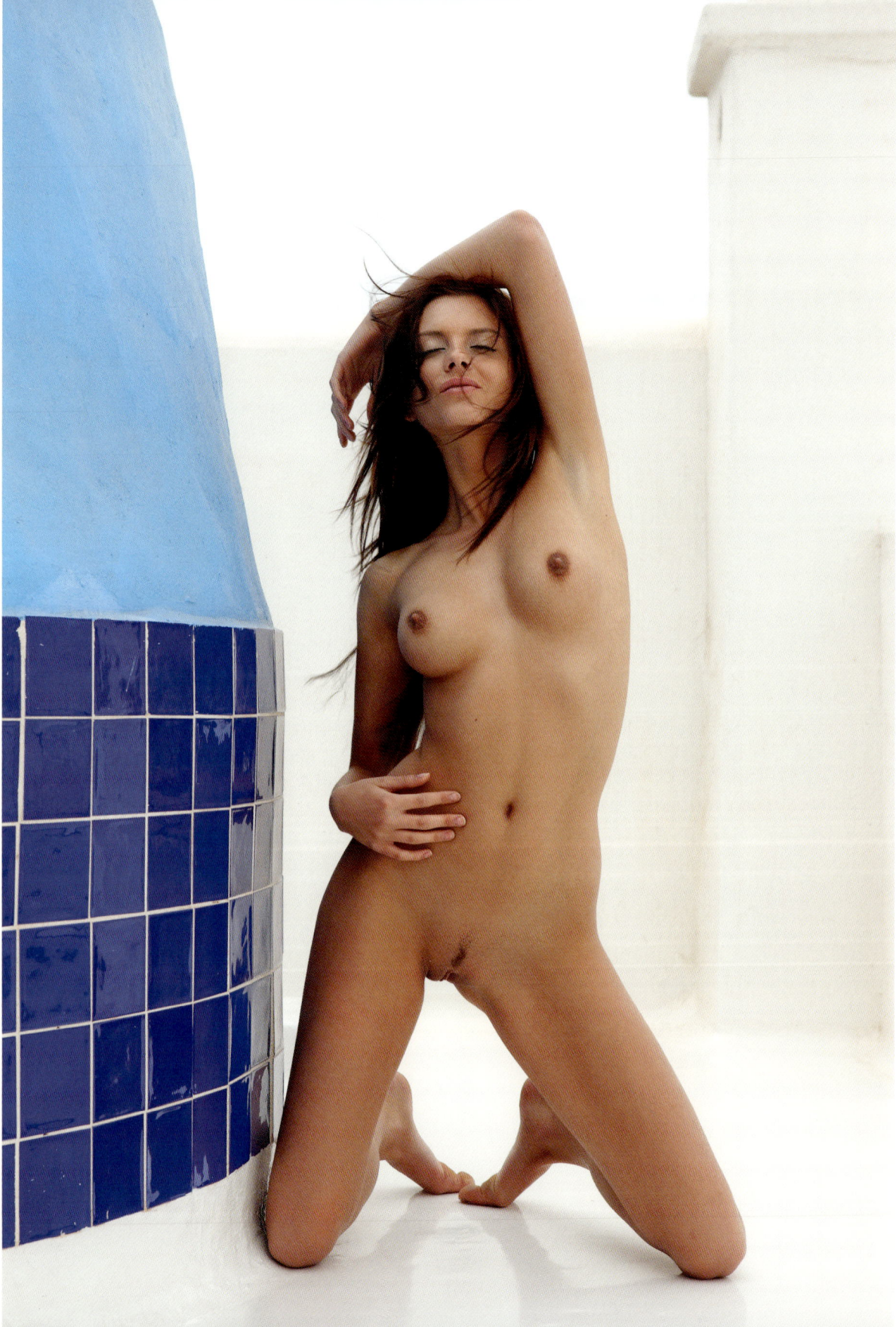

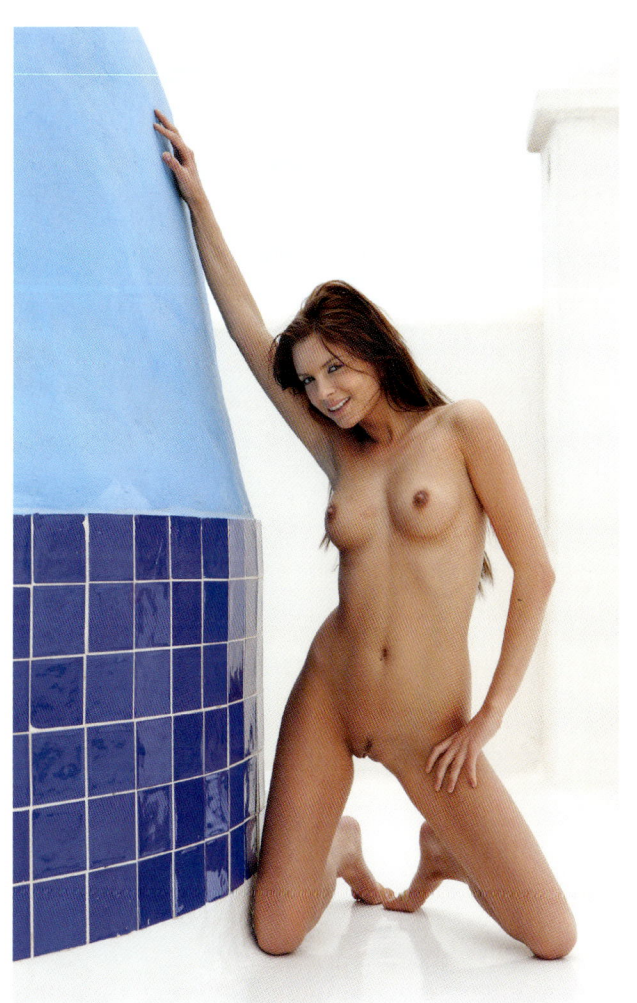

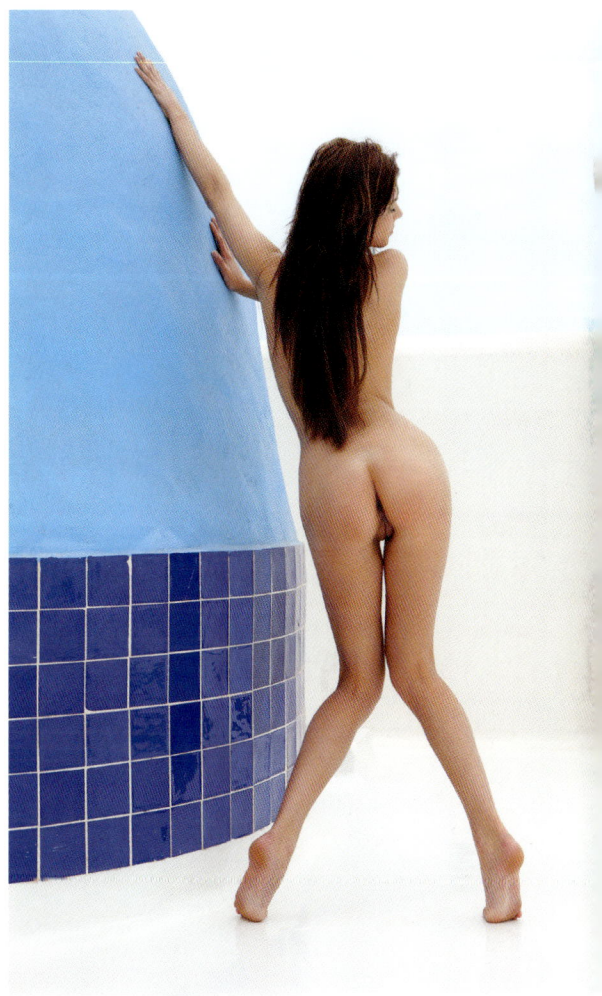

STACEY MONTANA BAJA, PLAYA BLANCA

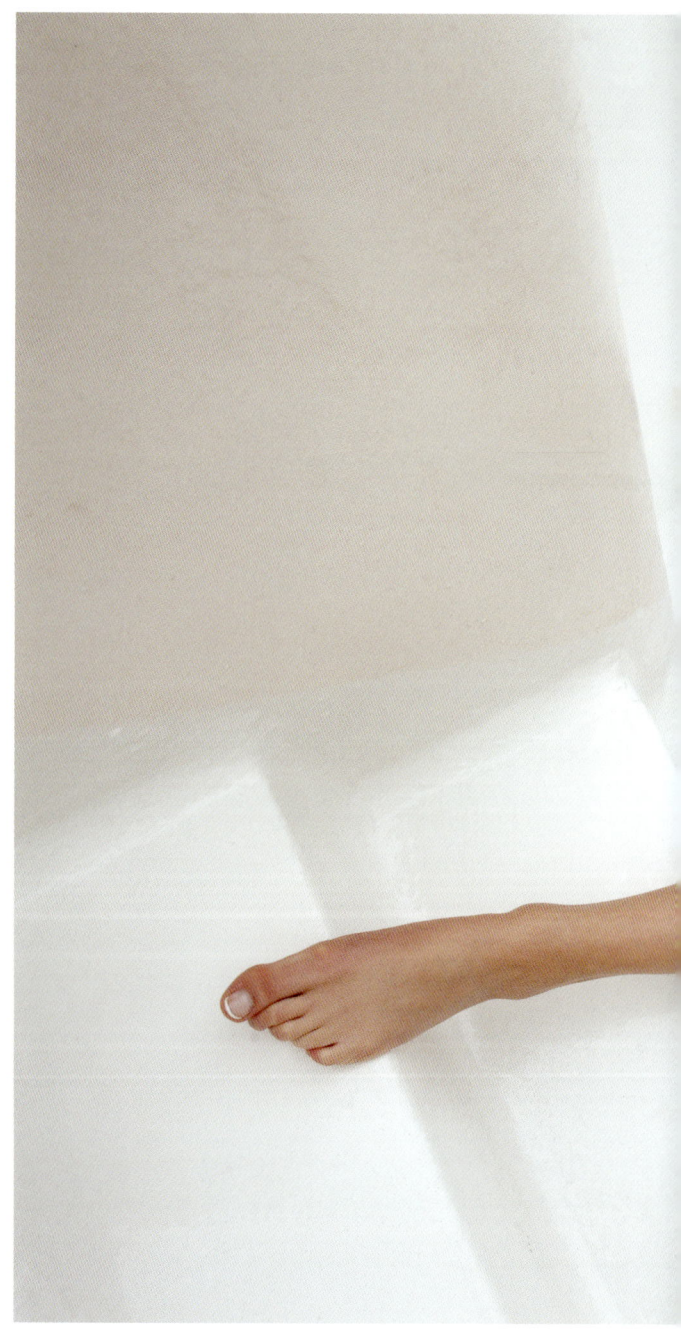

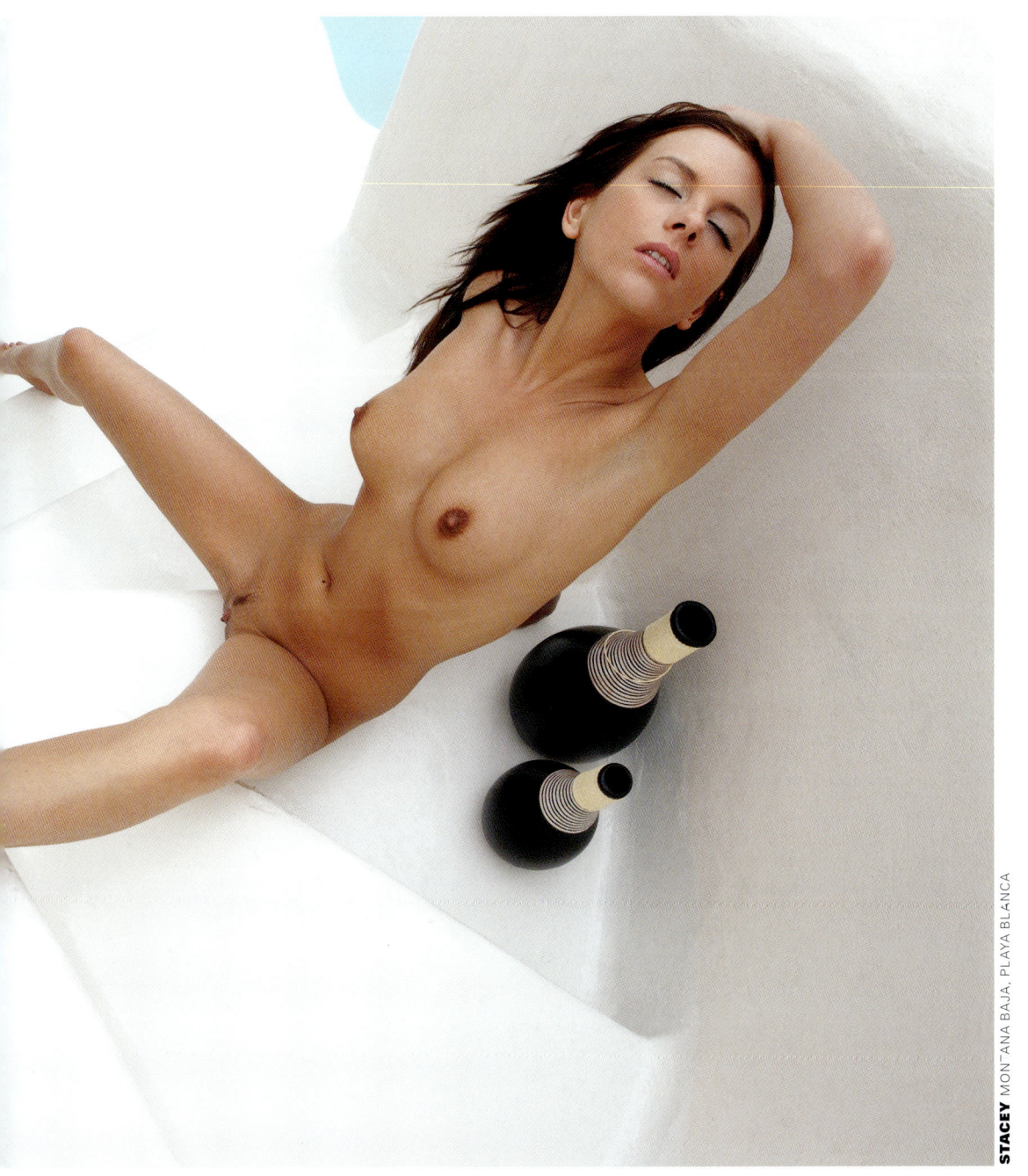

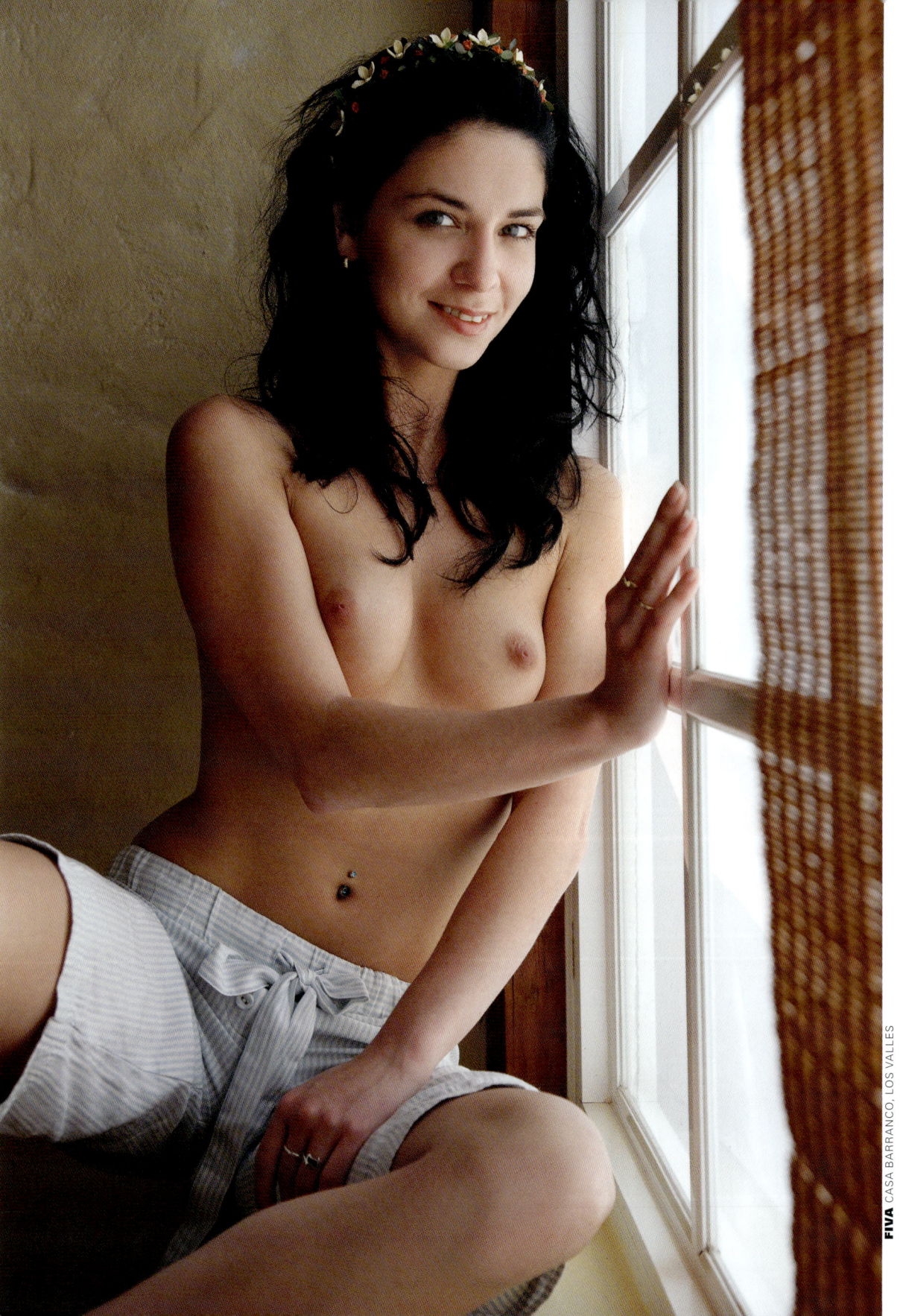

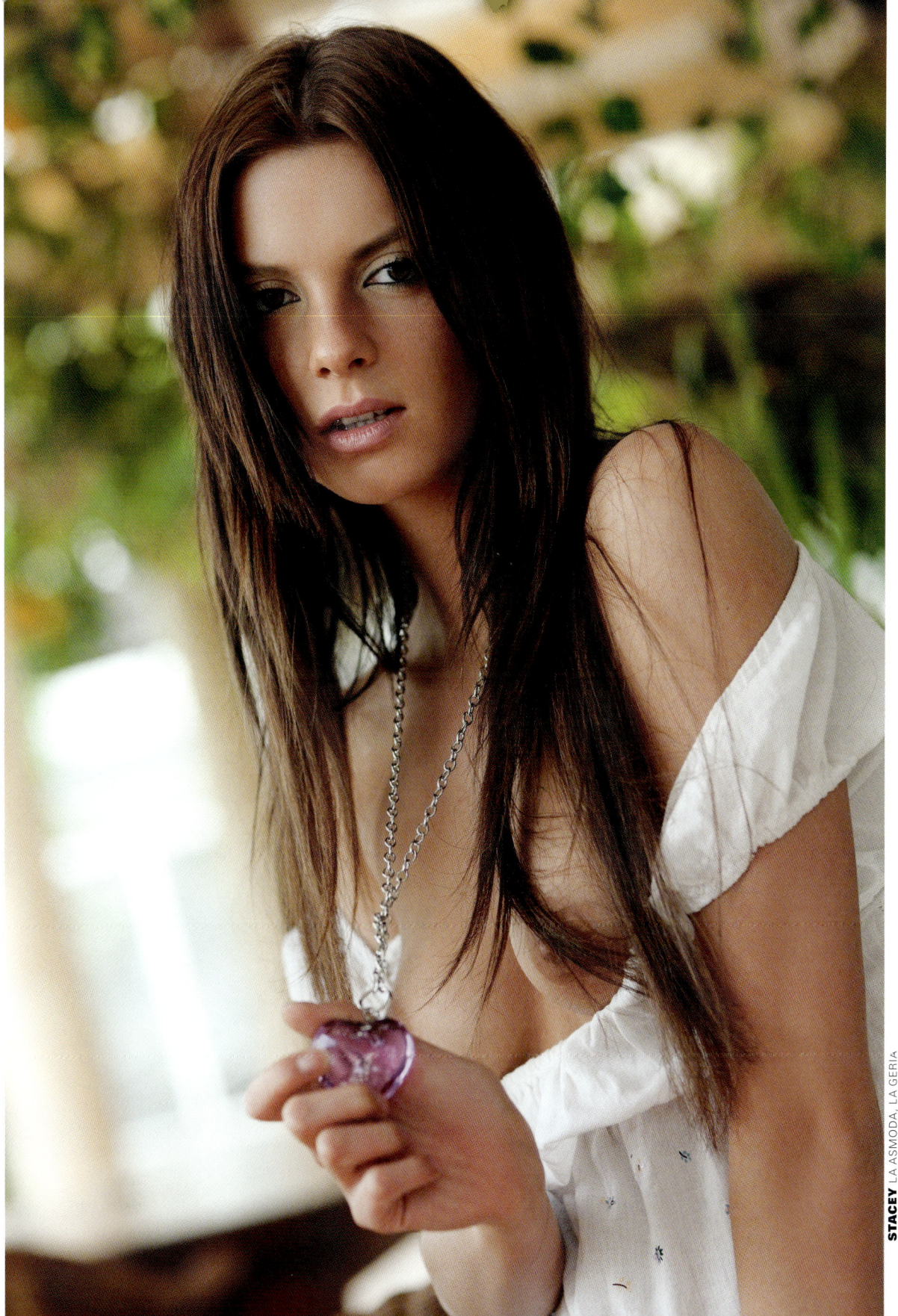

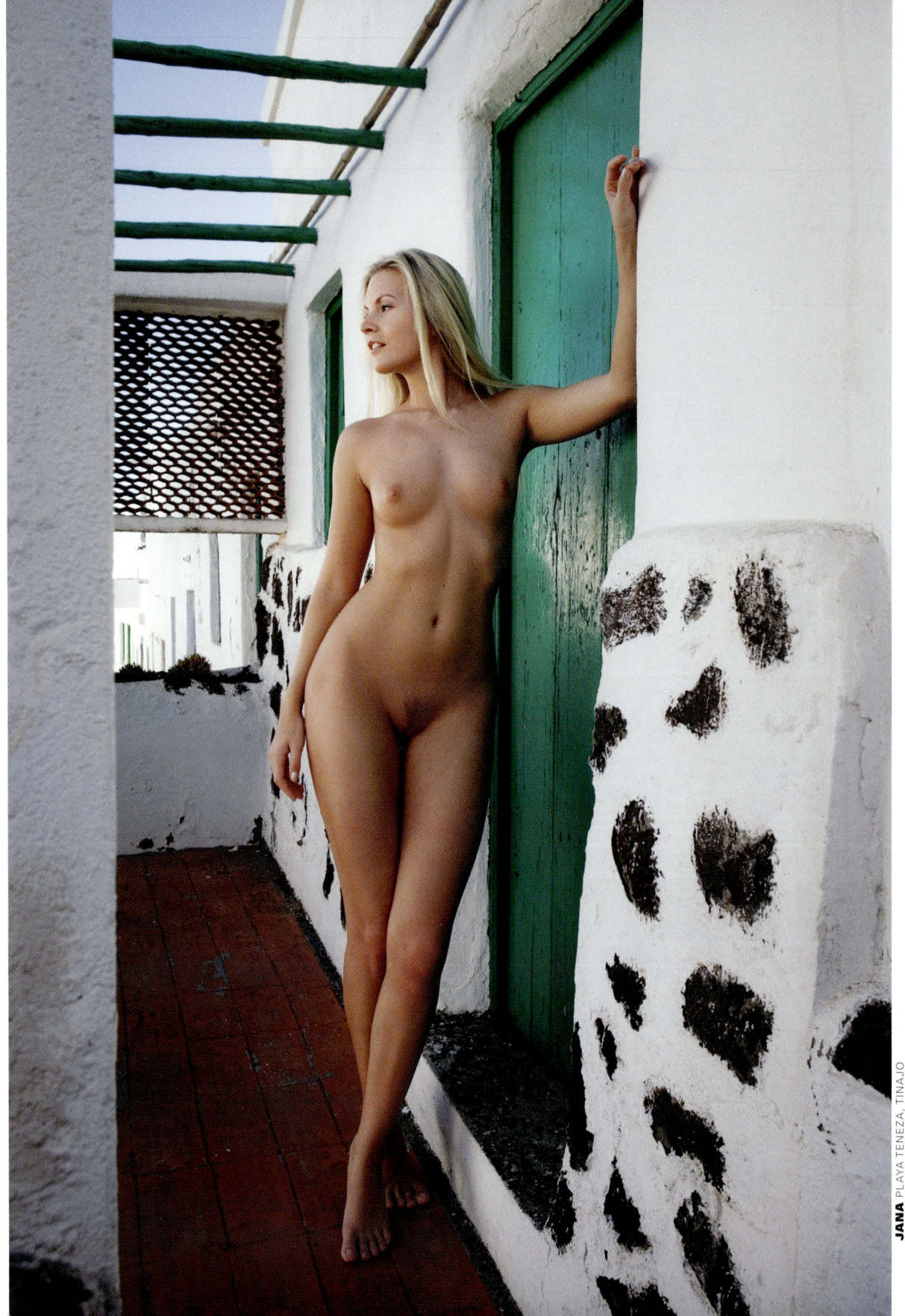

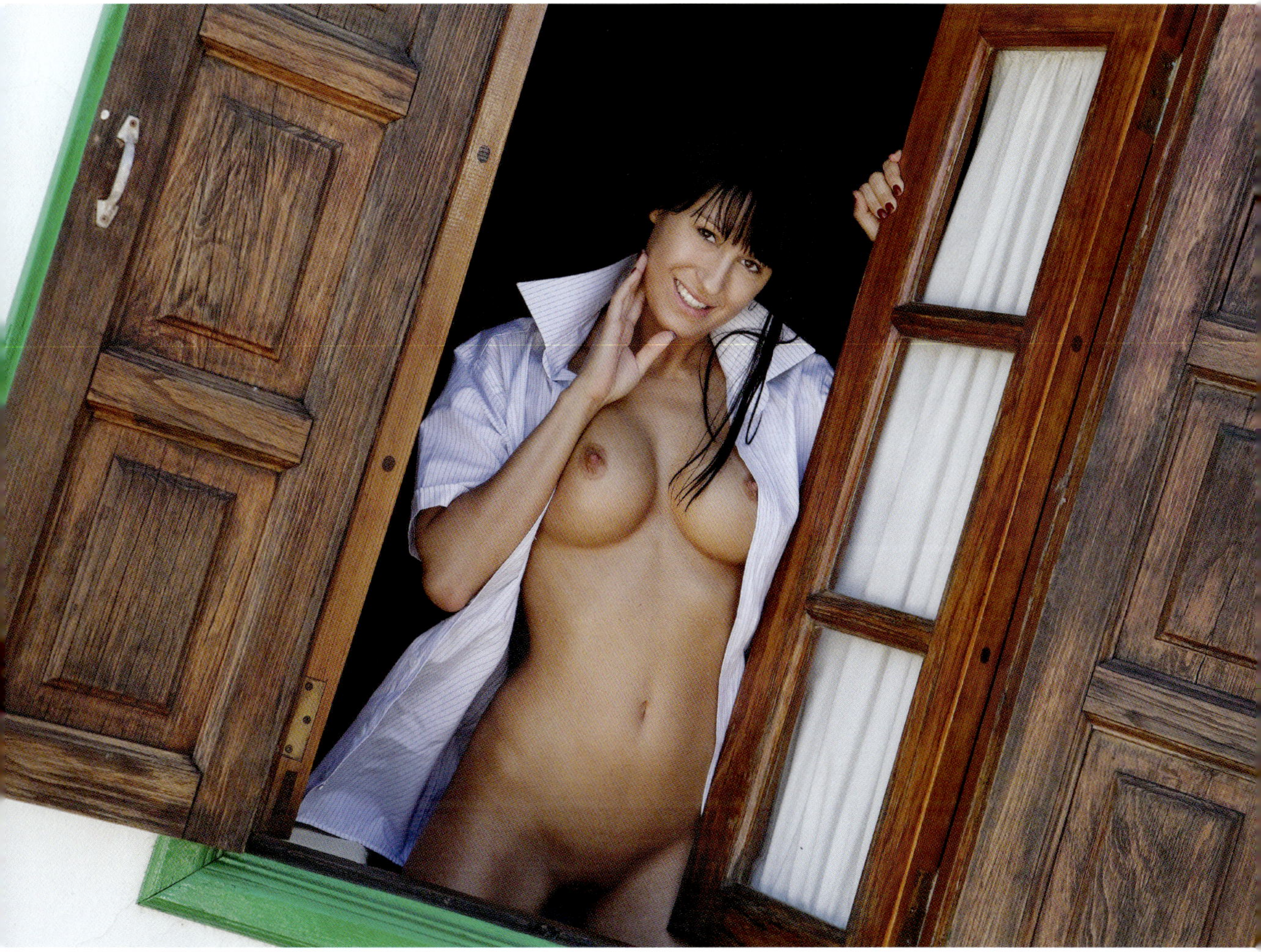

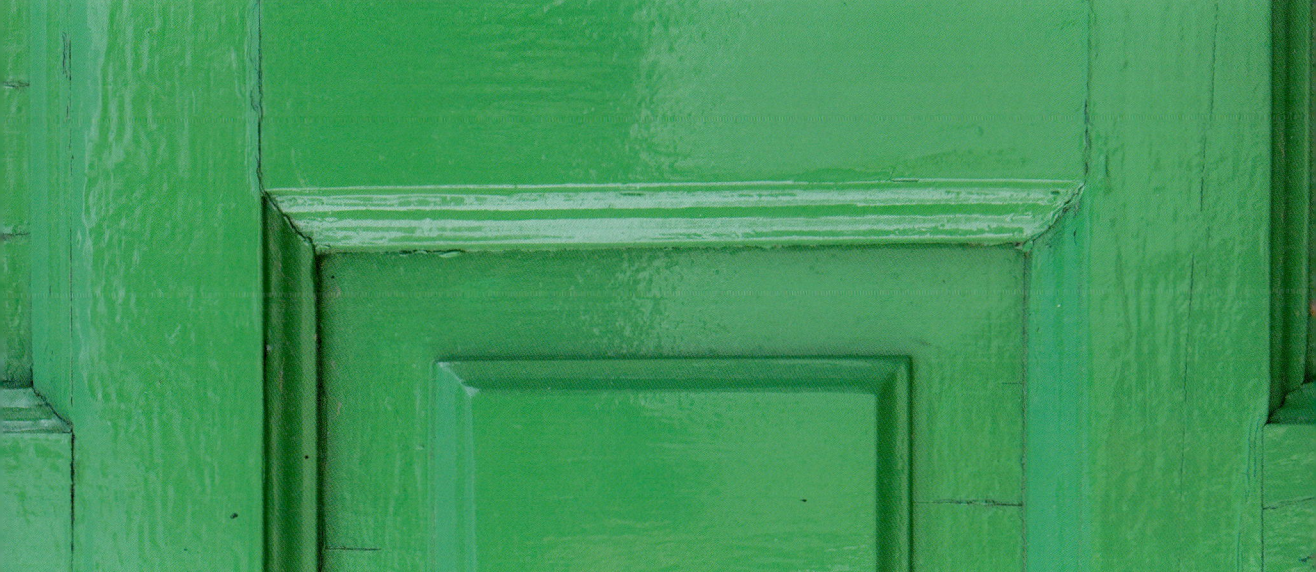

JAYLA CASA BARRANCO, LOS VALLES

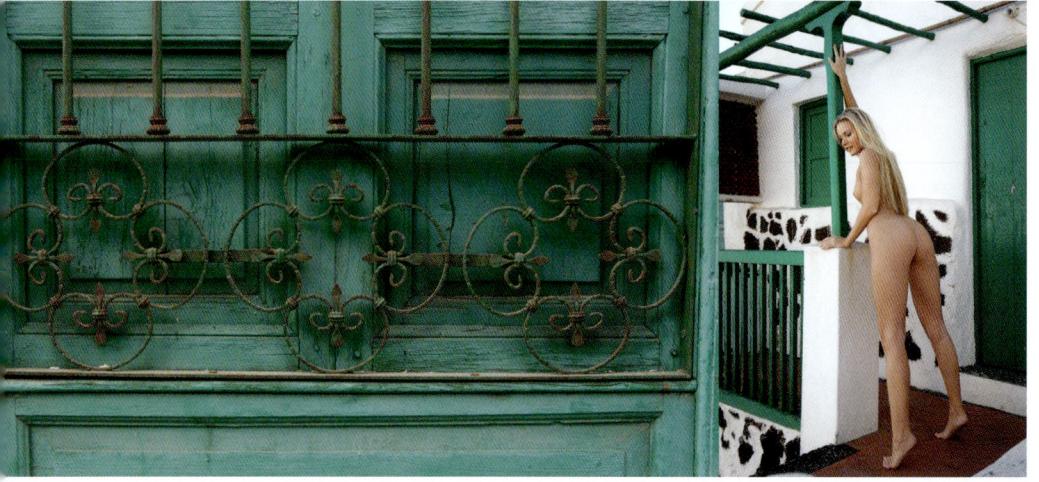
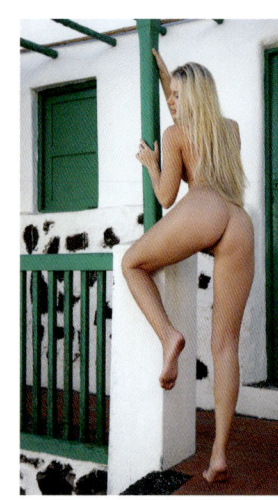

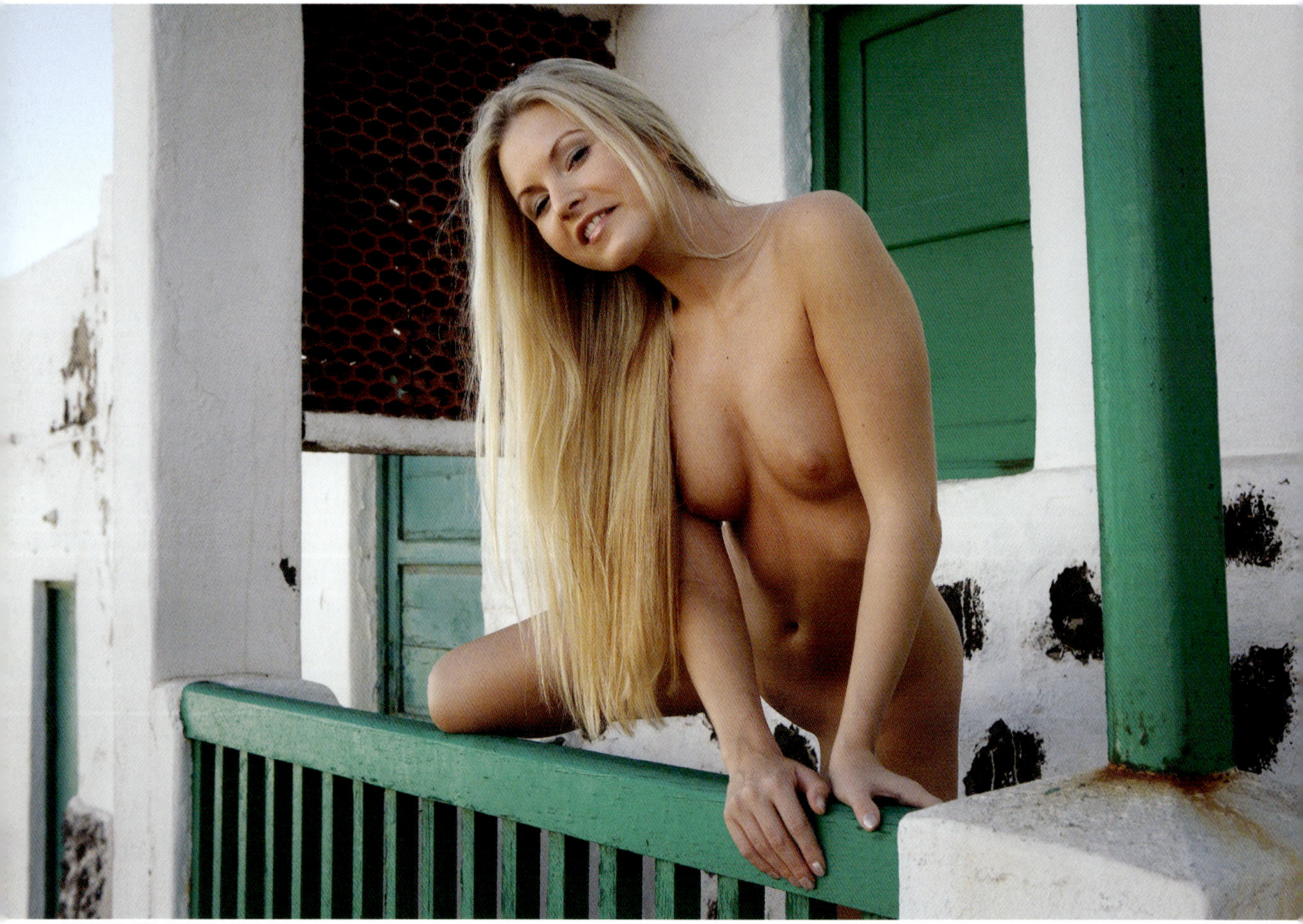

JANA PLAYA TENEZA, TINAJO

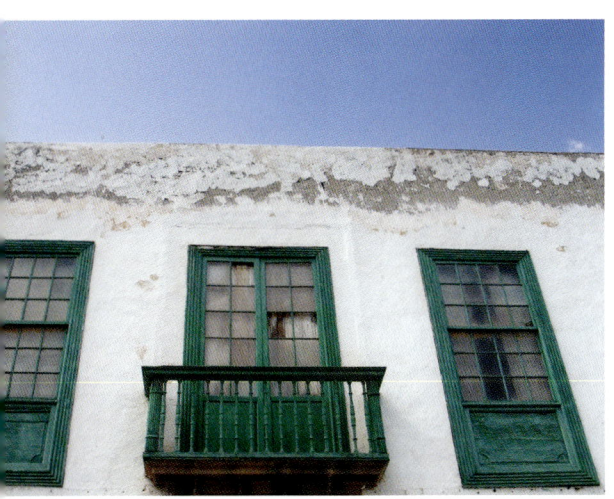
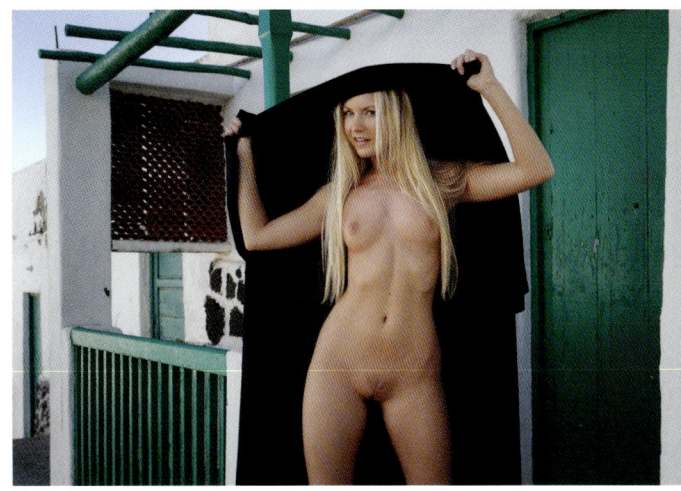

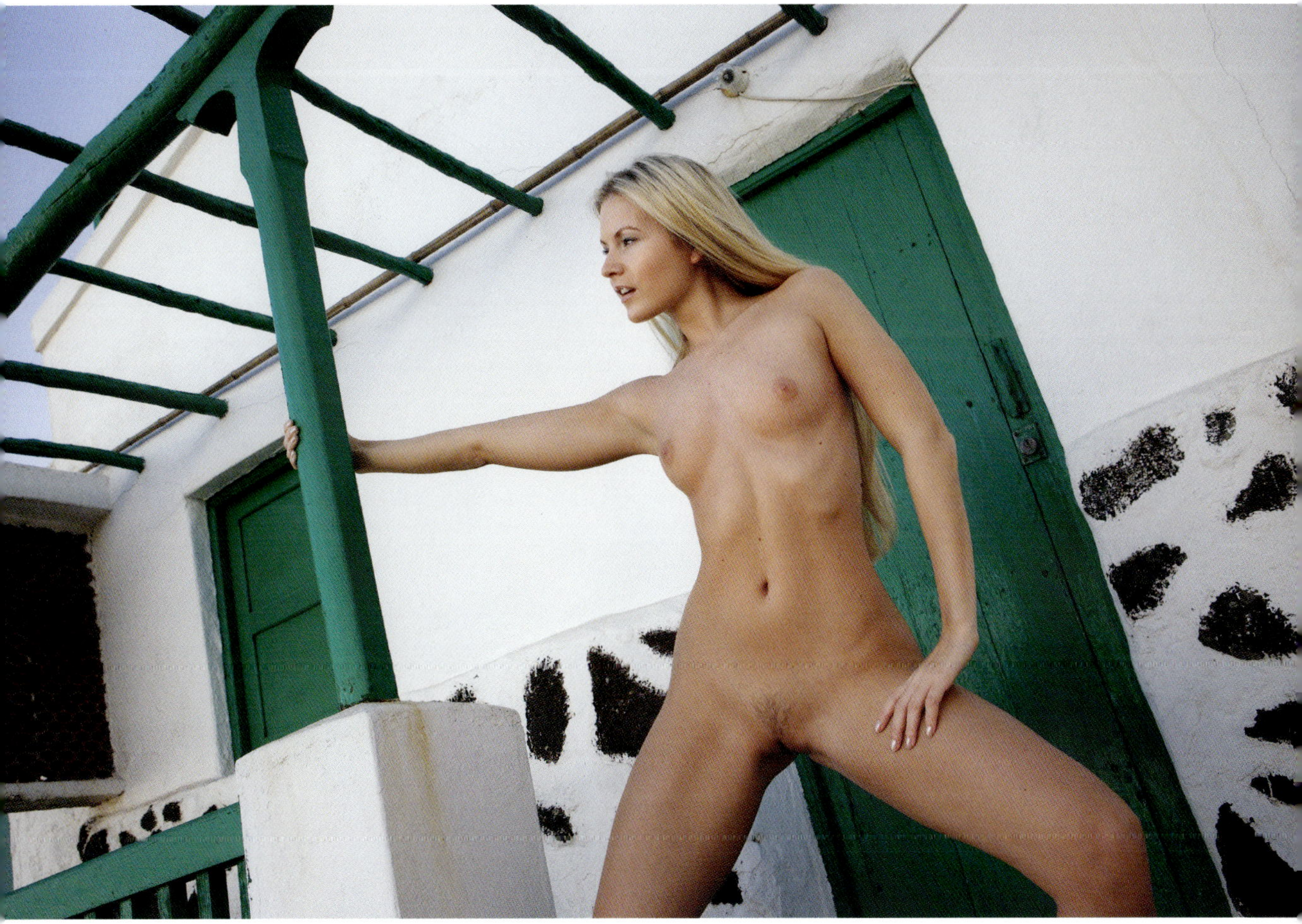

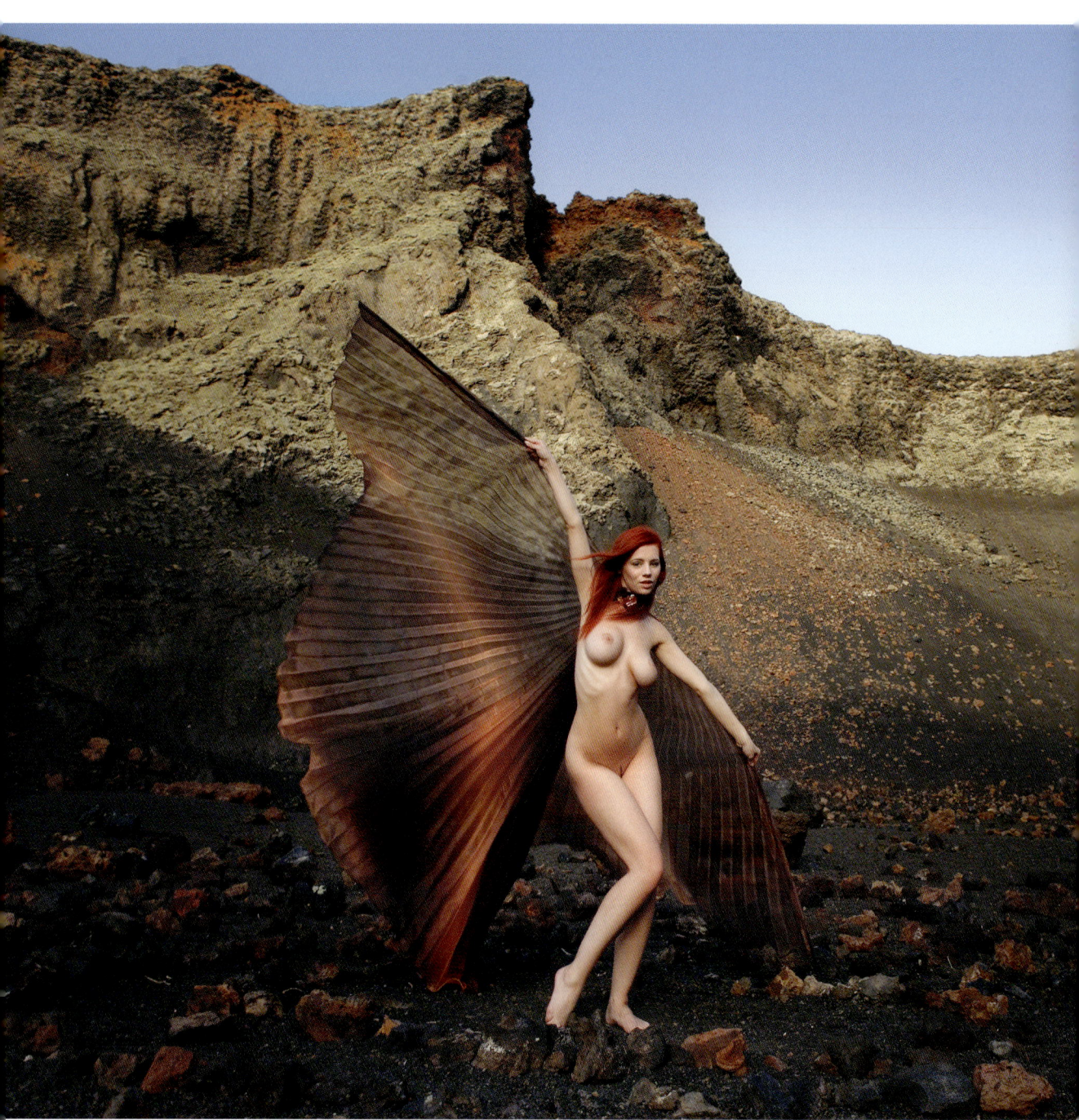

ARIEL CALDERA DE LAS CUEVOS, PARQUE NACIONAL DE TIMANFAYA

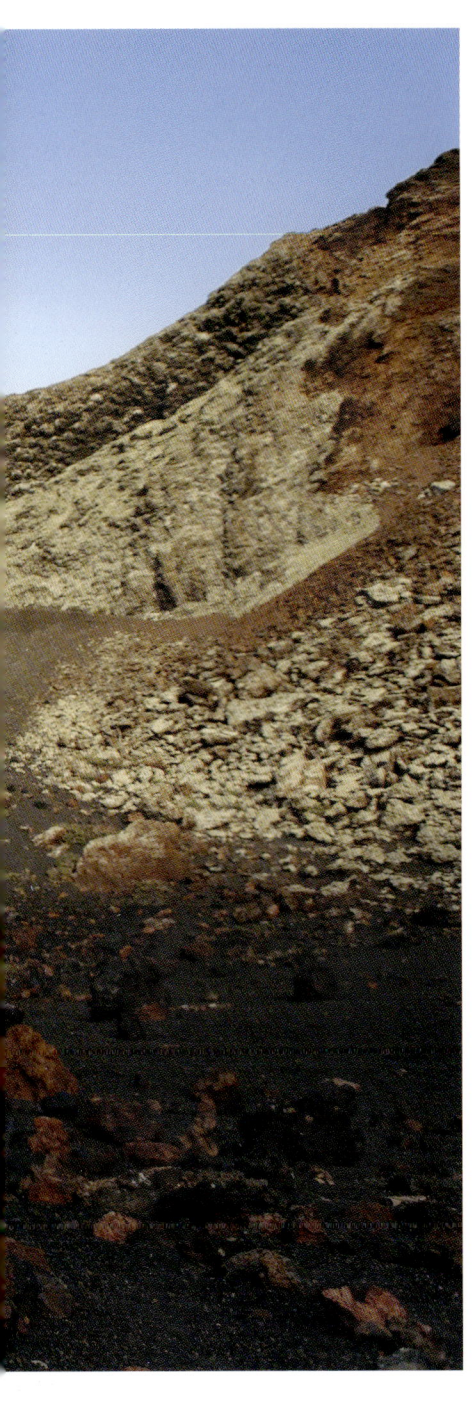

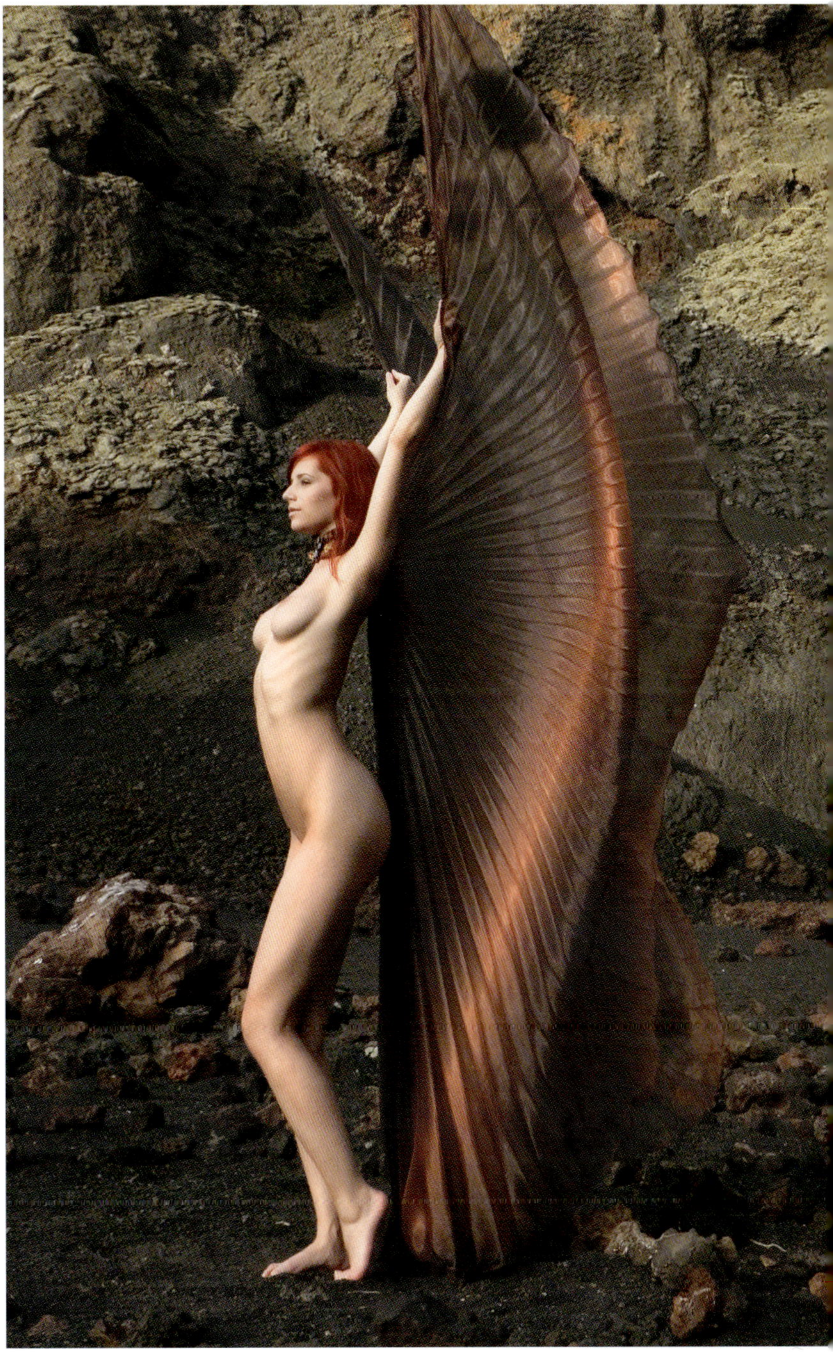

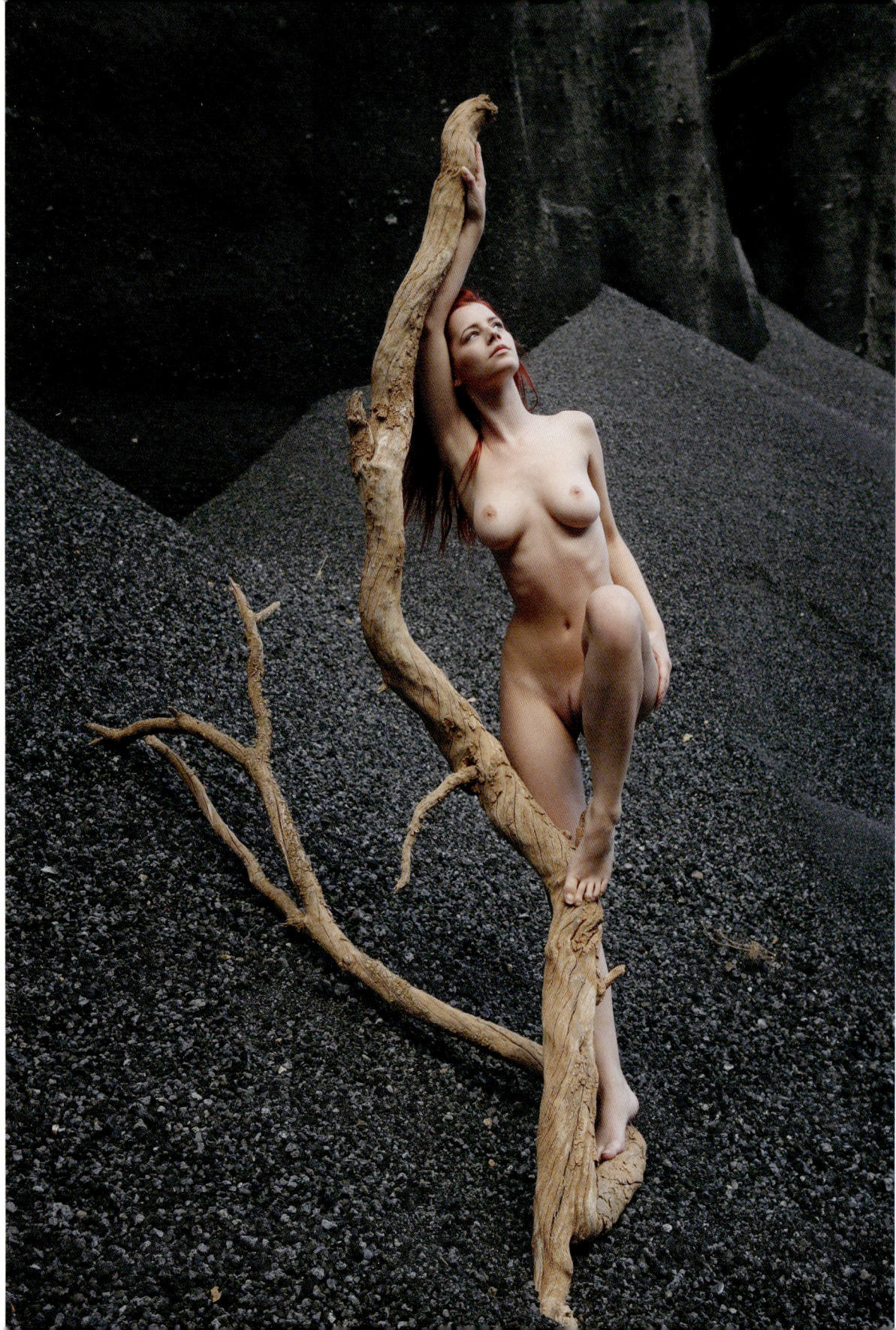

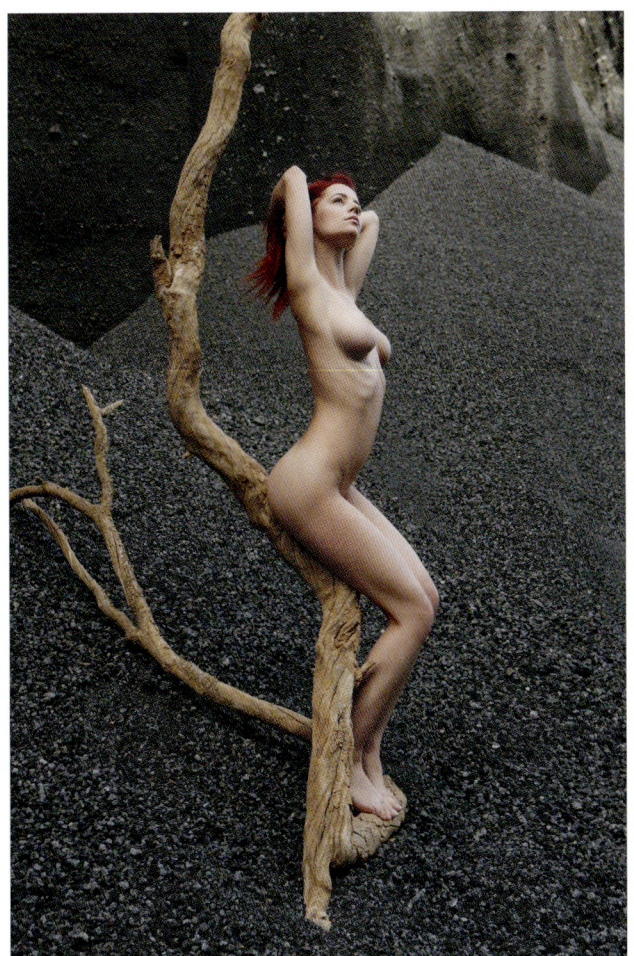

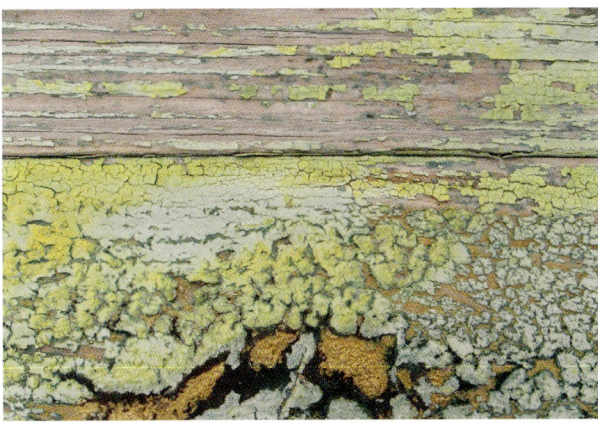

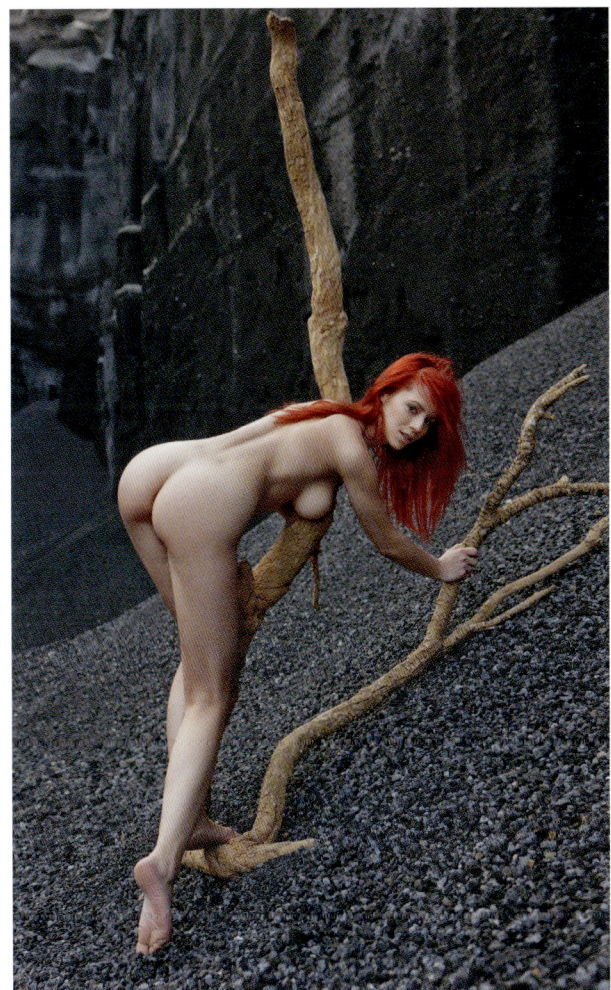

ARIEL ALAPILLI QUARY, TAO

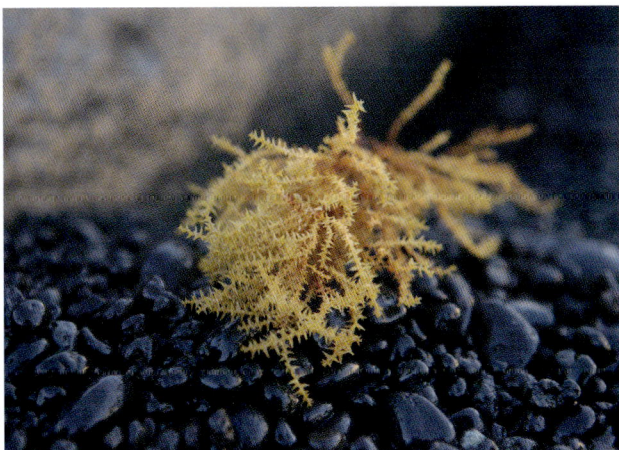

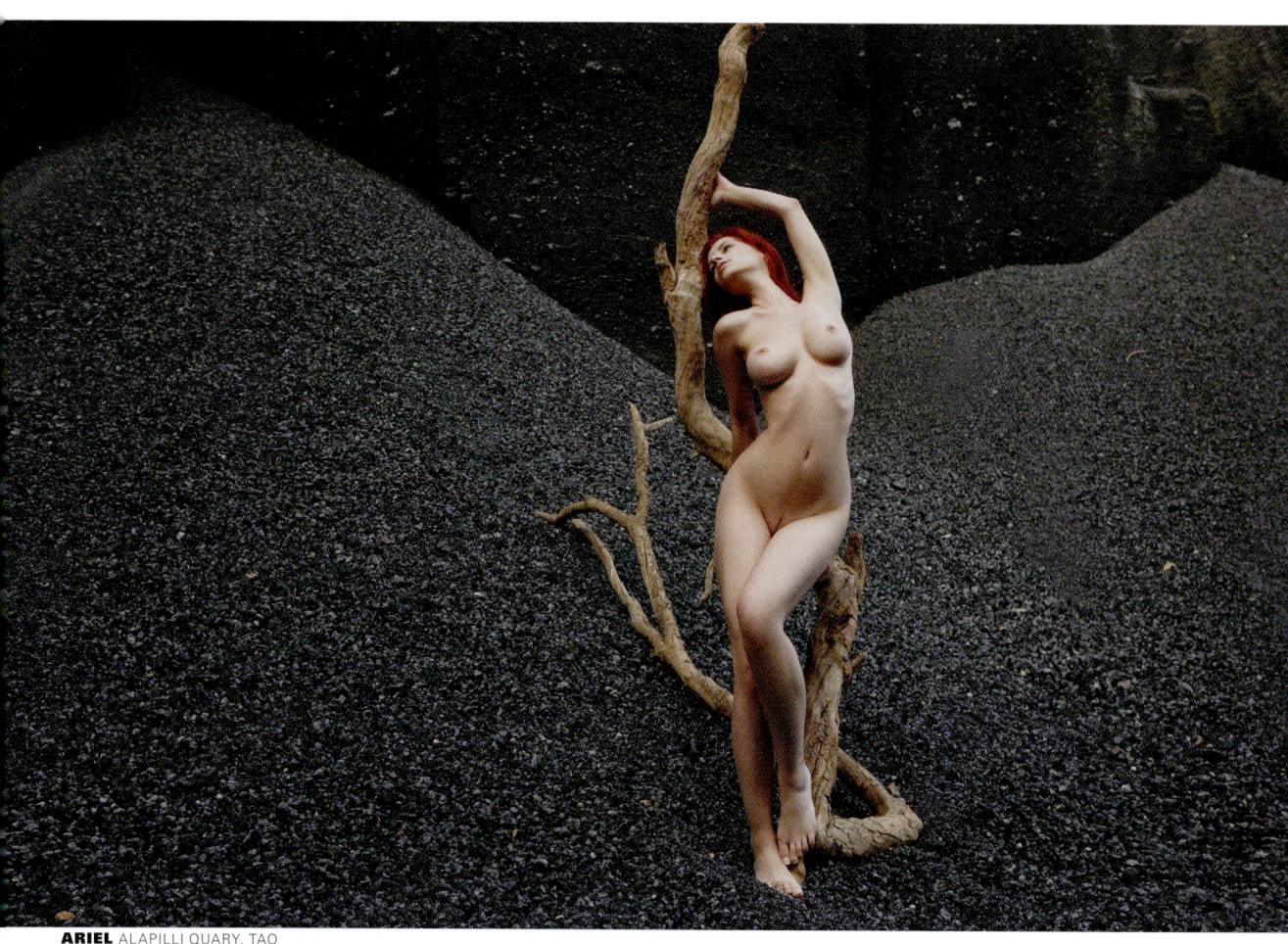

ARIEL ALAPILLI QUARY, TAO

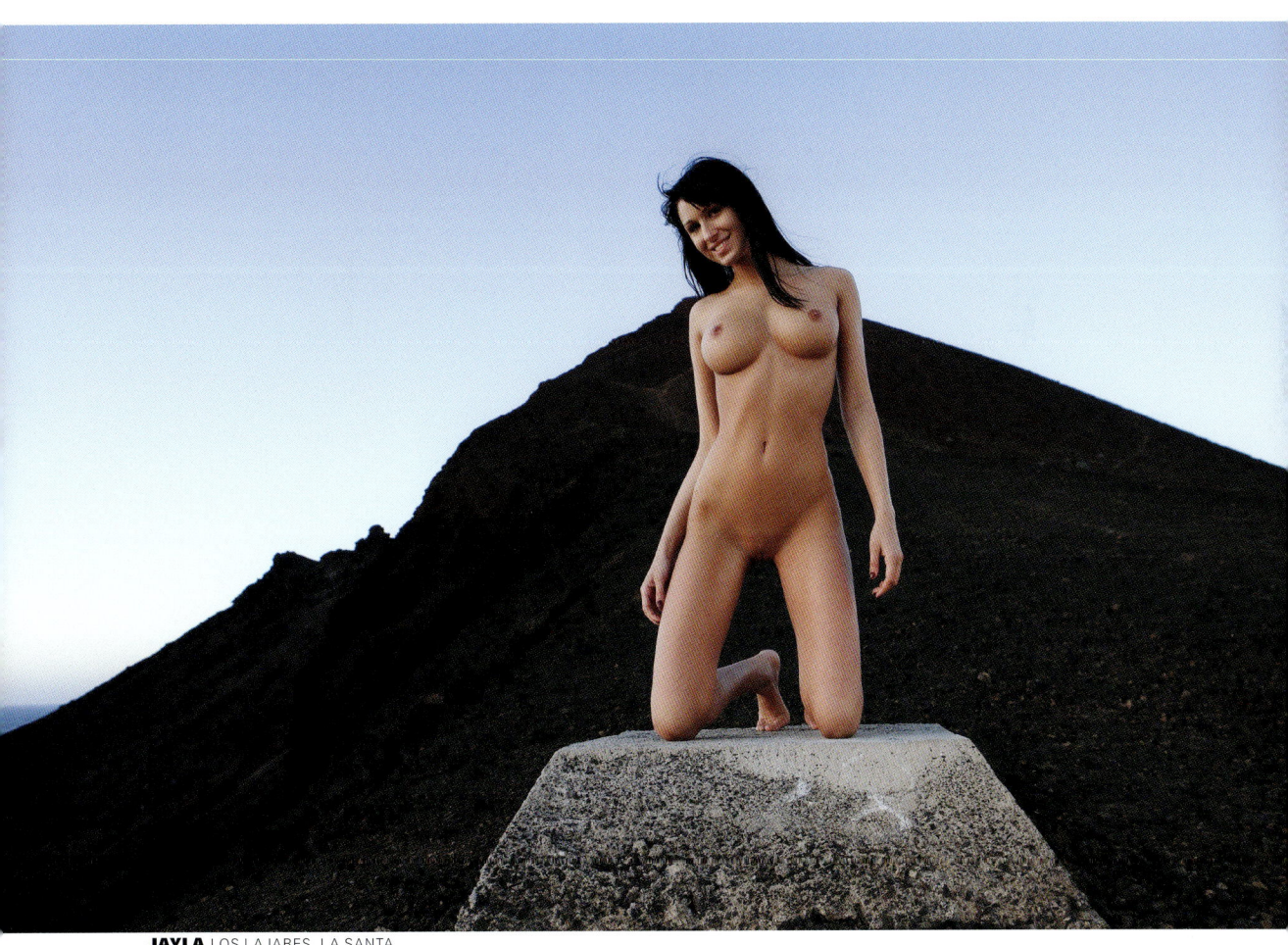

JAYLA LOS LAJARES, LA SANTA

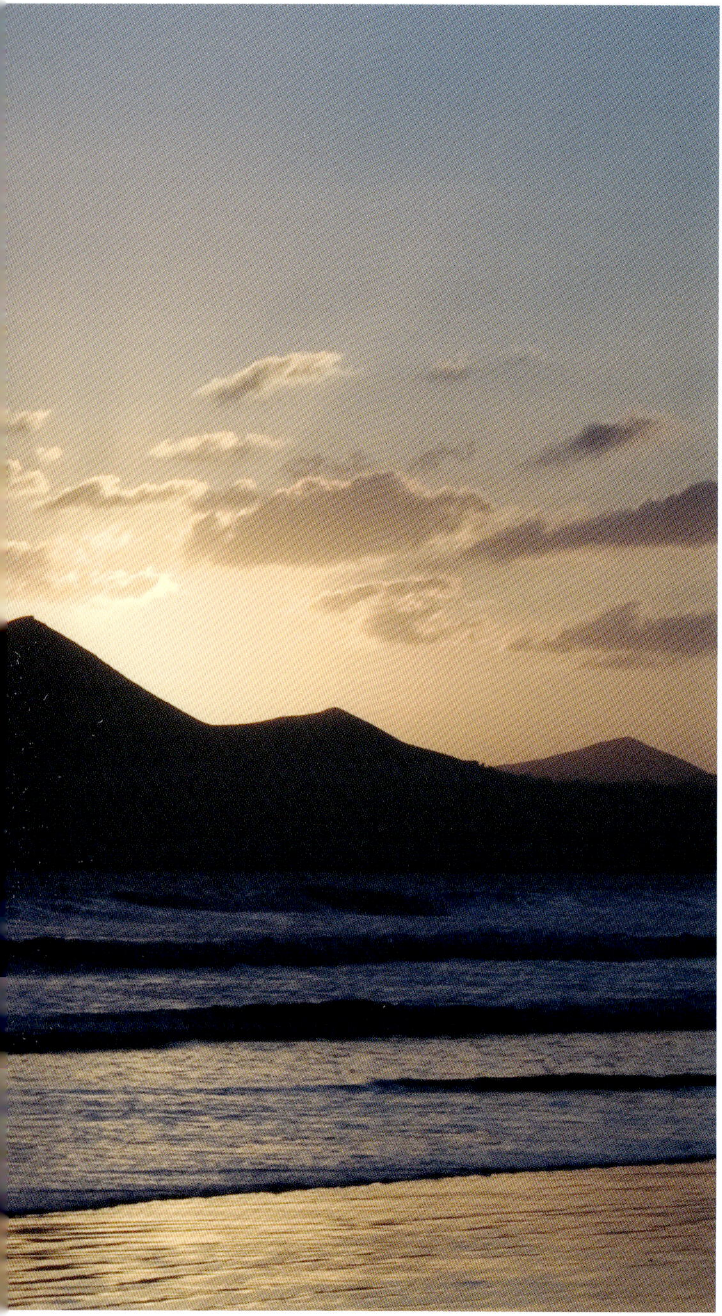

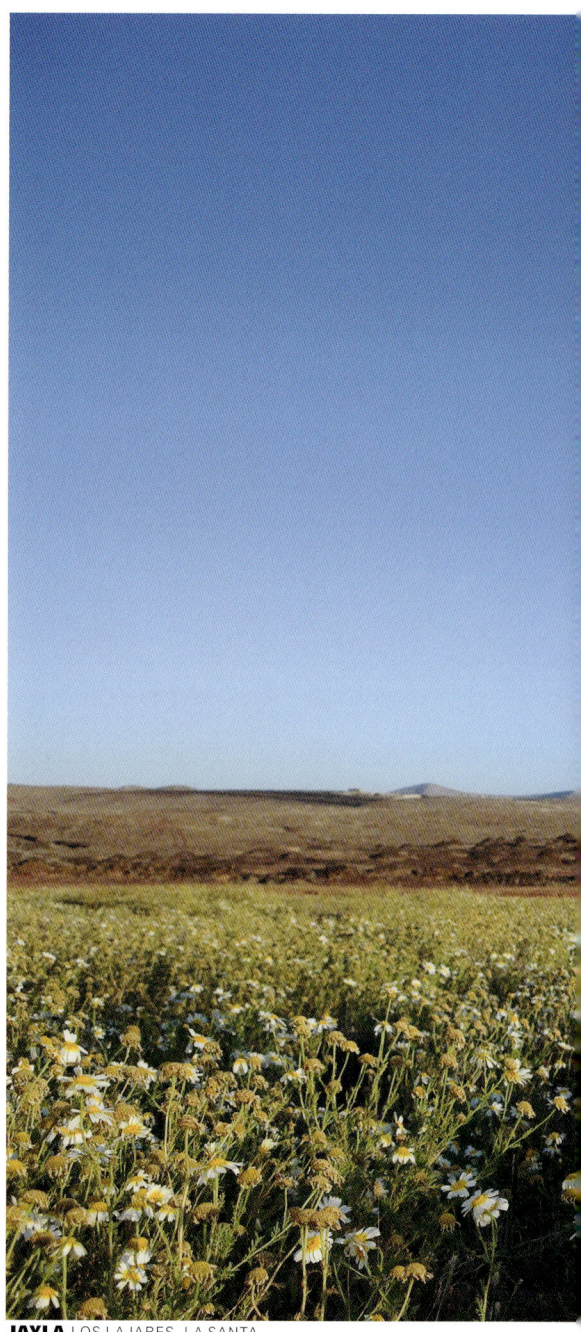

JAYLA LOS LAJARES, LA SANTA

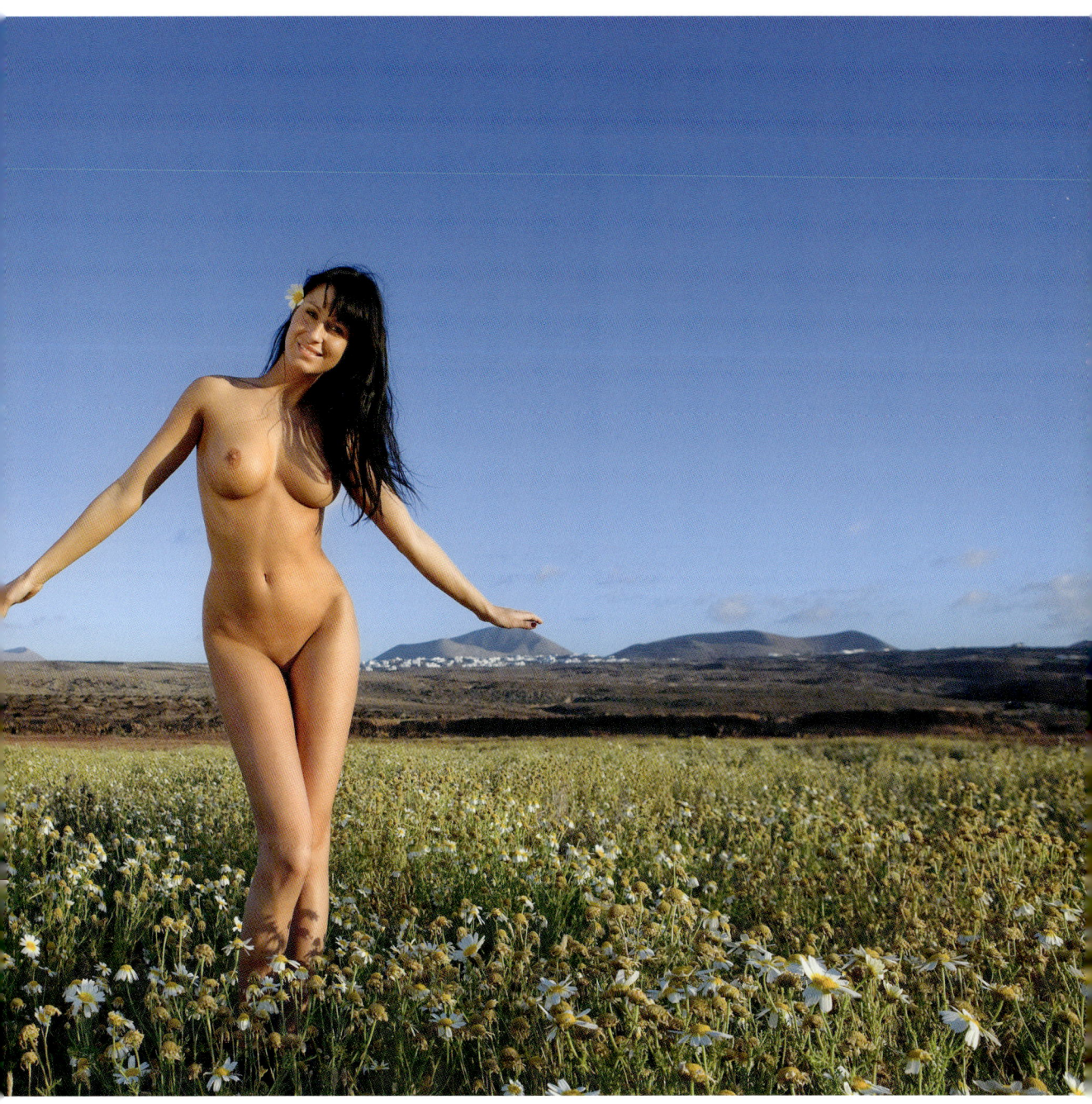

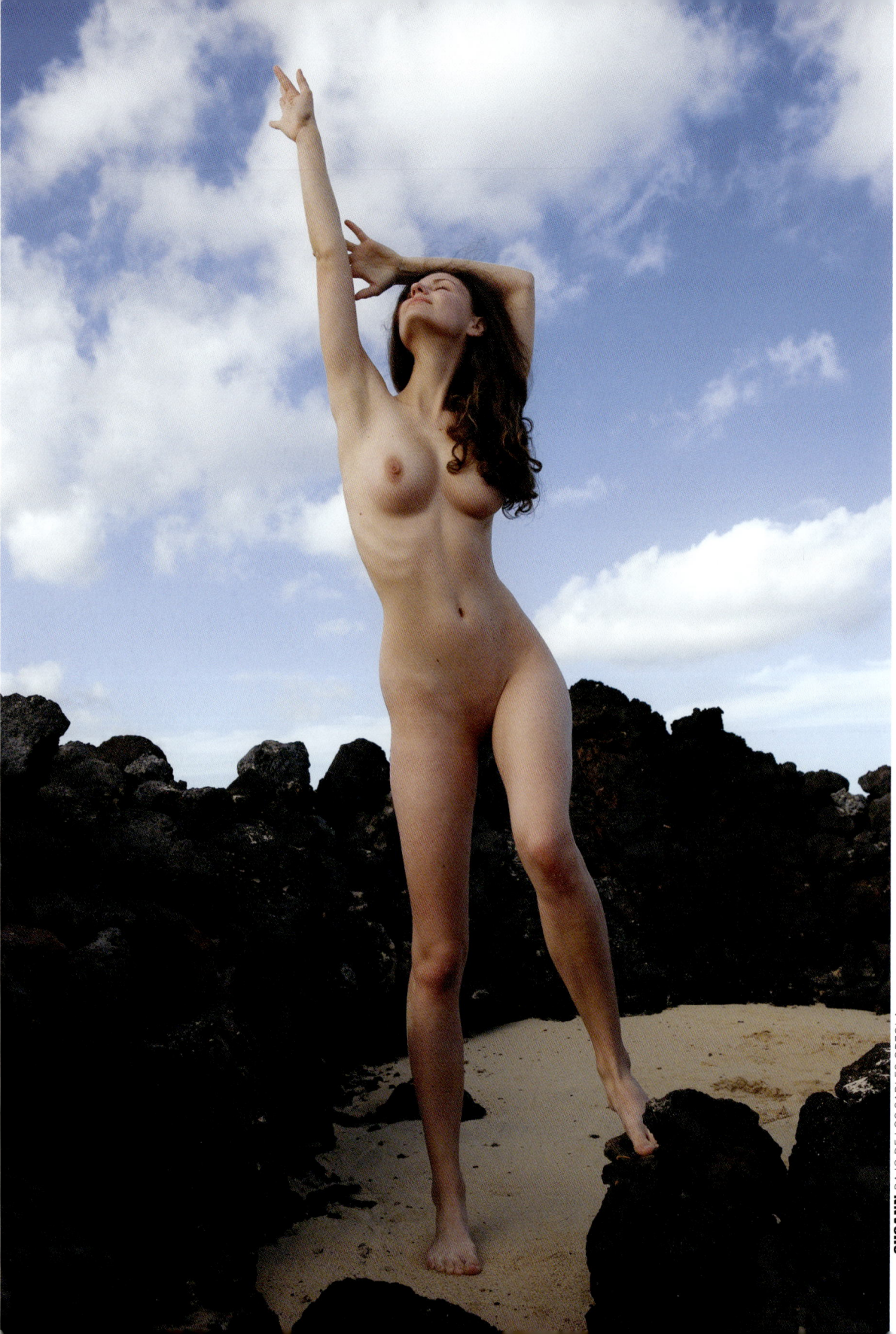

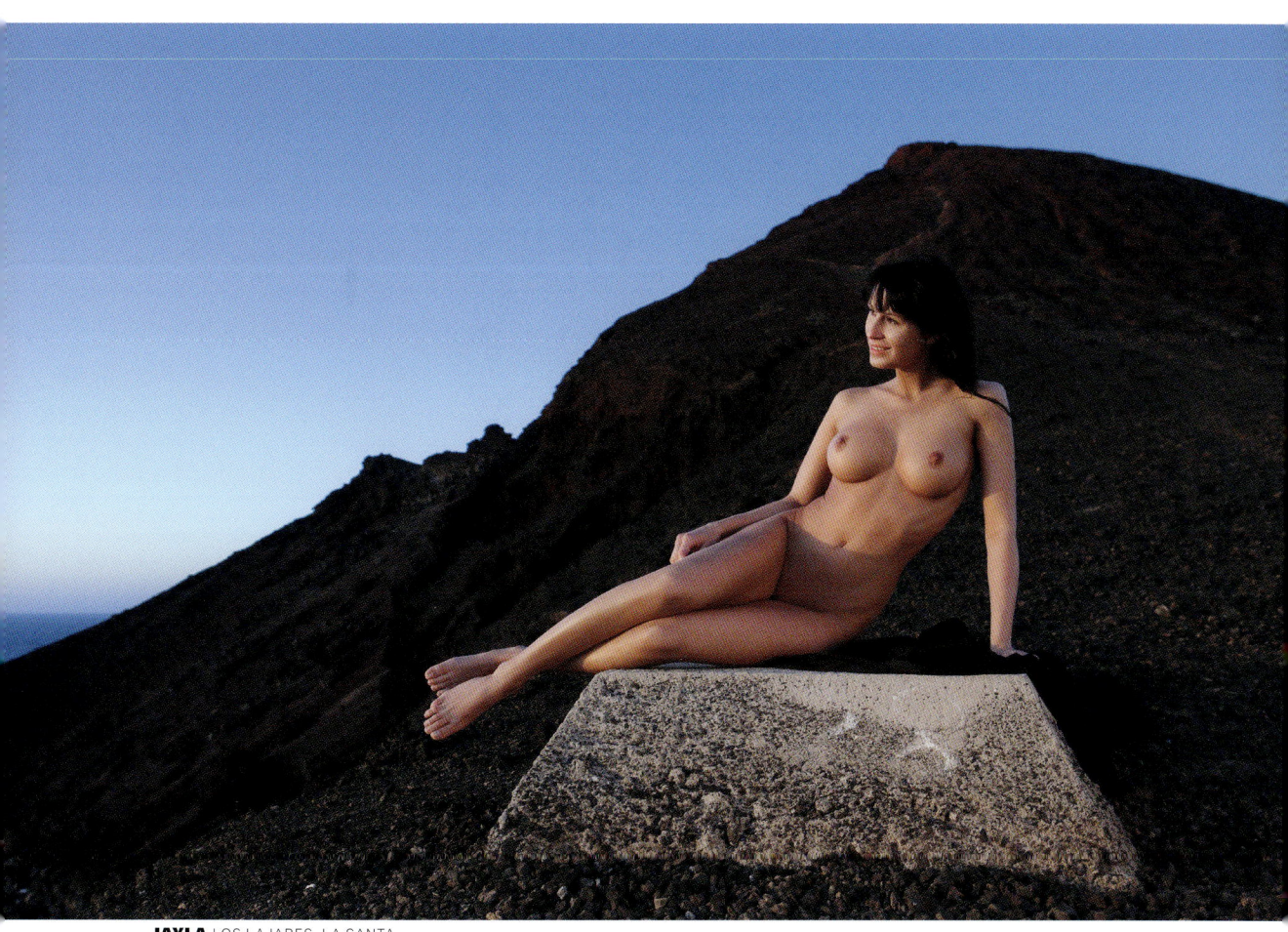

JAYLA LOS LAJARES, LA SANTA

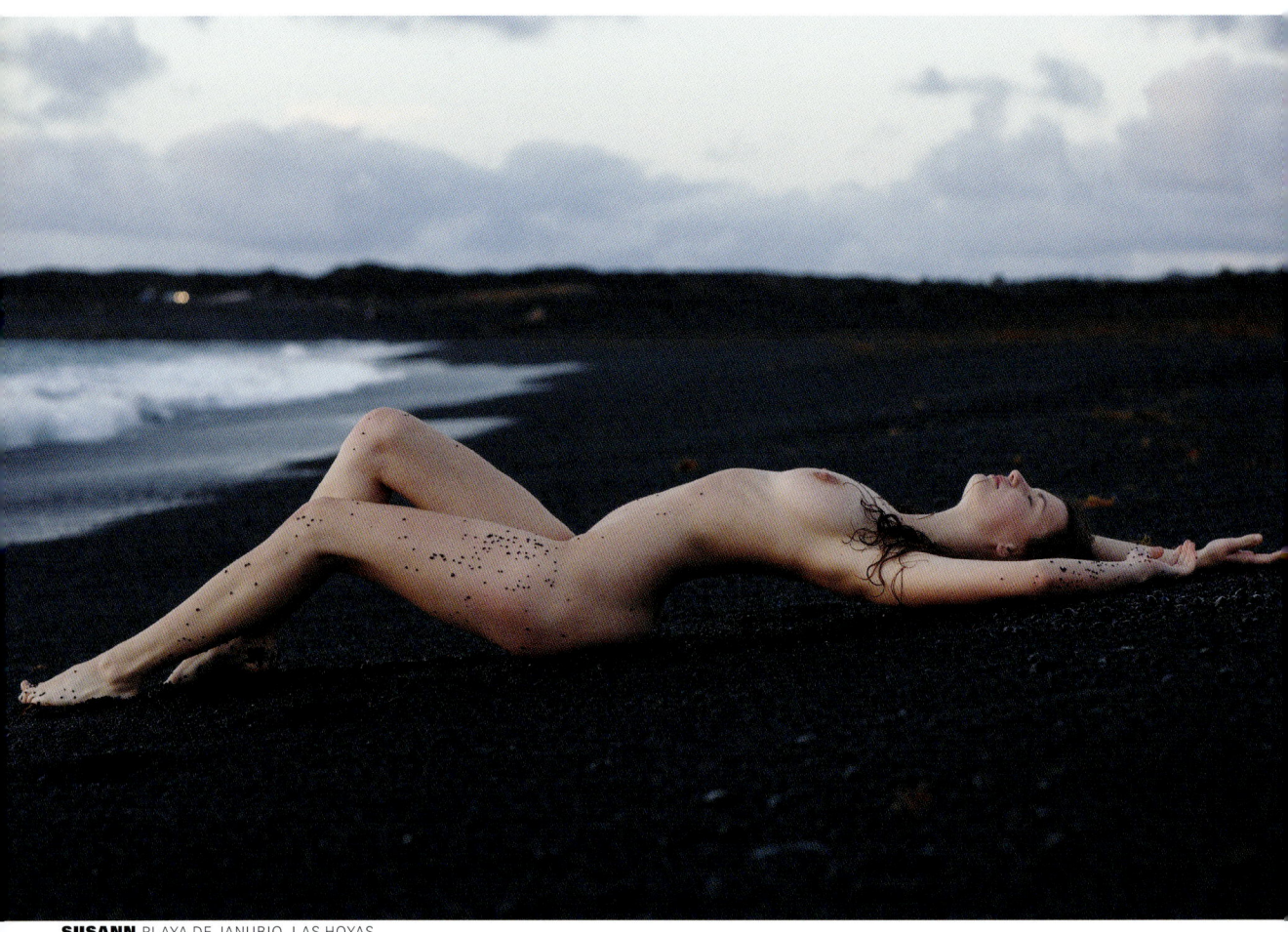

SUSANN PLAYA DE JANUBIO, LAS HOYAS

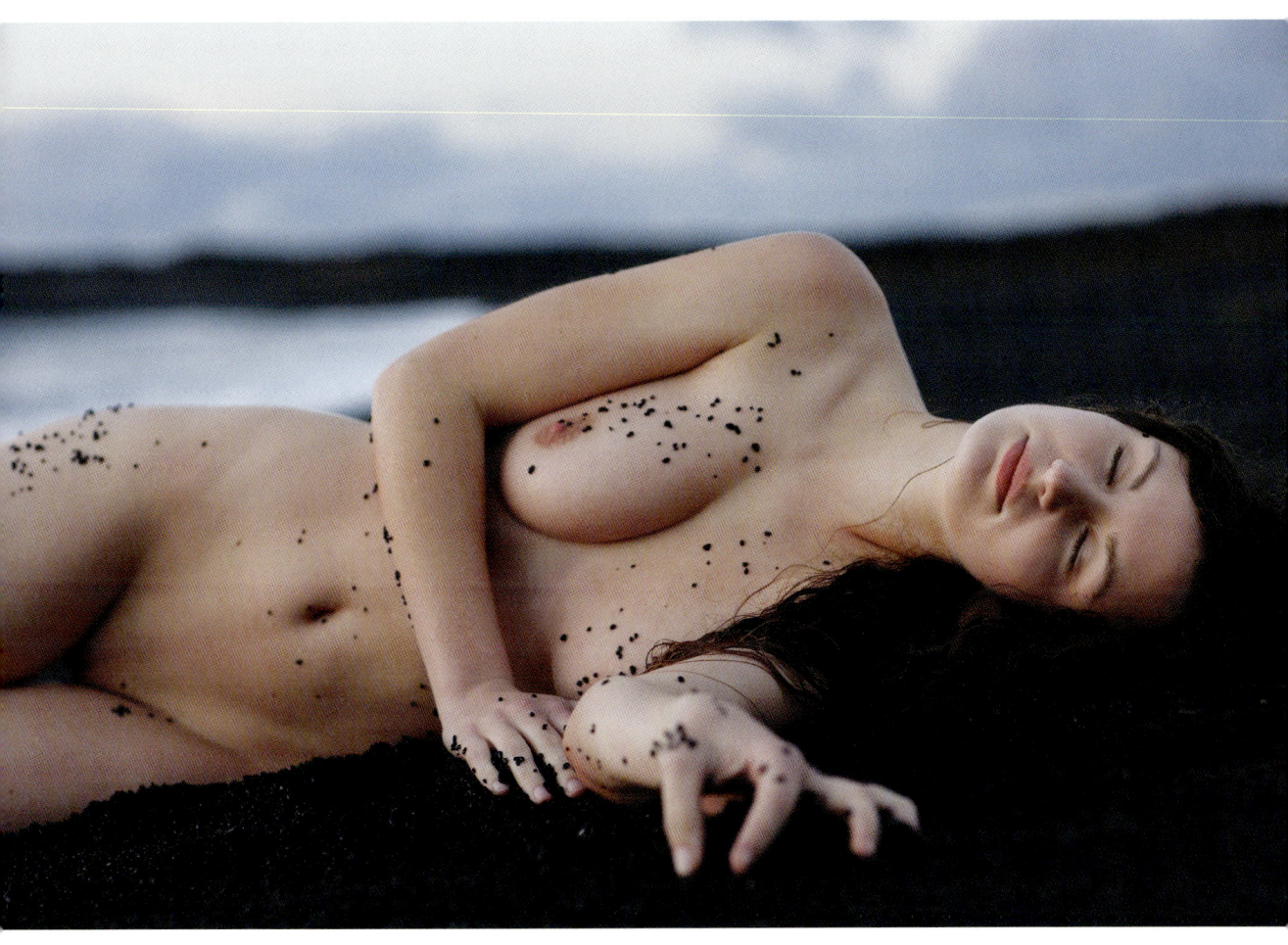

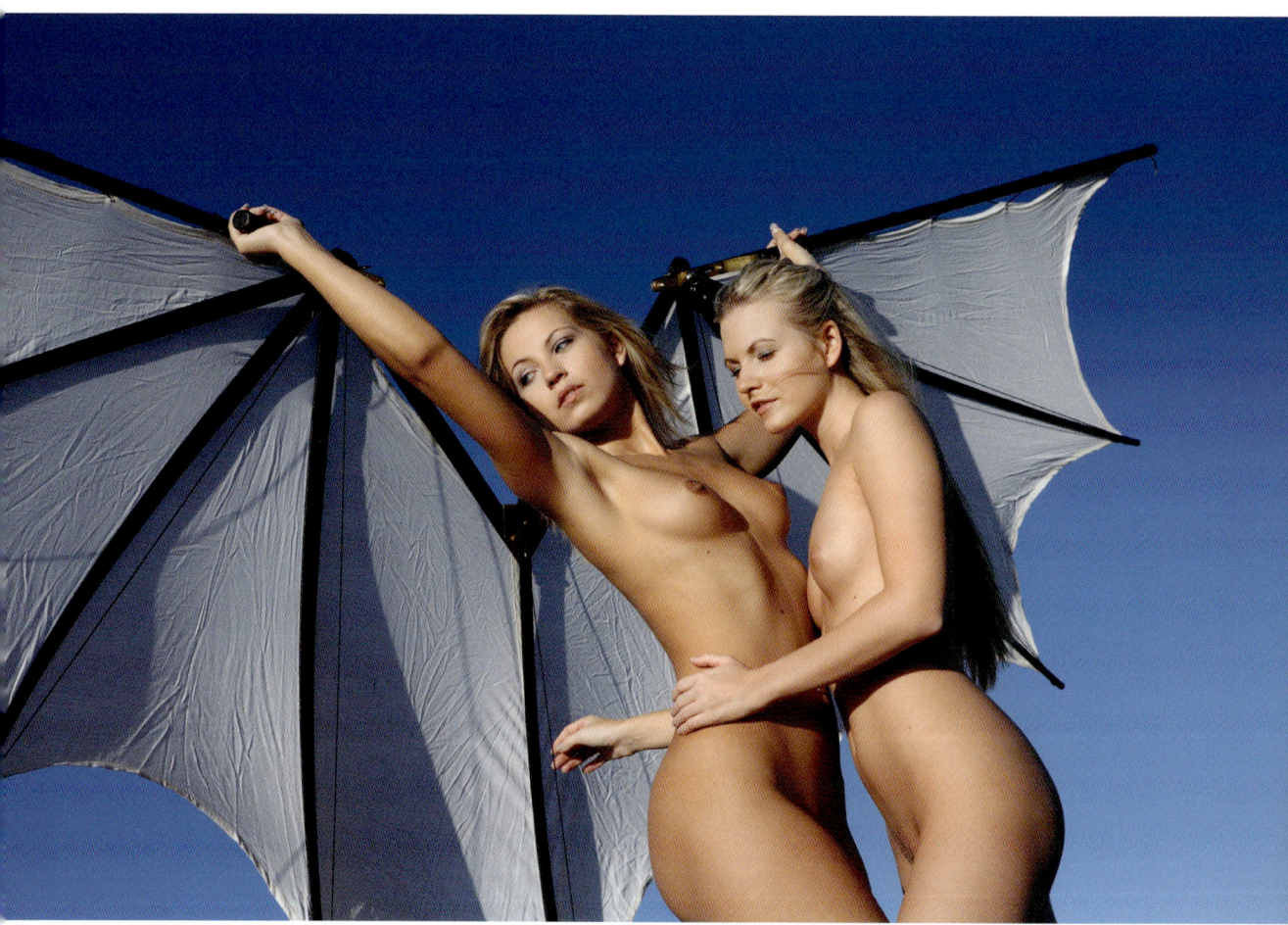

JANA JENNI CALDERA DE LAS CUEVOS, VEGAS DE TEGOYO

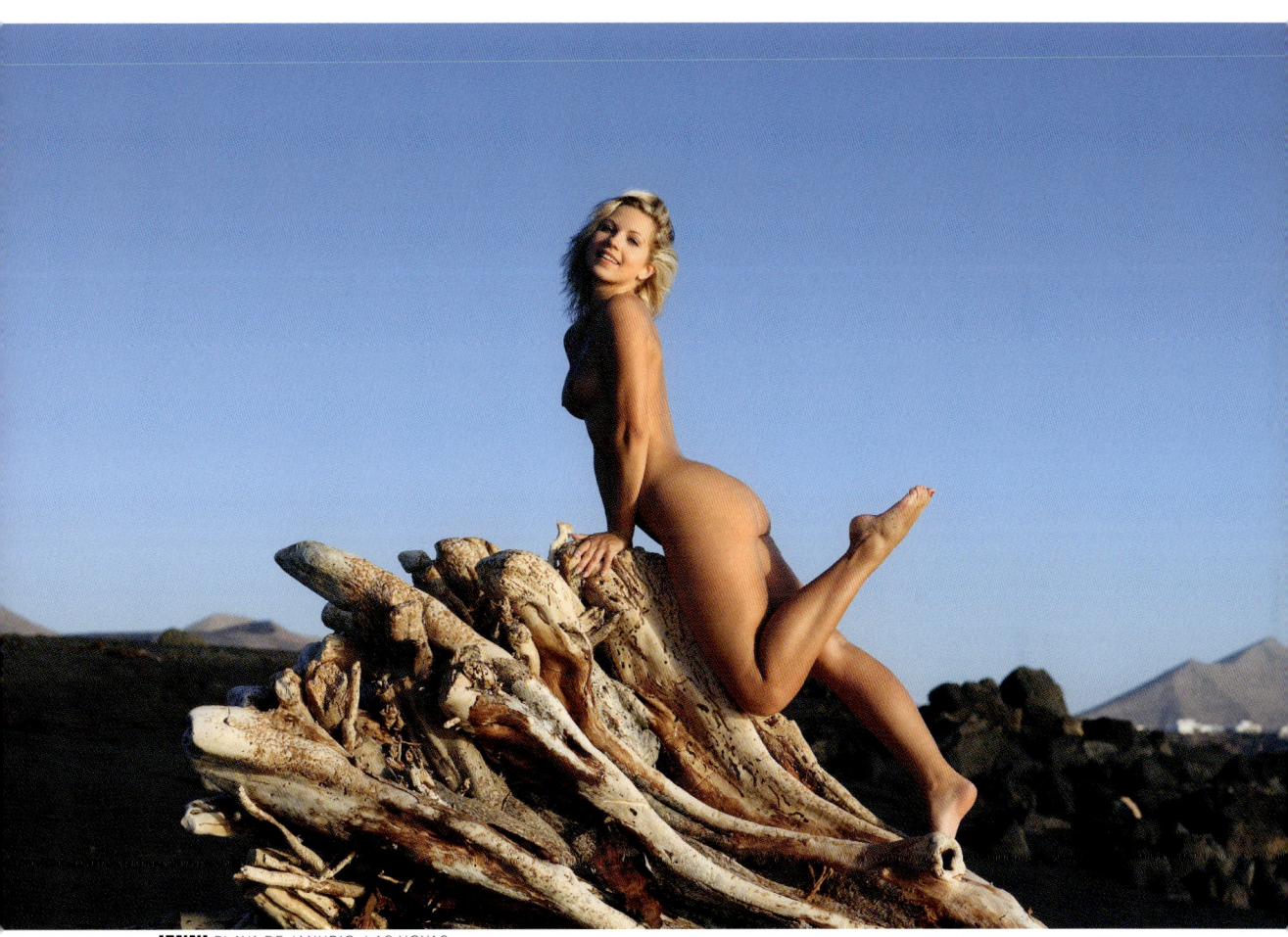

JENNI PLAYA DE JANUBIO, LAS HOYAS

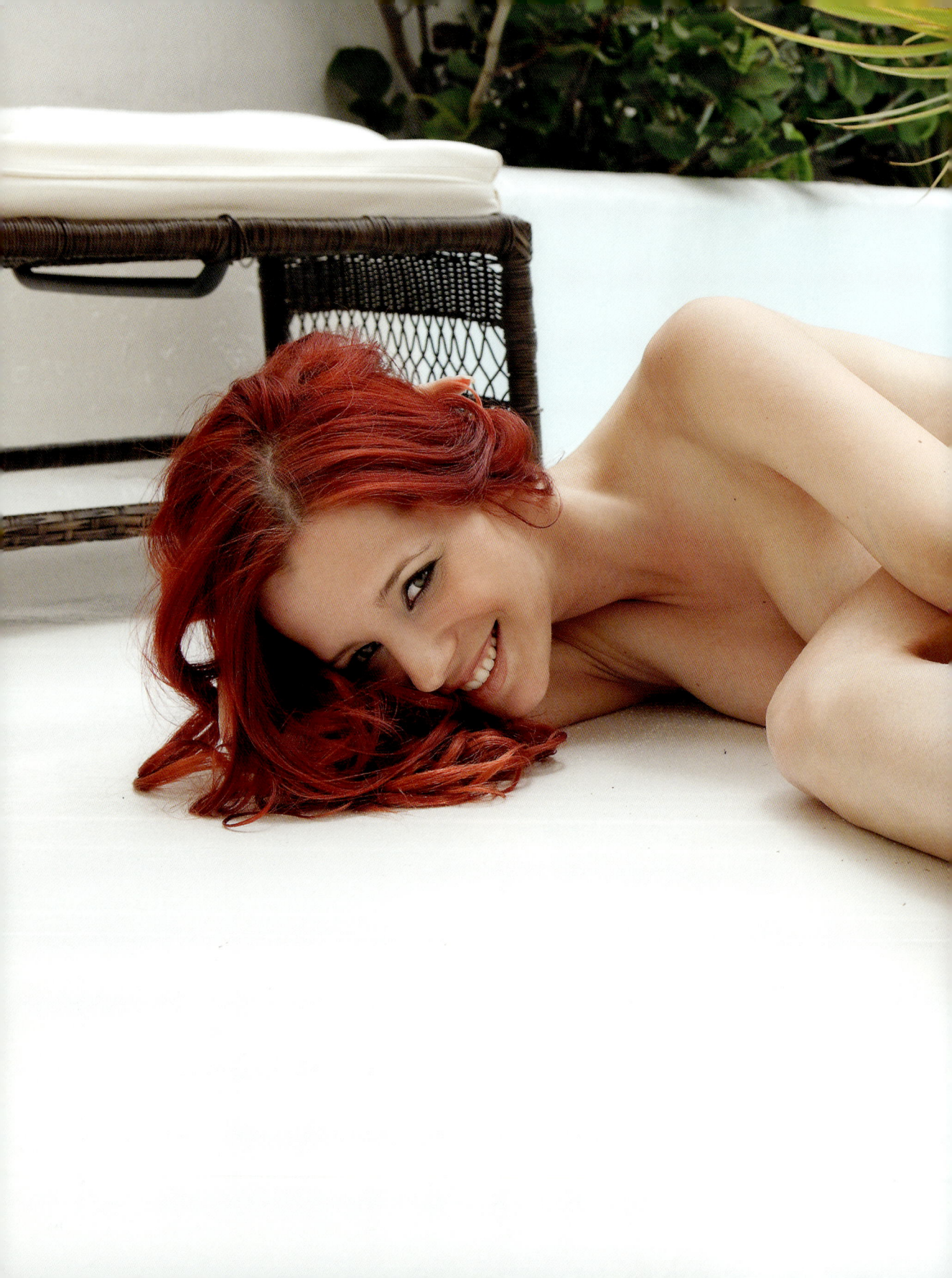

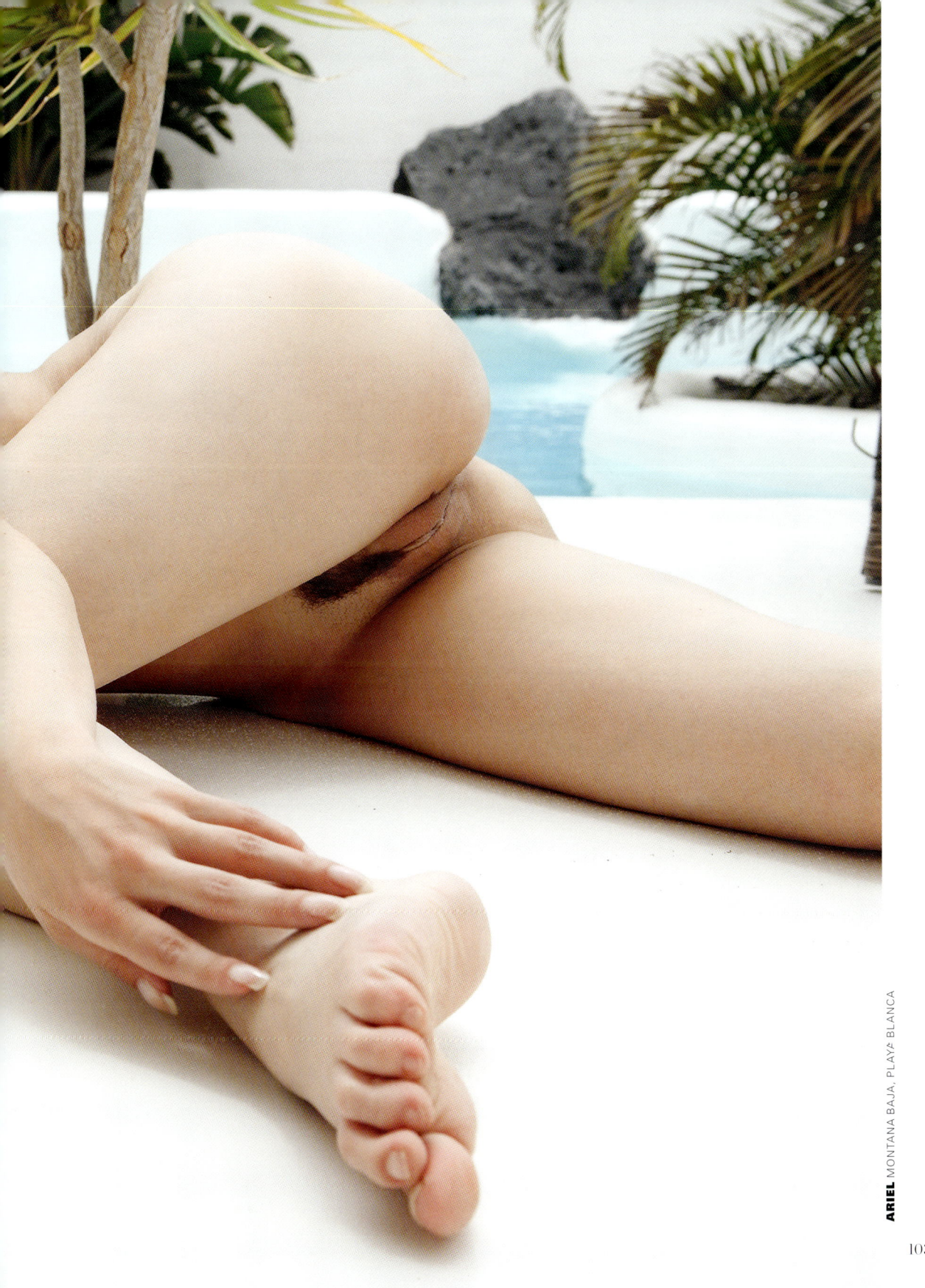

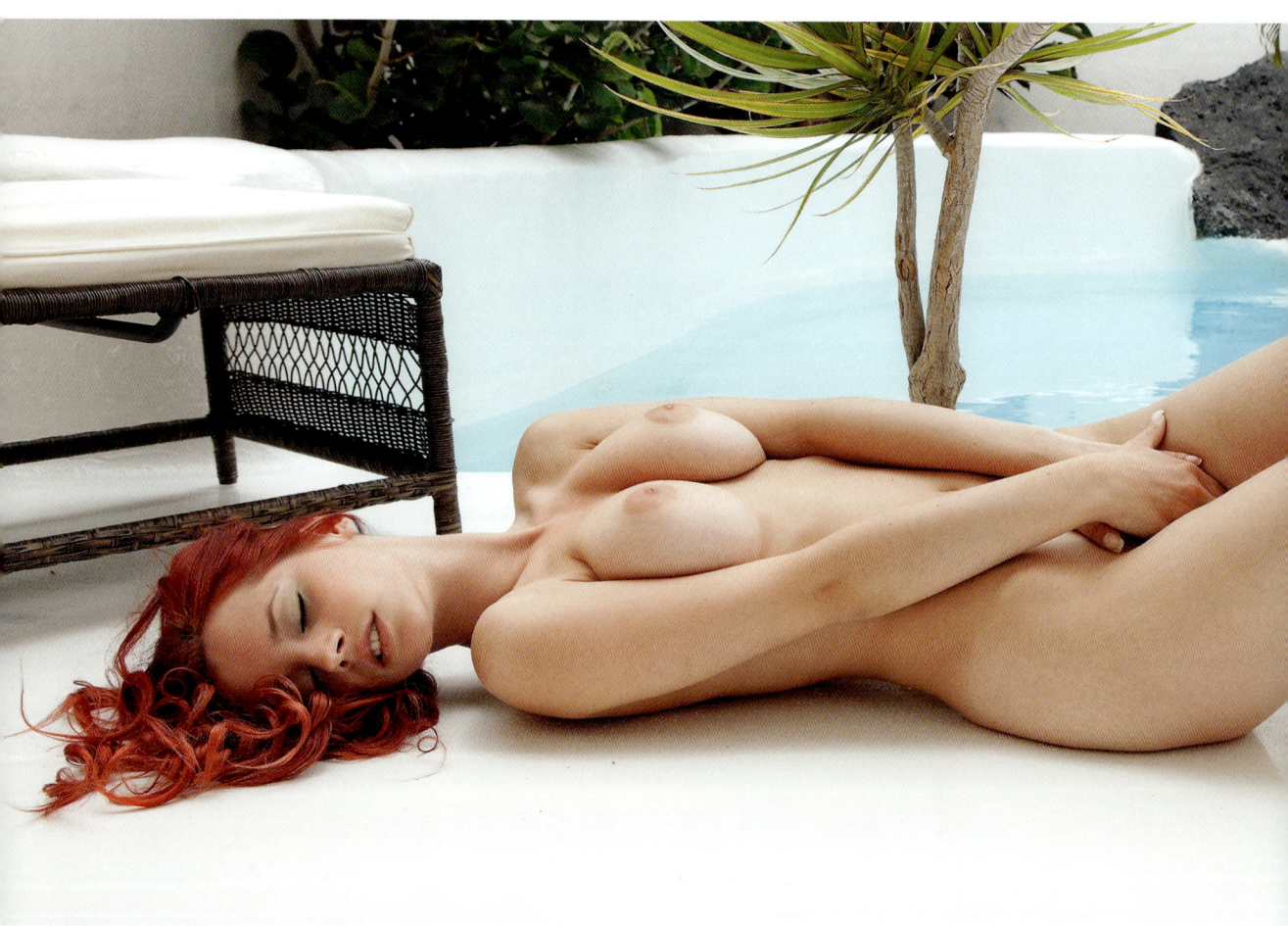

ARIEL MONTANA BAJA, PLAYA BLANCA

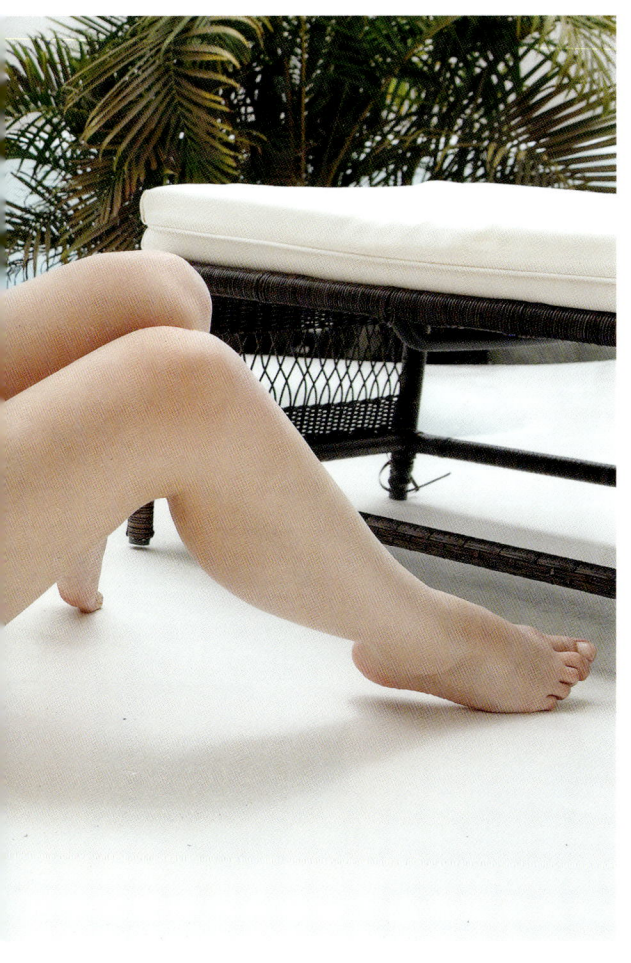

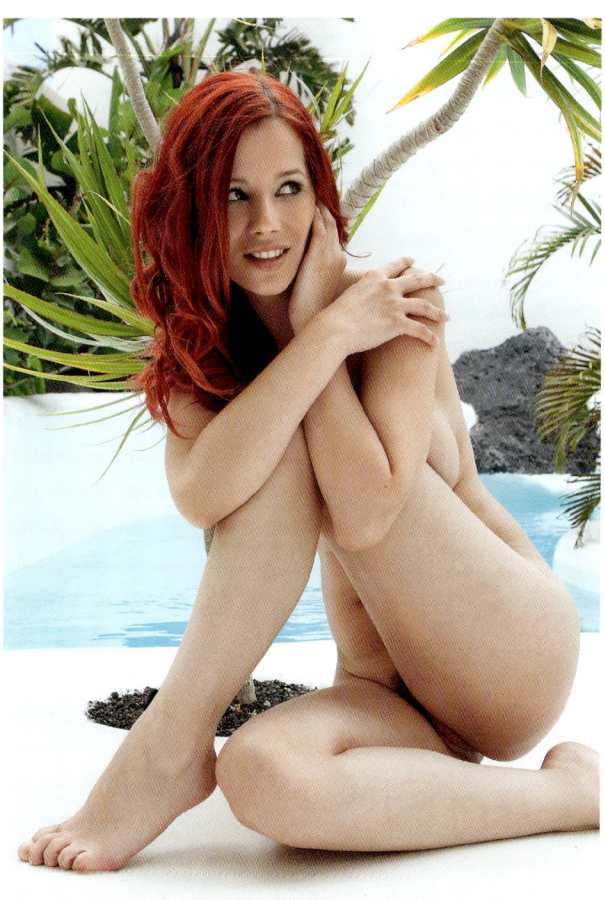

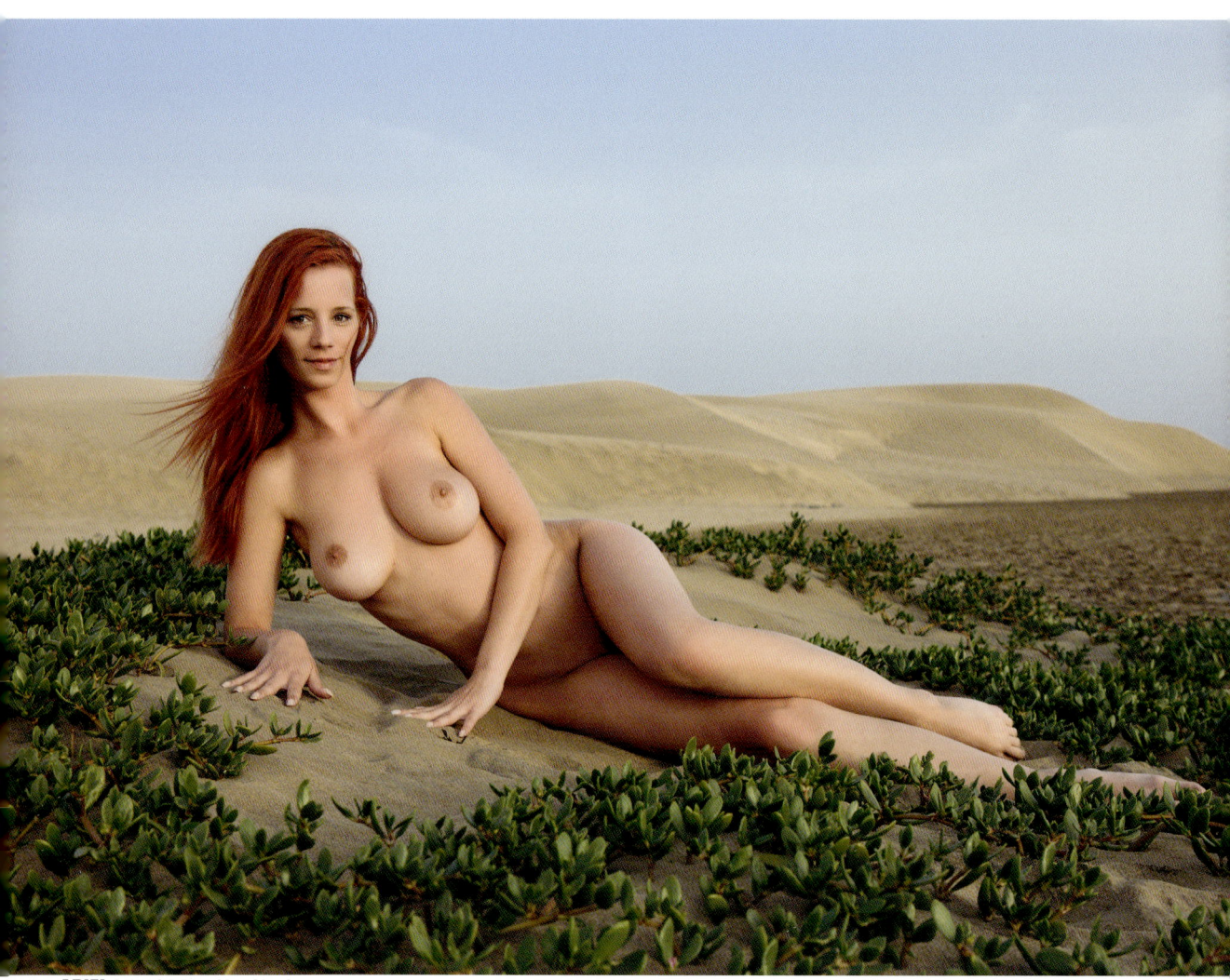

ARIEL DUNAS DE MASPALOMAS

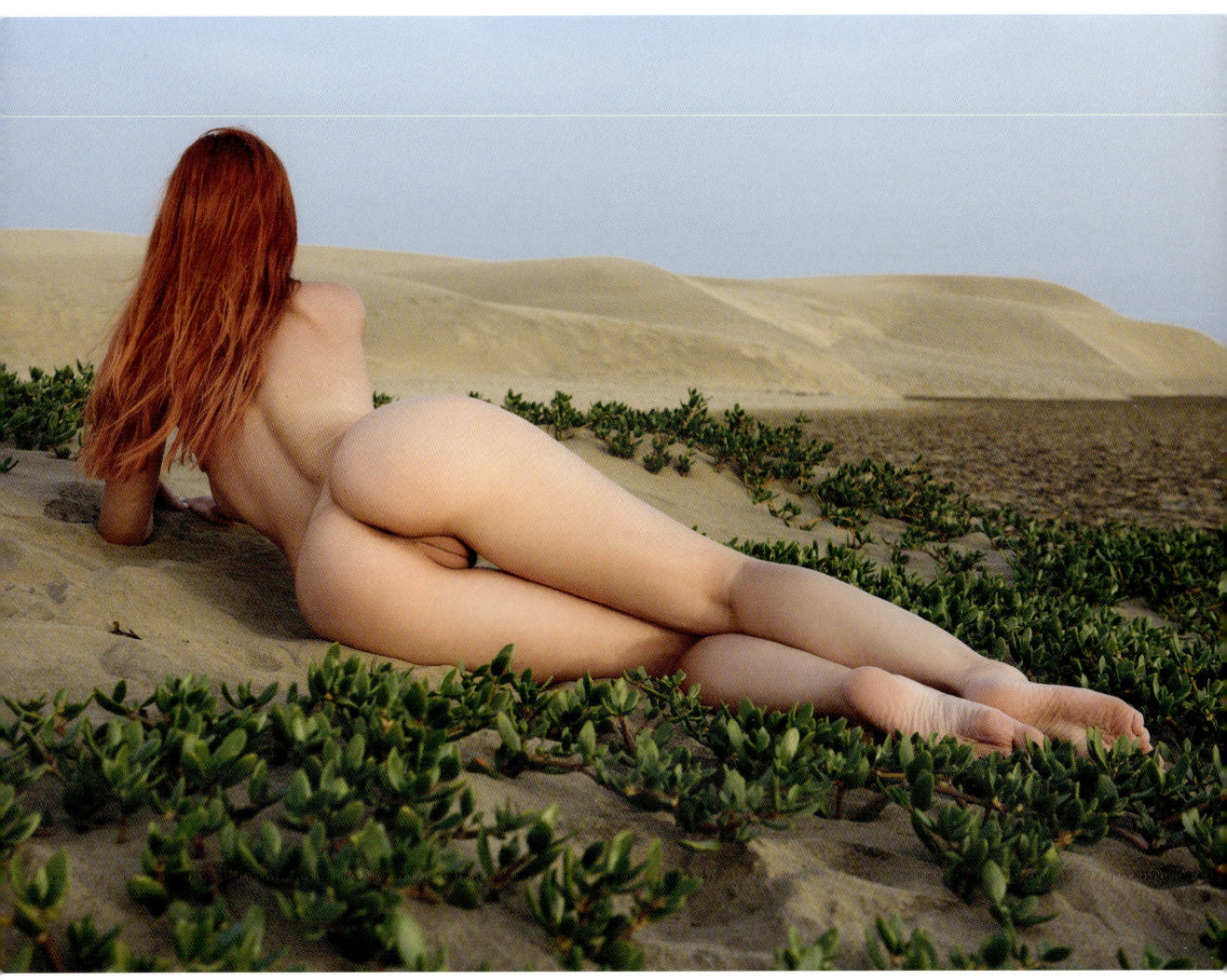

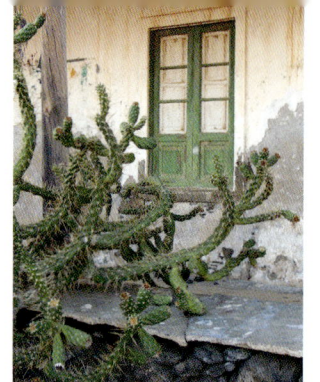

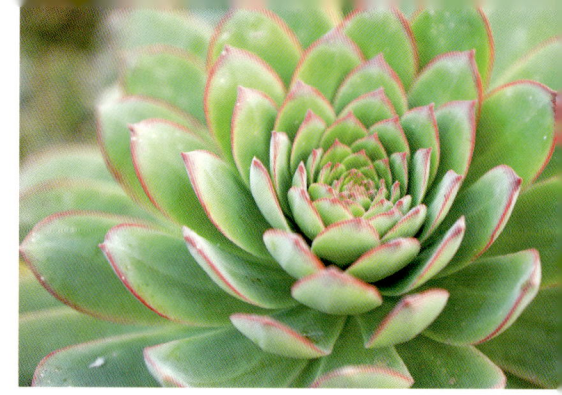

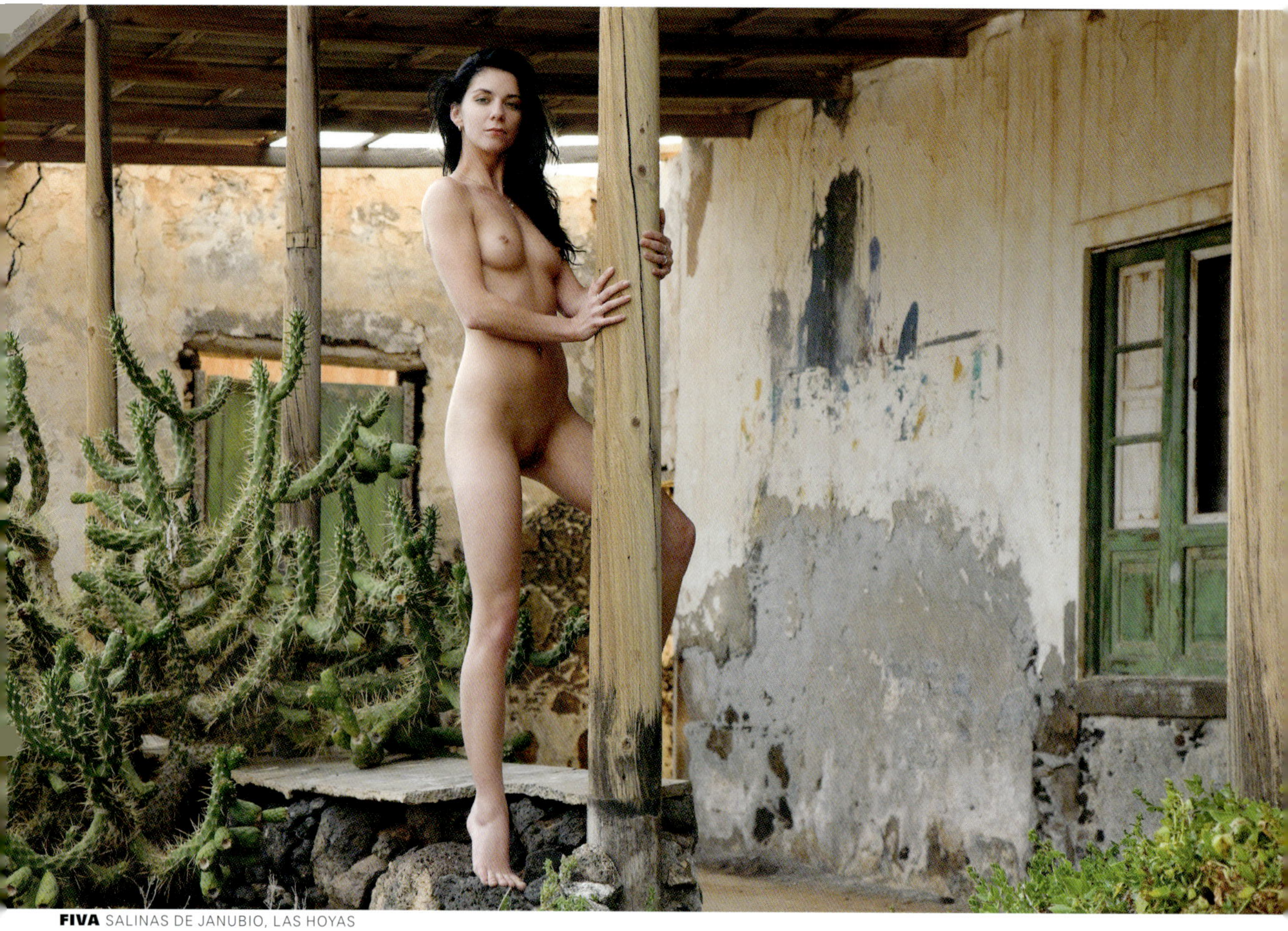

FIVA SALINAS DE JANUBIO, LAS HOYAS

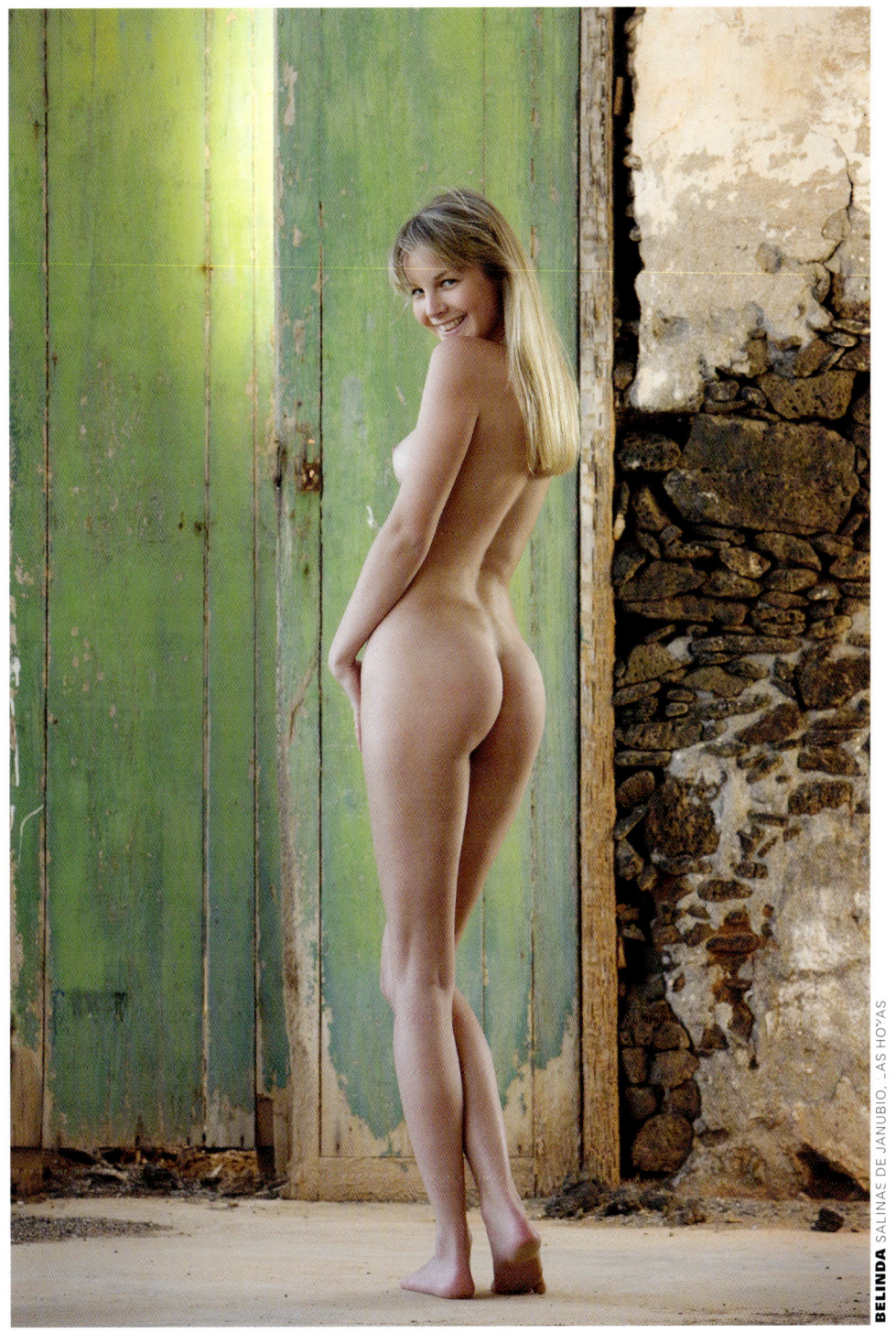

BELINDA SALINAS DE JANUBIO. _AS HOYAS

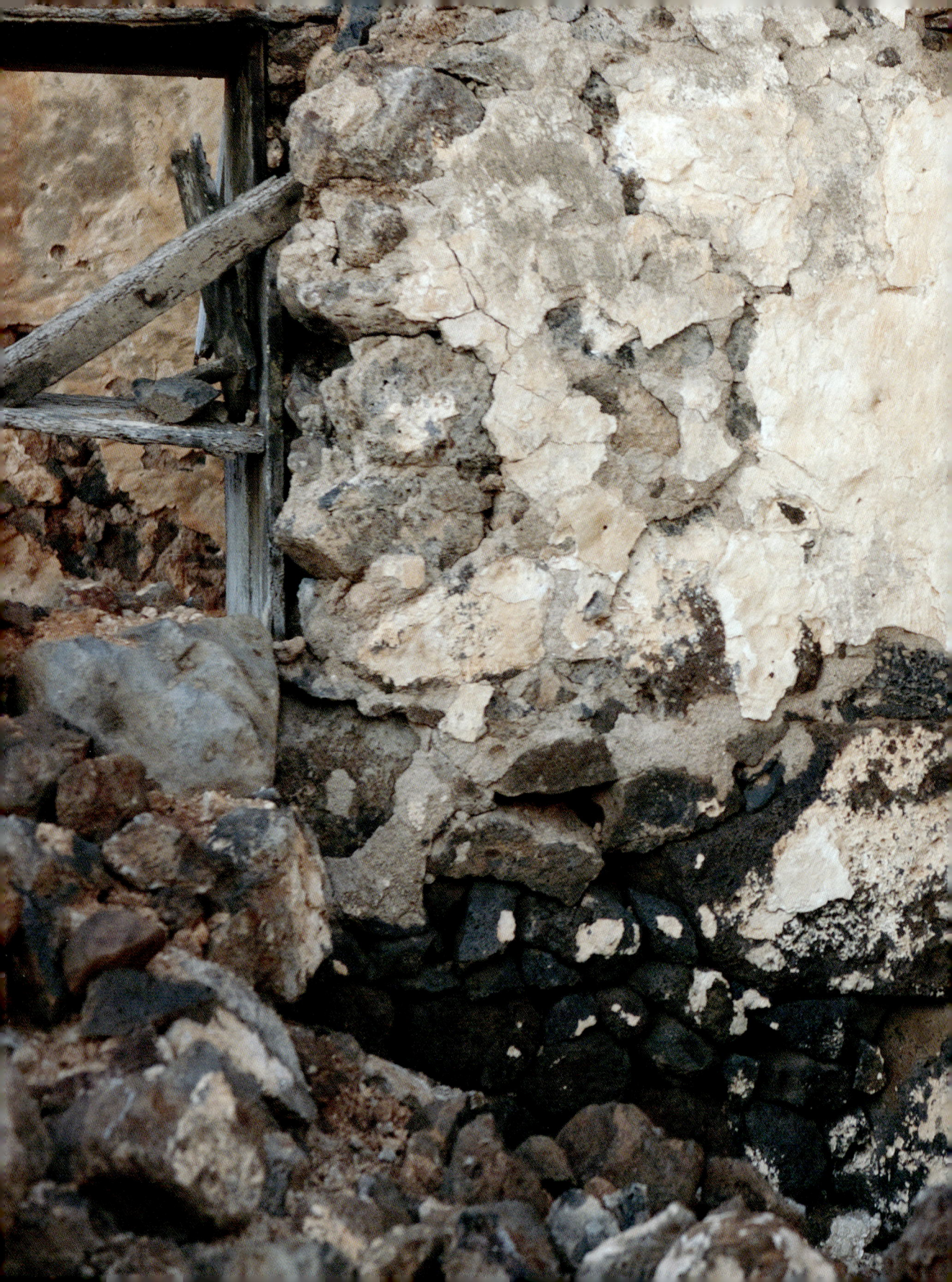

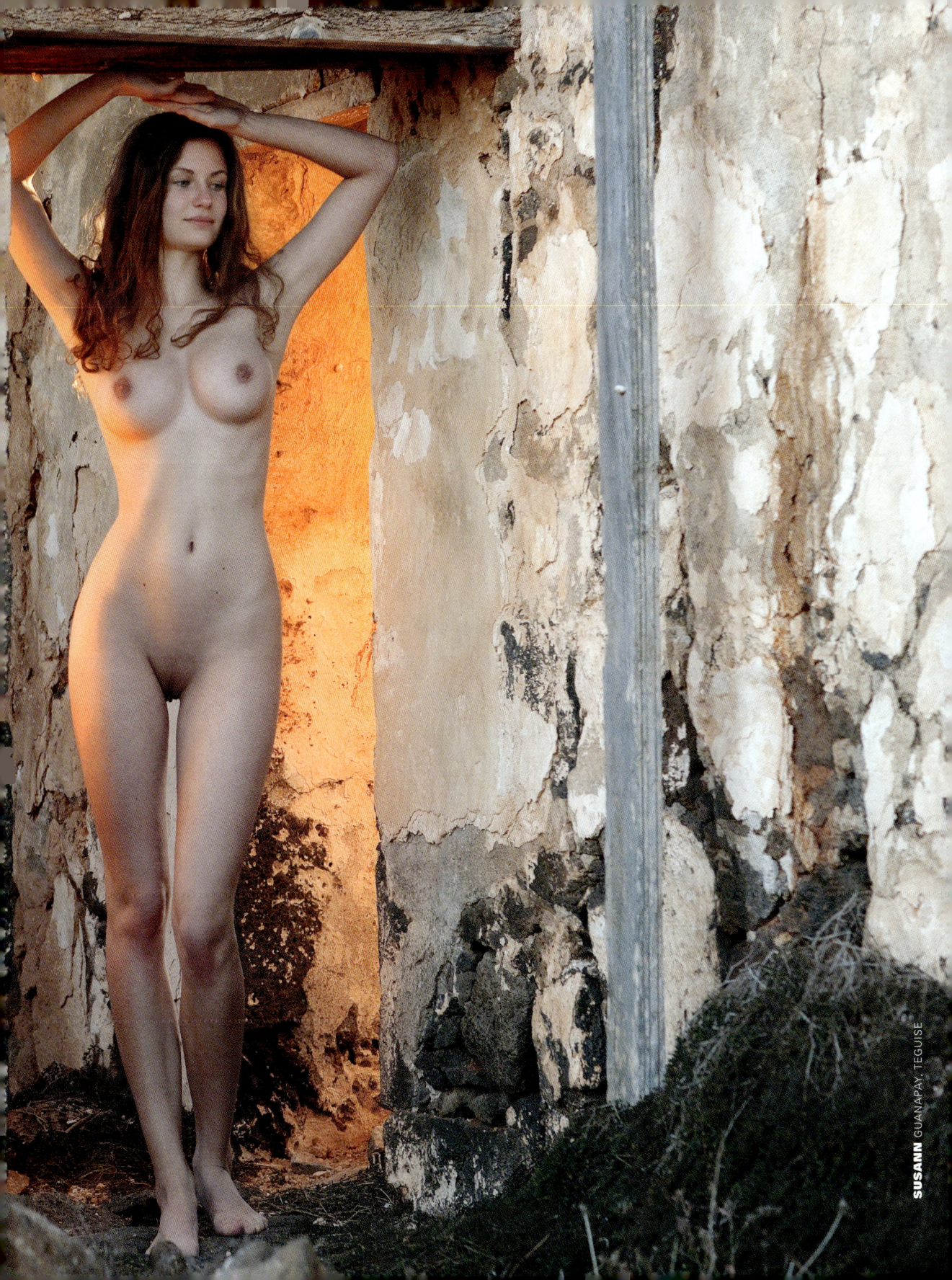

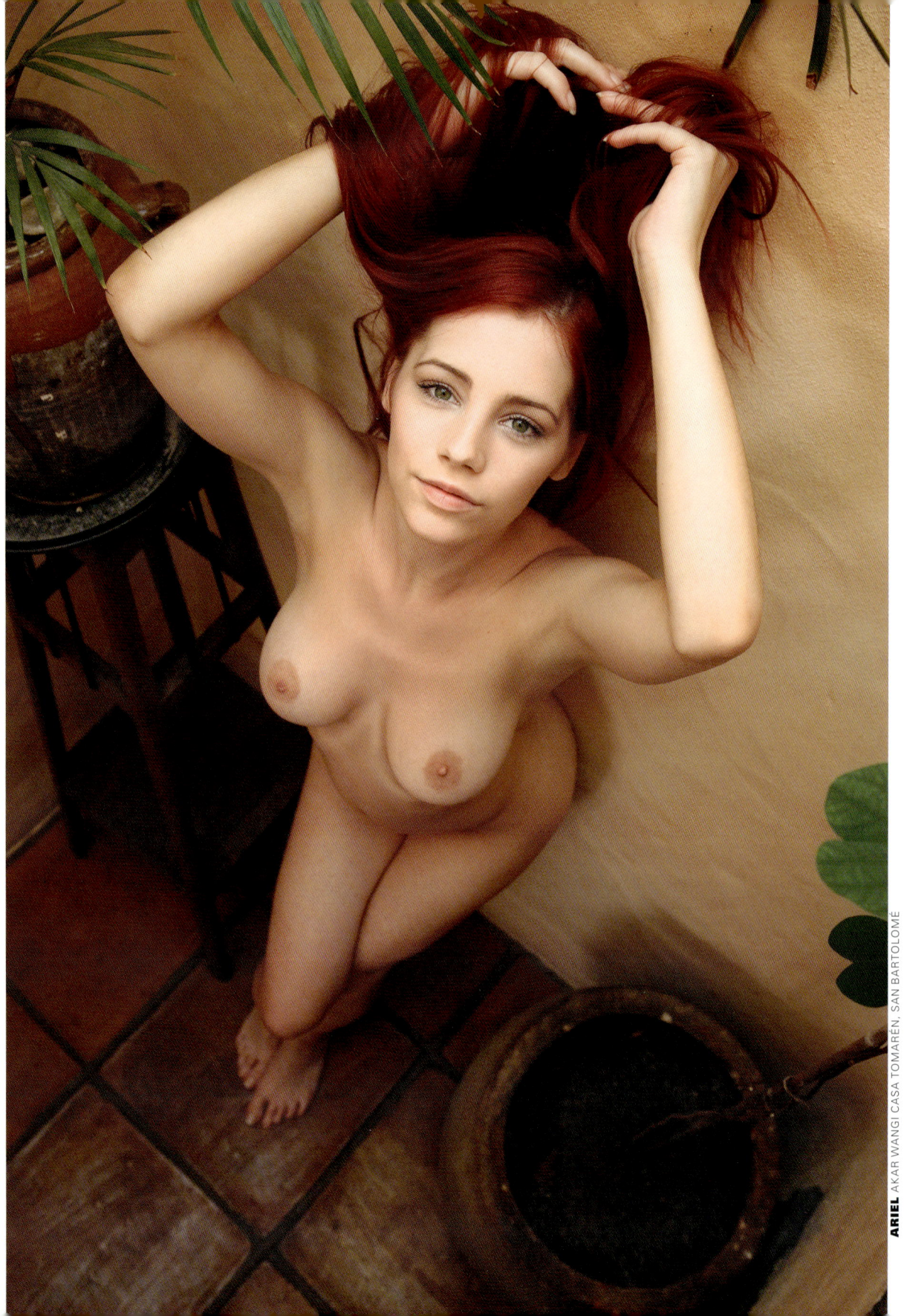

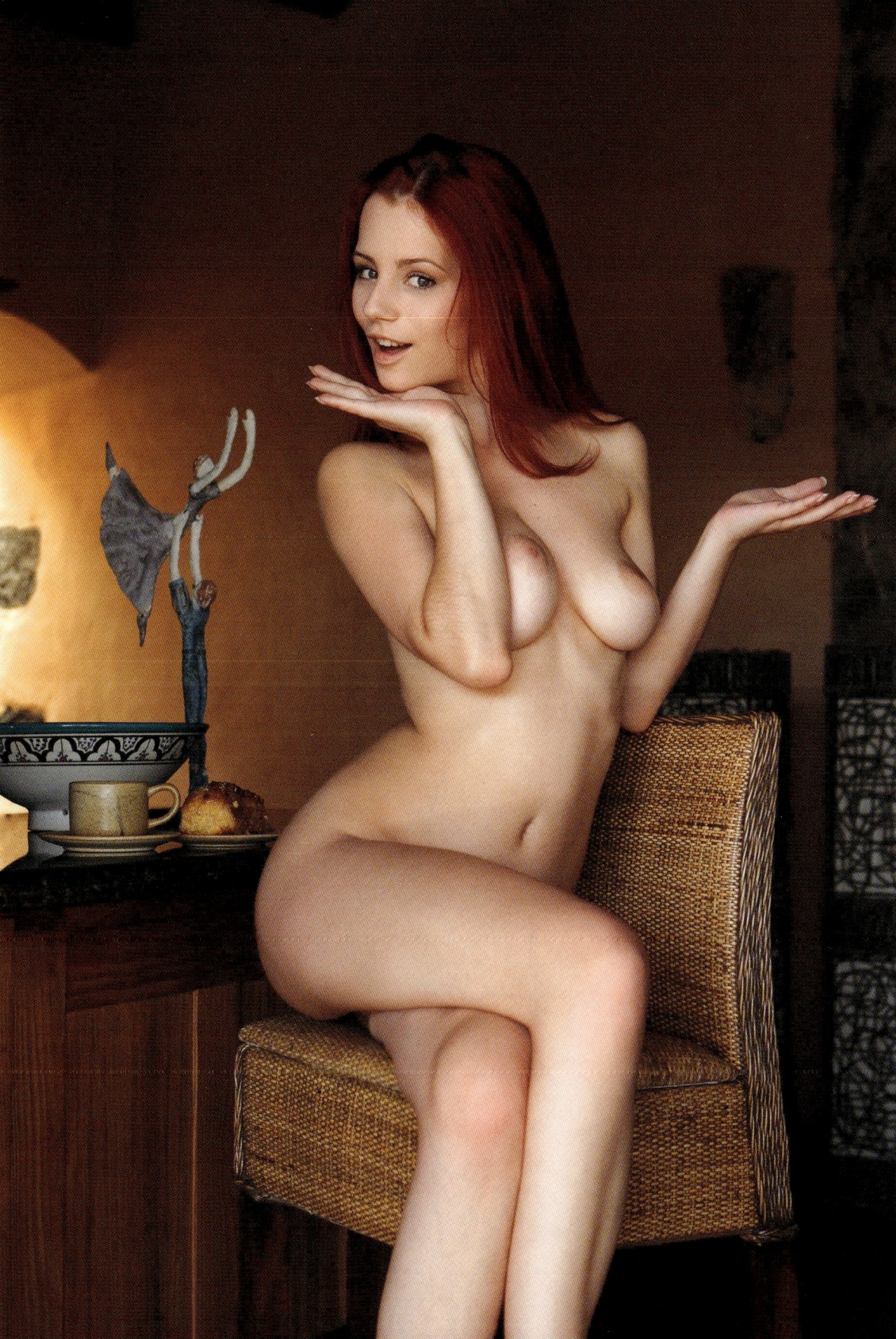

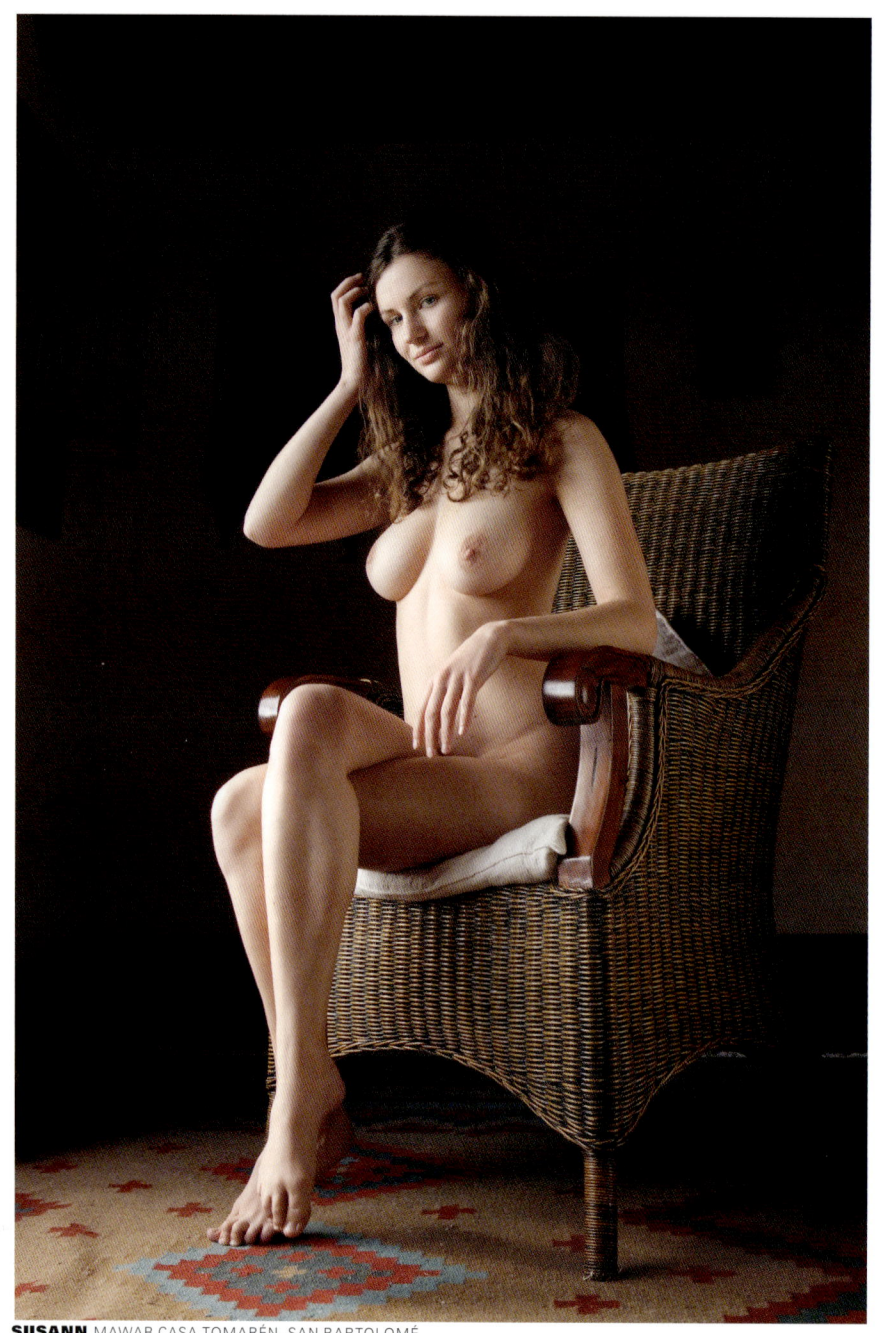

SUSANN MAWAR CASA TOMARÉN, SAN BARTOLOMÉ

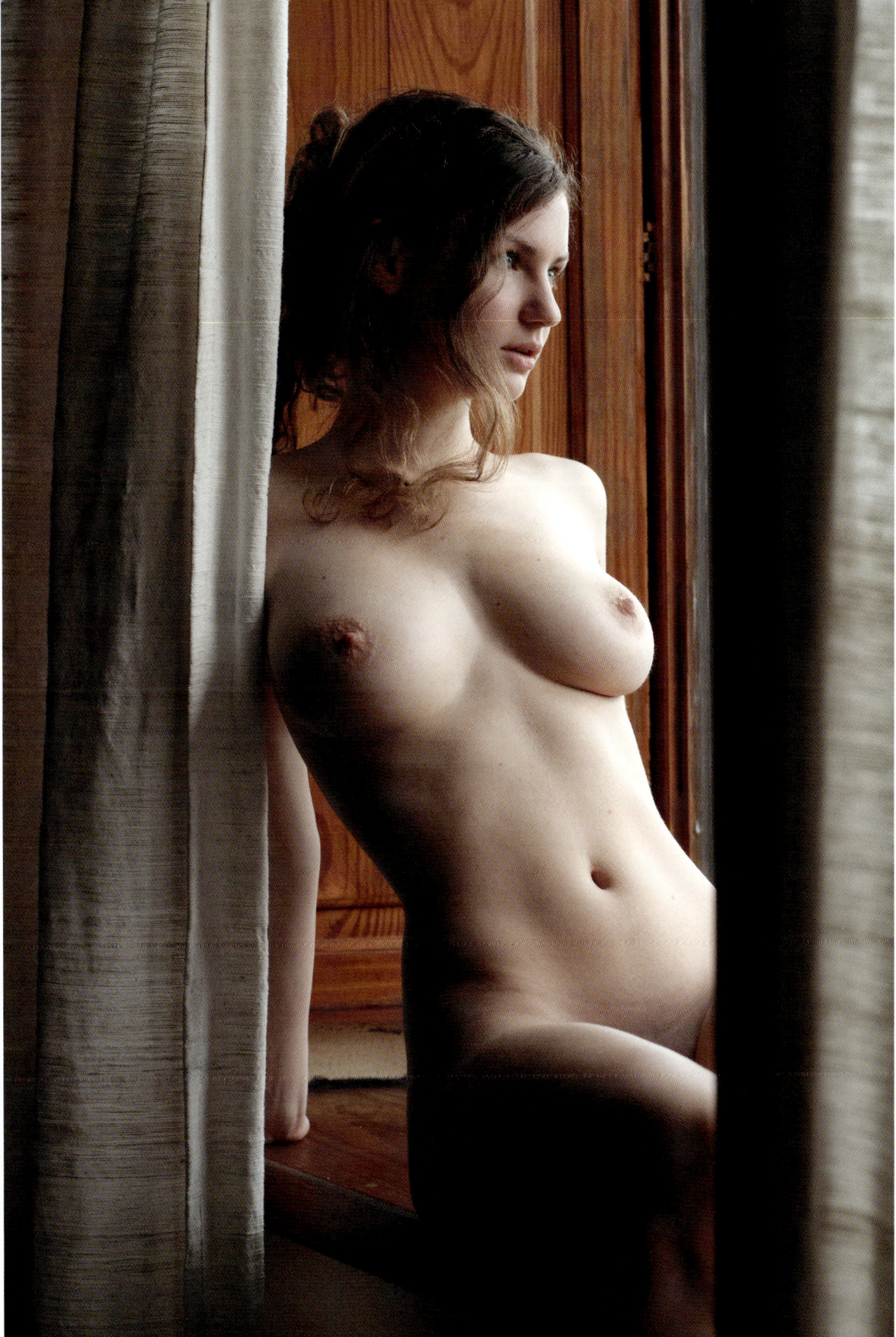

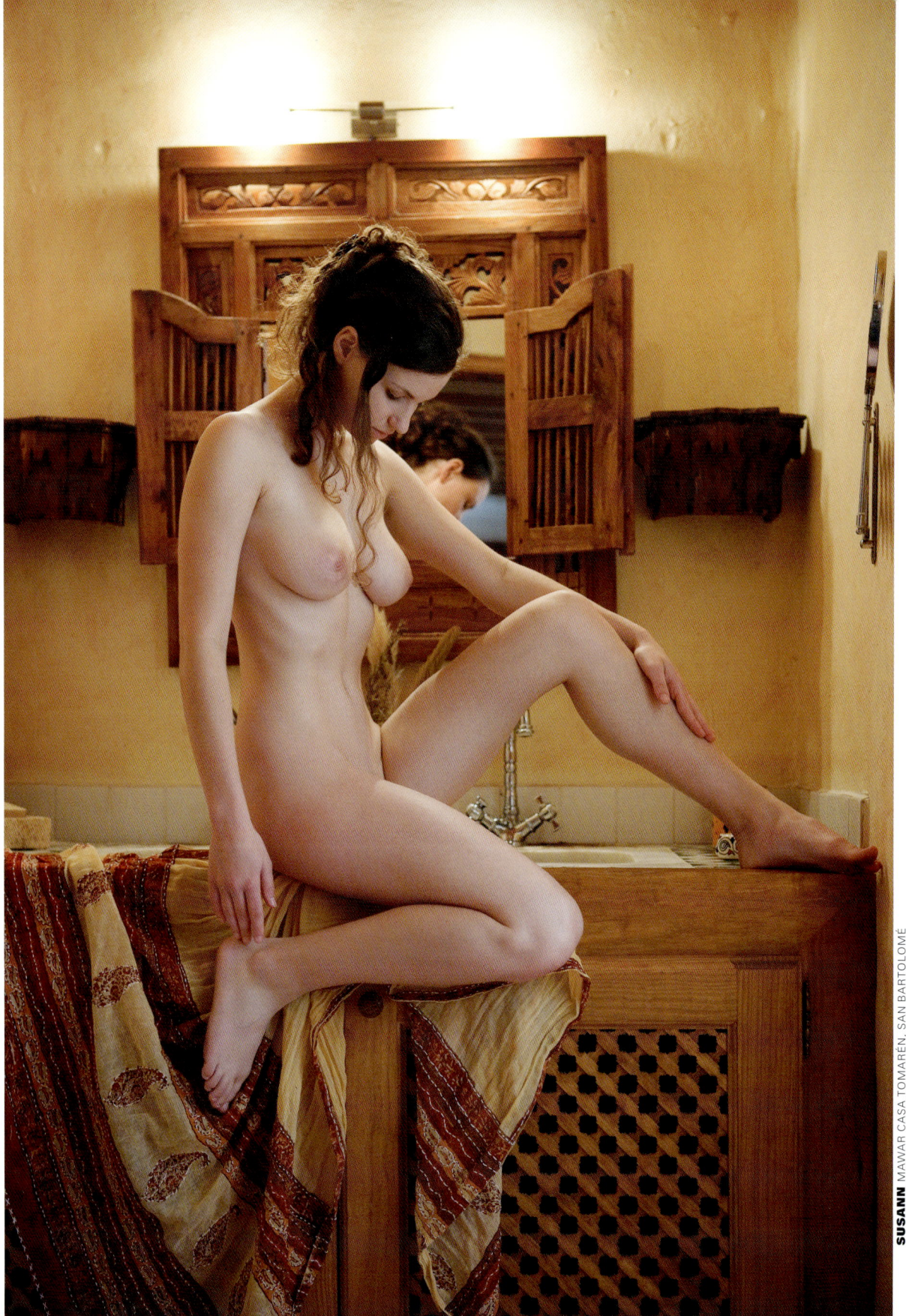

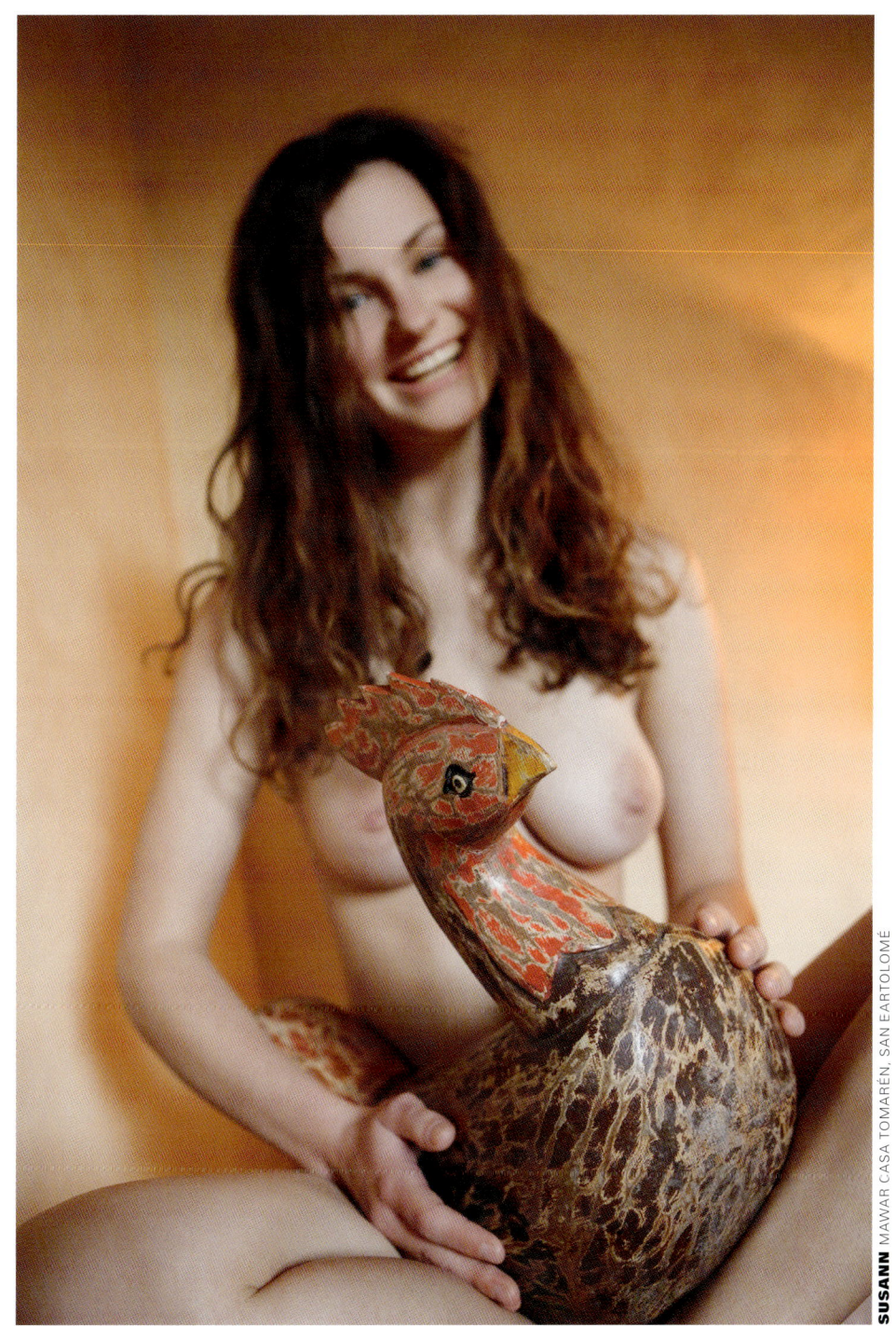

117

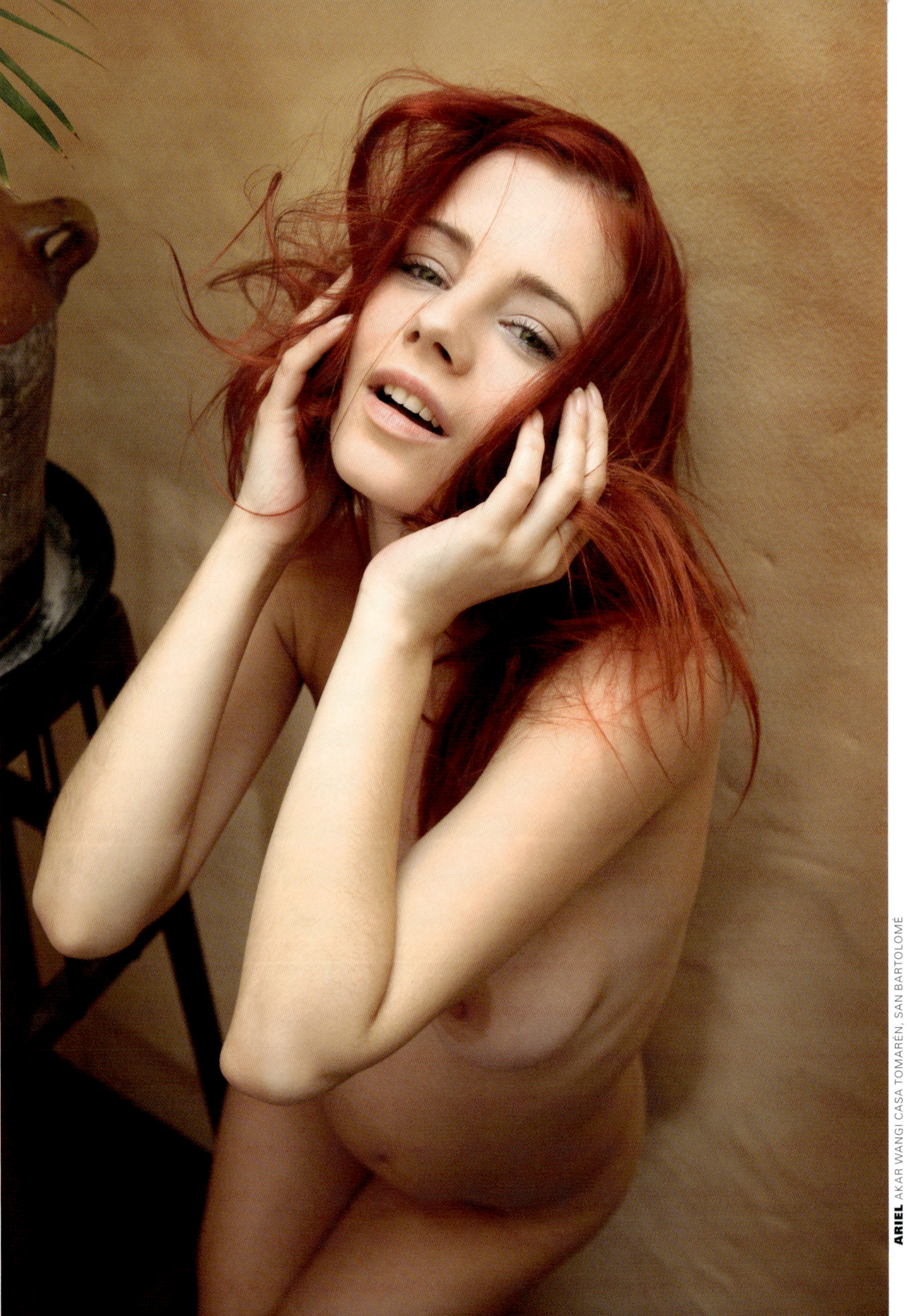

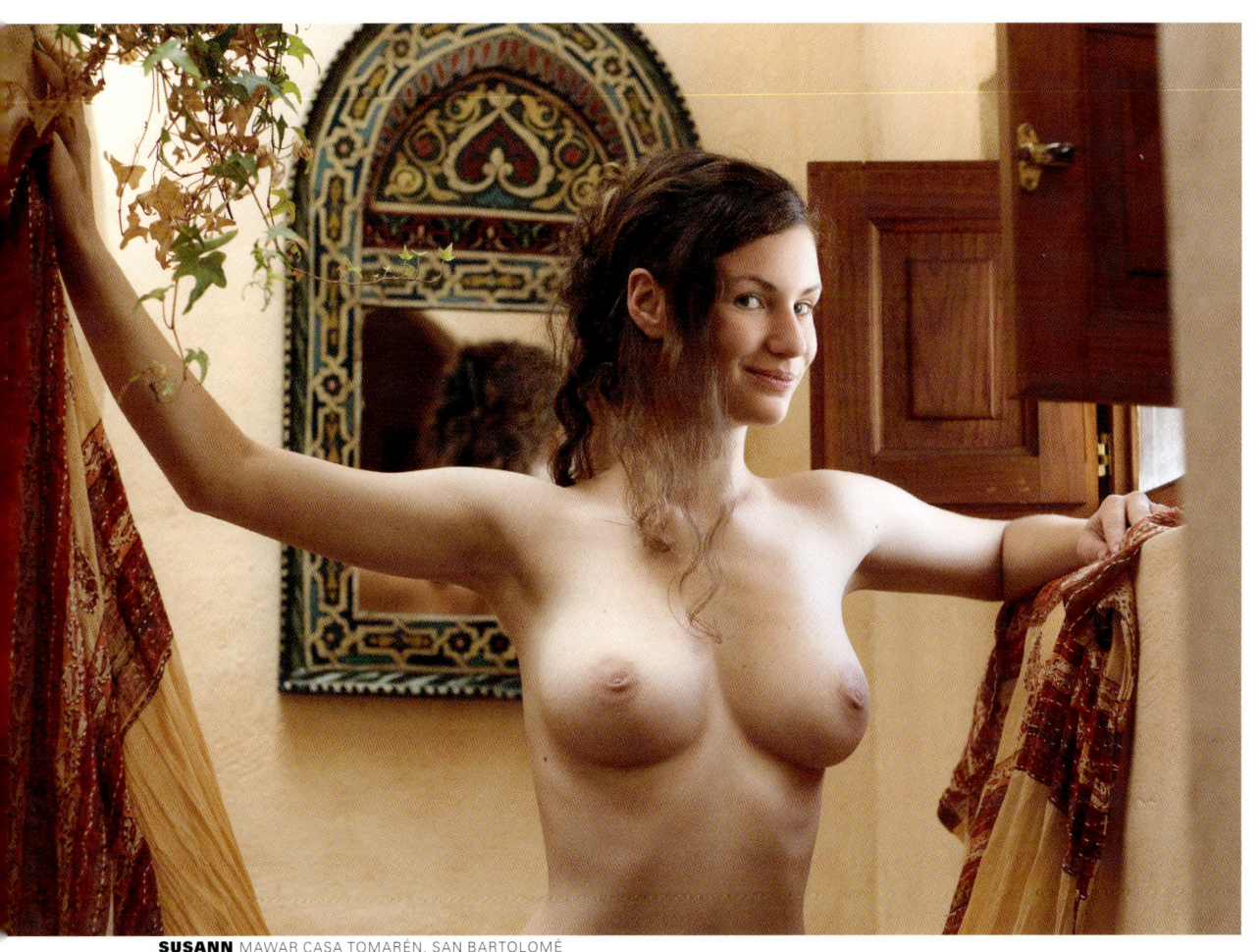

SUSANN MAWAR CASA TOMARÉN, SAN BARTOLOMÉ

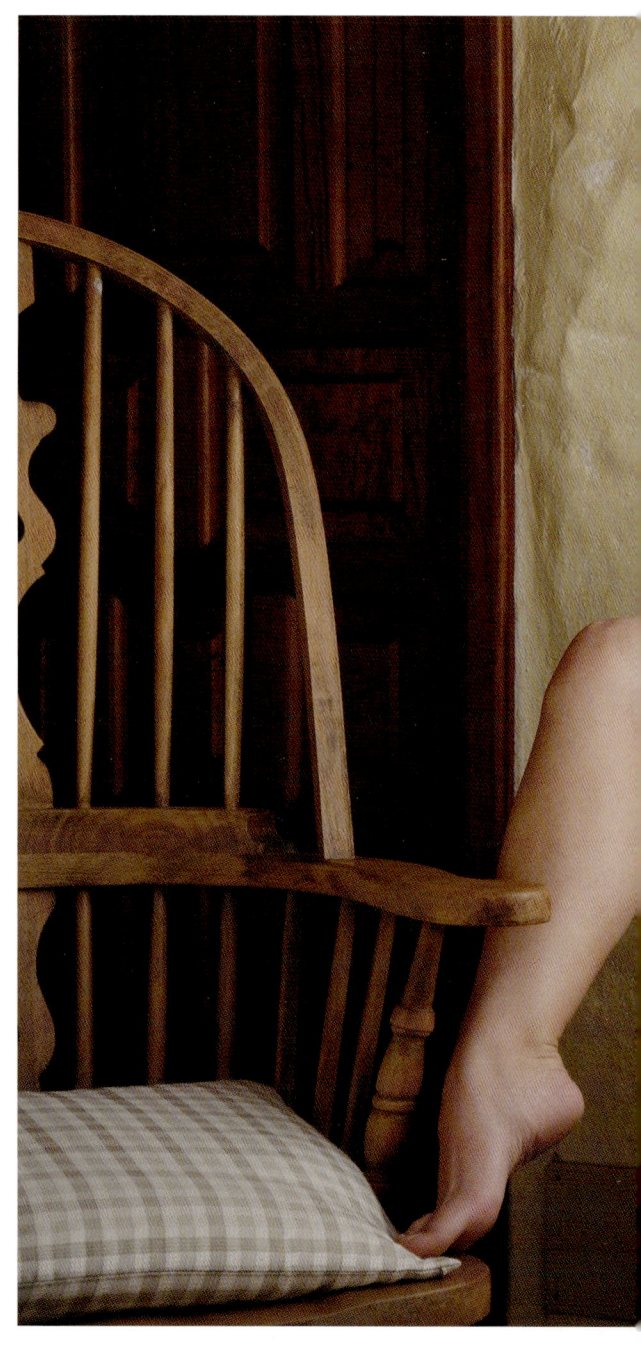

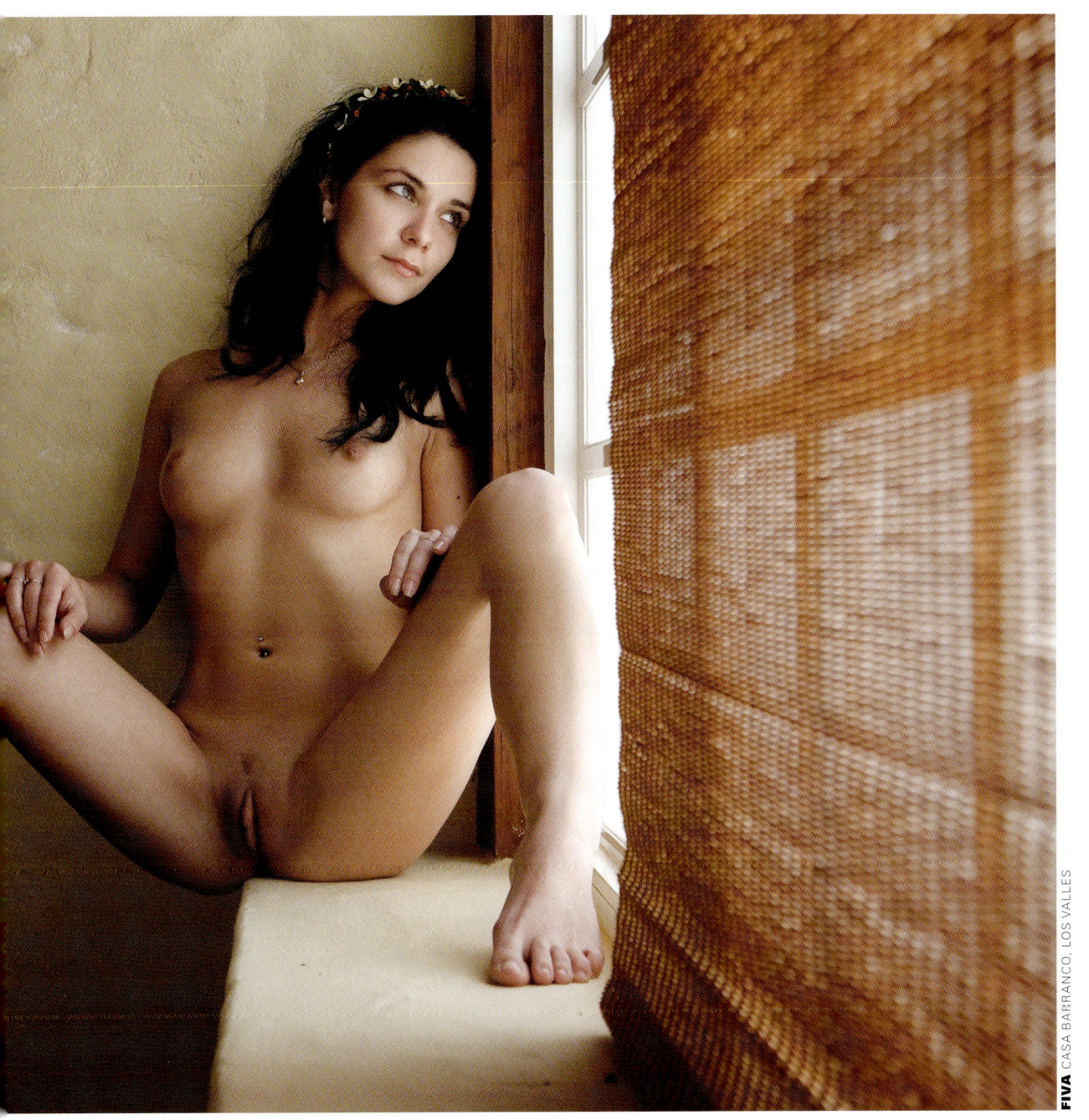

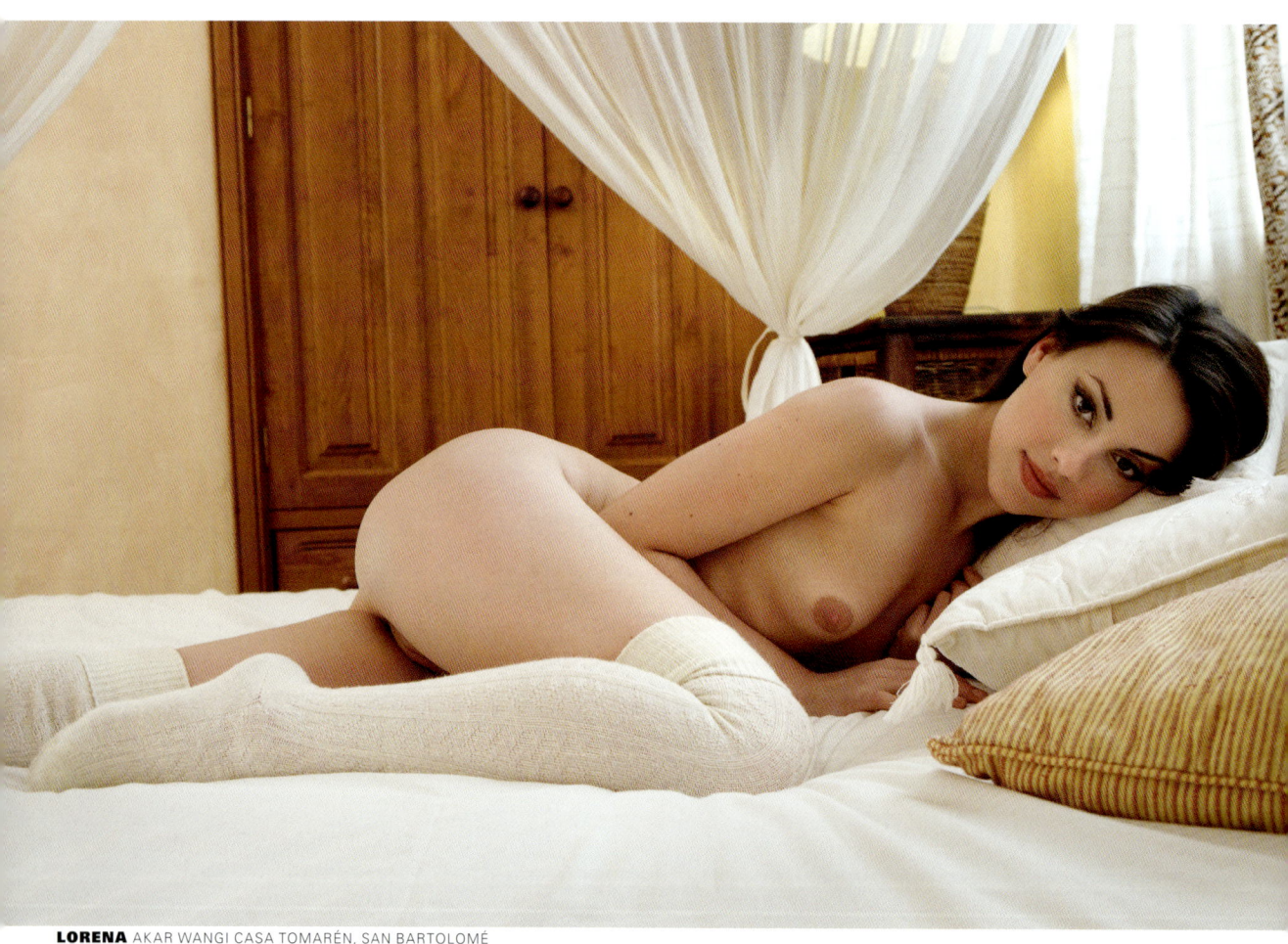

LORENA AKAR WANGI CASA TOMARÉN, SAN BARTOLOMÉ

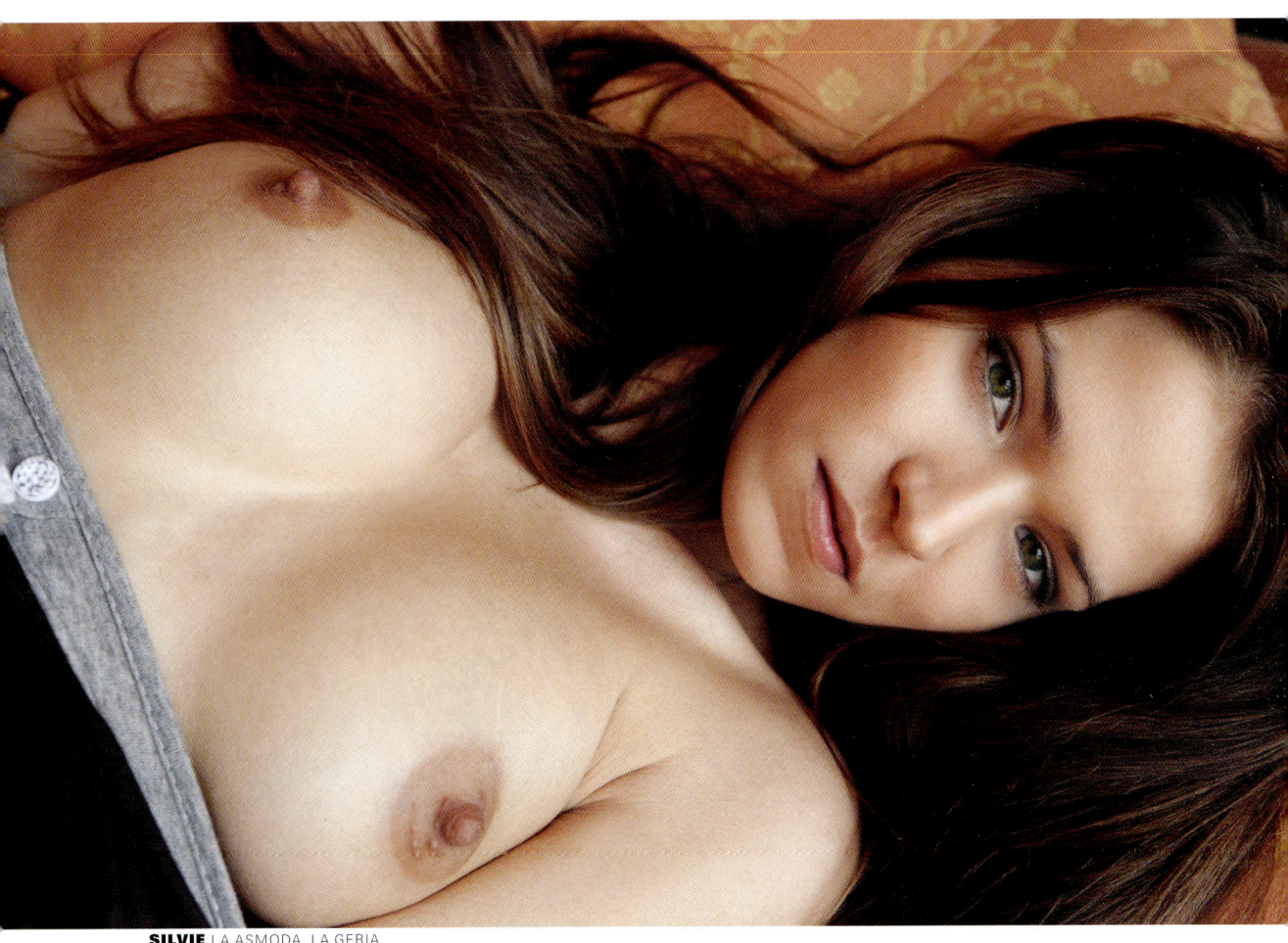

SILVIE LA ASMODA, LA GERIA

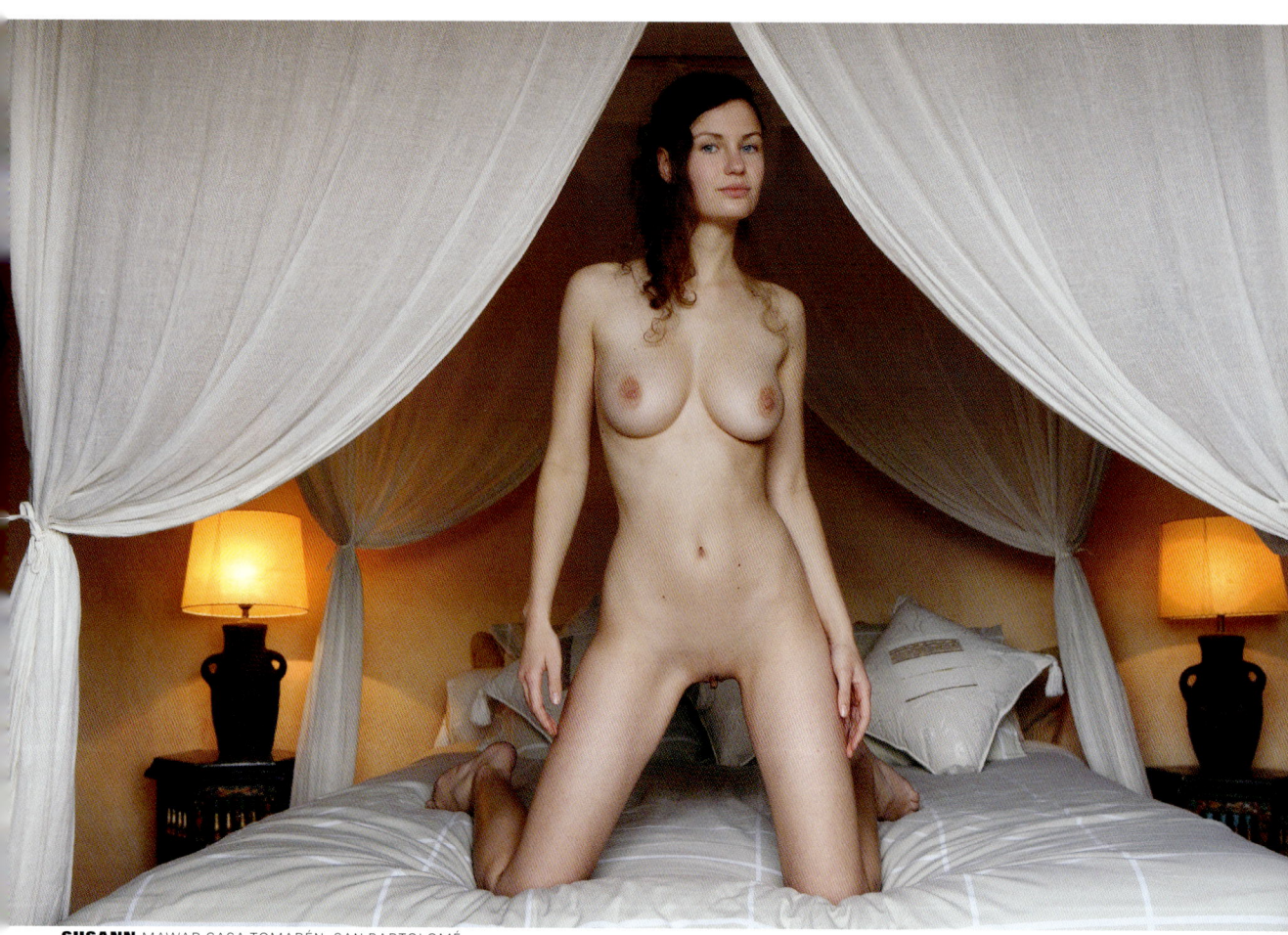

SUSANN MAWAR CASA TOMARÉN, SAN BARTOLOMÉ

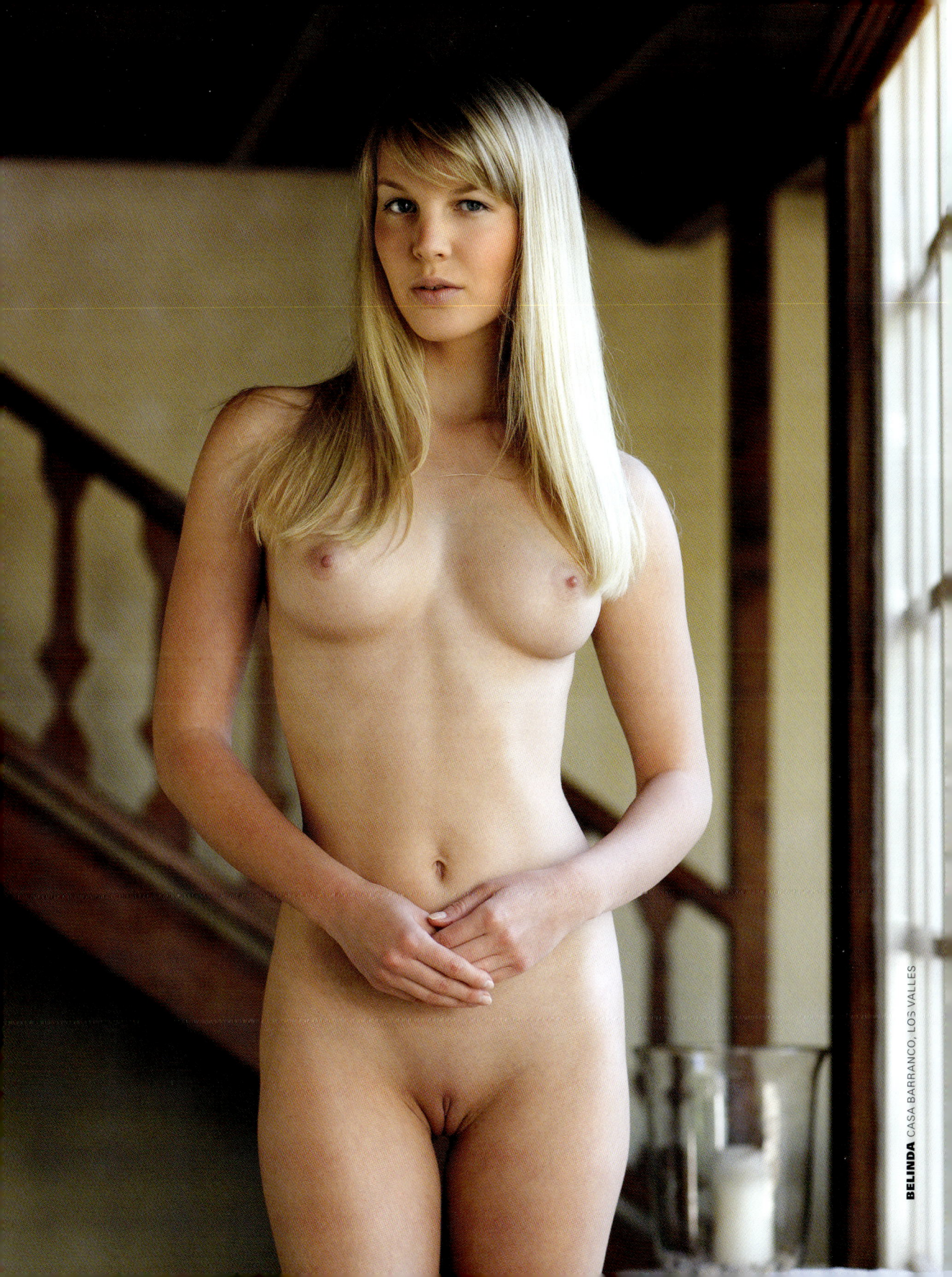

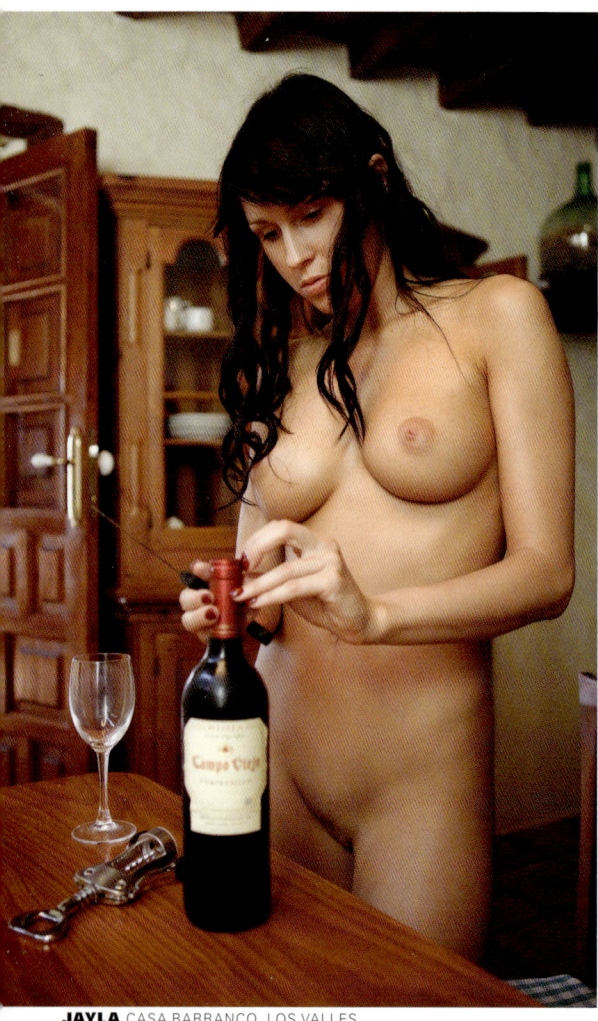
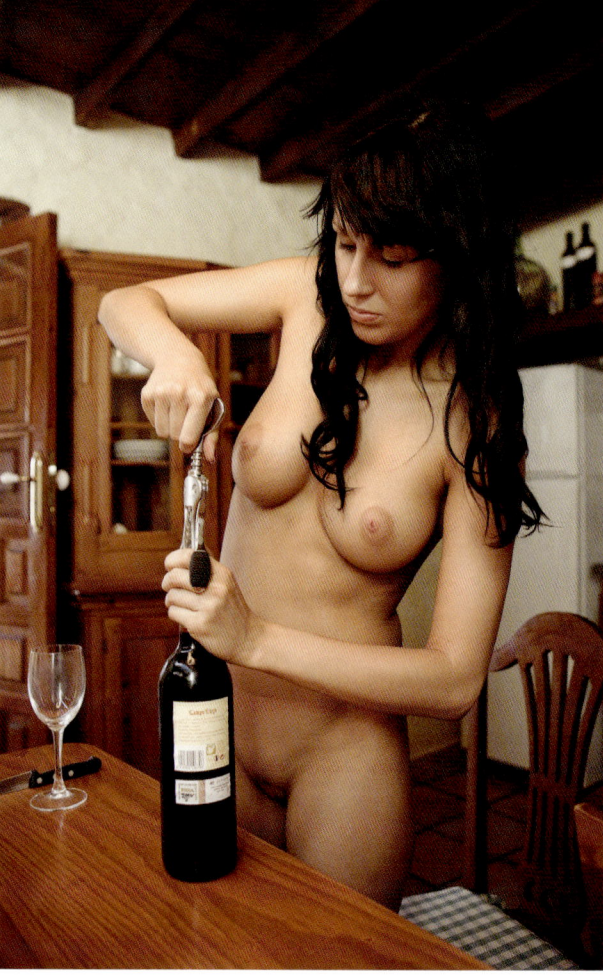

JAYLA CASA BARRANCO, LOS VALLES

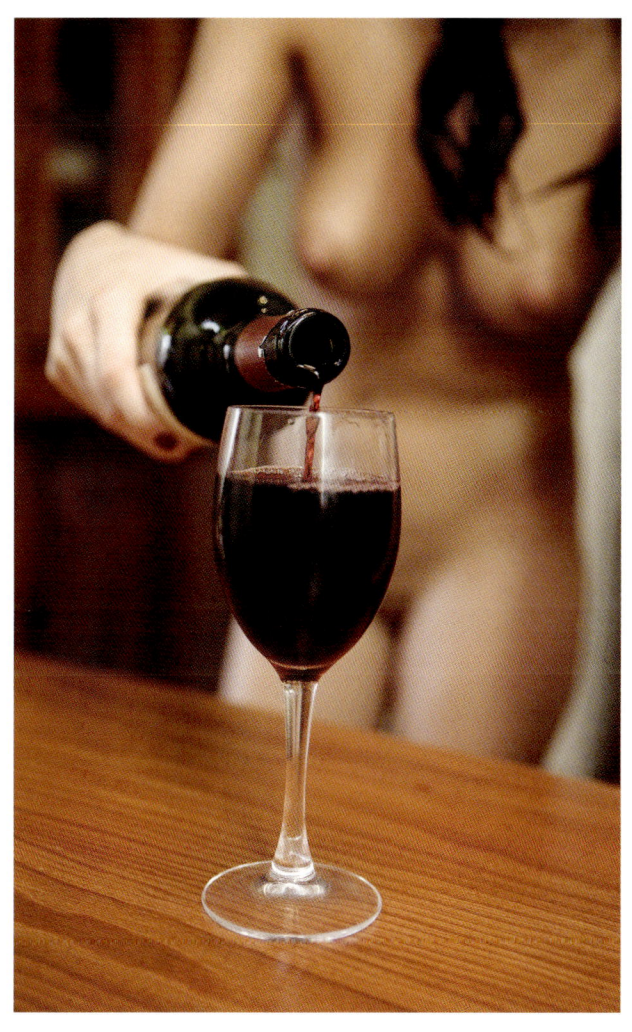
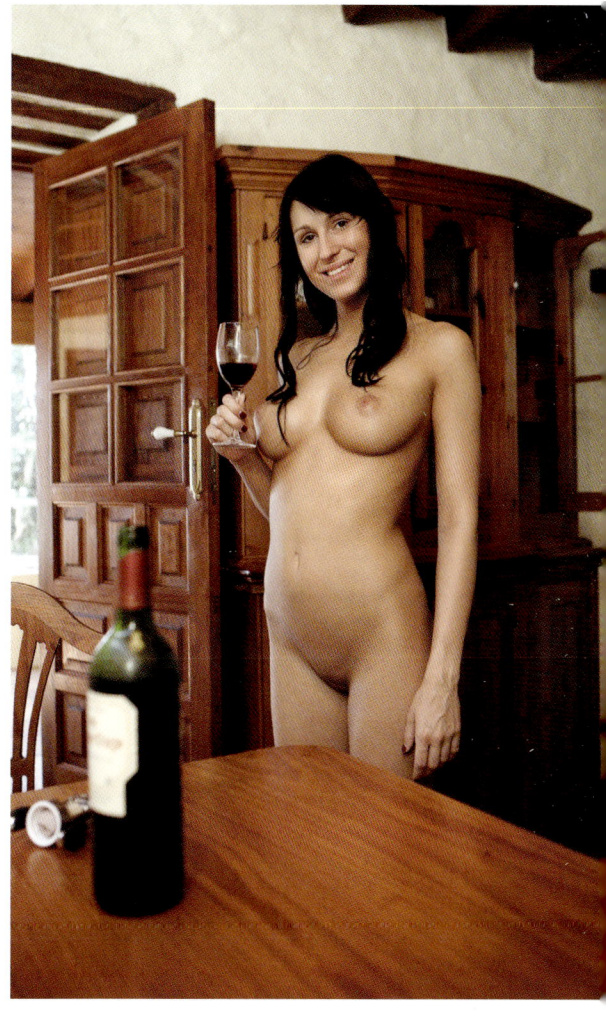

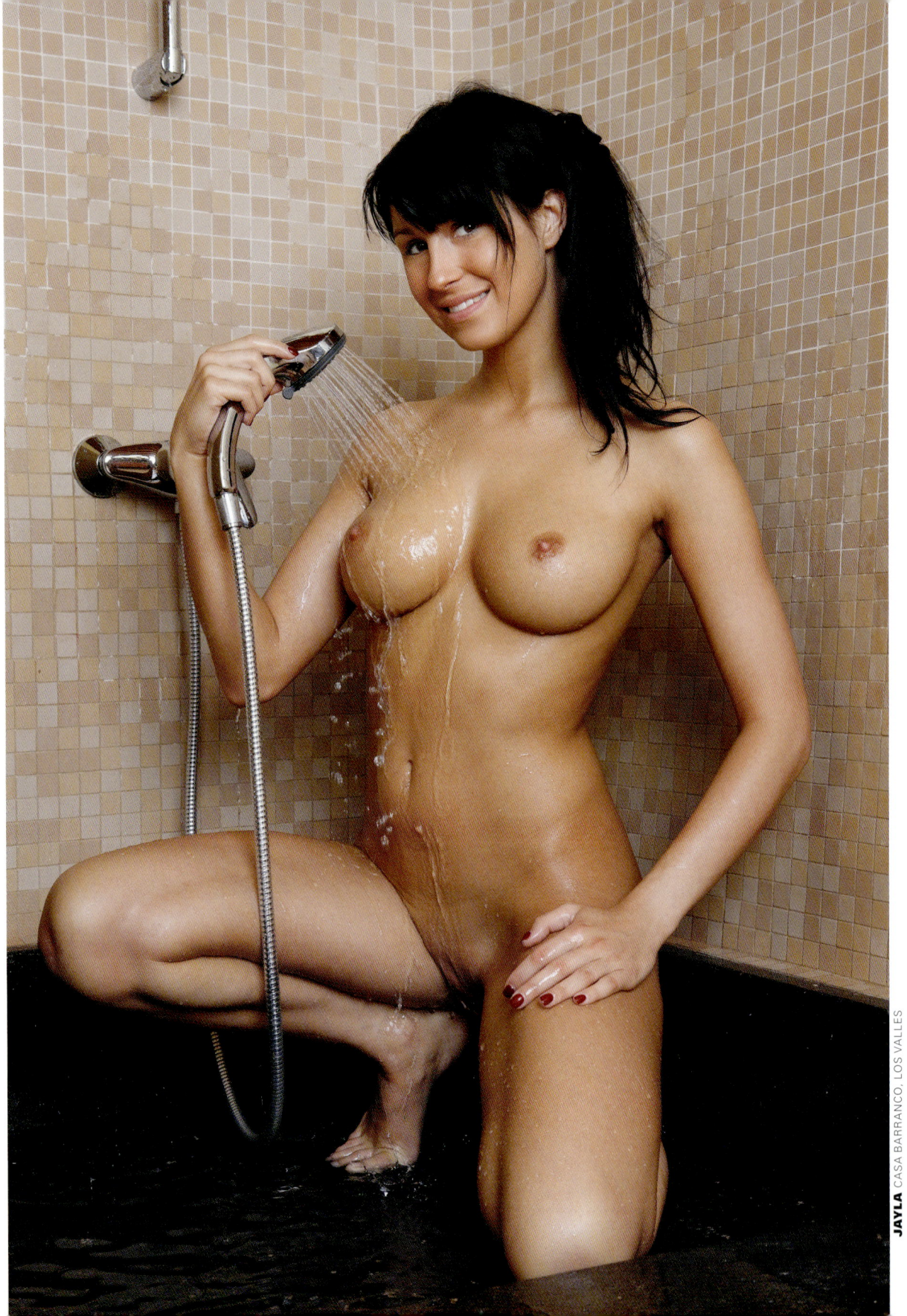

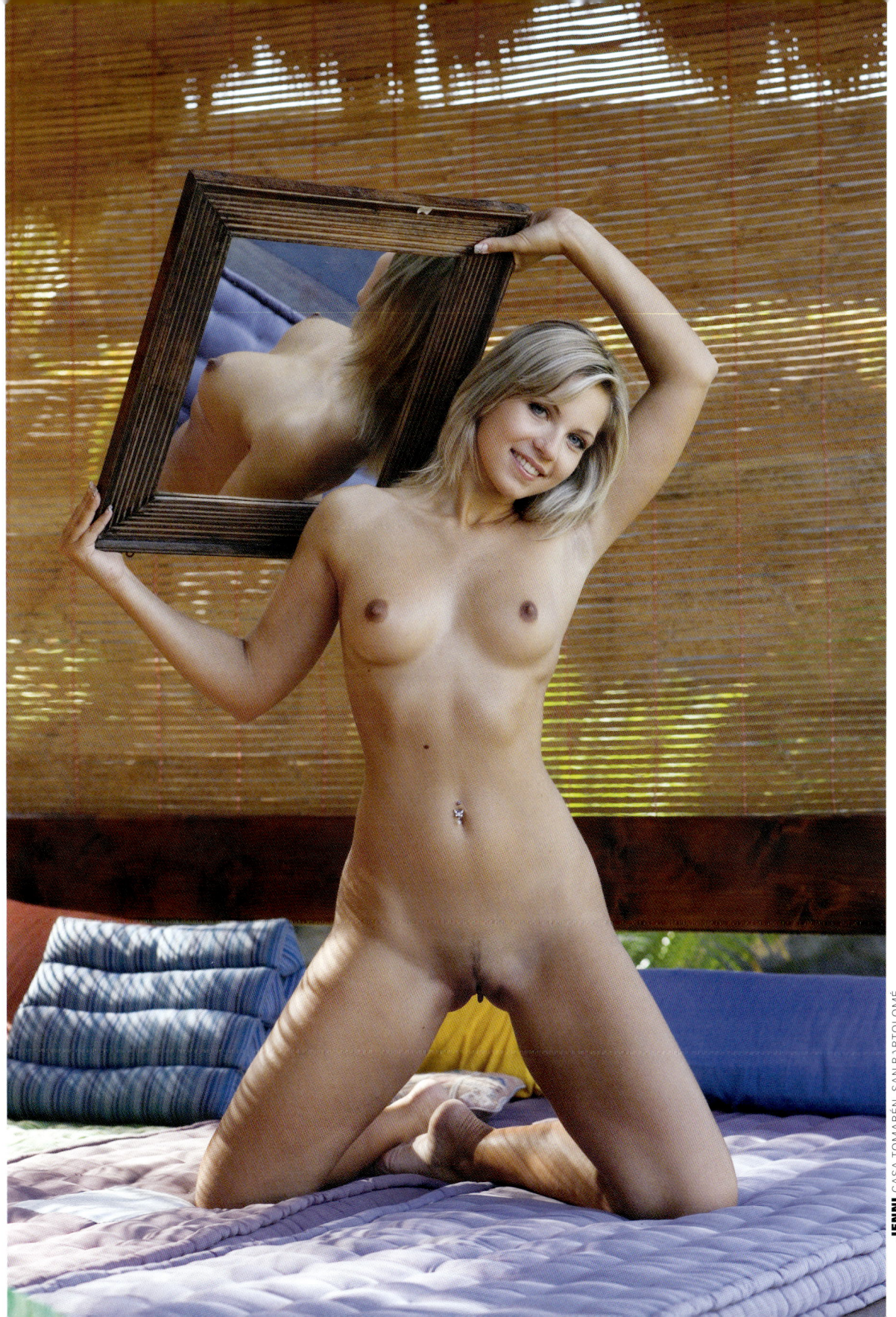

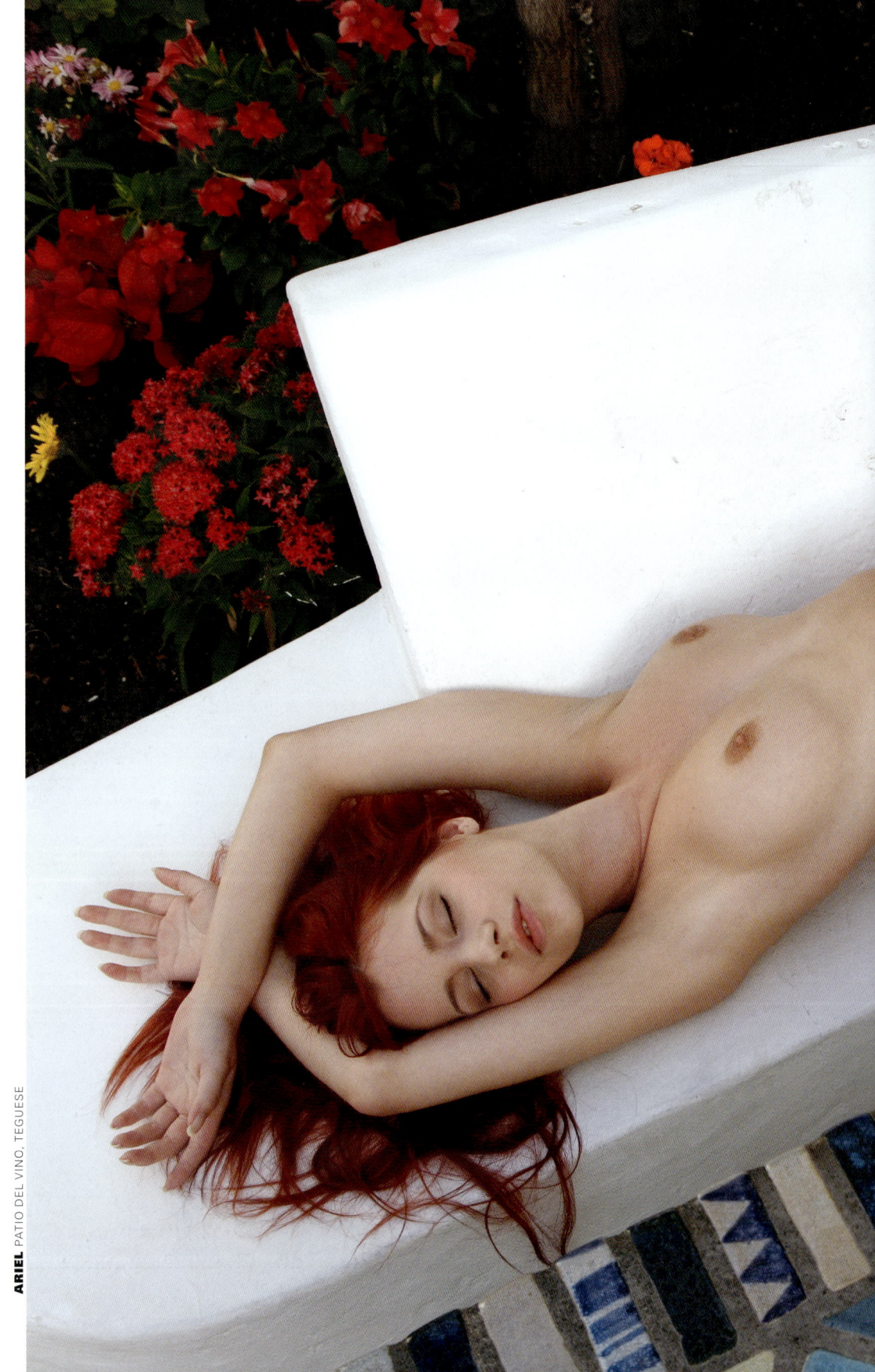

ARIEL PATIO DEL VINO, TEGUESE

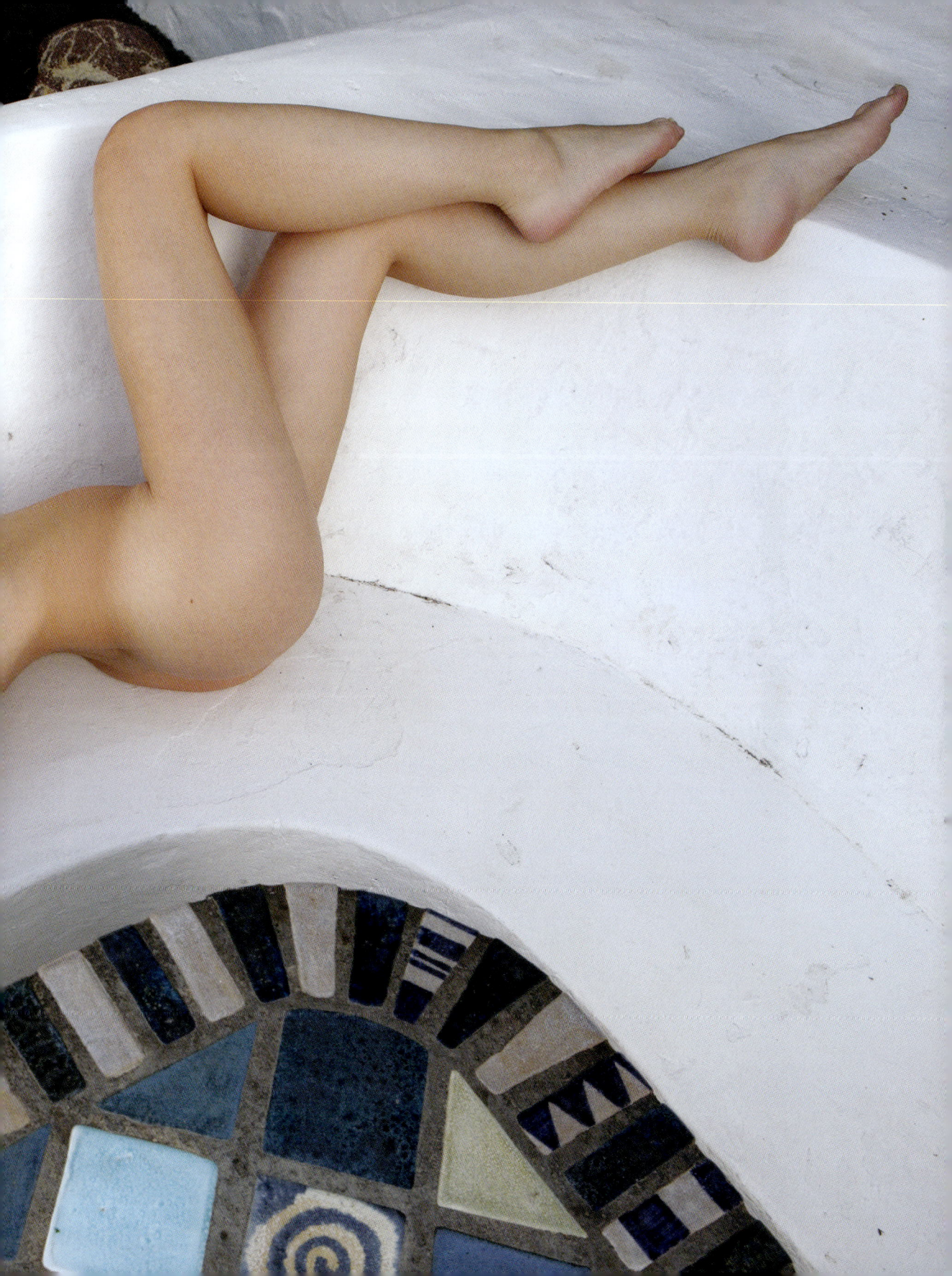

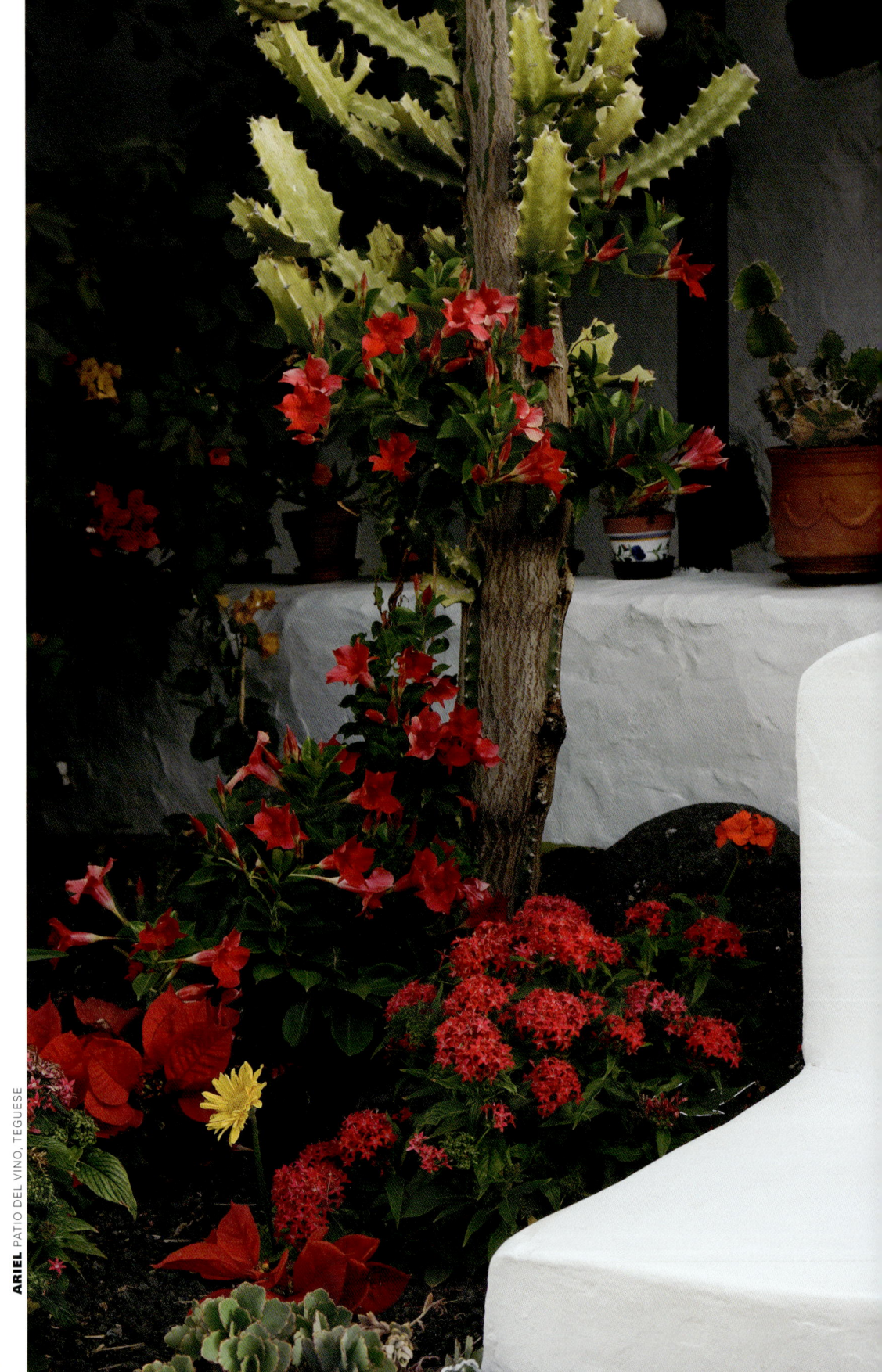

ARIEL PATIO DEL VINO, TEGUESE

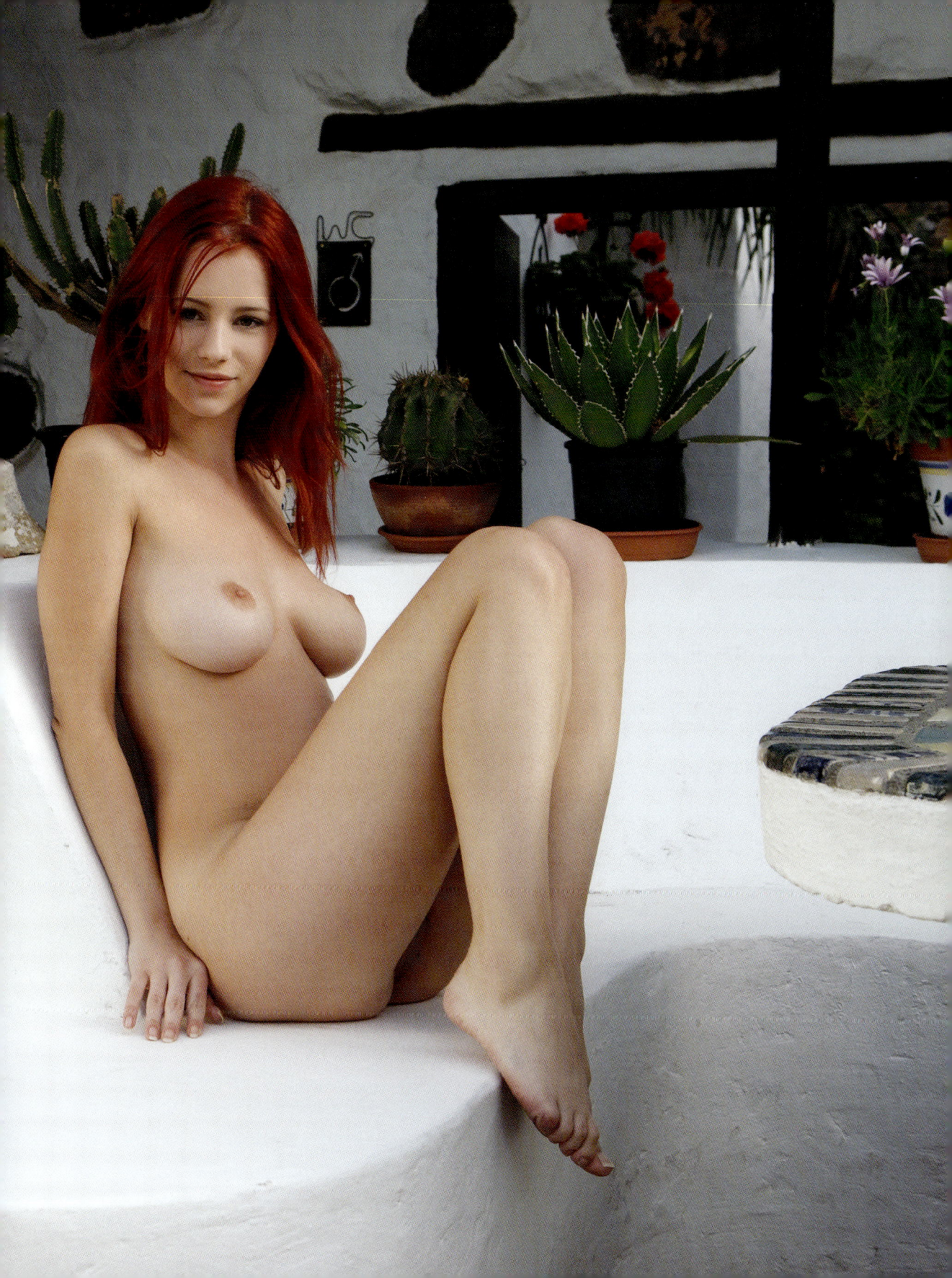

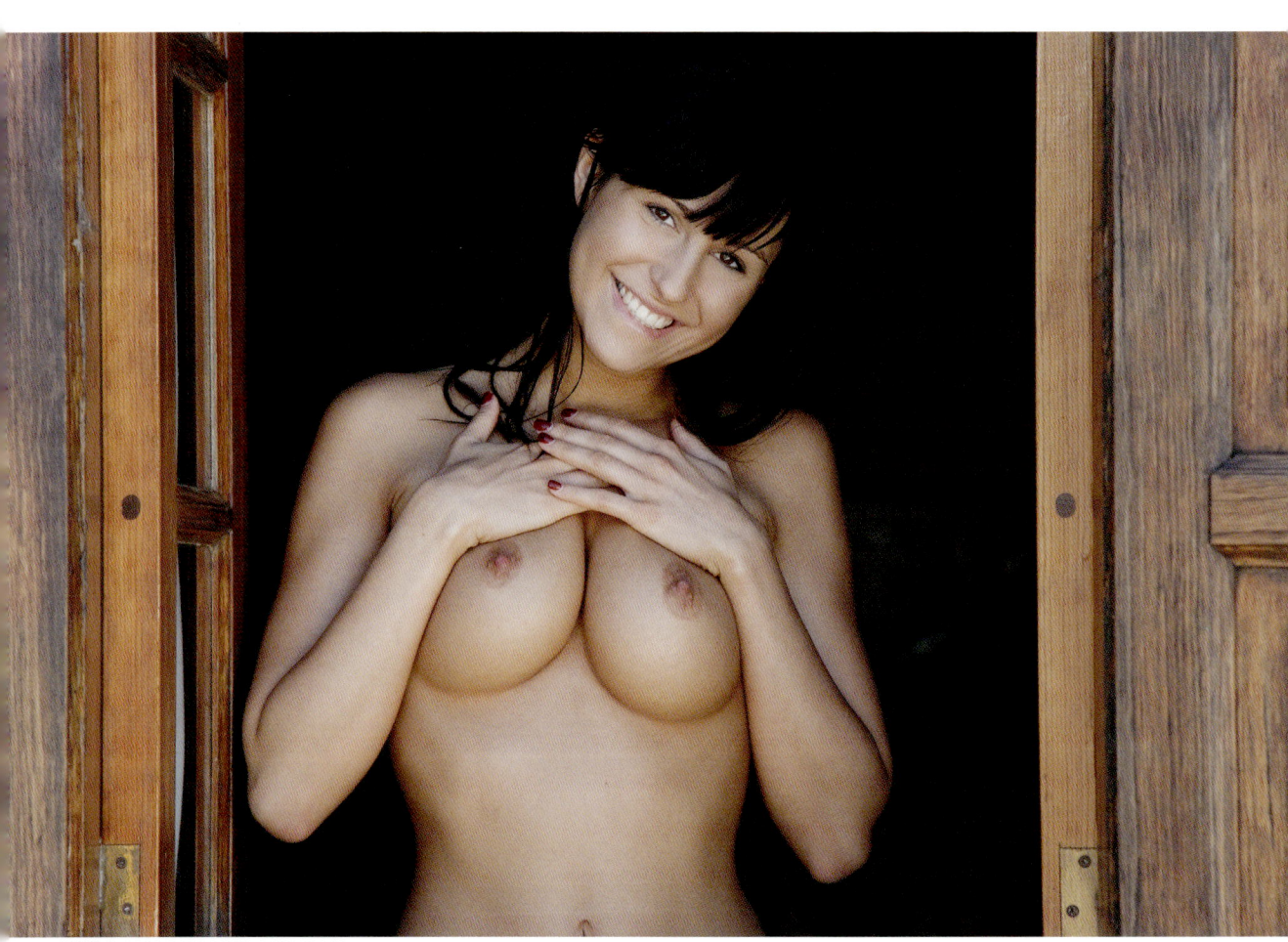

JAYLA CASA BARRANCO, LOS VALLES

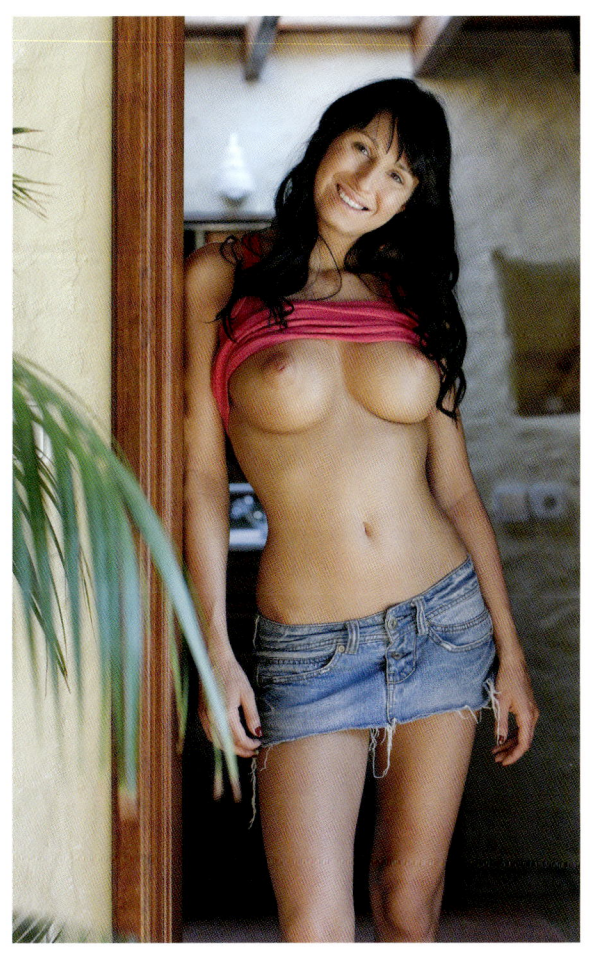
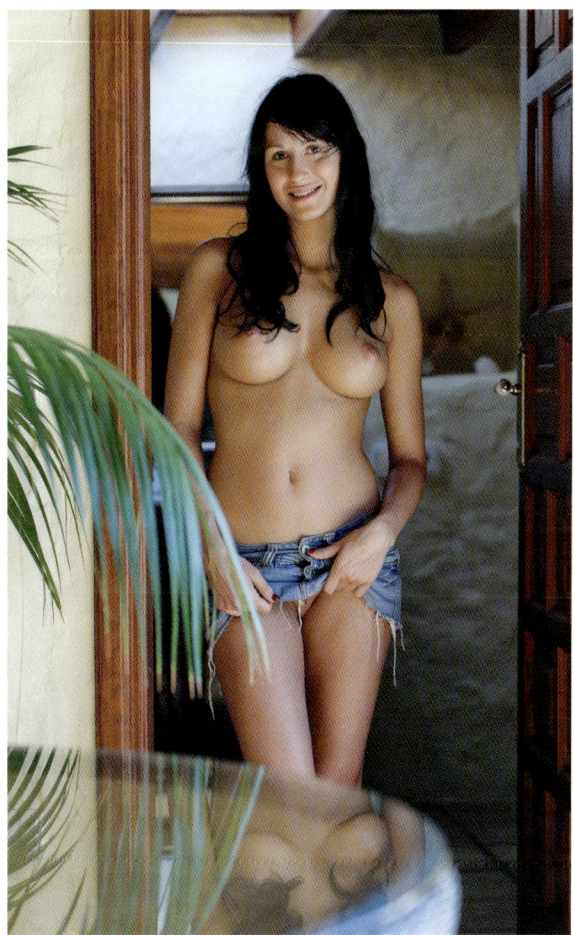

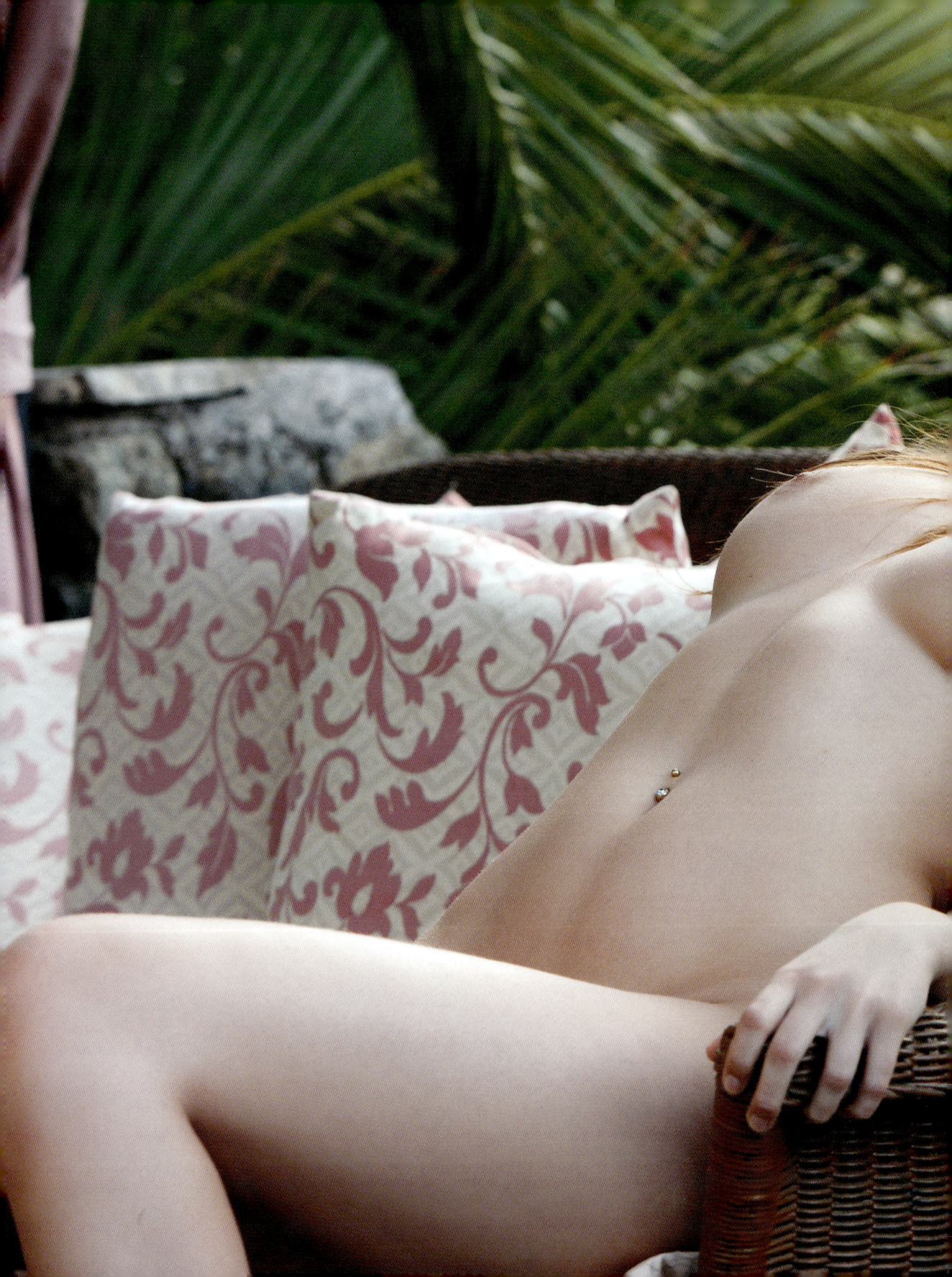

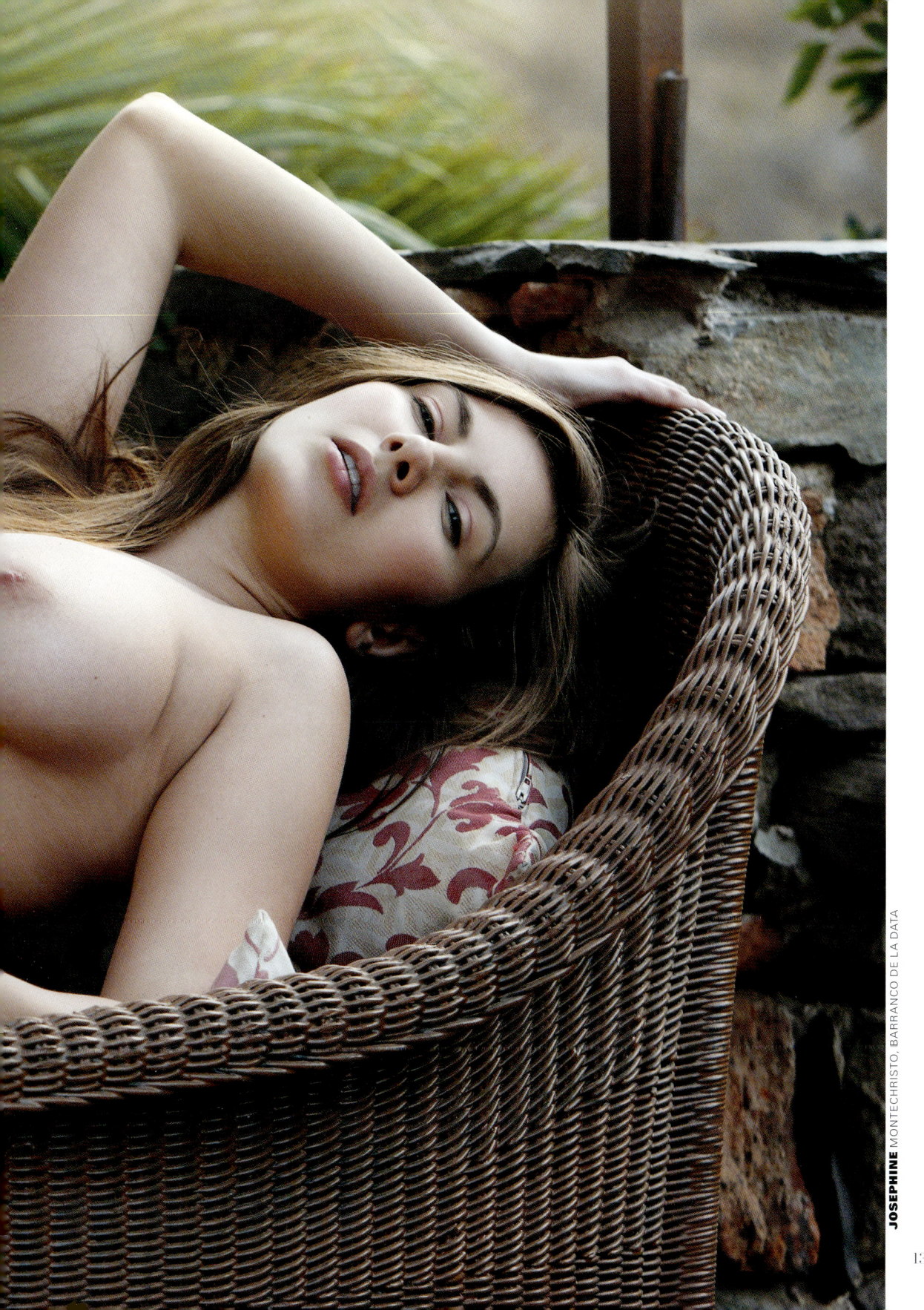

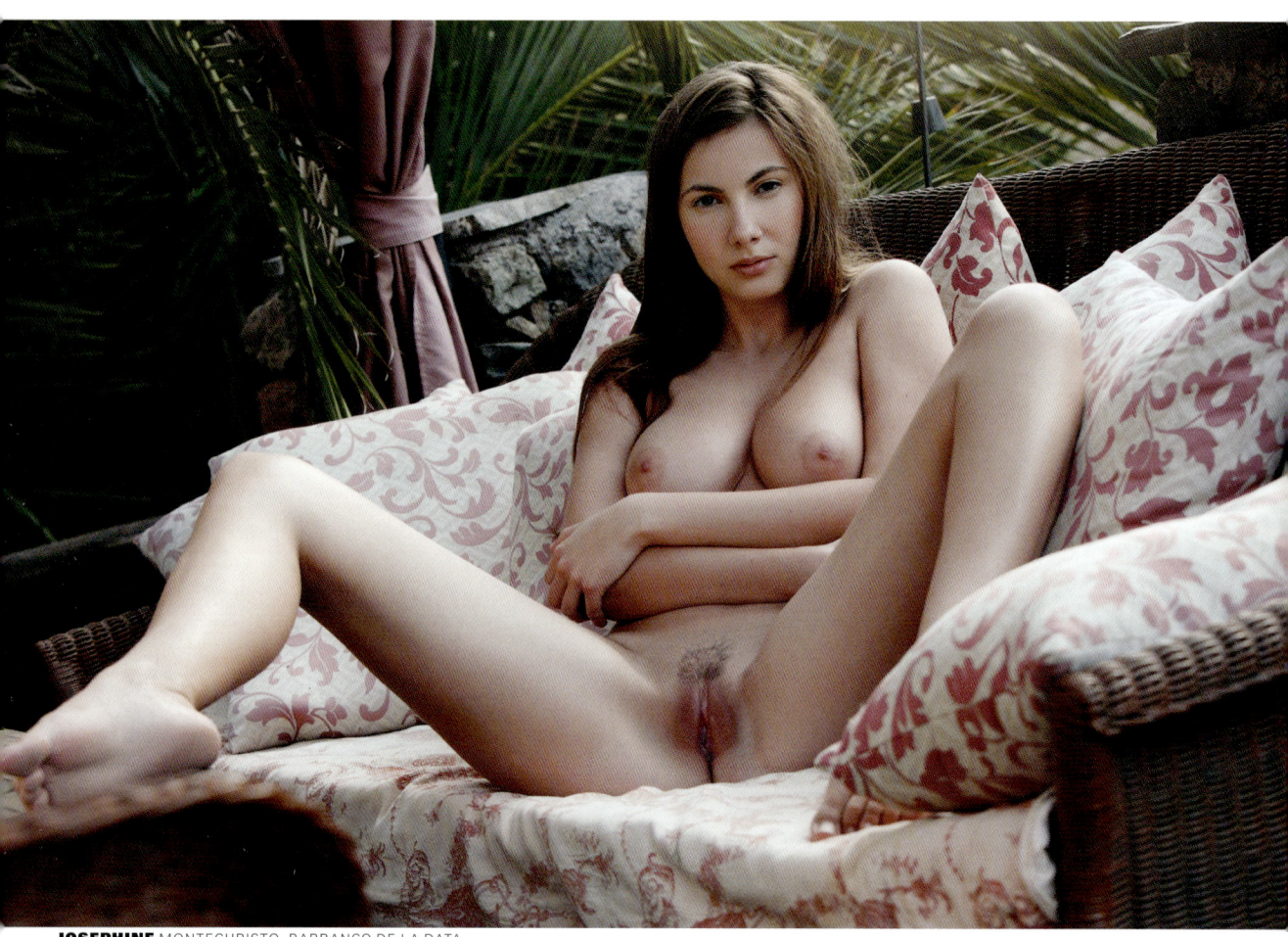

JOSEPHINE MONTECHRISTO, BARRANCO DE LA DATA

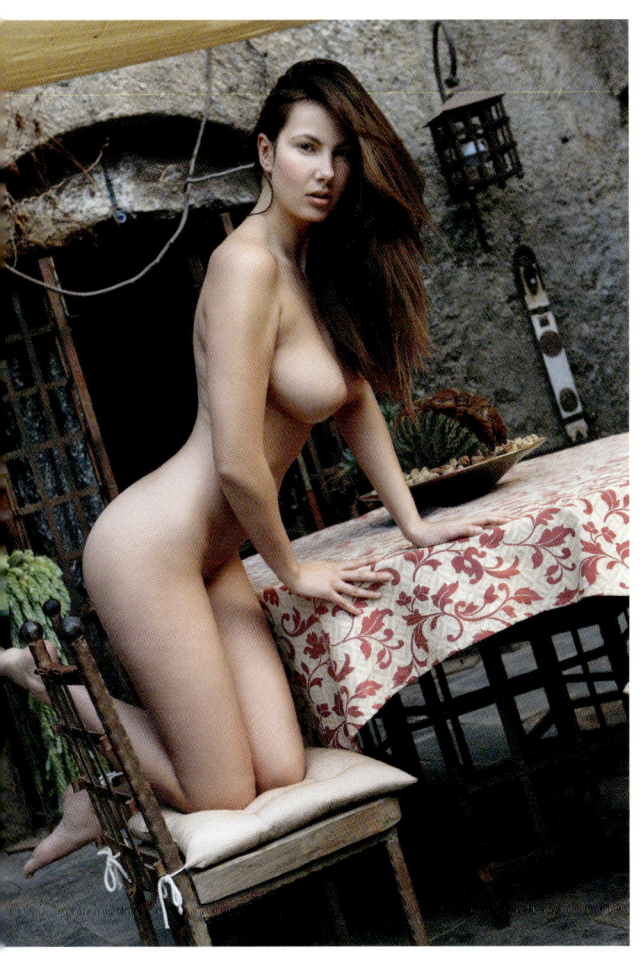
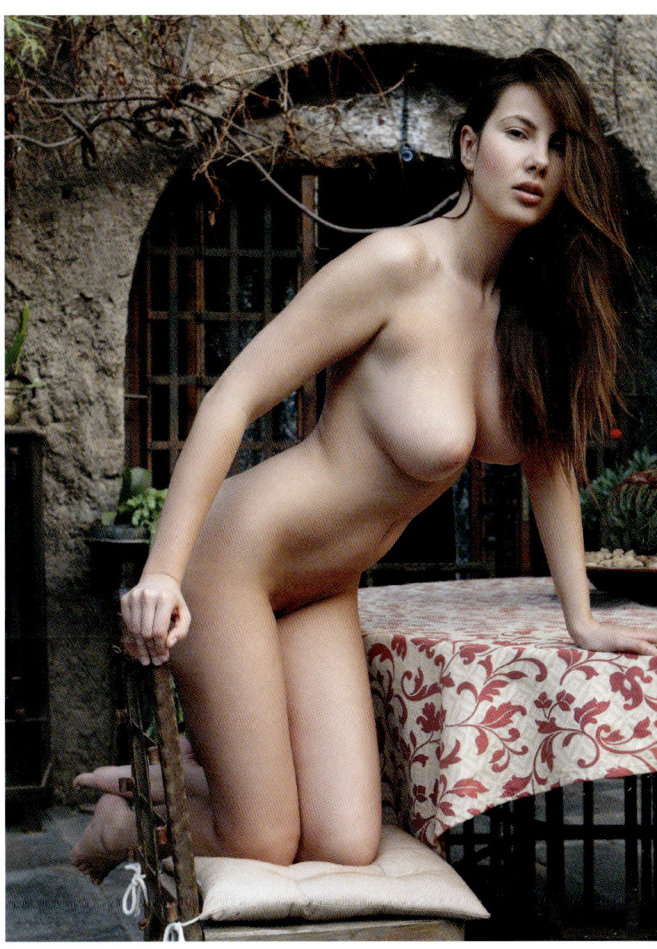

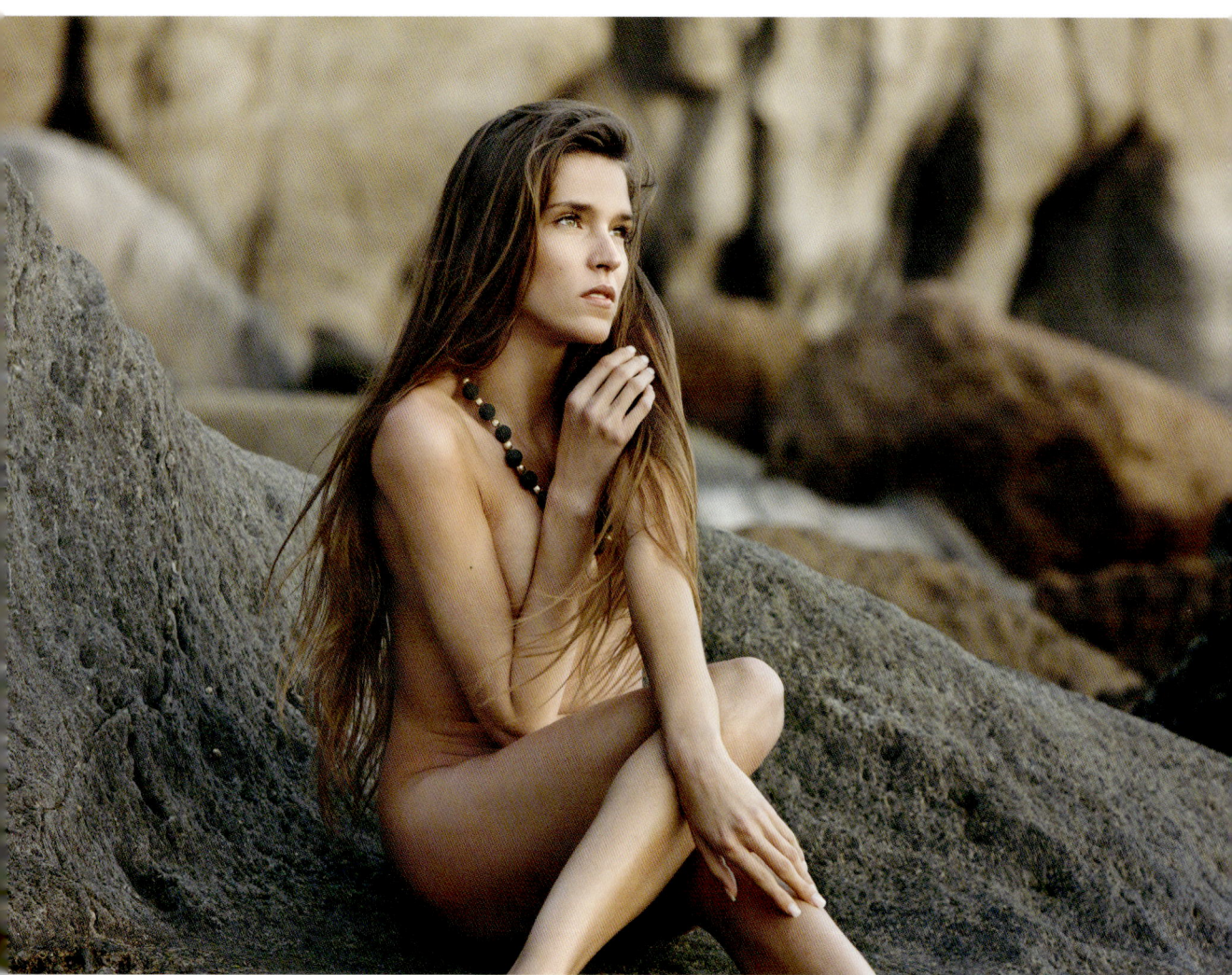

SIMONA PLAYA DE TIRITAÑA

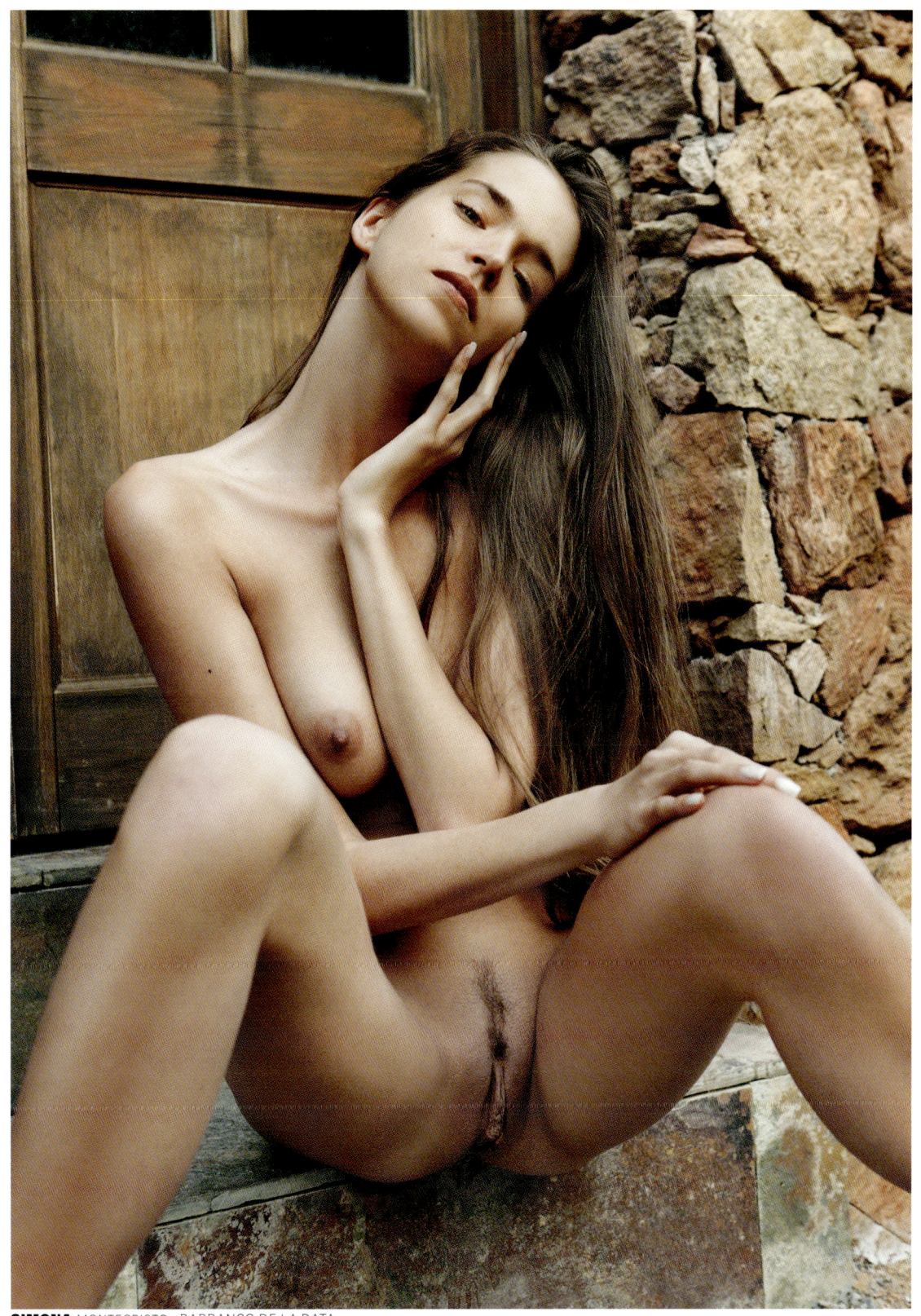

SIMONA MONTECRISTO, BARRANCO DE LA DATA

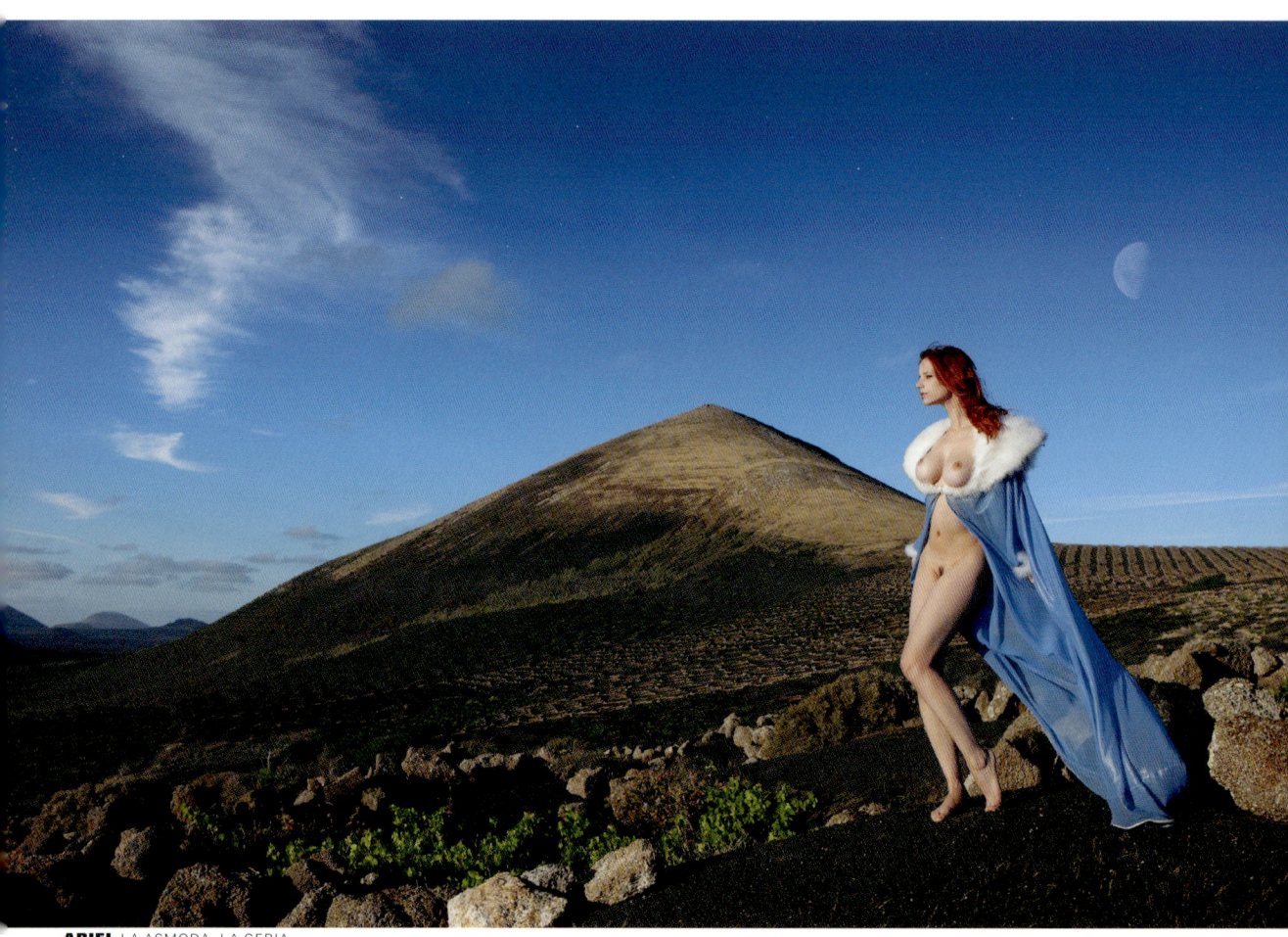

ARIEL LA ASMODA, LA GERIA

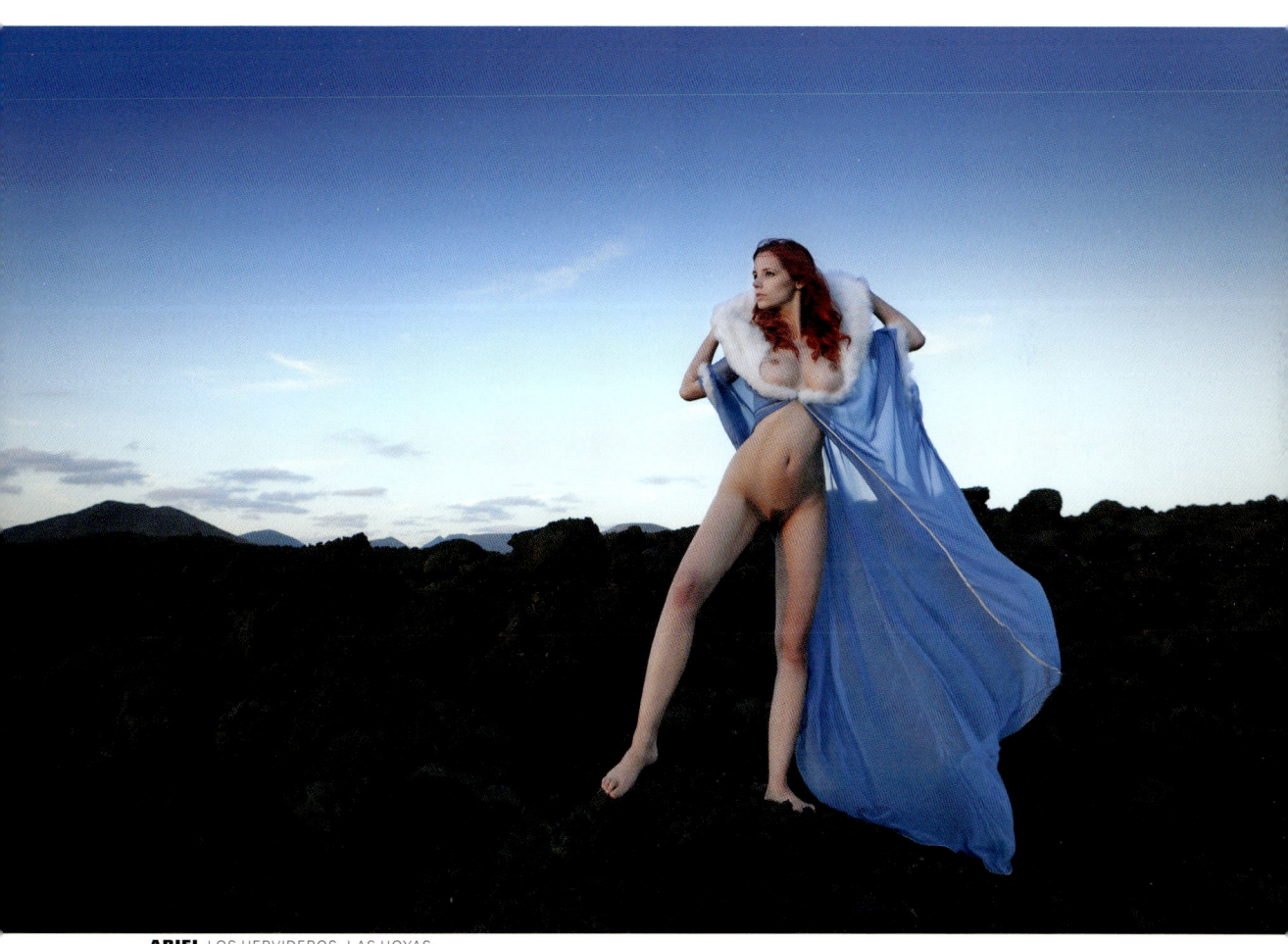

ARIEL LOS HERVIDEROS, LAS HOYAS

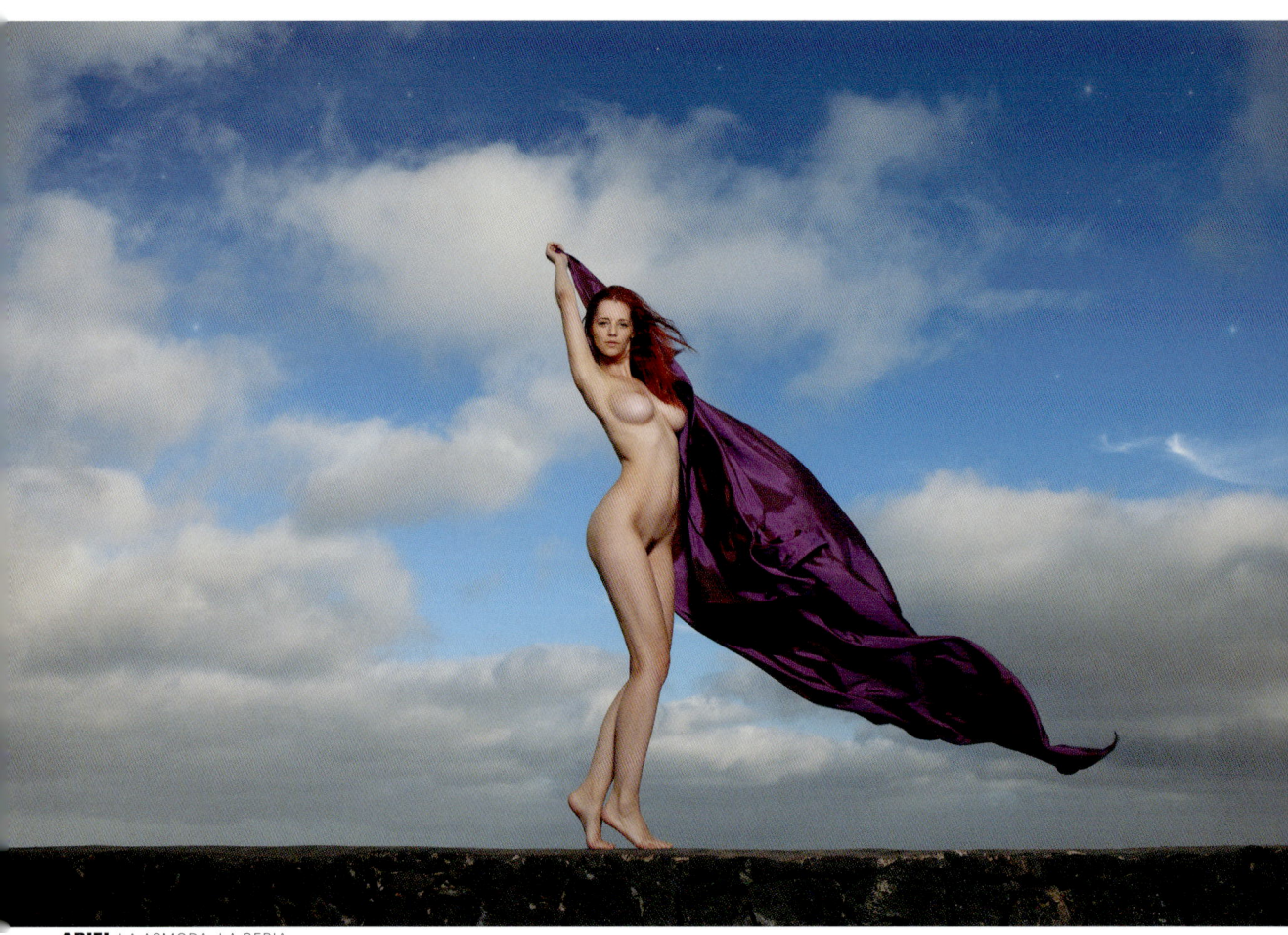

ARIEL LA ASMODA, LA GERIA

144

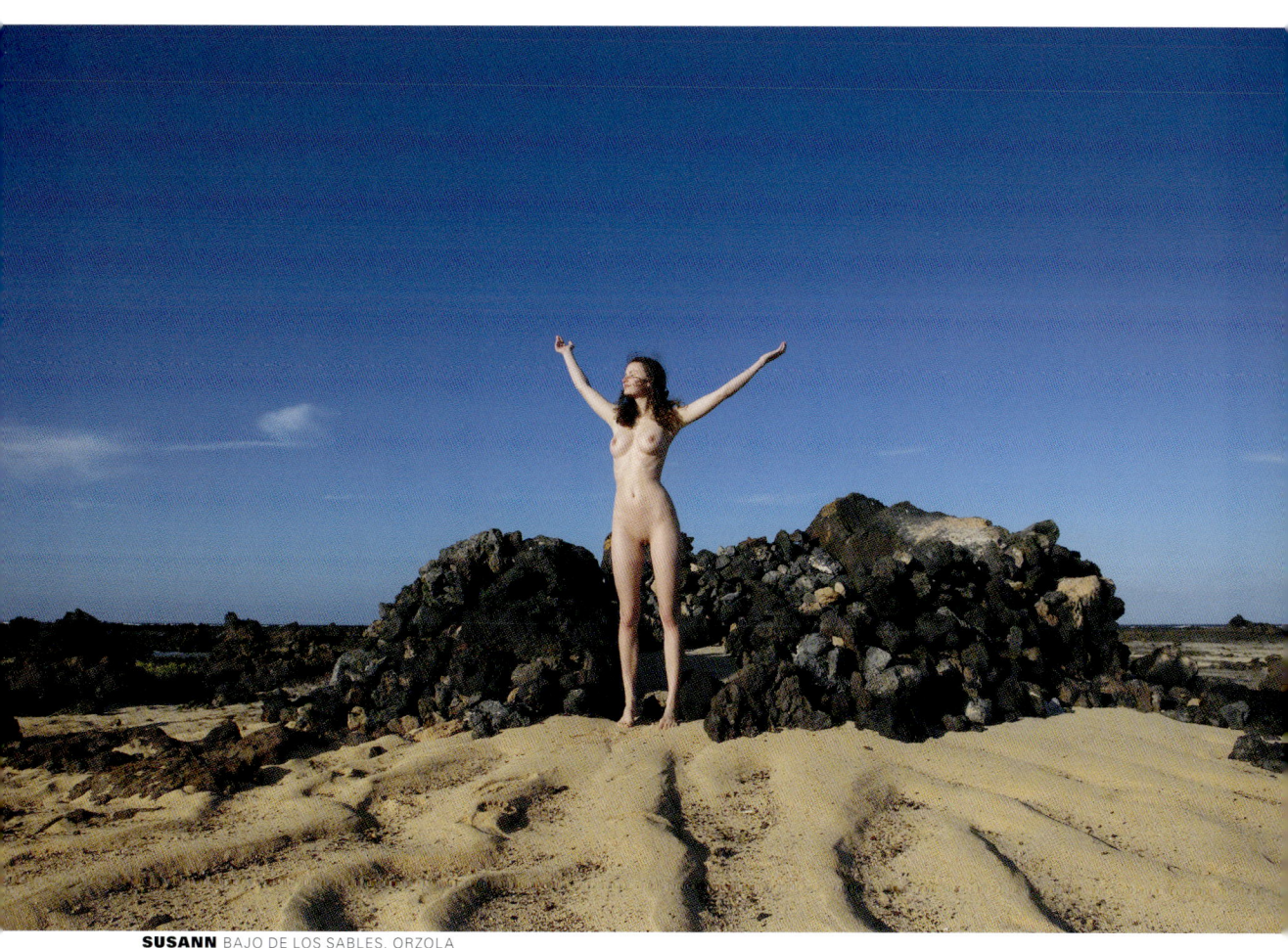

SUSANN BAJO DE LOS SABLES, ORZOLA

JAYLA LOS LAJARES, LA SANTA

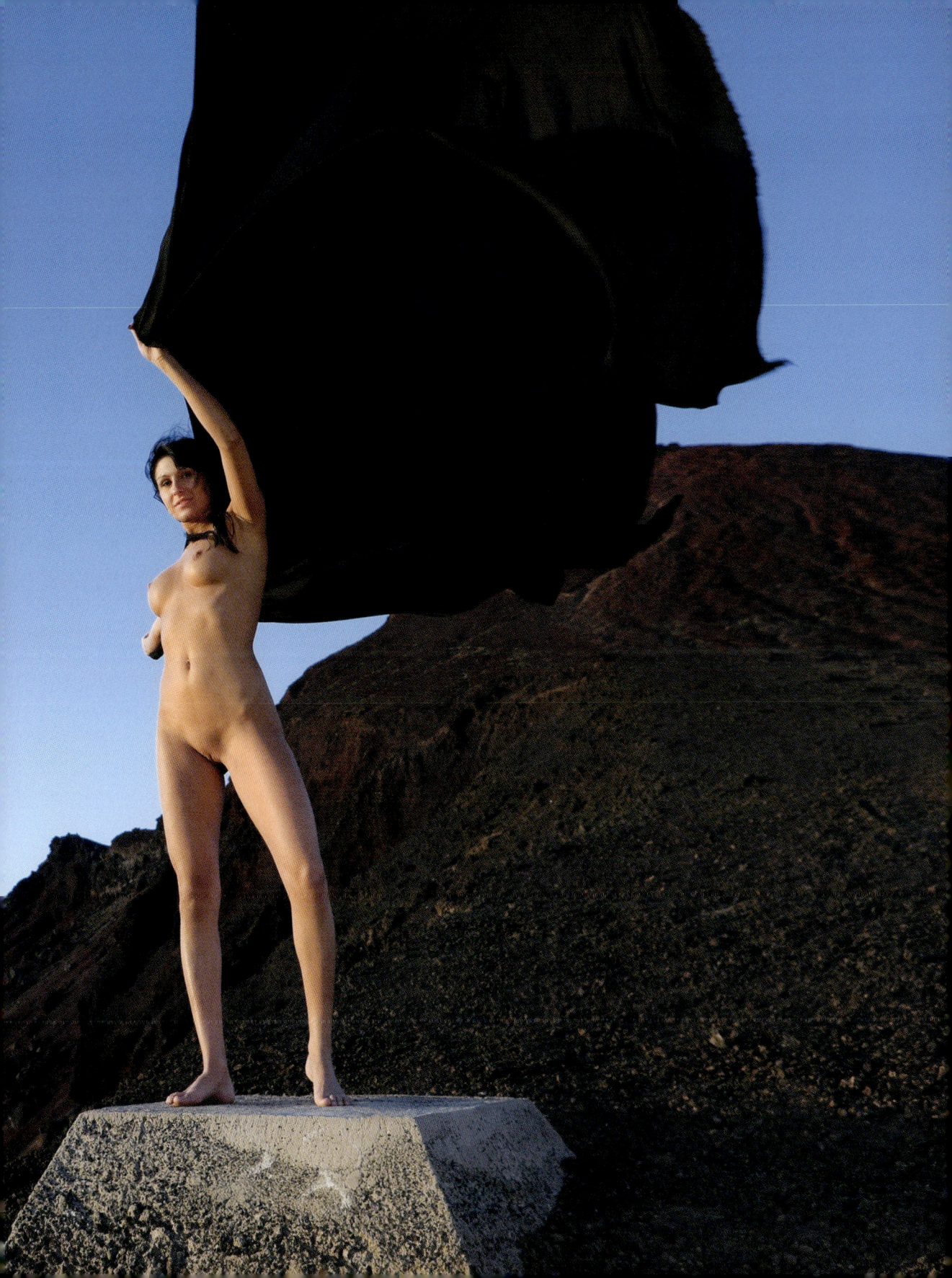

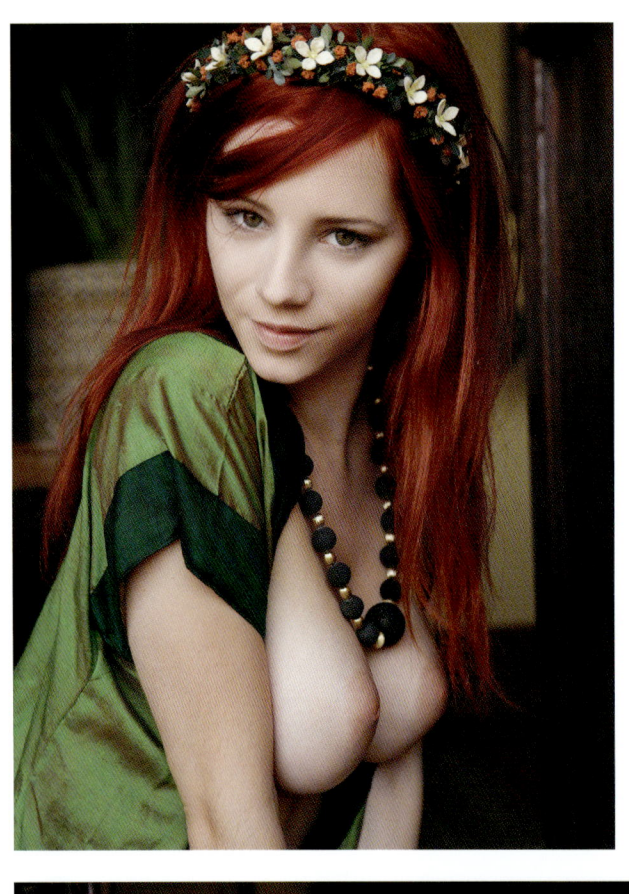

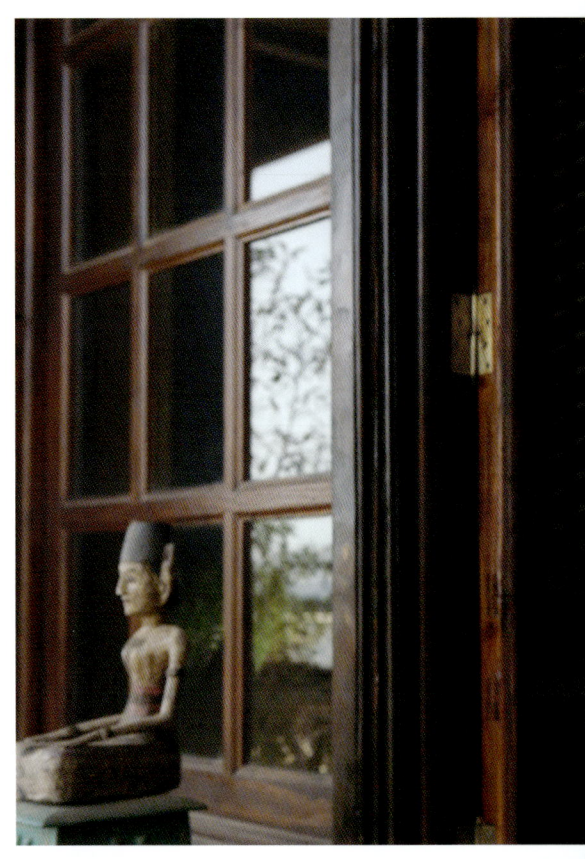

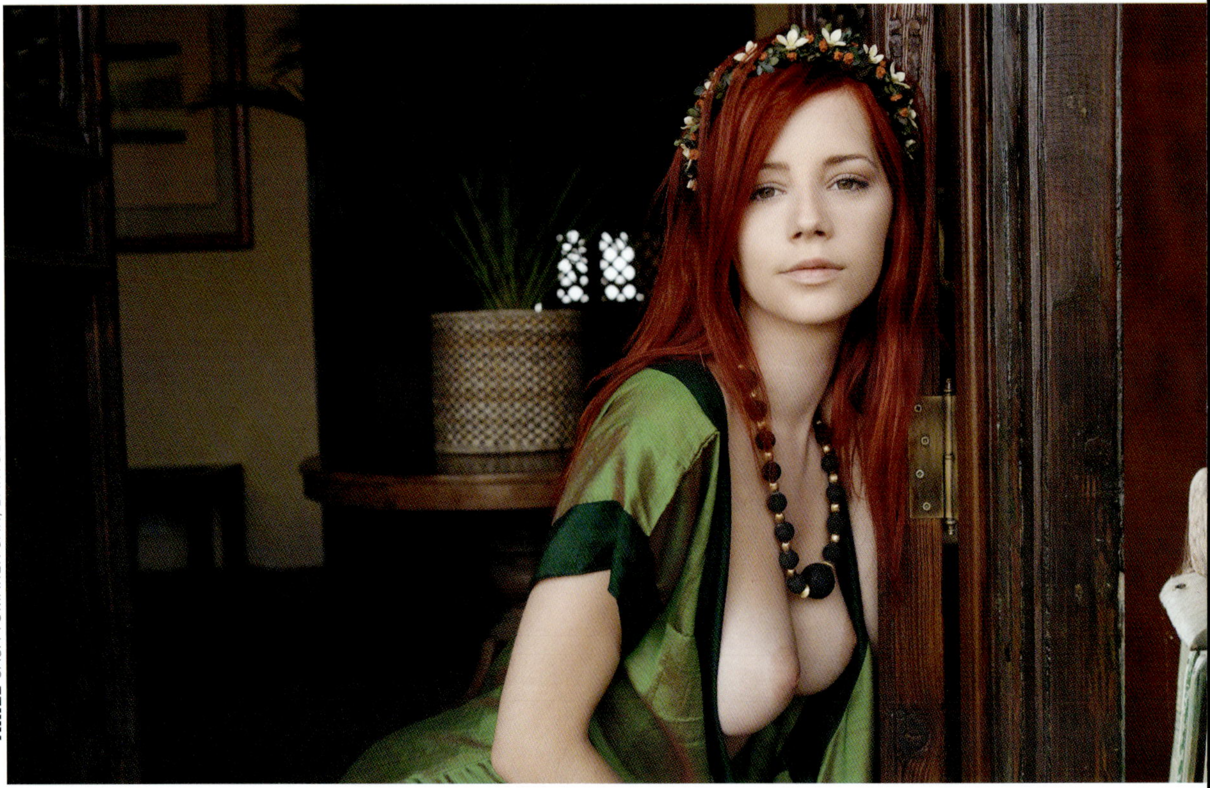

ARIEL CASA TOMARÉN SAN, BARTOLOMÉ

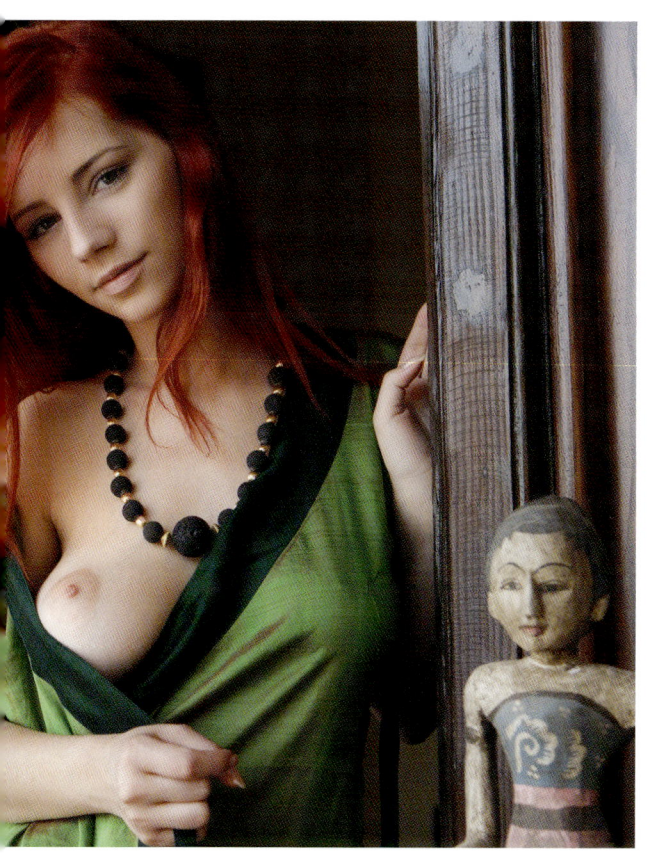
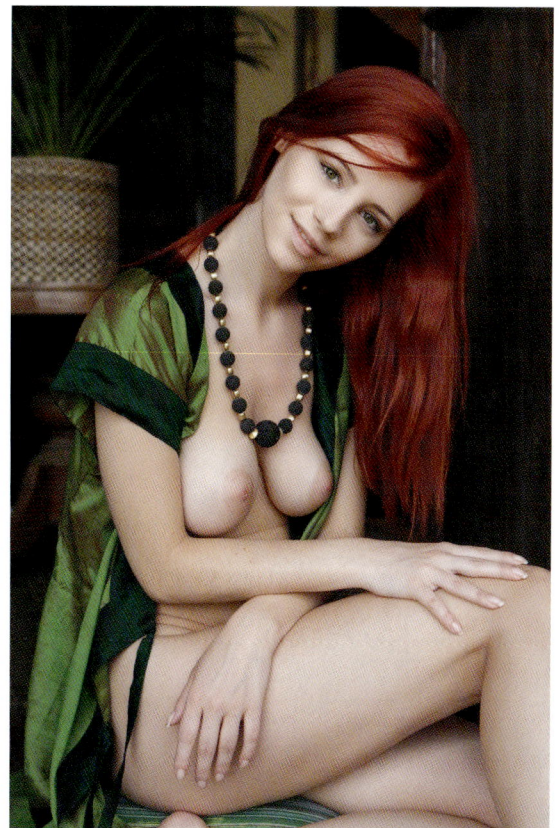
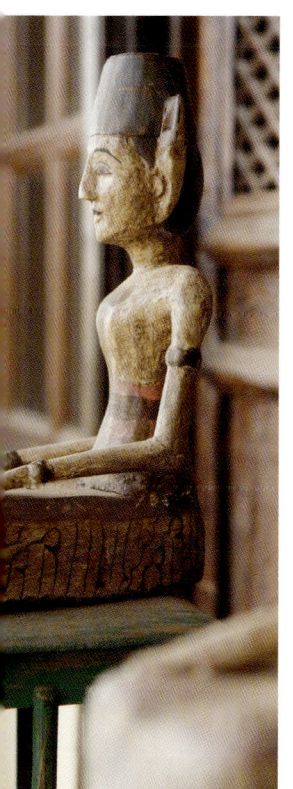
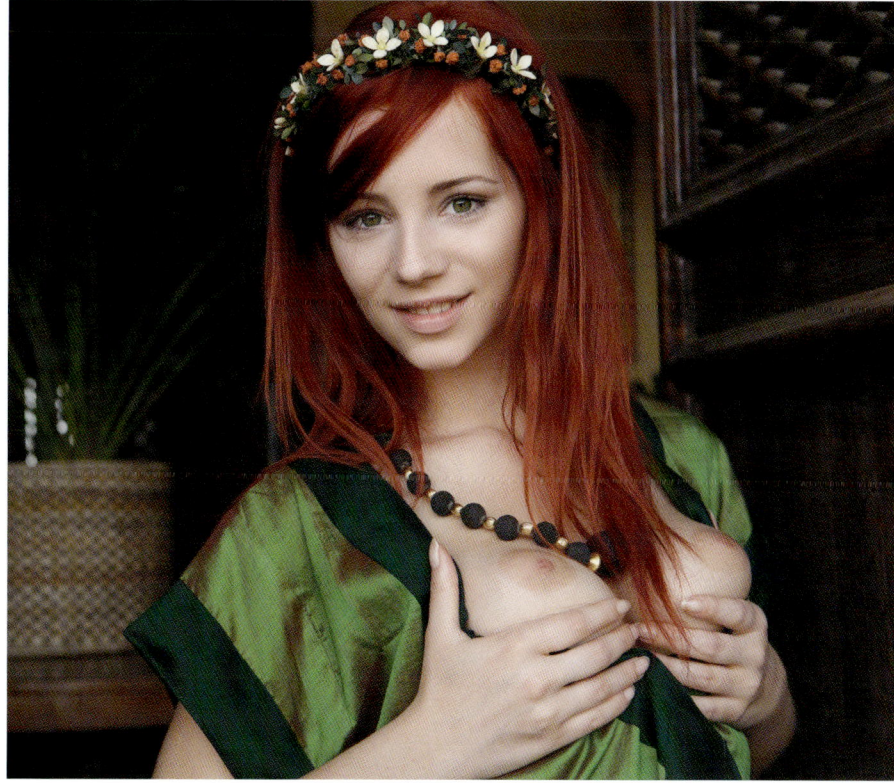

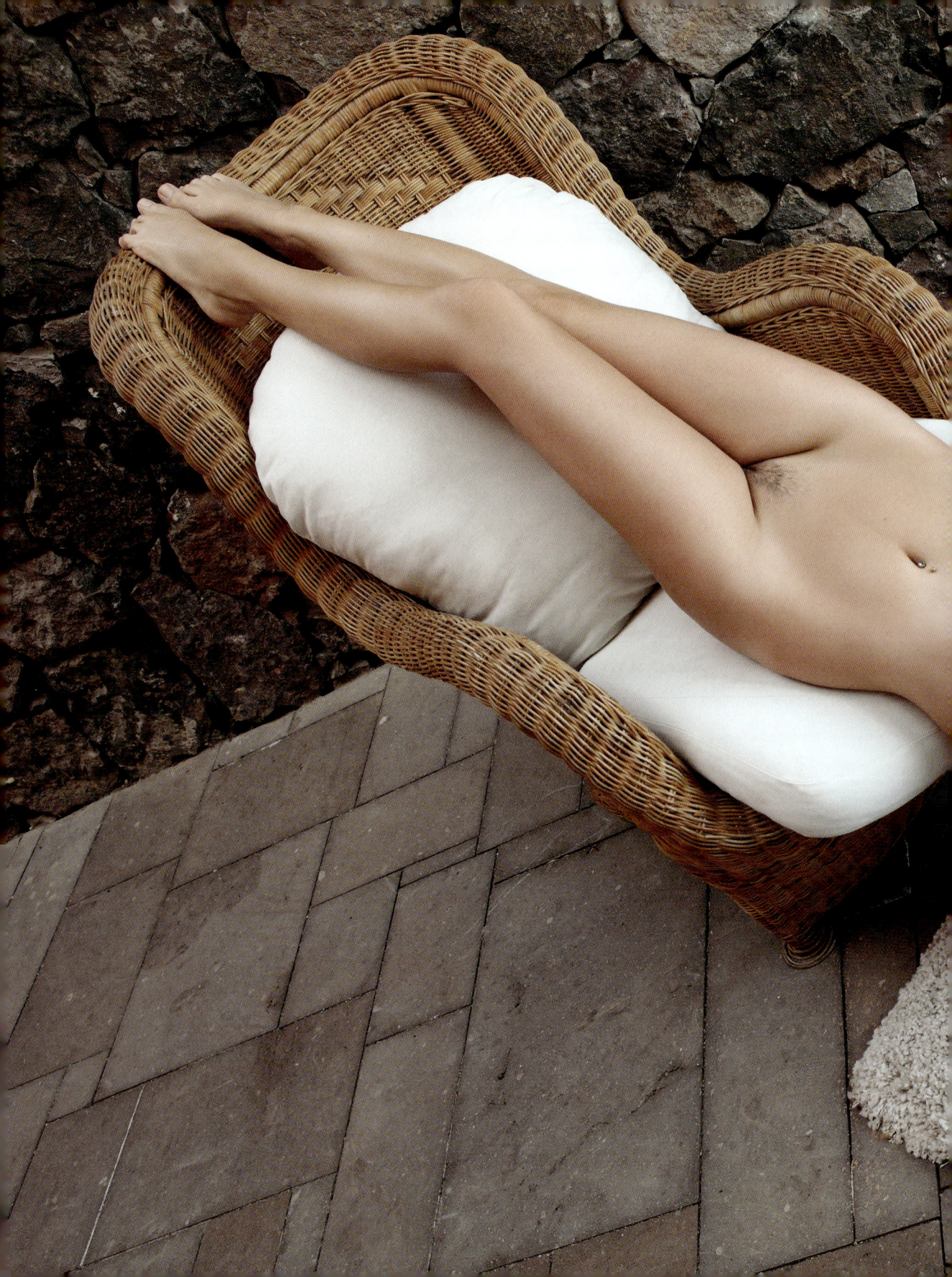

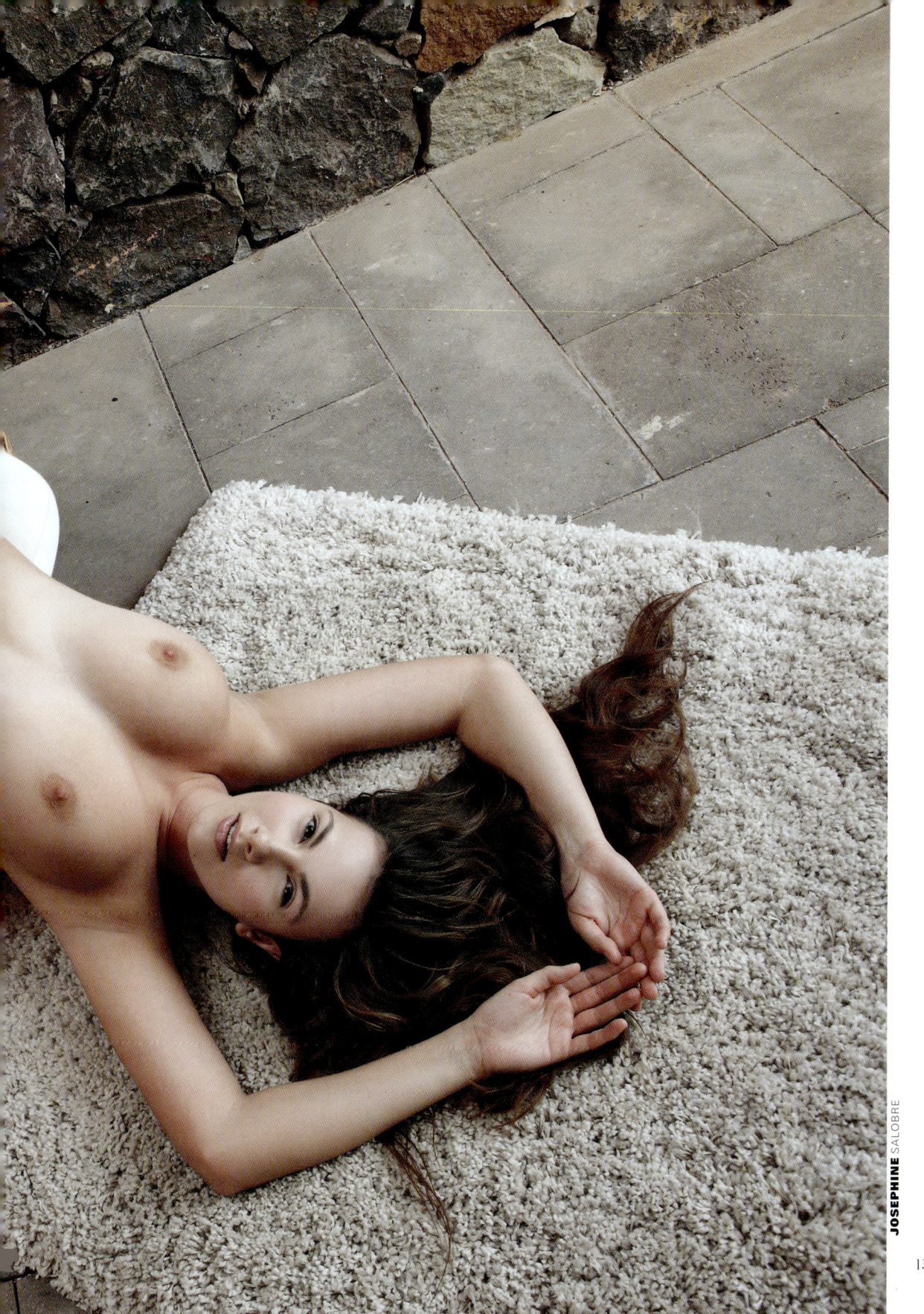

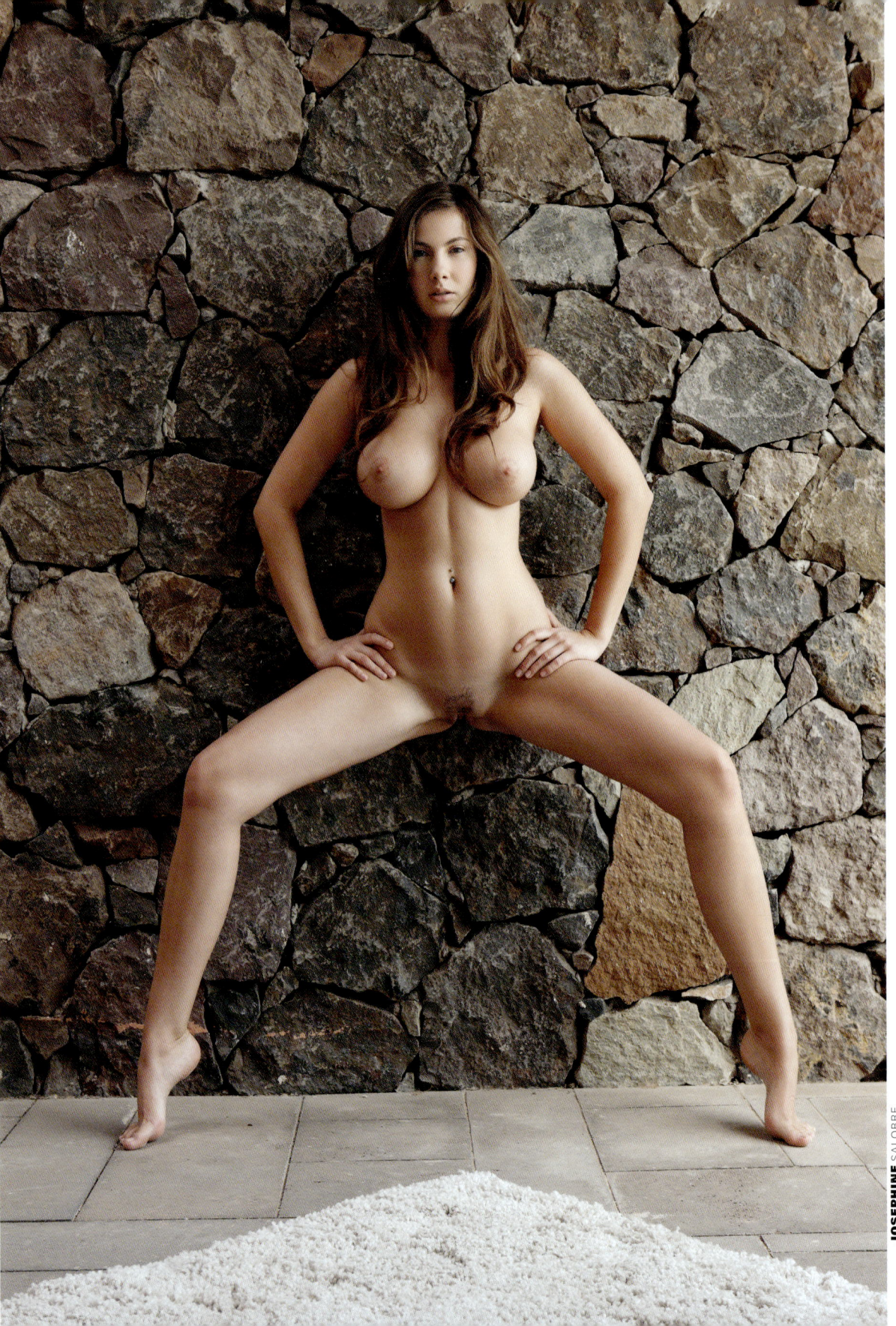

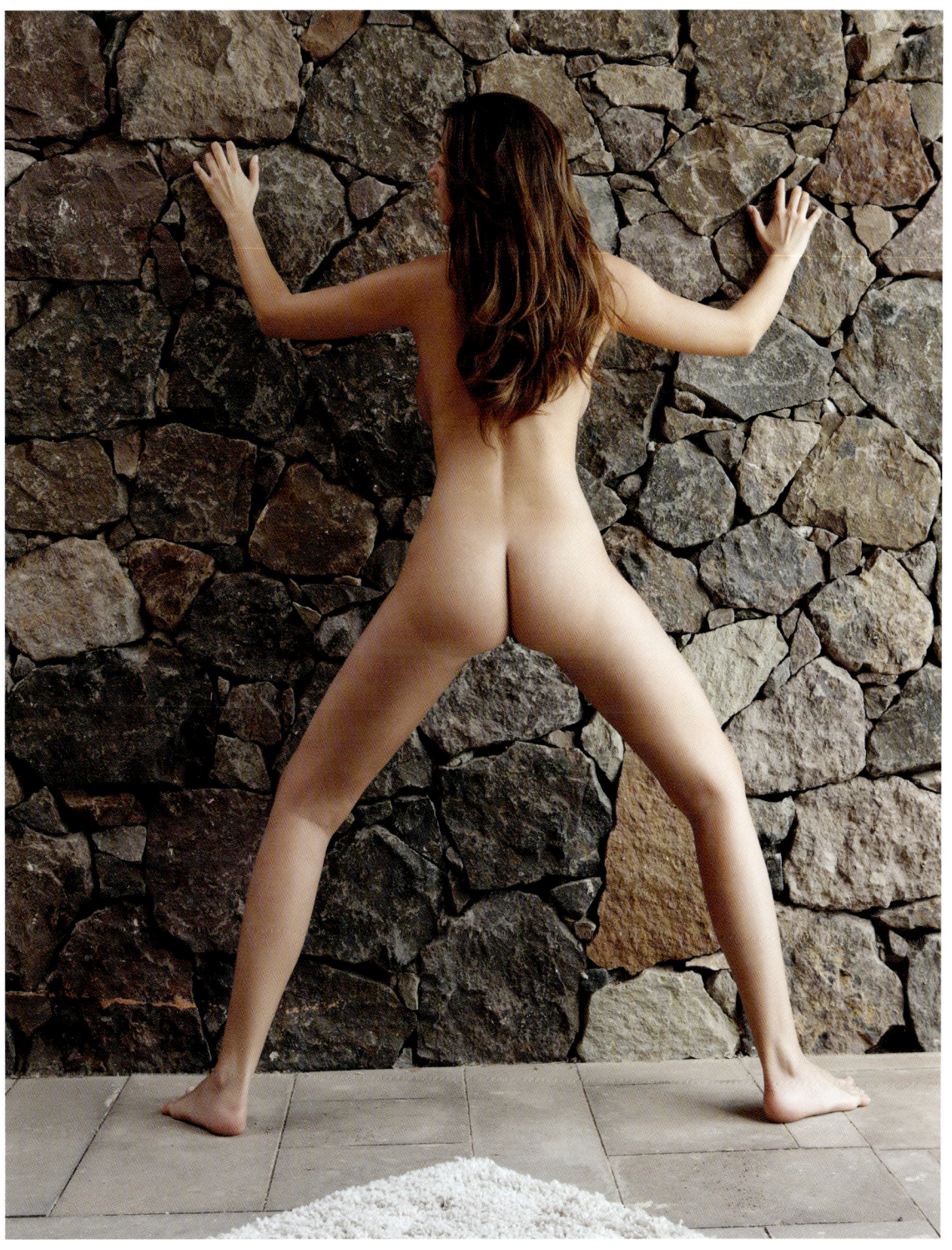

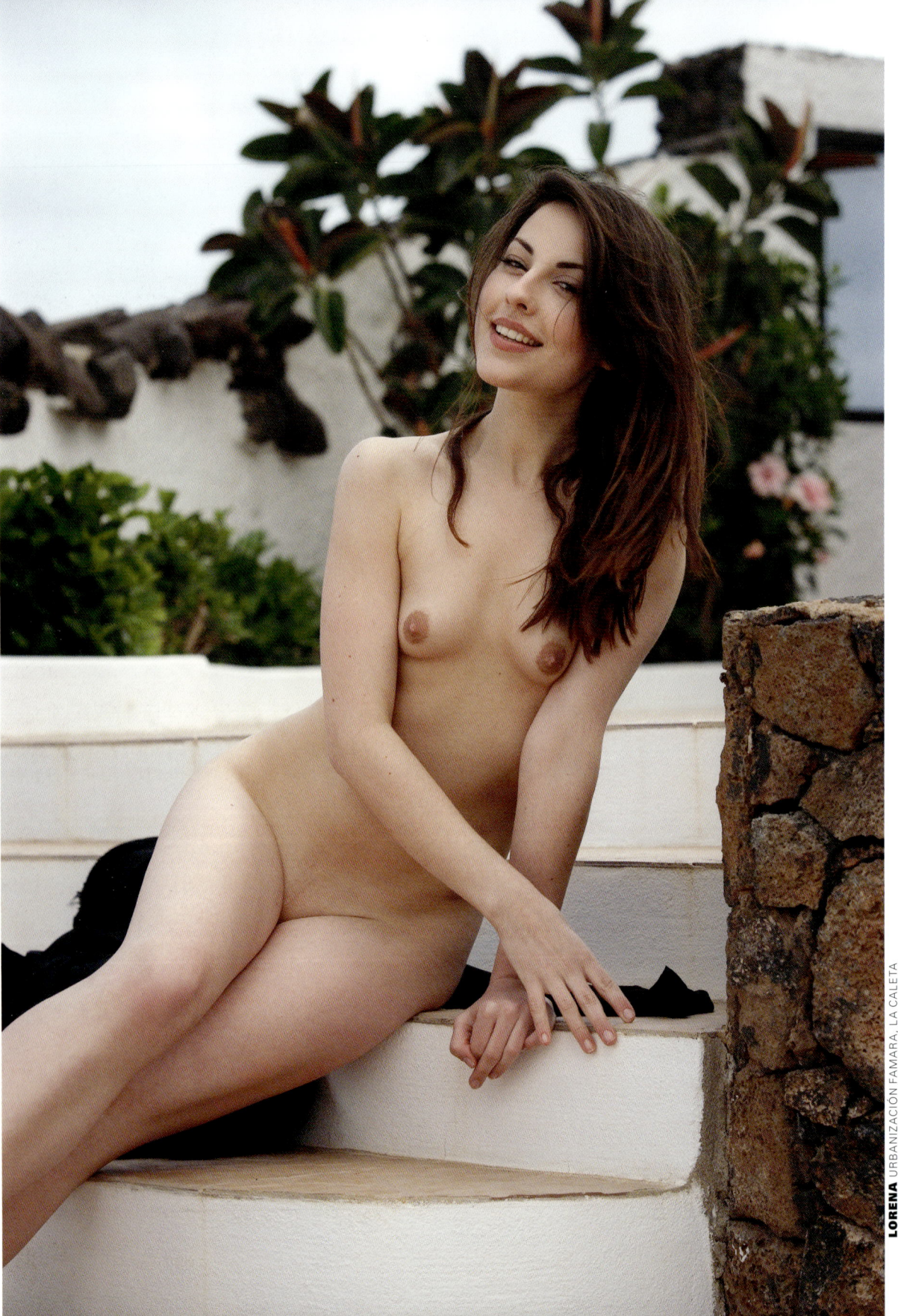

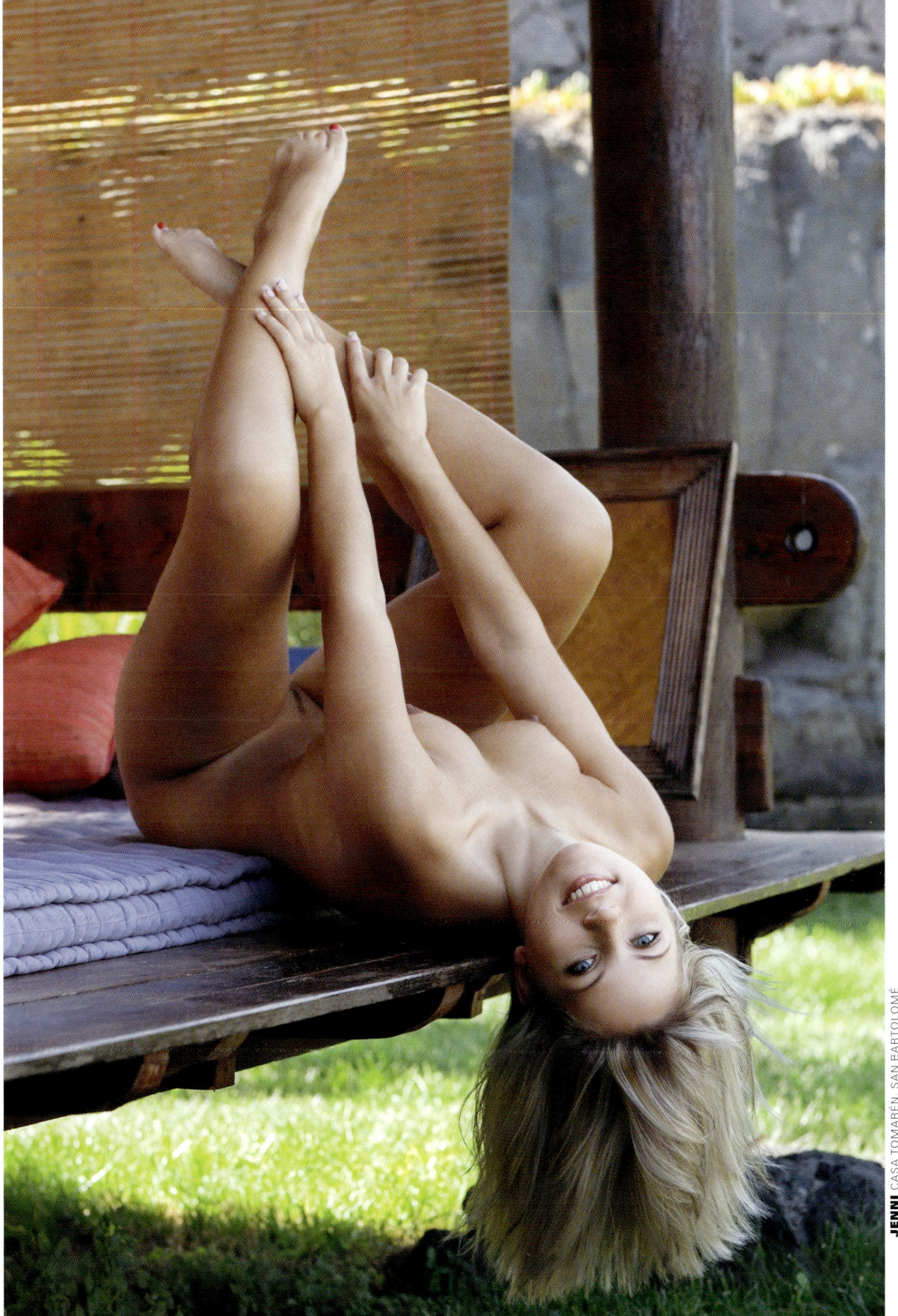

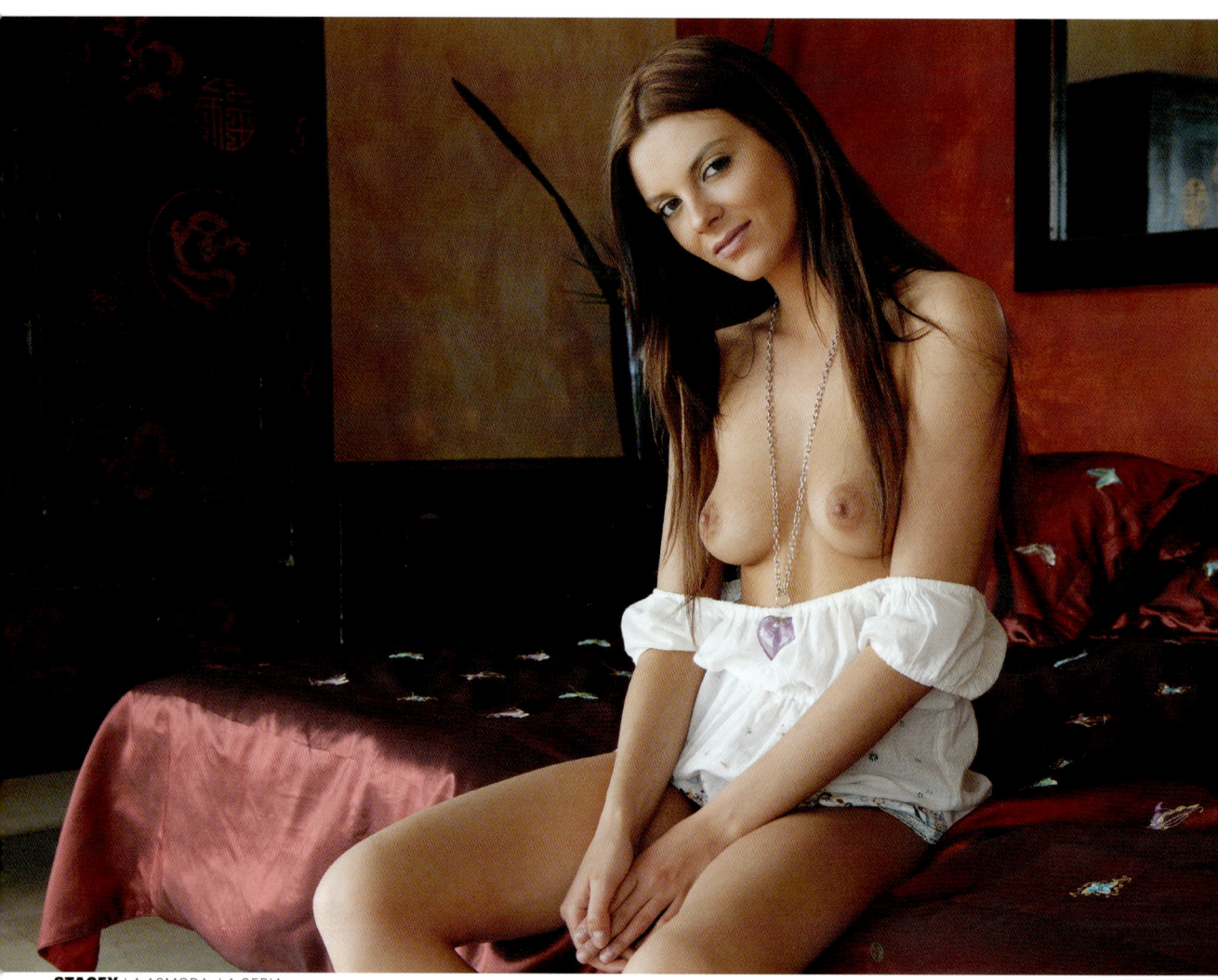

STACEY LA ASMODA, LA GERIA

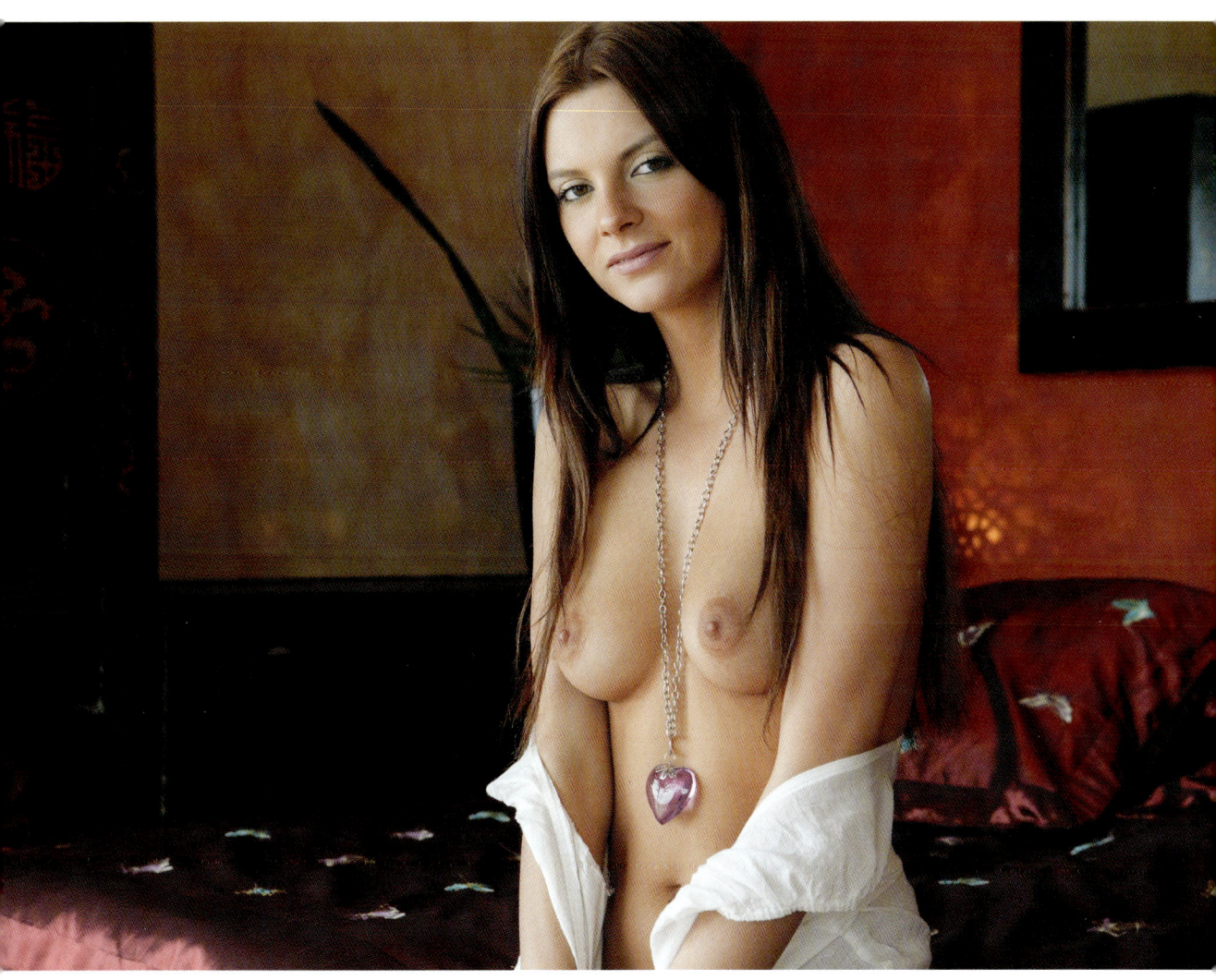

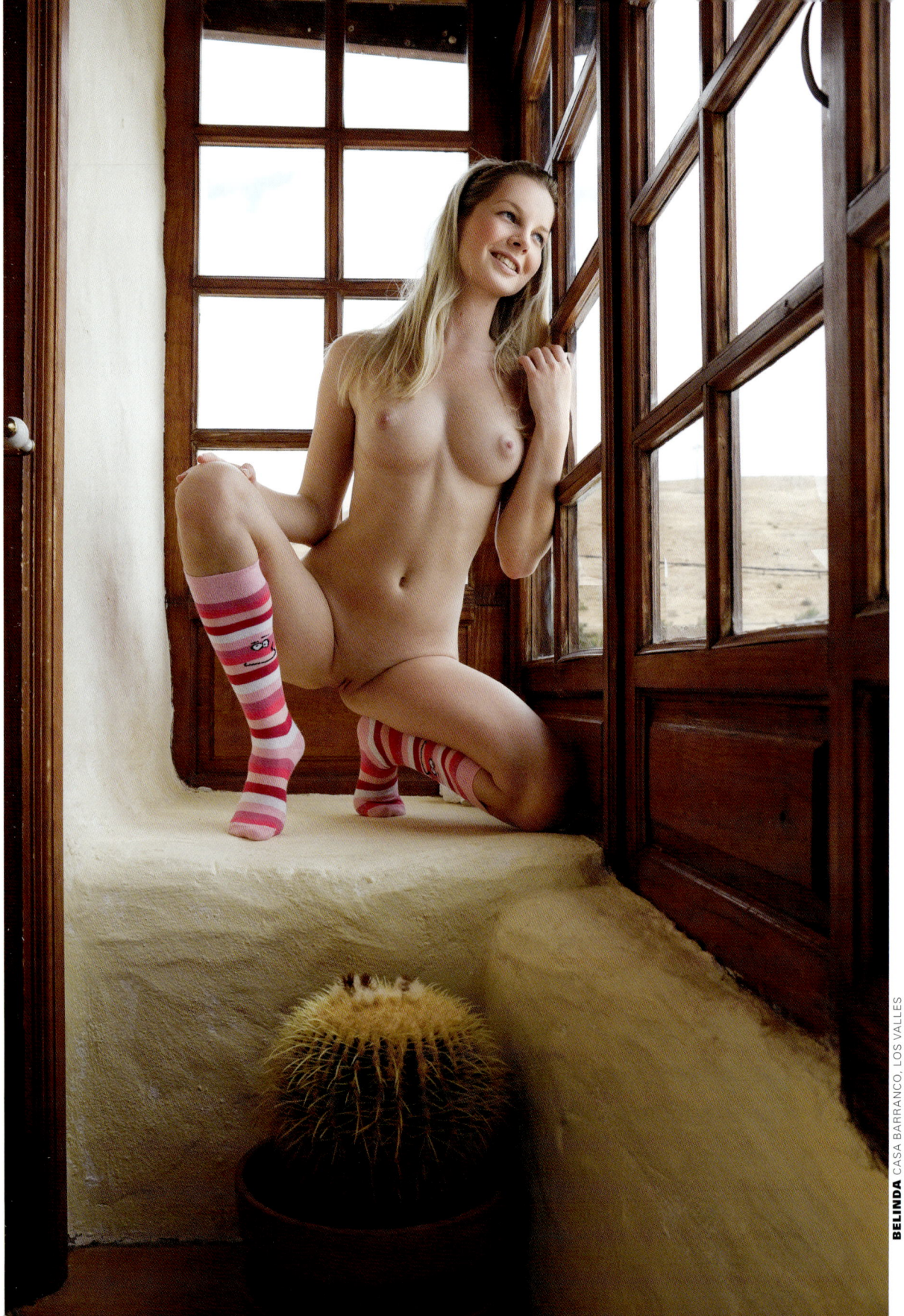

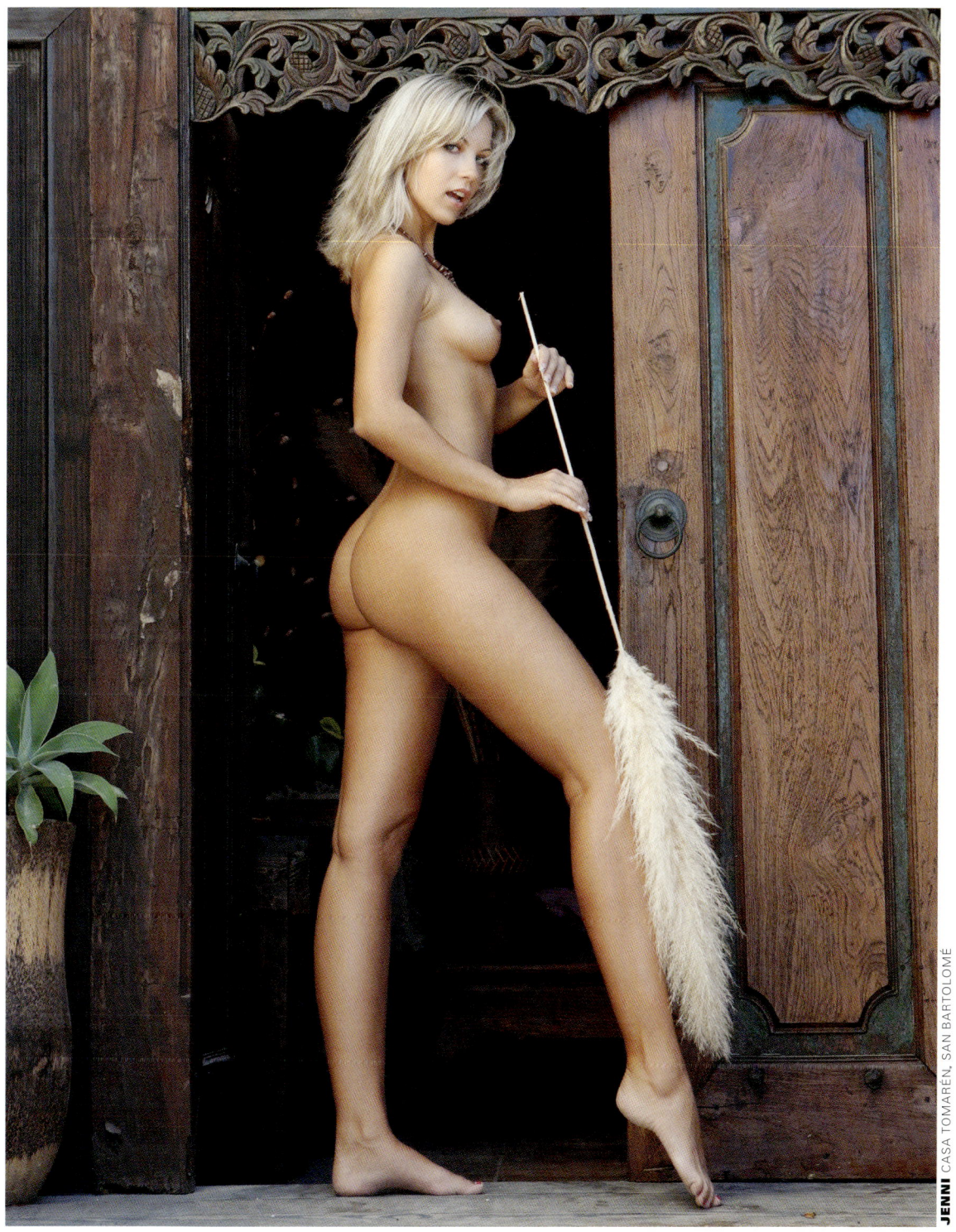

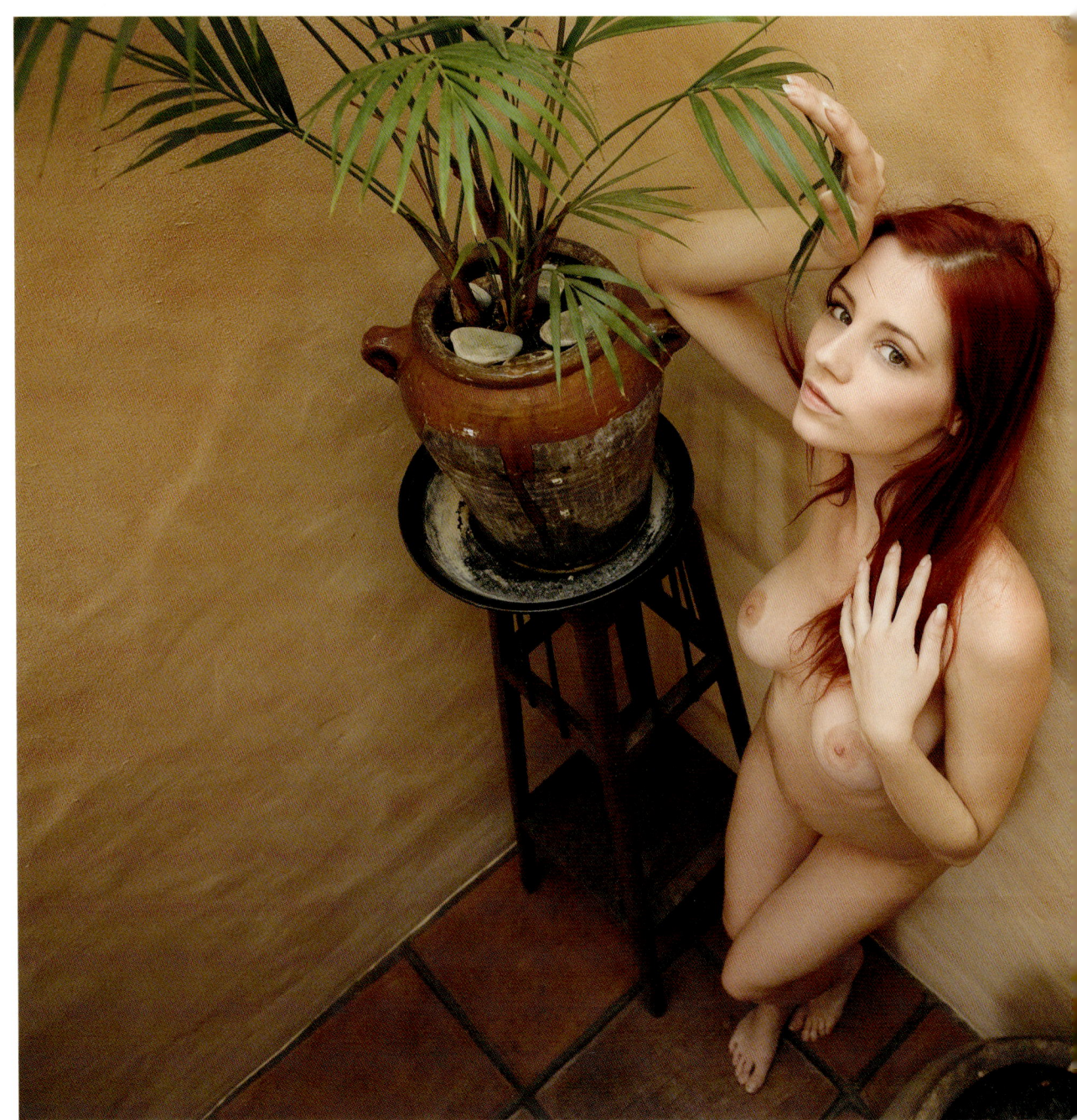

ARIEL AKAR WANGI CASA TOMARÉN, SAN BARTOLOMÉ

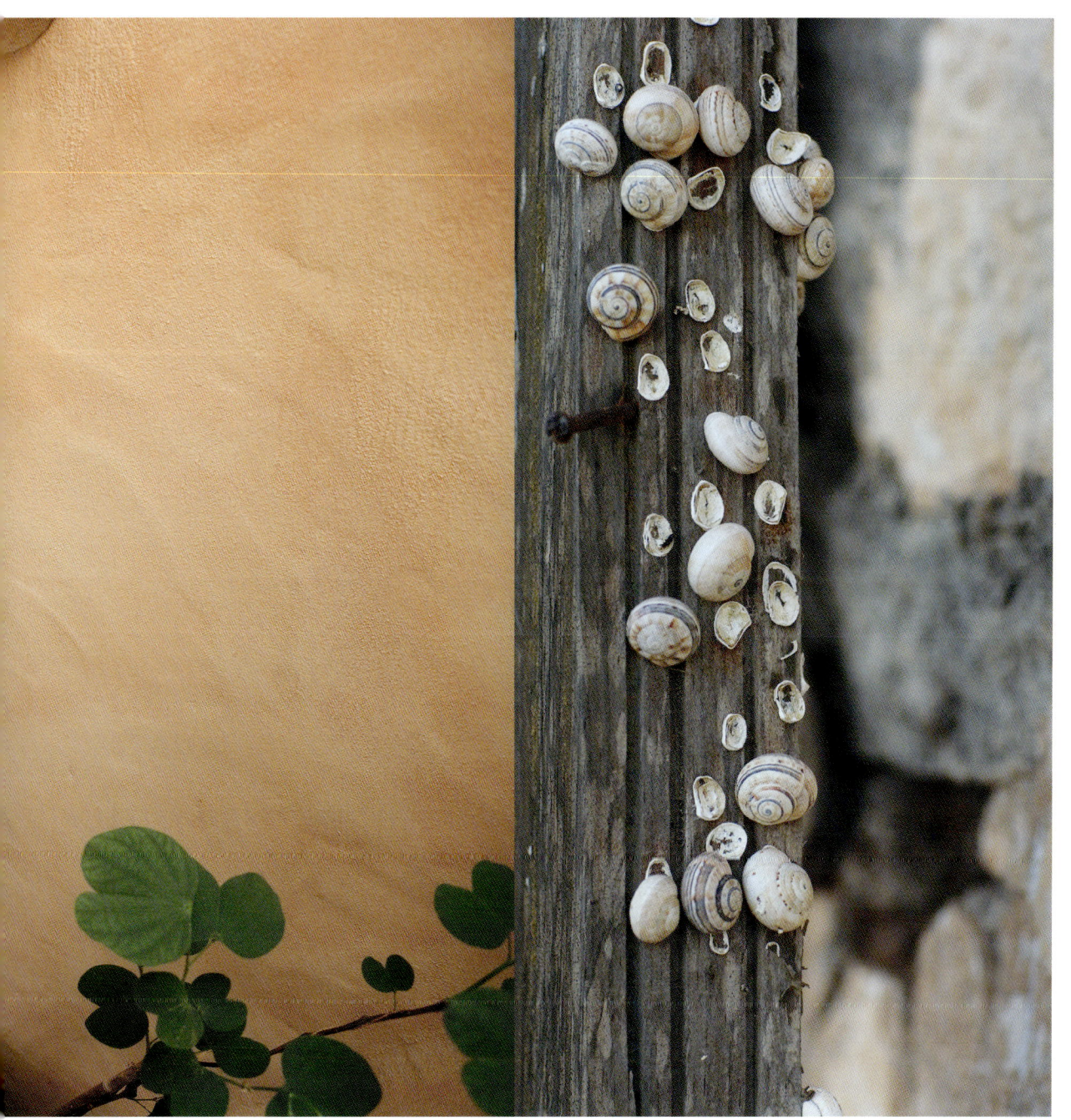

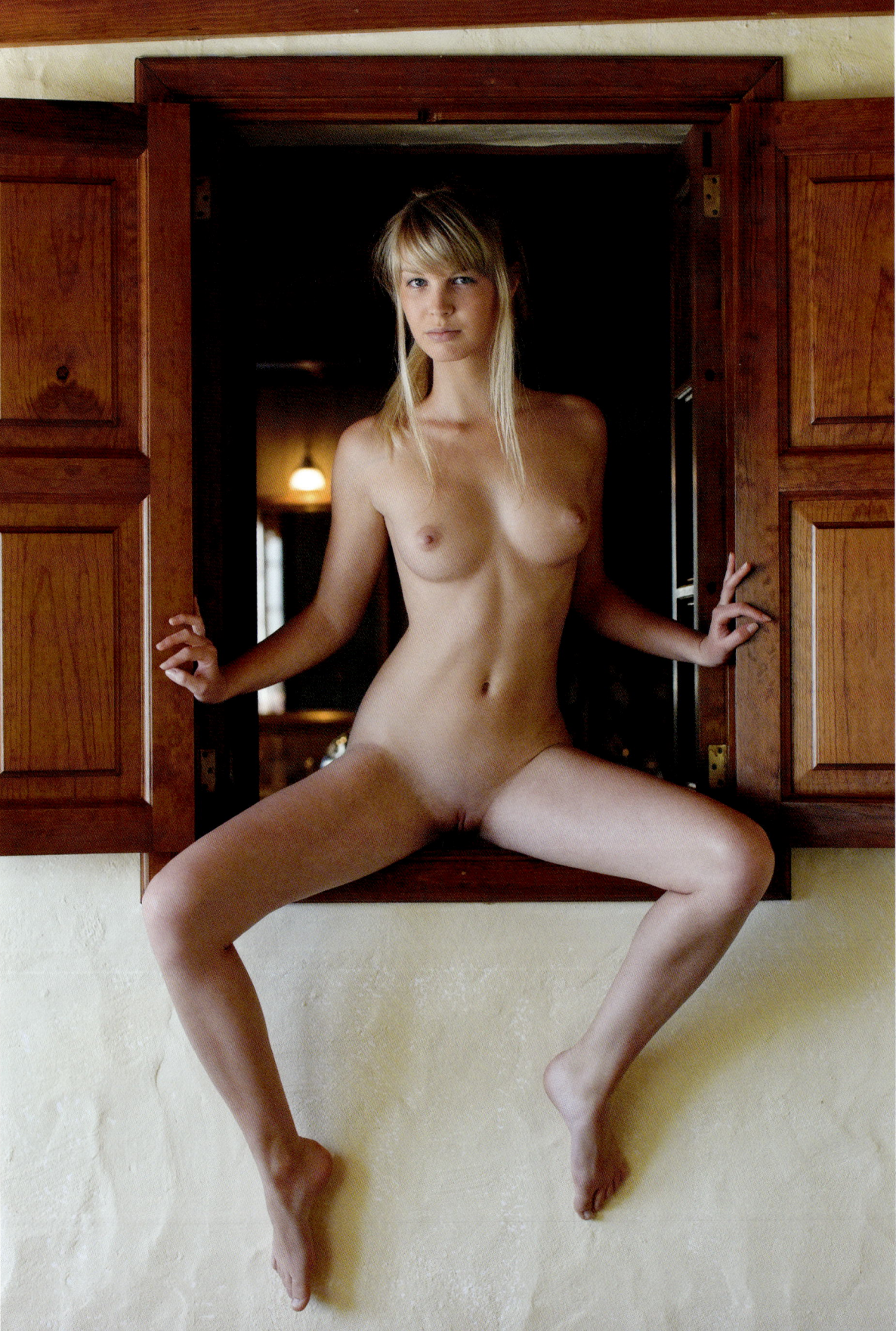

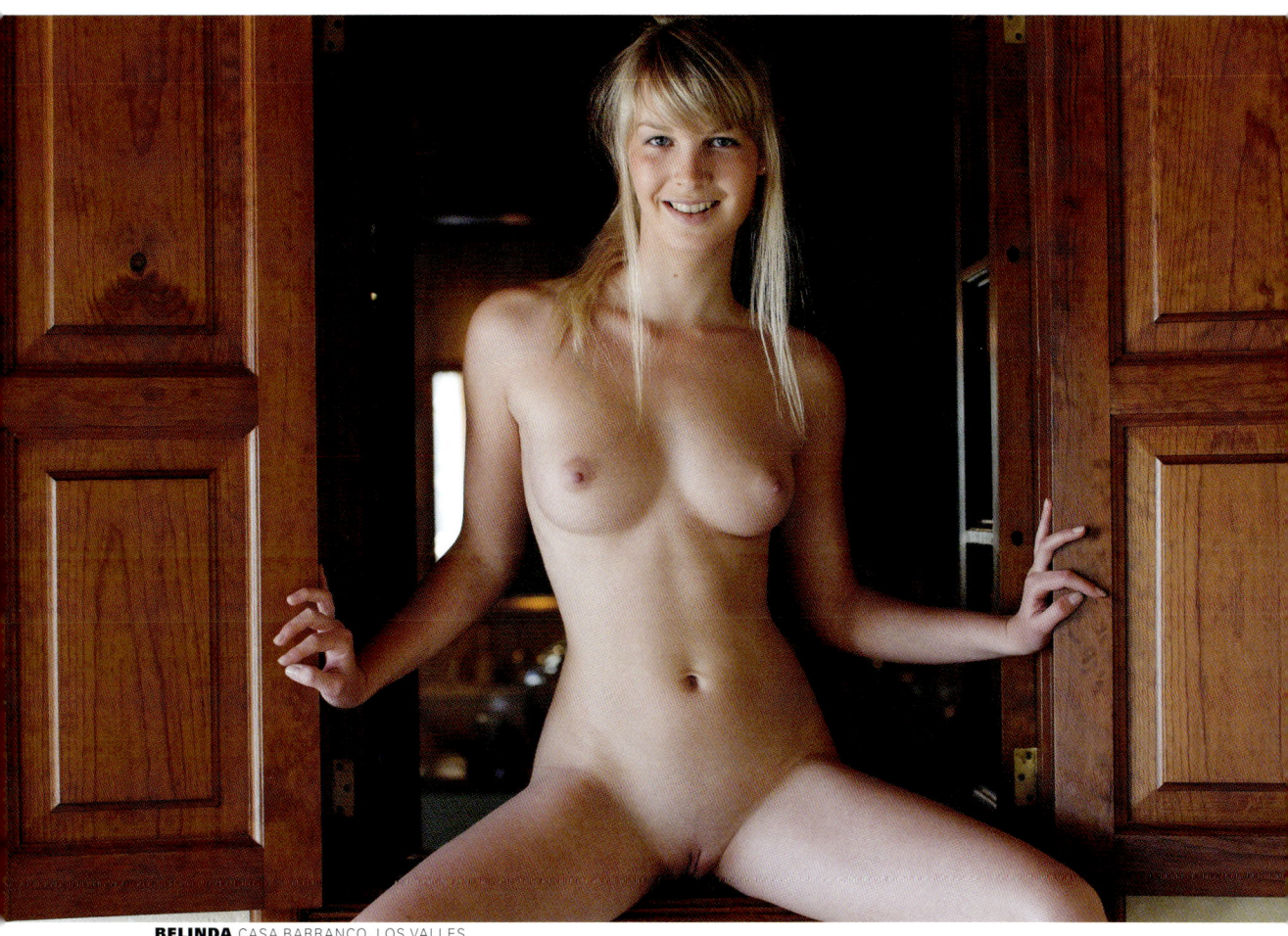

BELINDA CASA BARRANCO, LOS VALLES

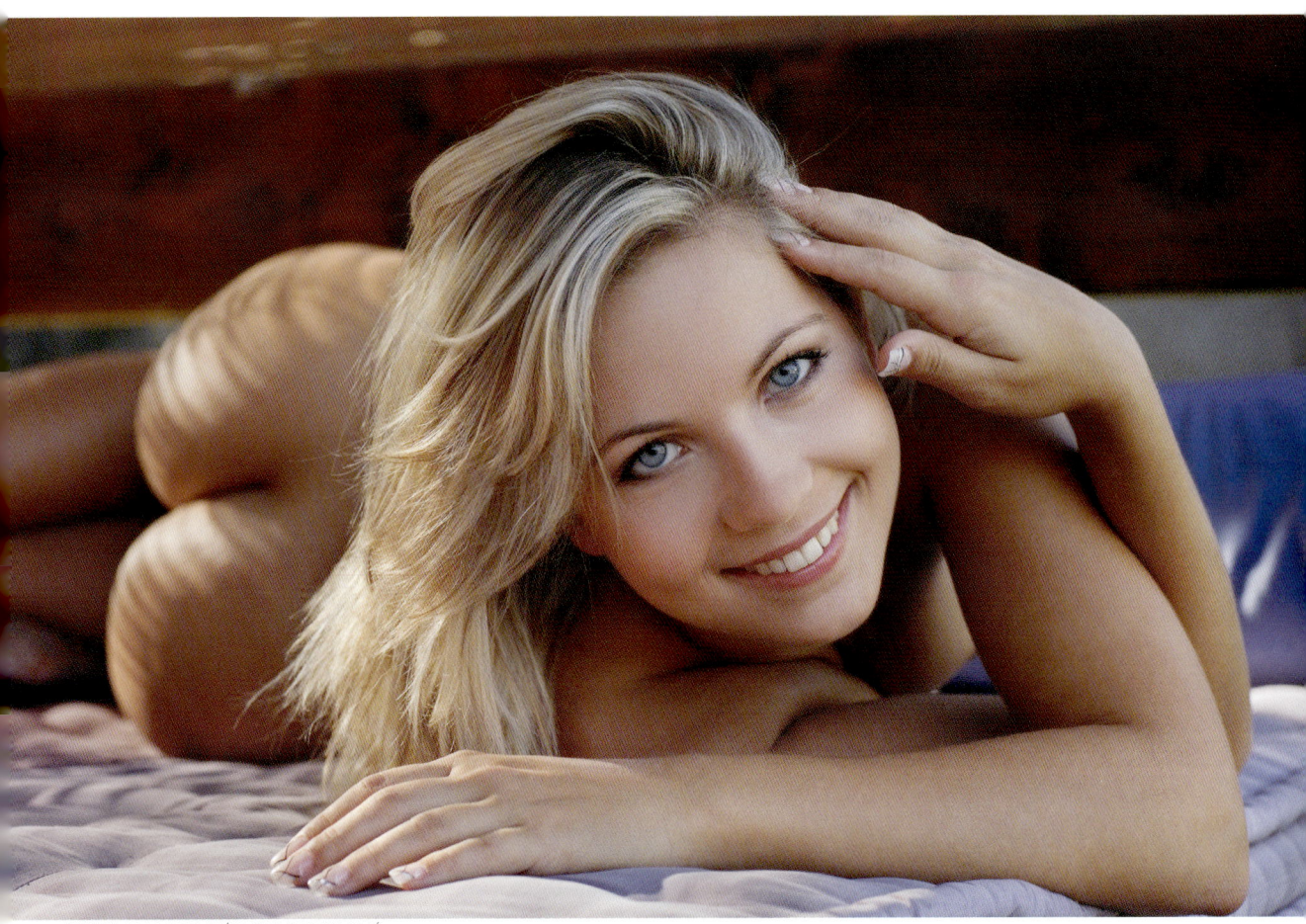

JENNI CASA TOMARÉN, SAN BARTOLOMÉ

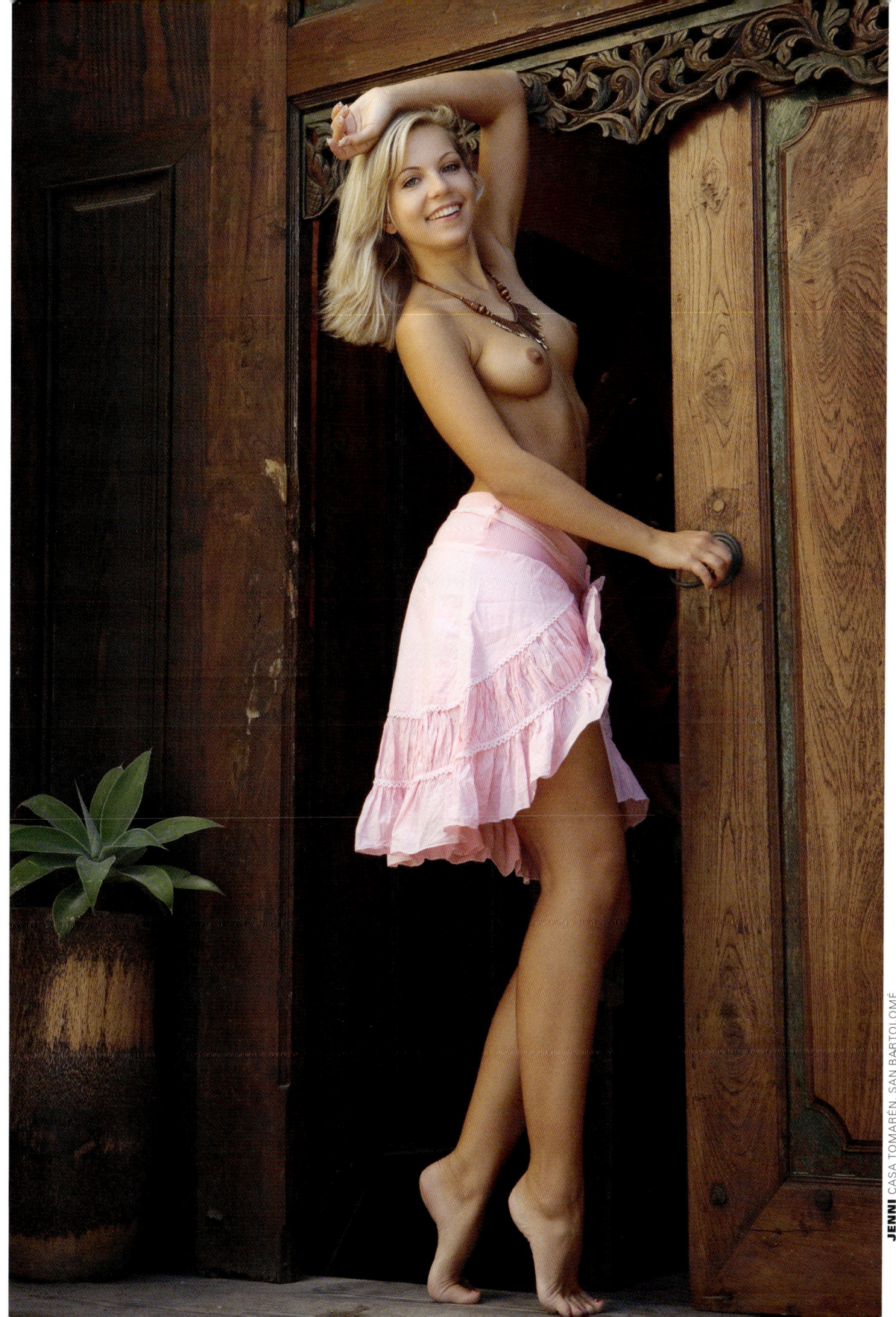

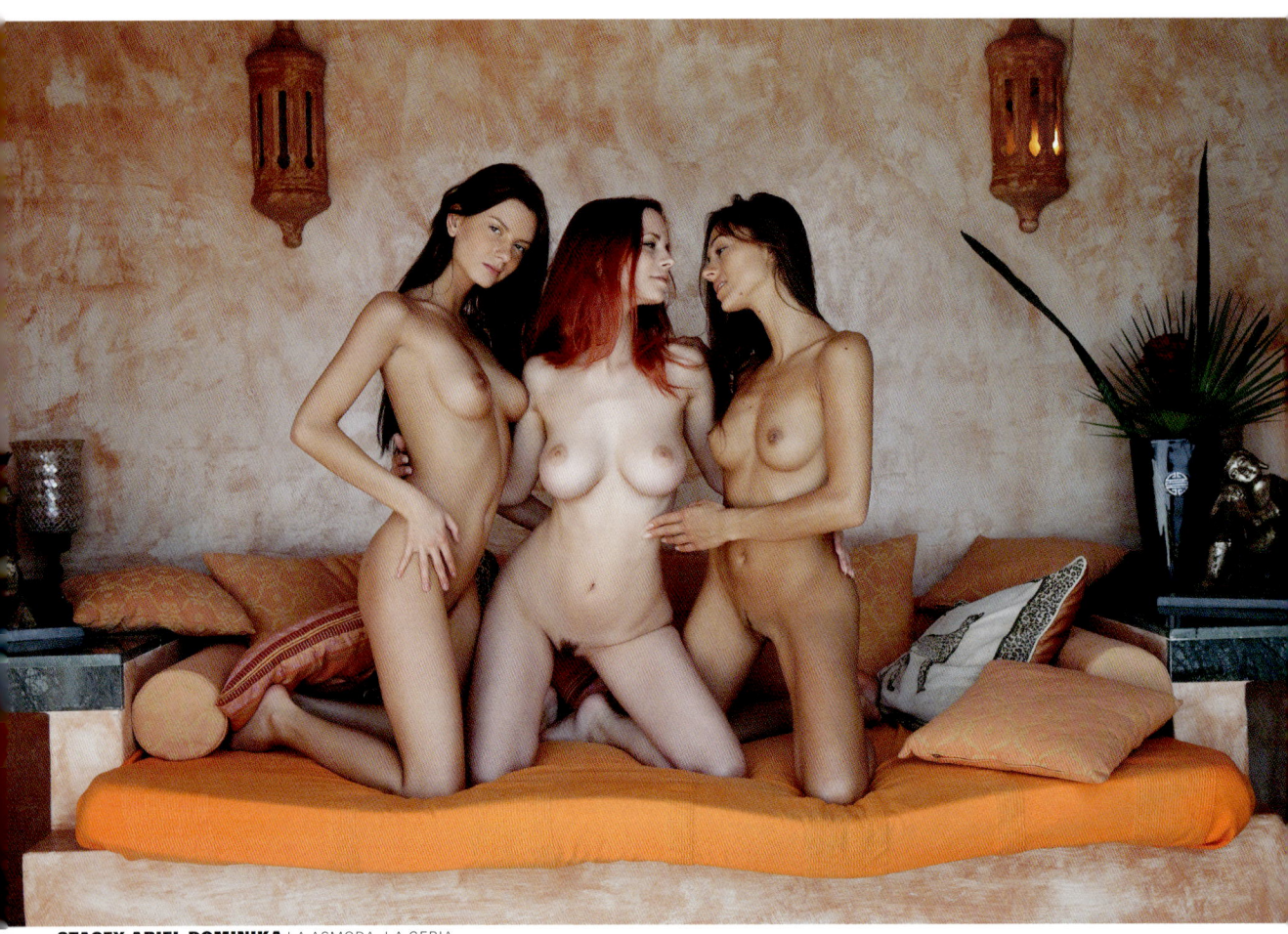

STACEY ARIEL DOMINIKA LA ASMODA, LA GERIA

166

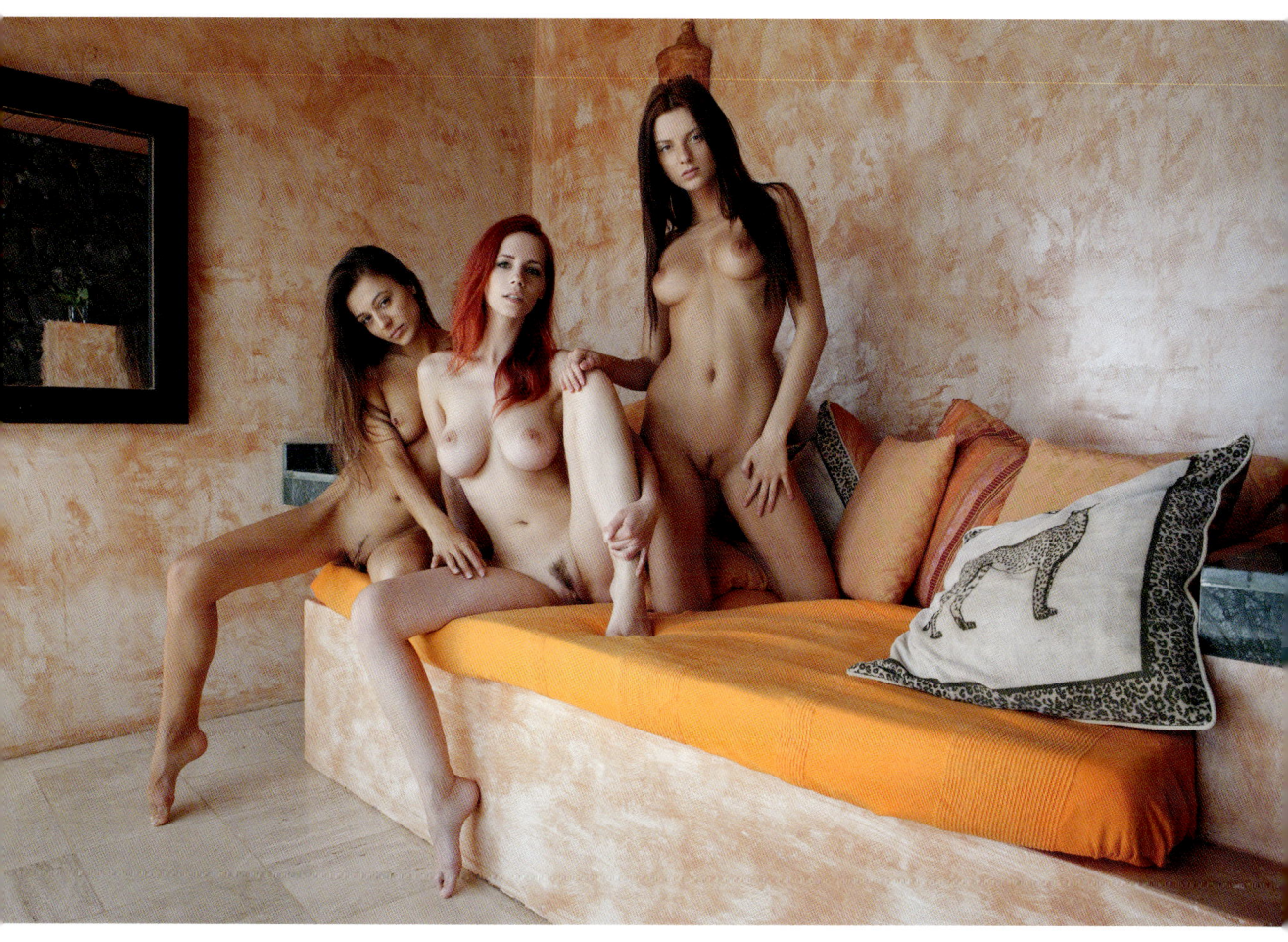

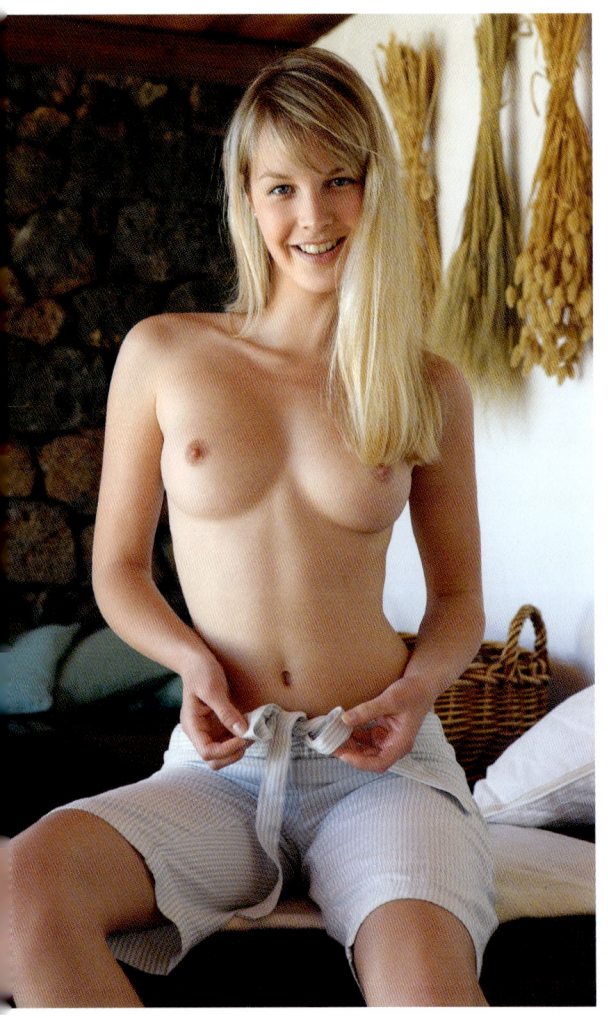

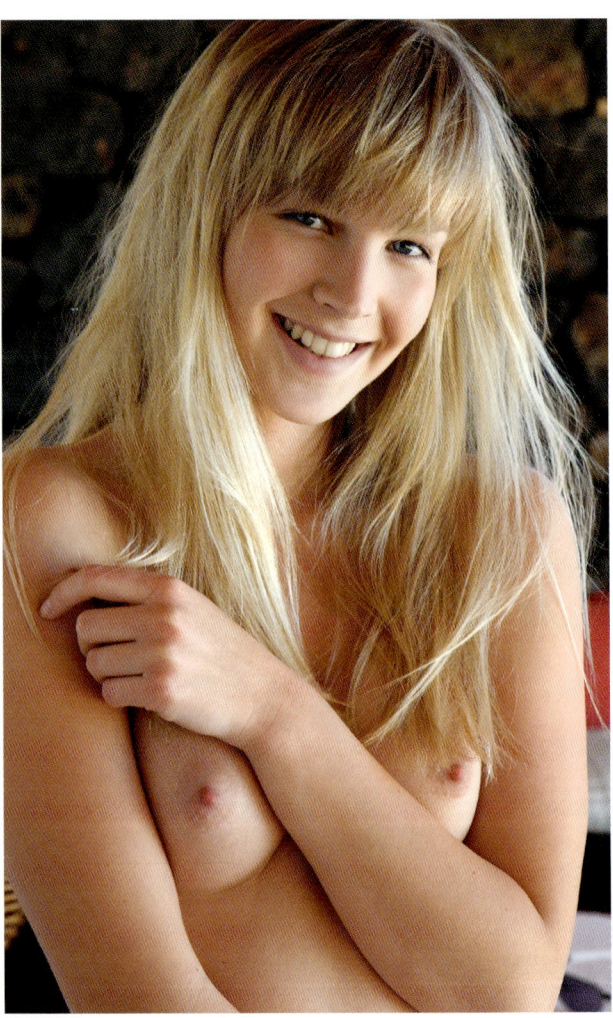

BELINDA LA ASMODA, LA GERIA

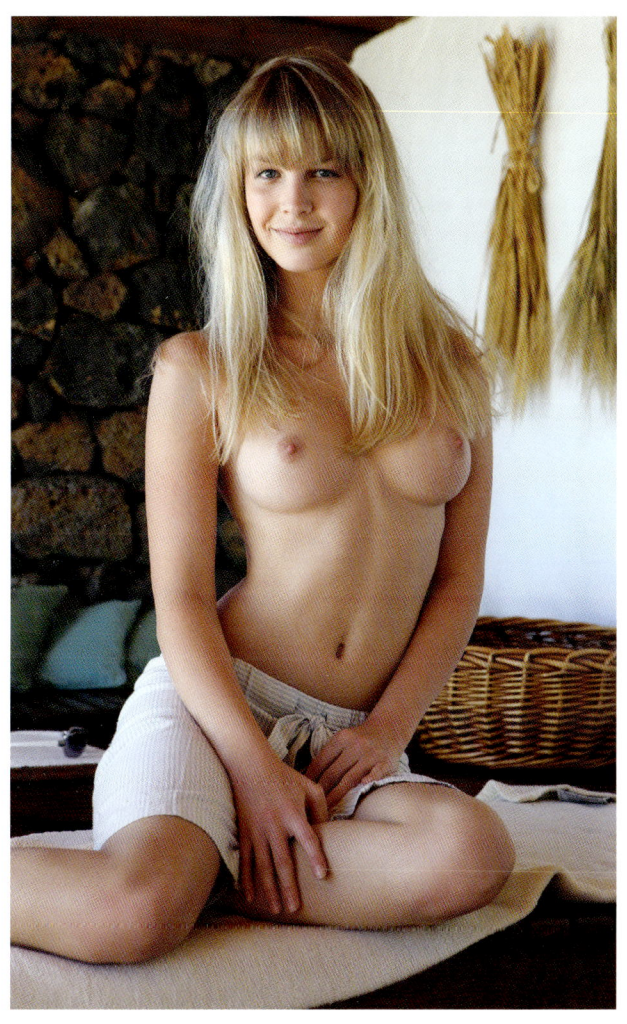

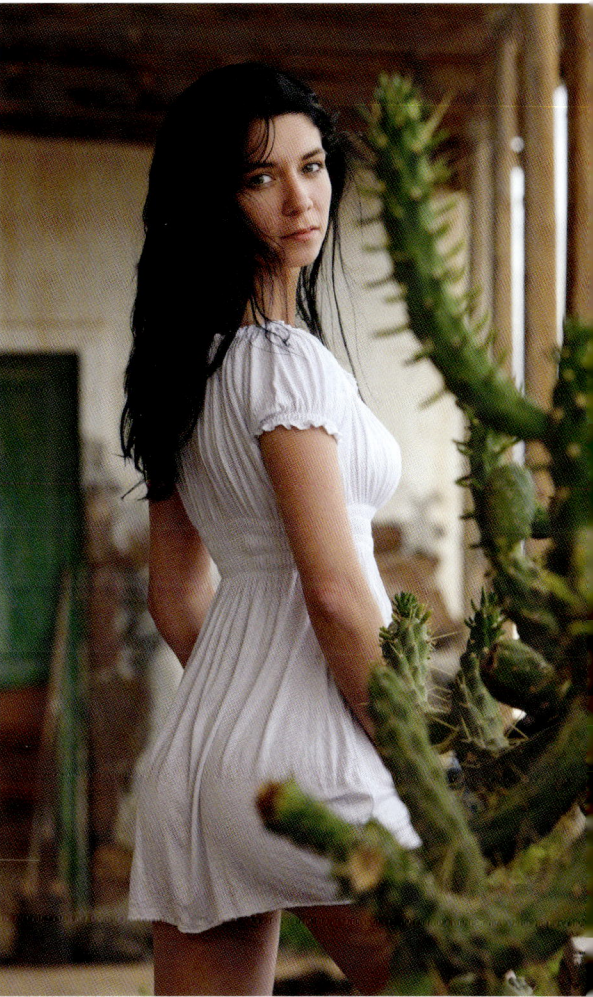

FIVA SALINAS DE JANUBIO, LAS HOYAS

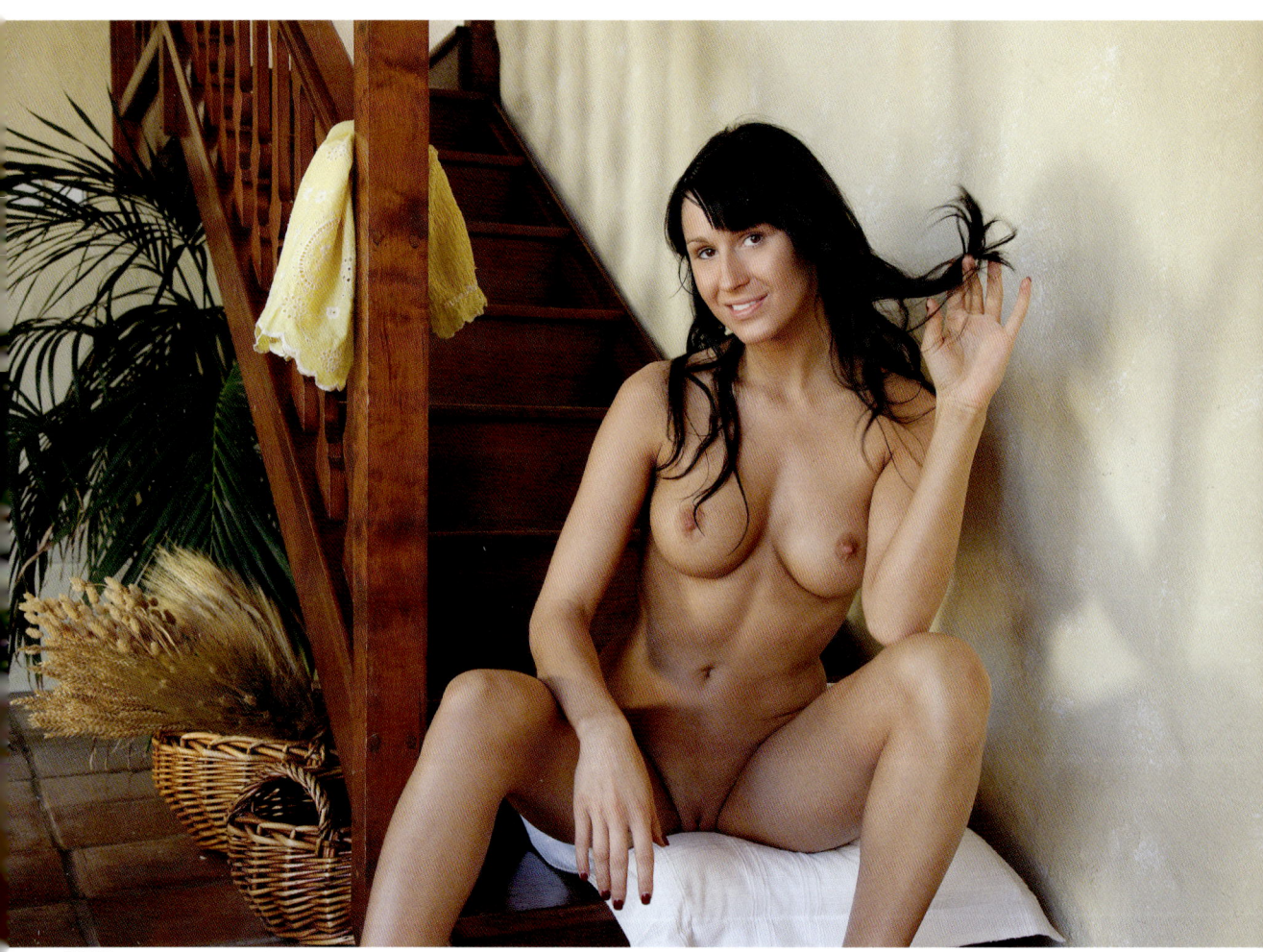

JAYLA CASA BARRANCO, LOS VALLES

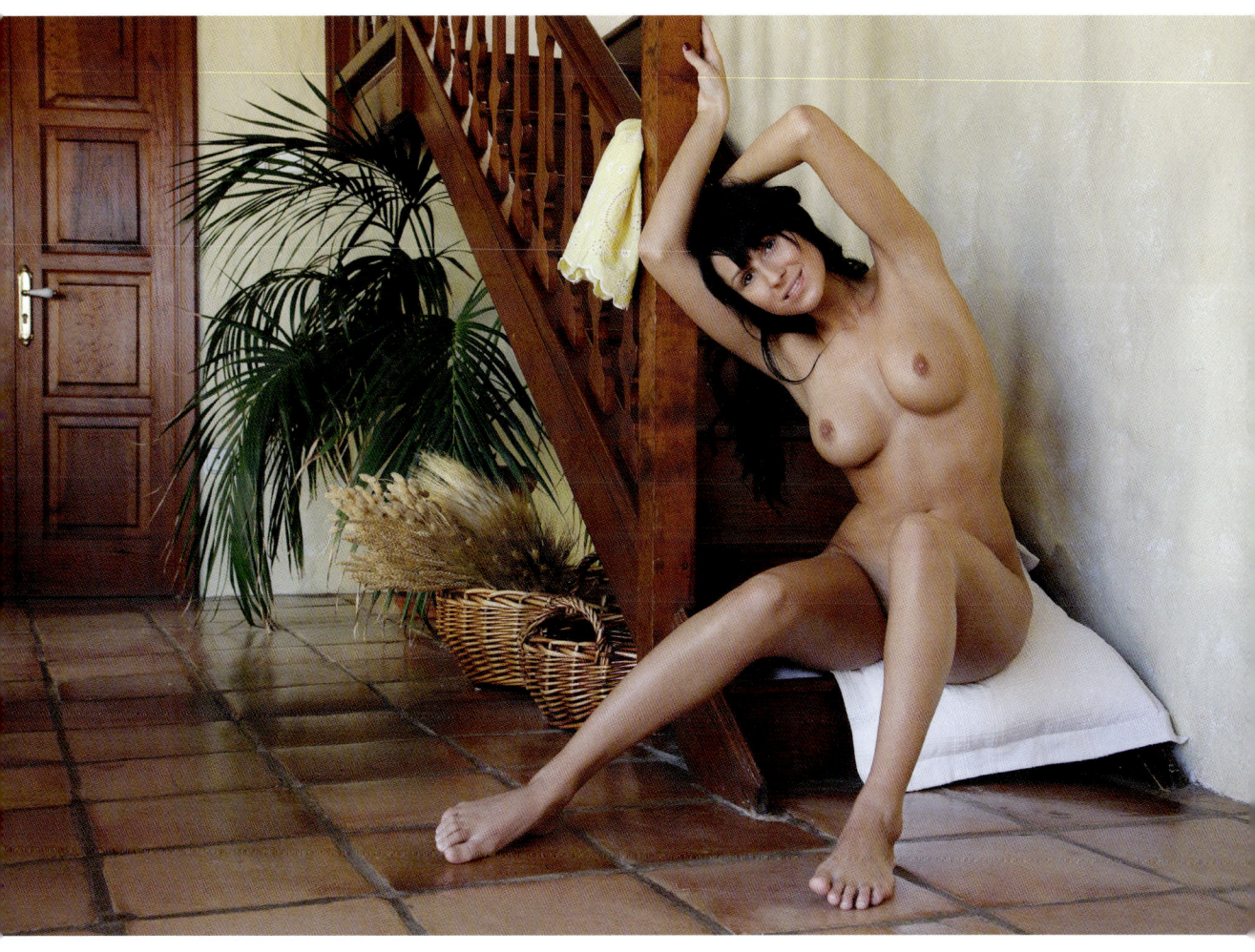

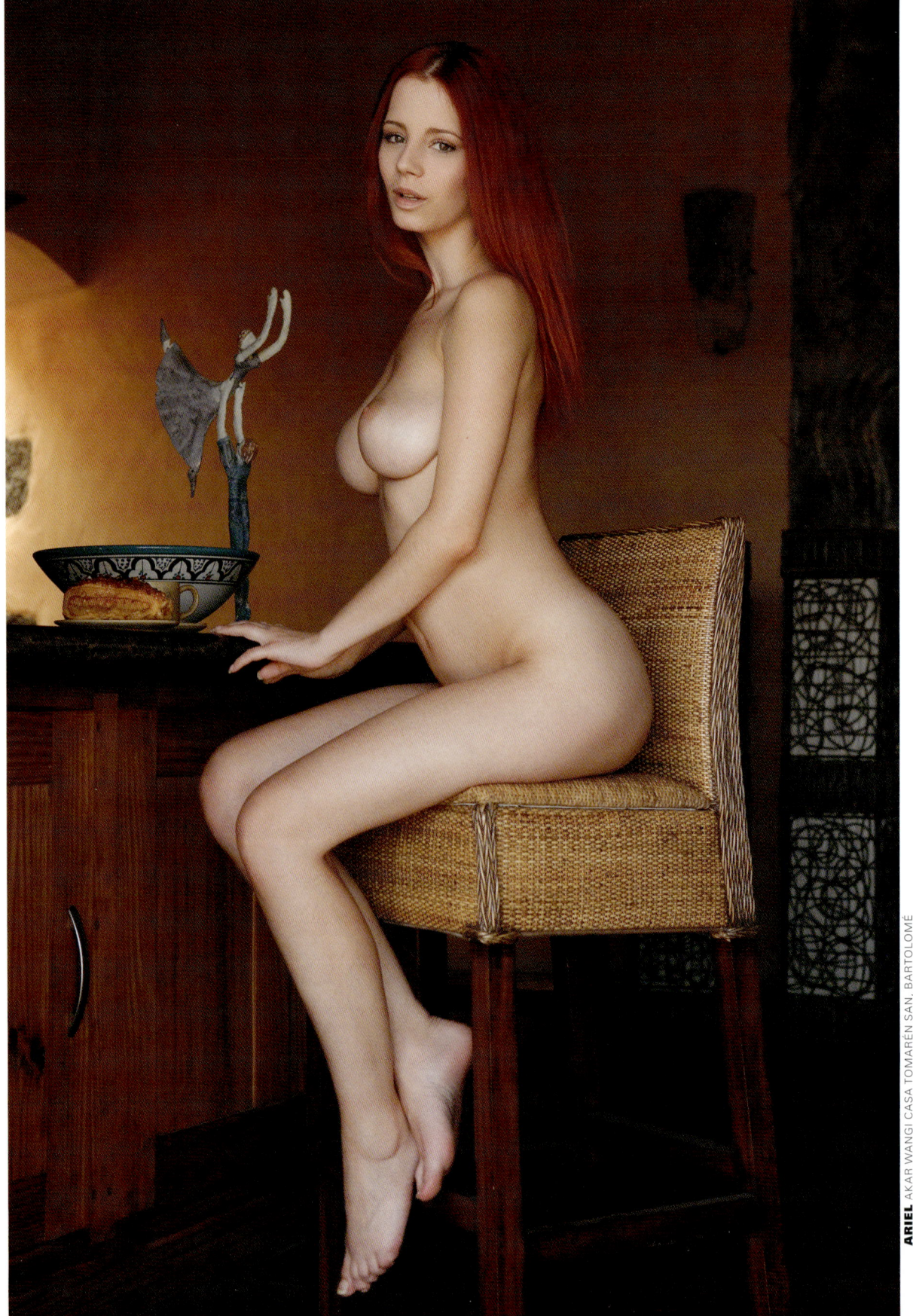

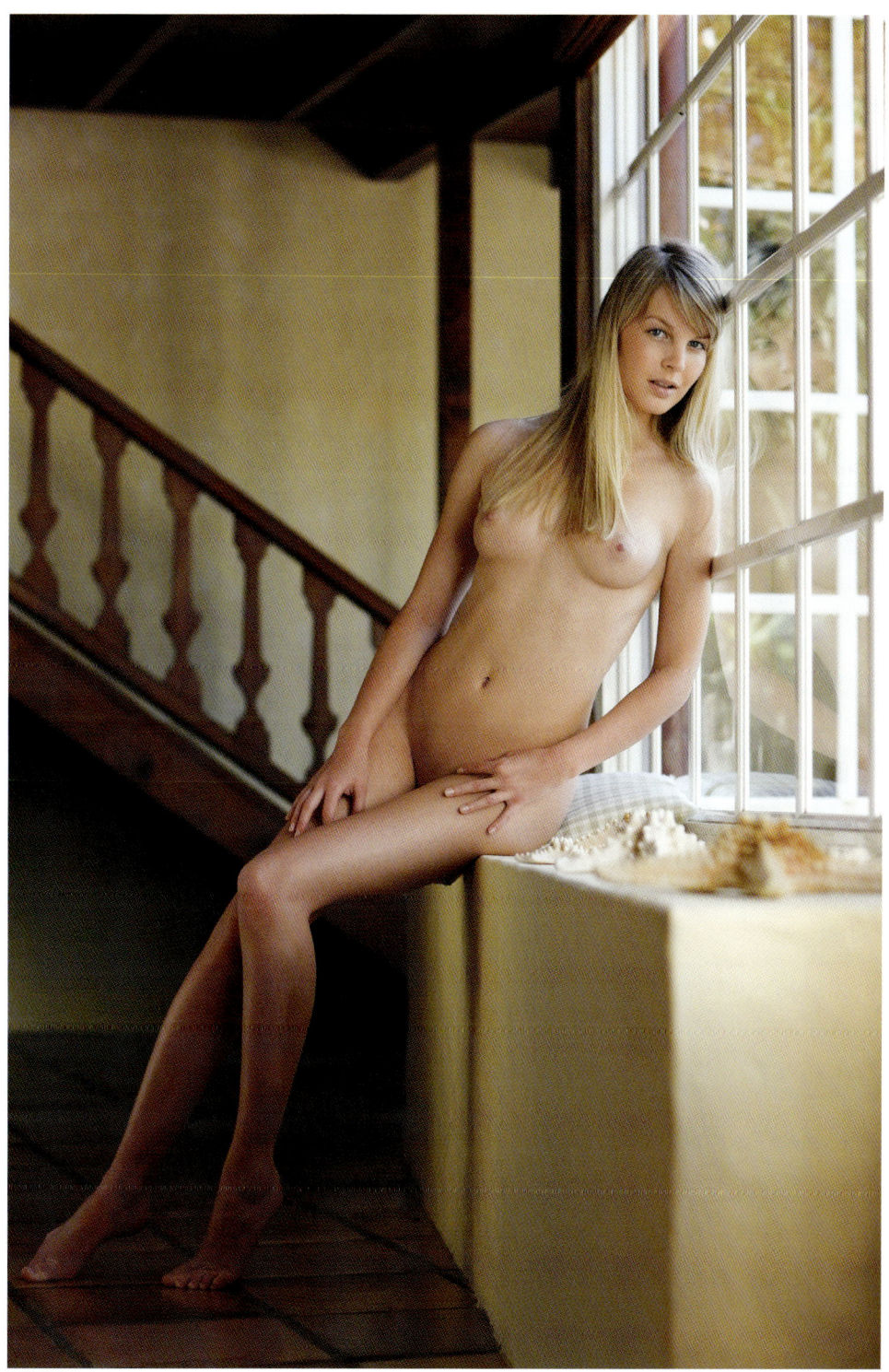

BELINDA CASA BARRANCO, LOS VALLES

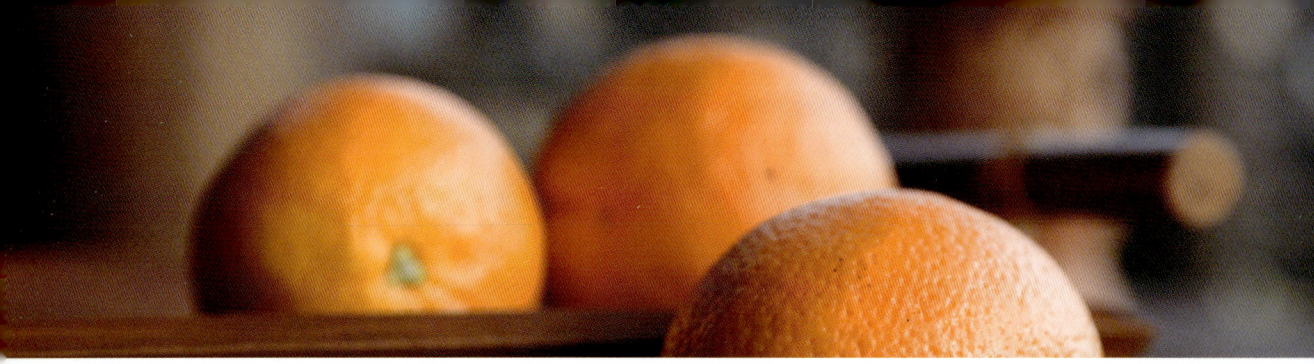

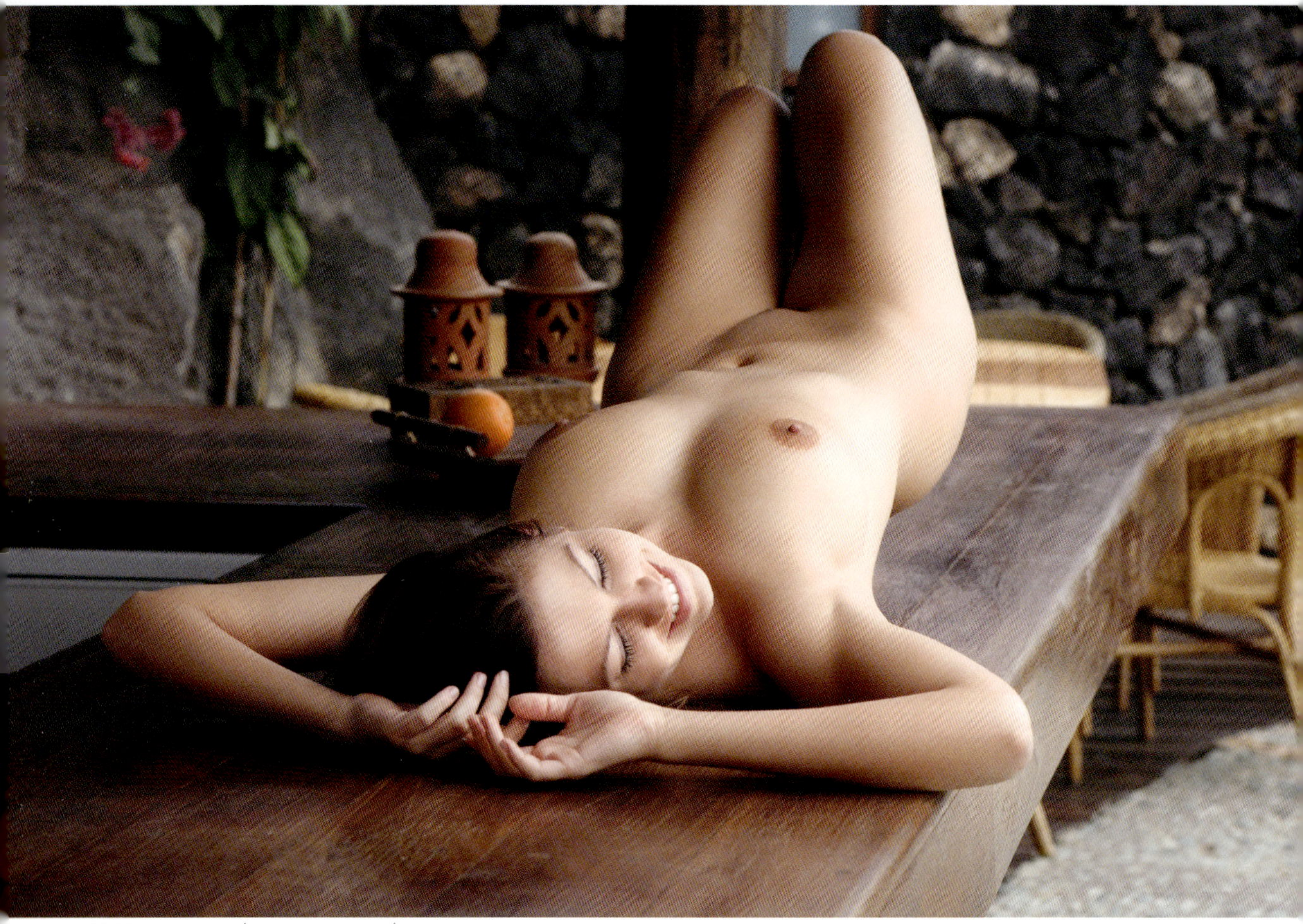

EUFRAT CASA TOMARÉN, SAN BARTOLOMÉ

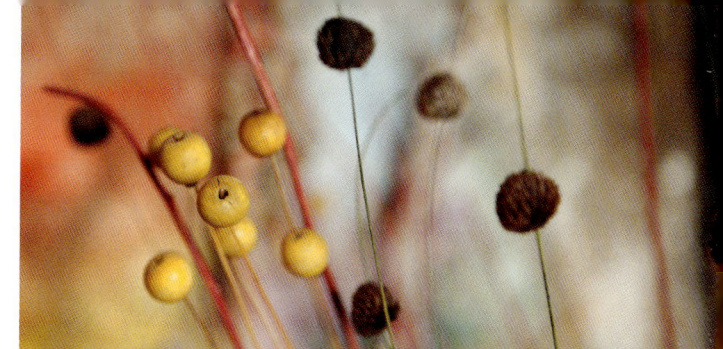

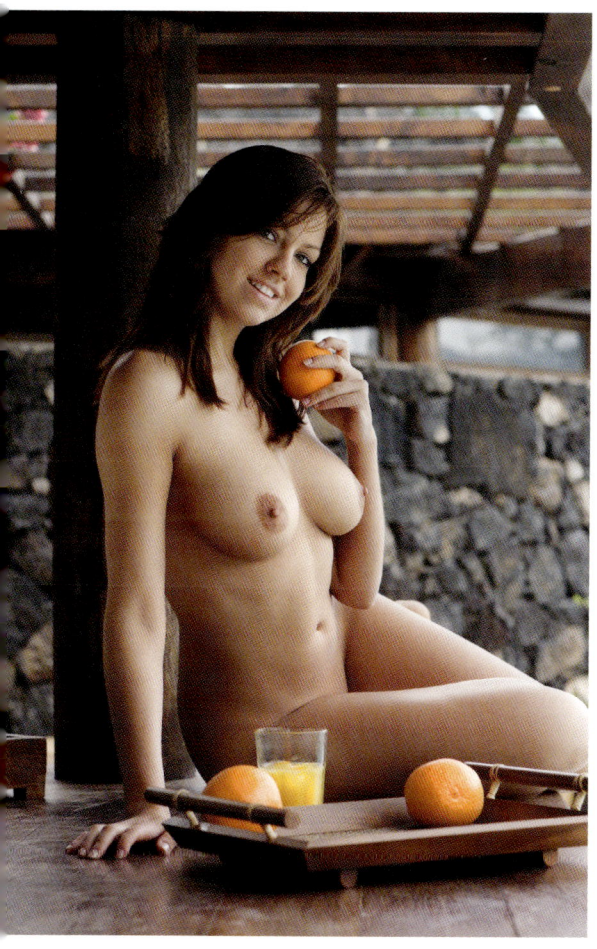

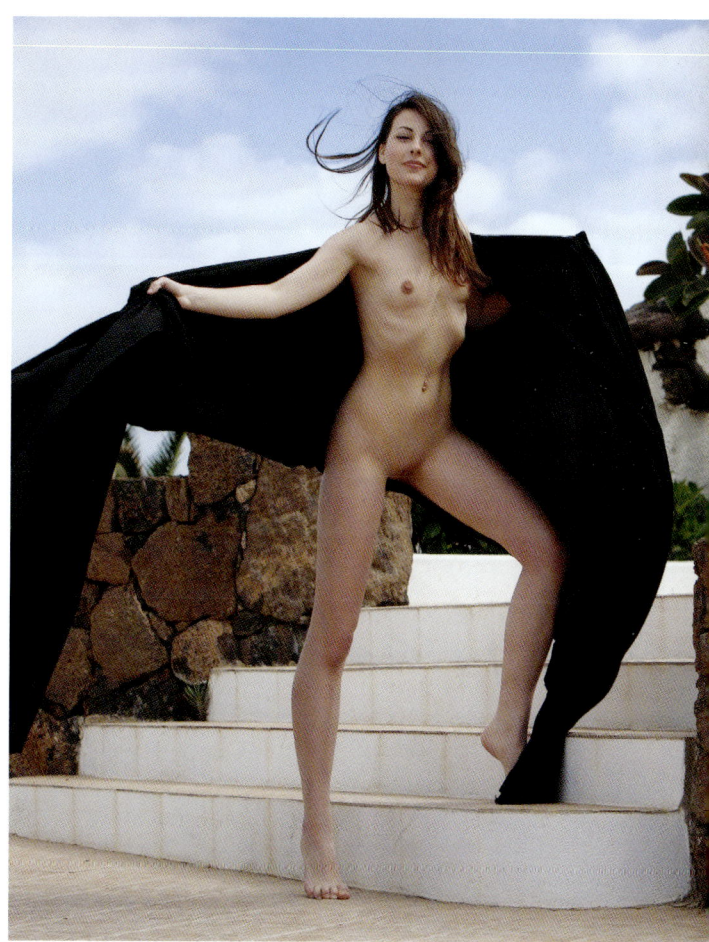

LORENA URBANIZACIÓN FAMARA, LA CALETA

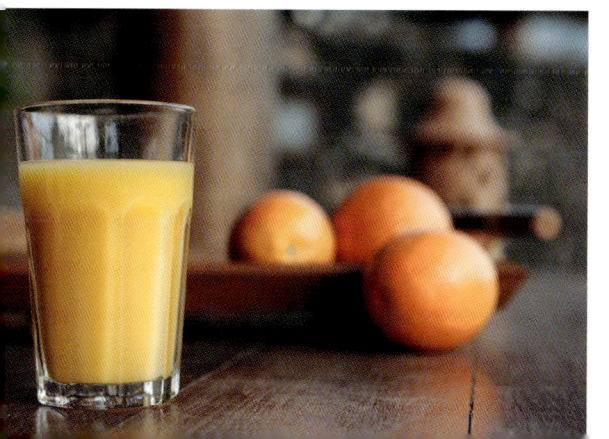

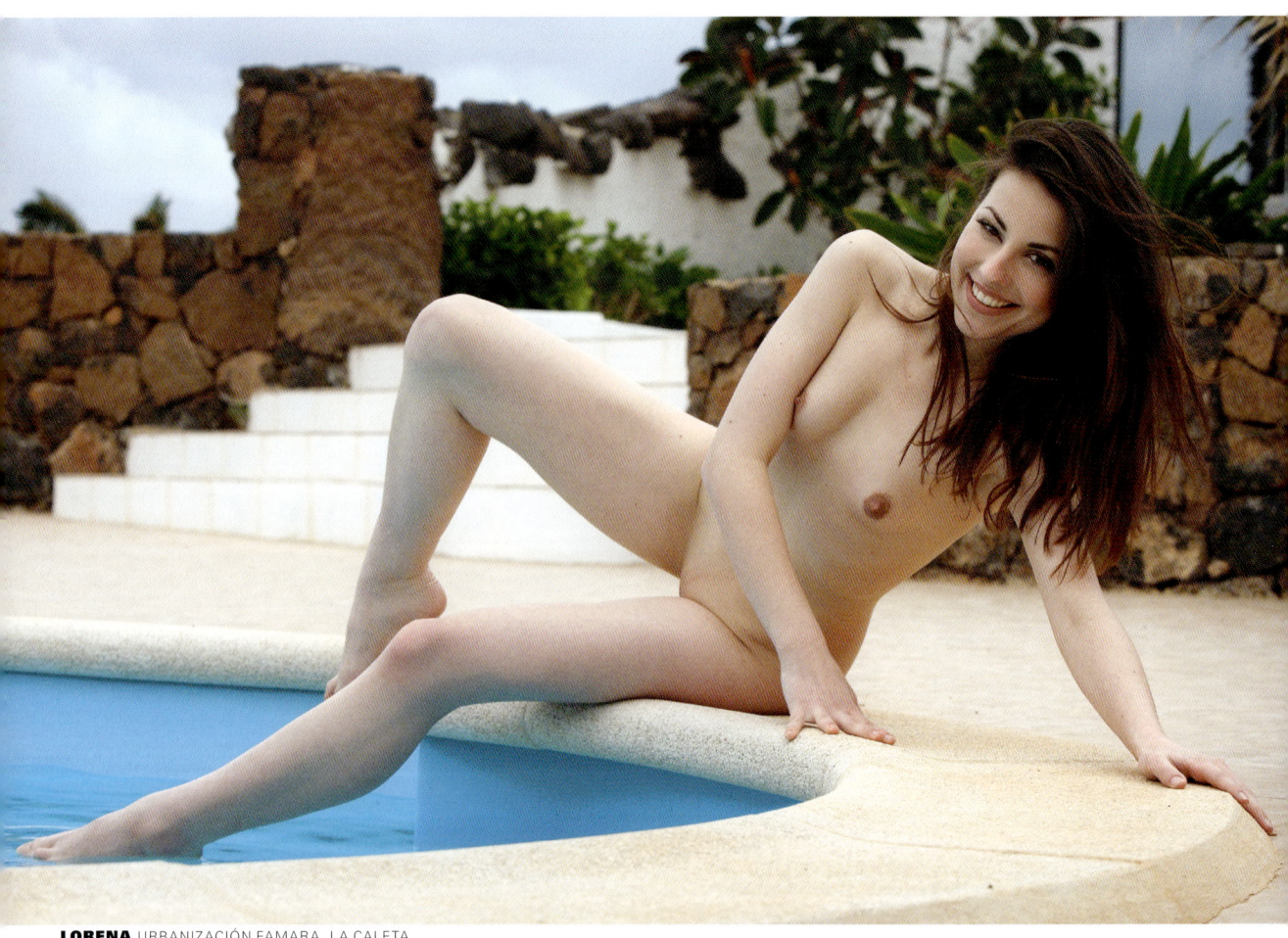

LORENA URBANIZACIÓN FAMARA, LA CALETA

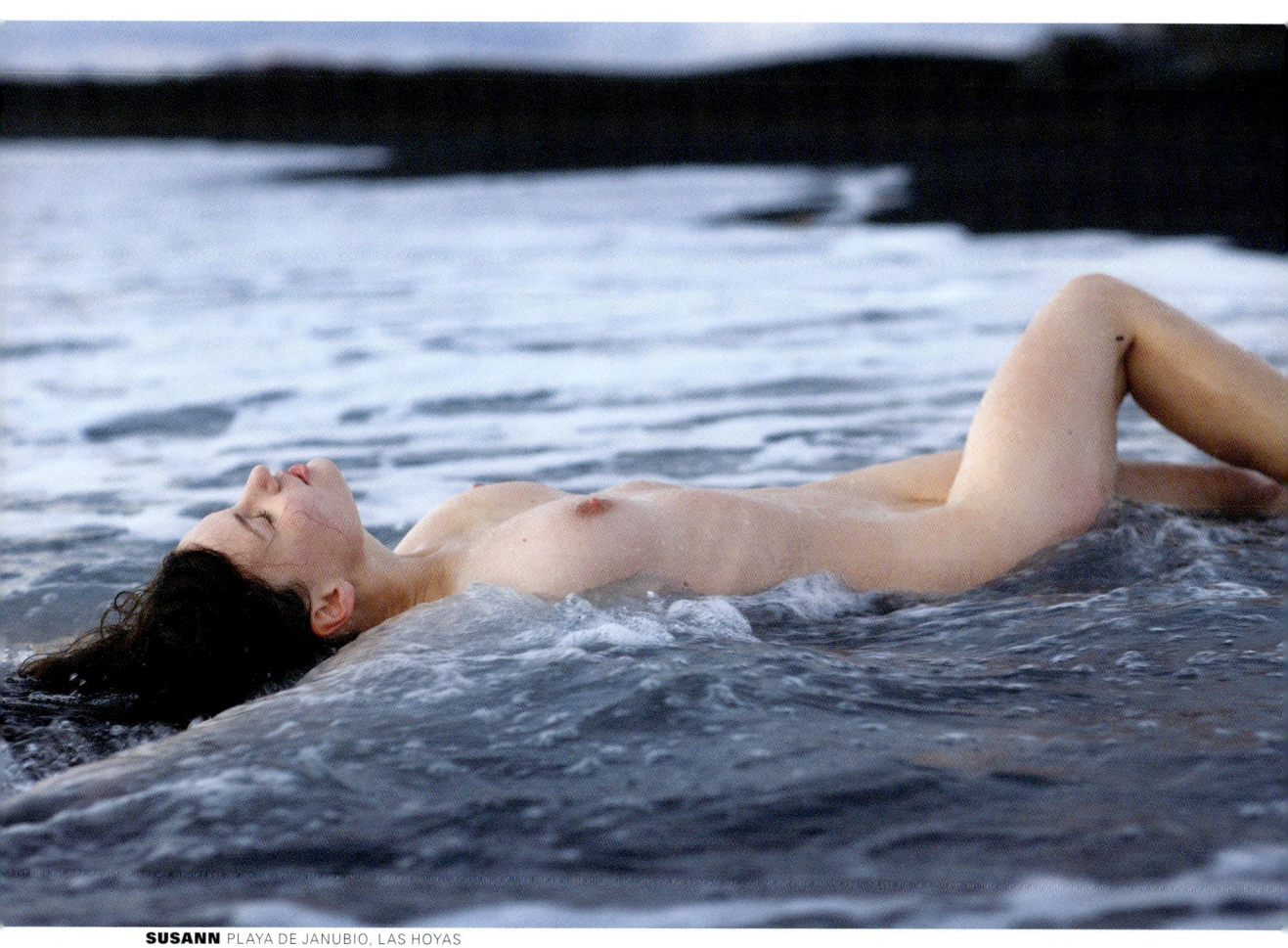

SUSANN PLAYA DE JANUBIO, LAS HOYAS

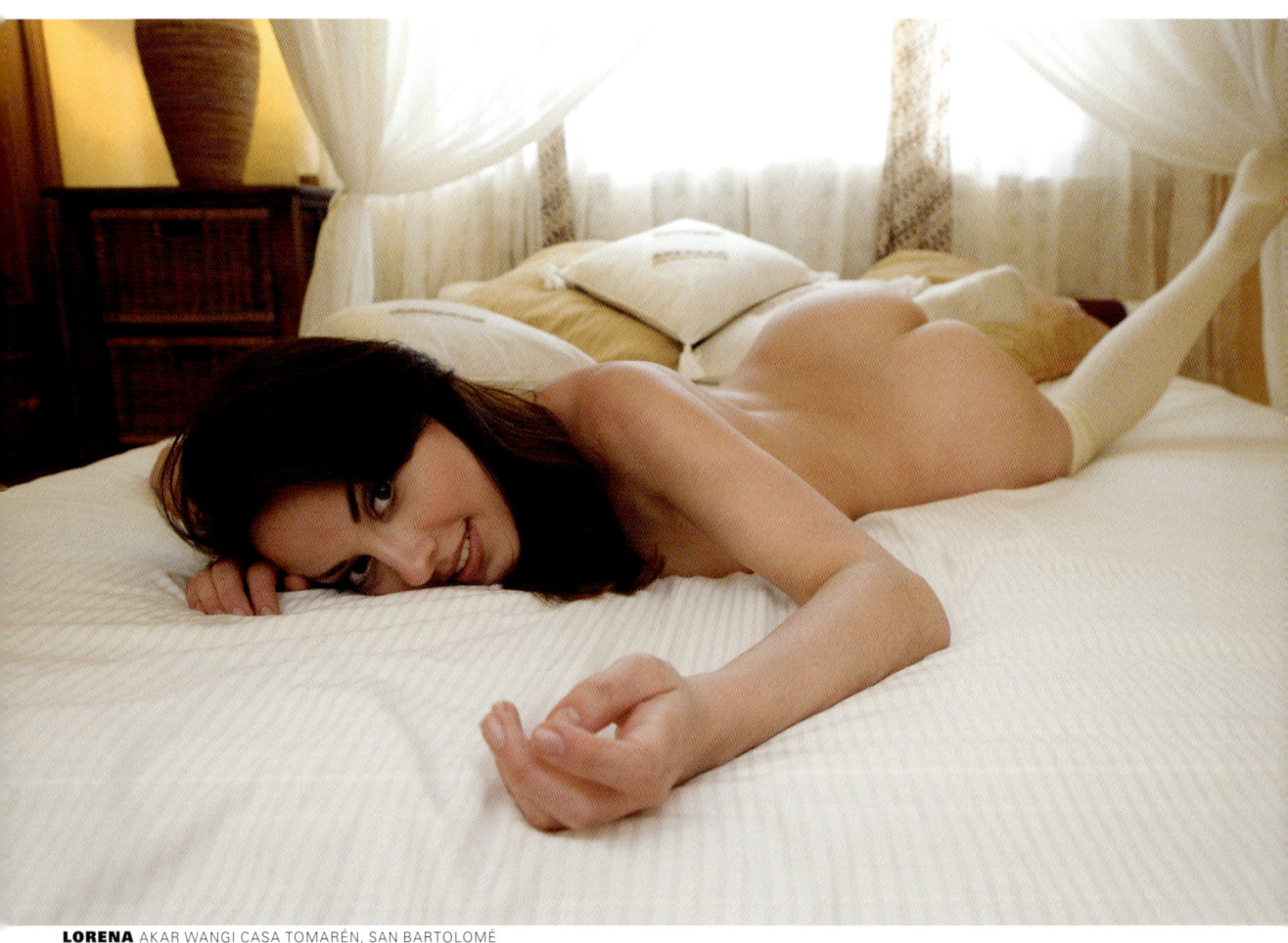

LORENA AKAR WANGI CASA TOMARÉN, SAN BARTOLOMÉ

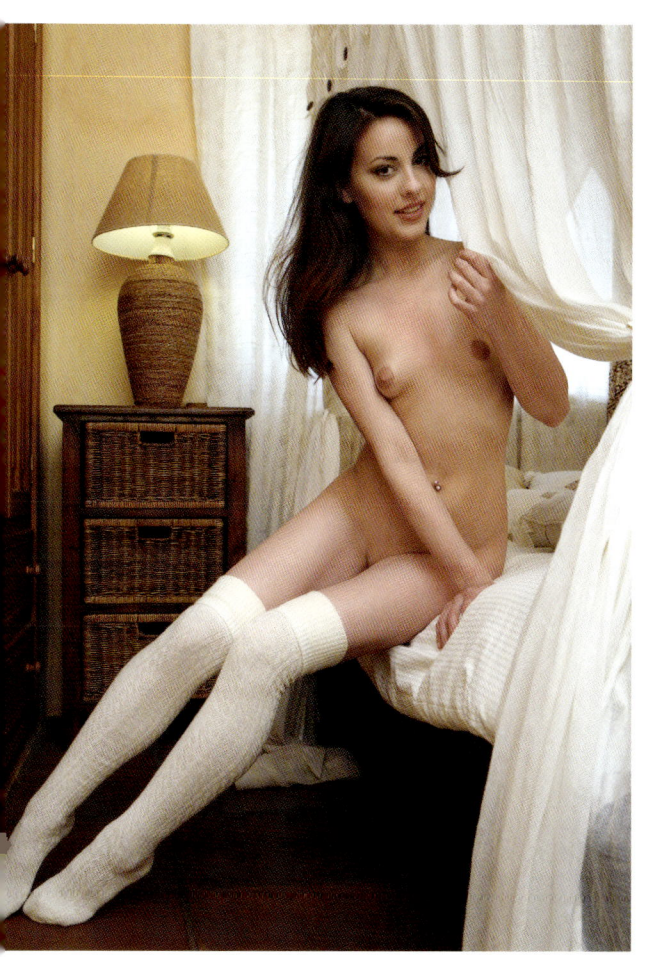
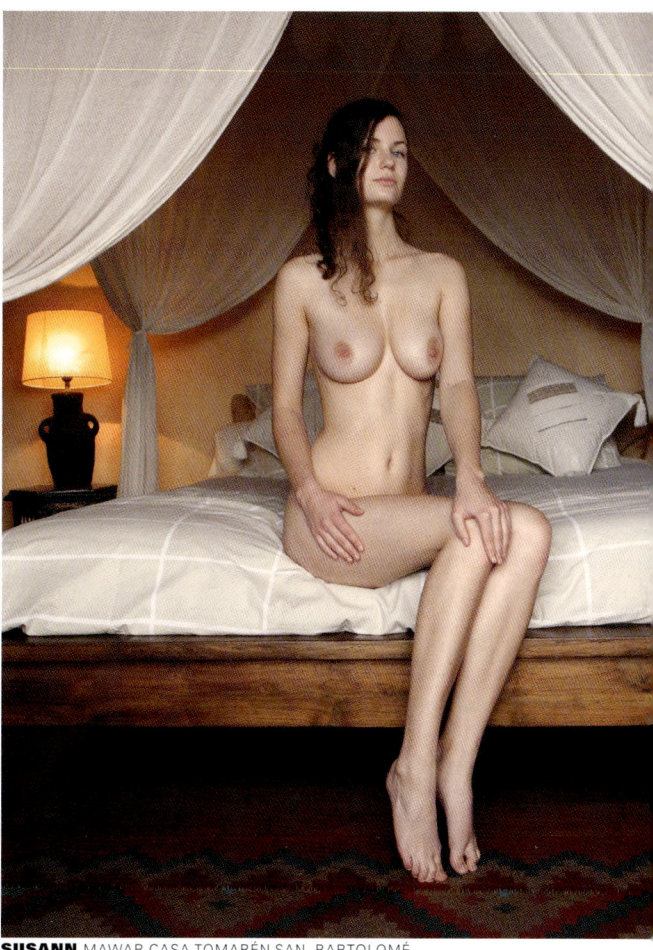

SUSANN MAWAR CASA TOMARÉN SAN, BARTOLOMÉ

179

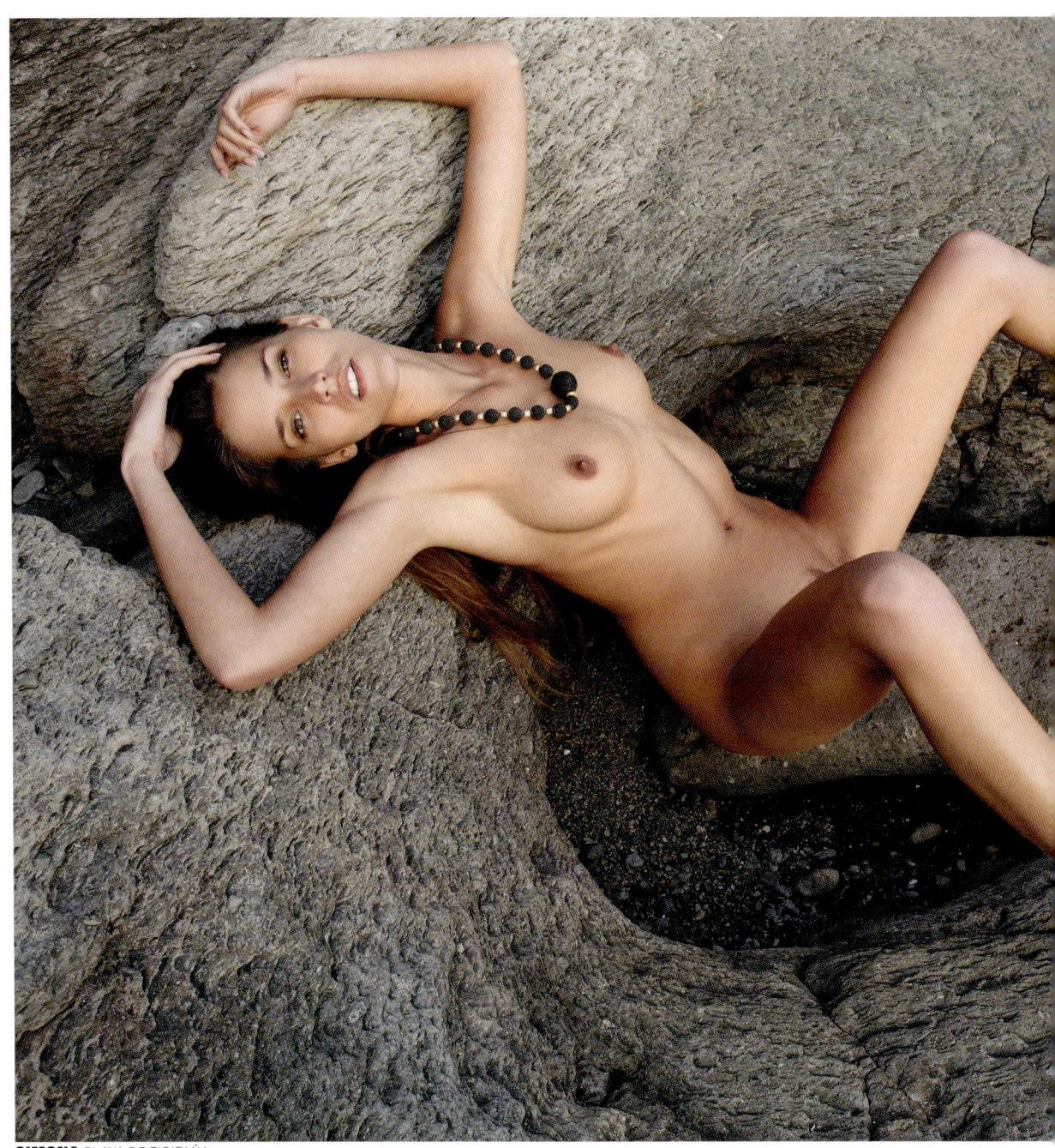

SIMONA PLAYA DE TIRITAÑA

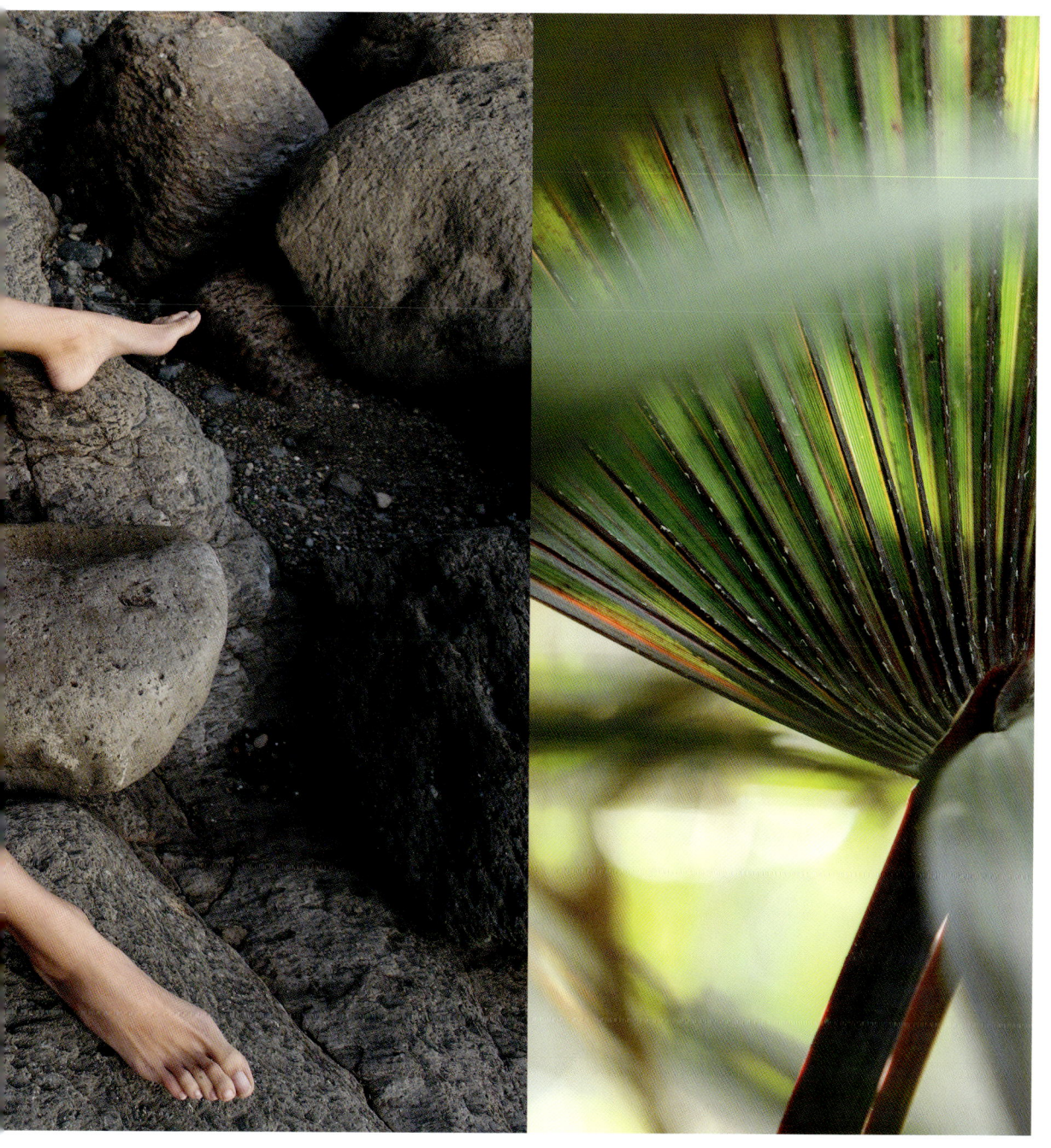

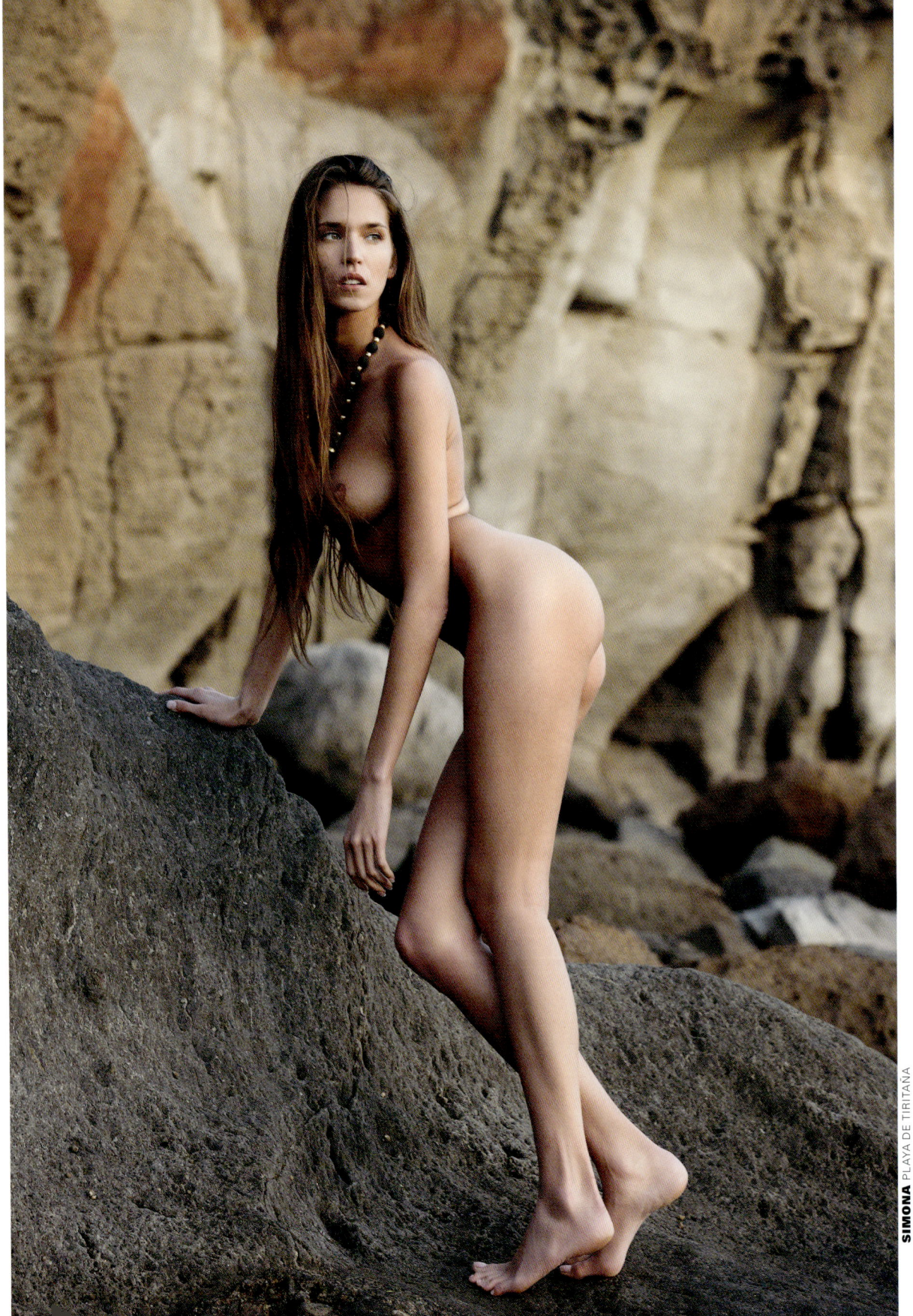

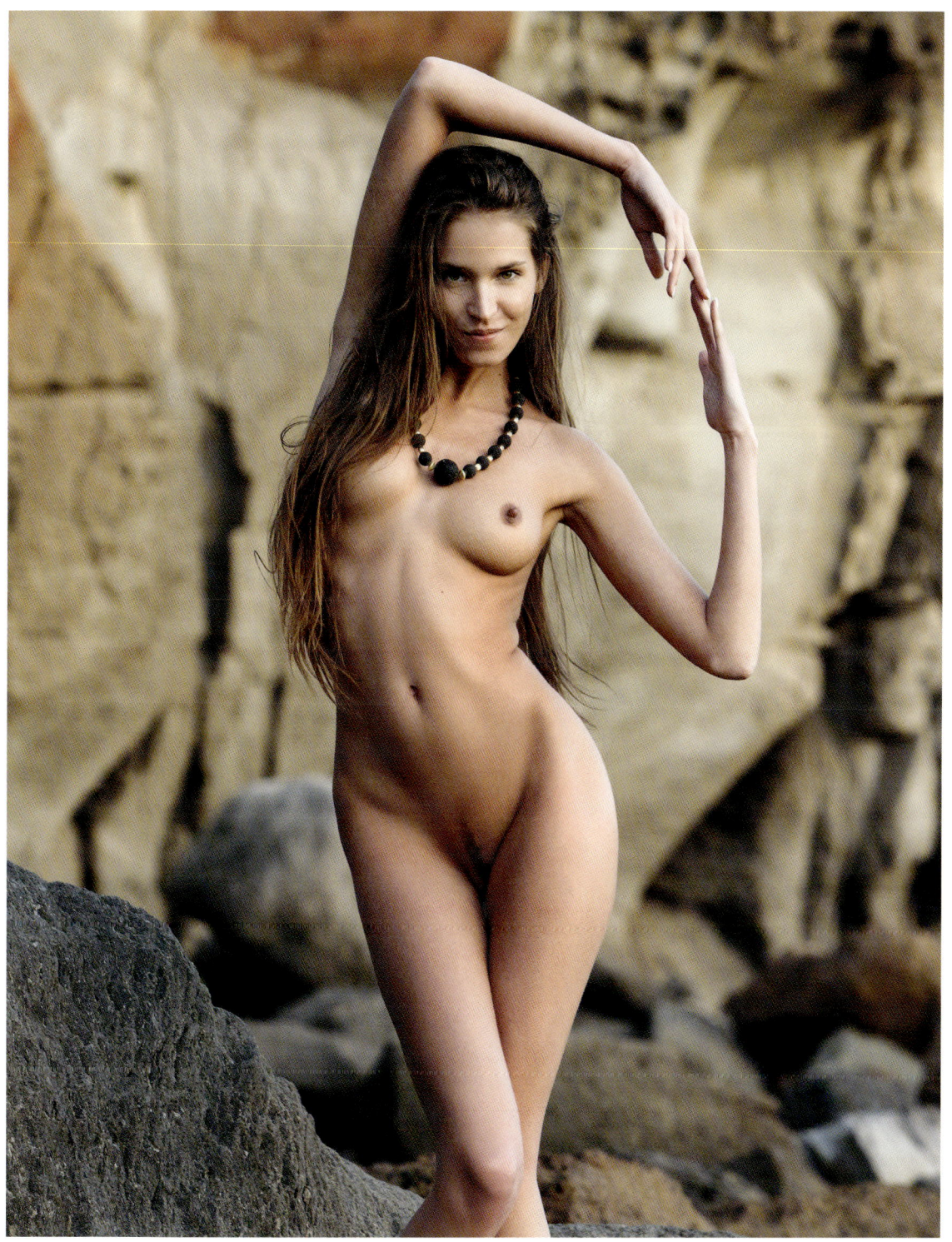

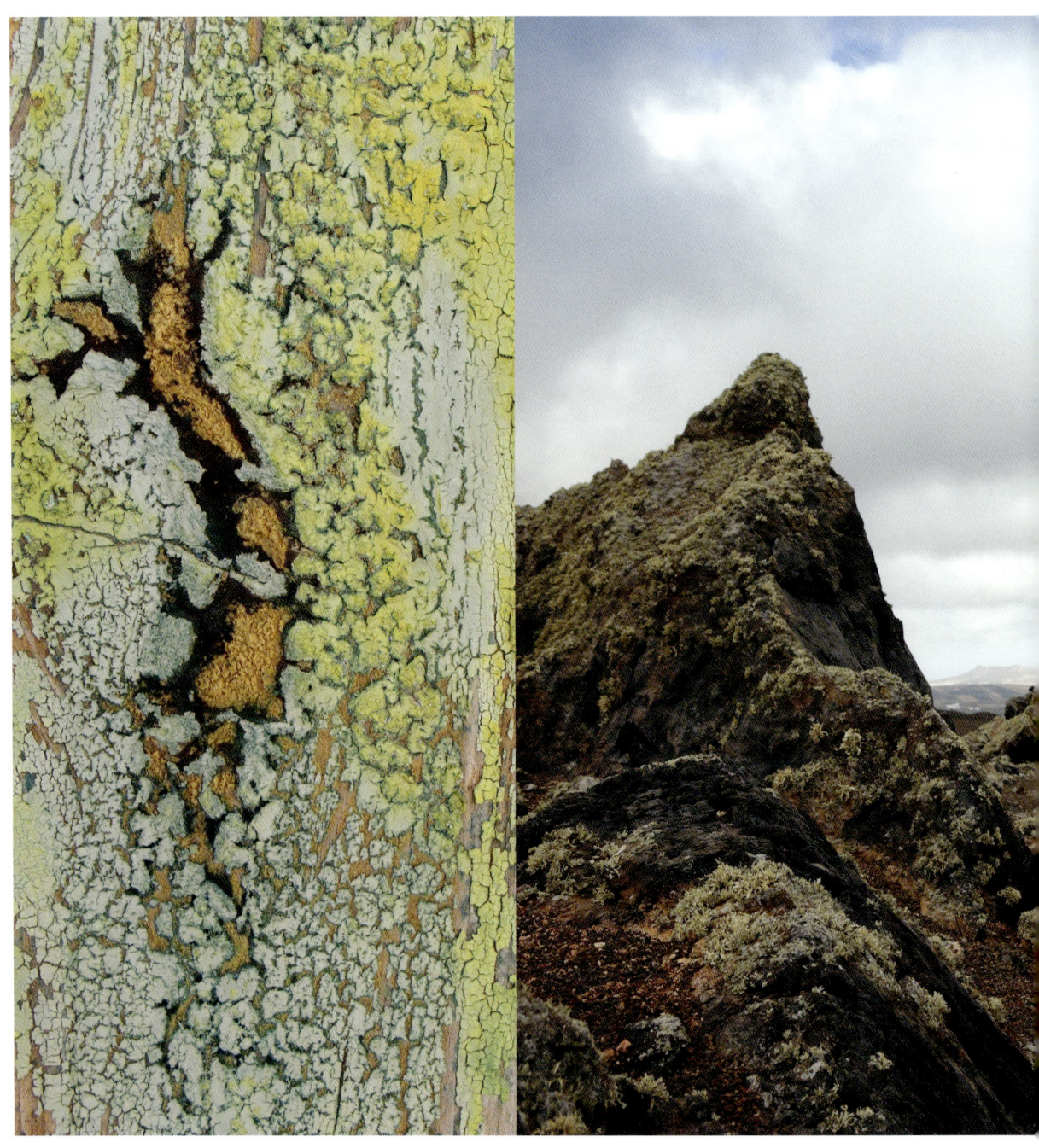

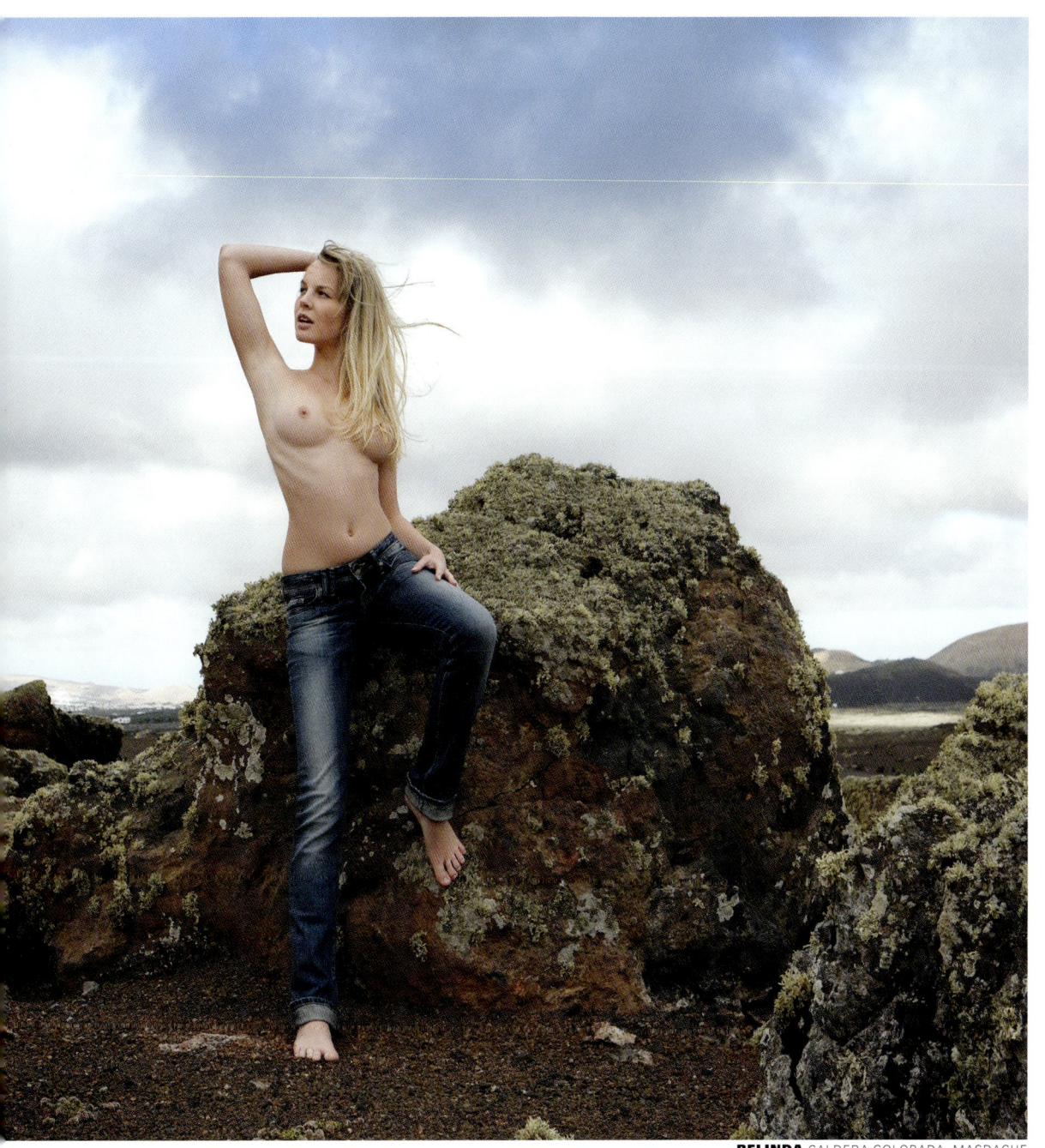

BELINDA CALDERA COLORADA, MASDACHE

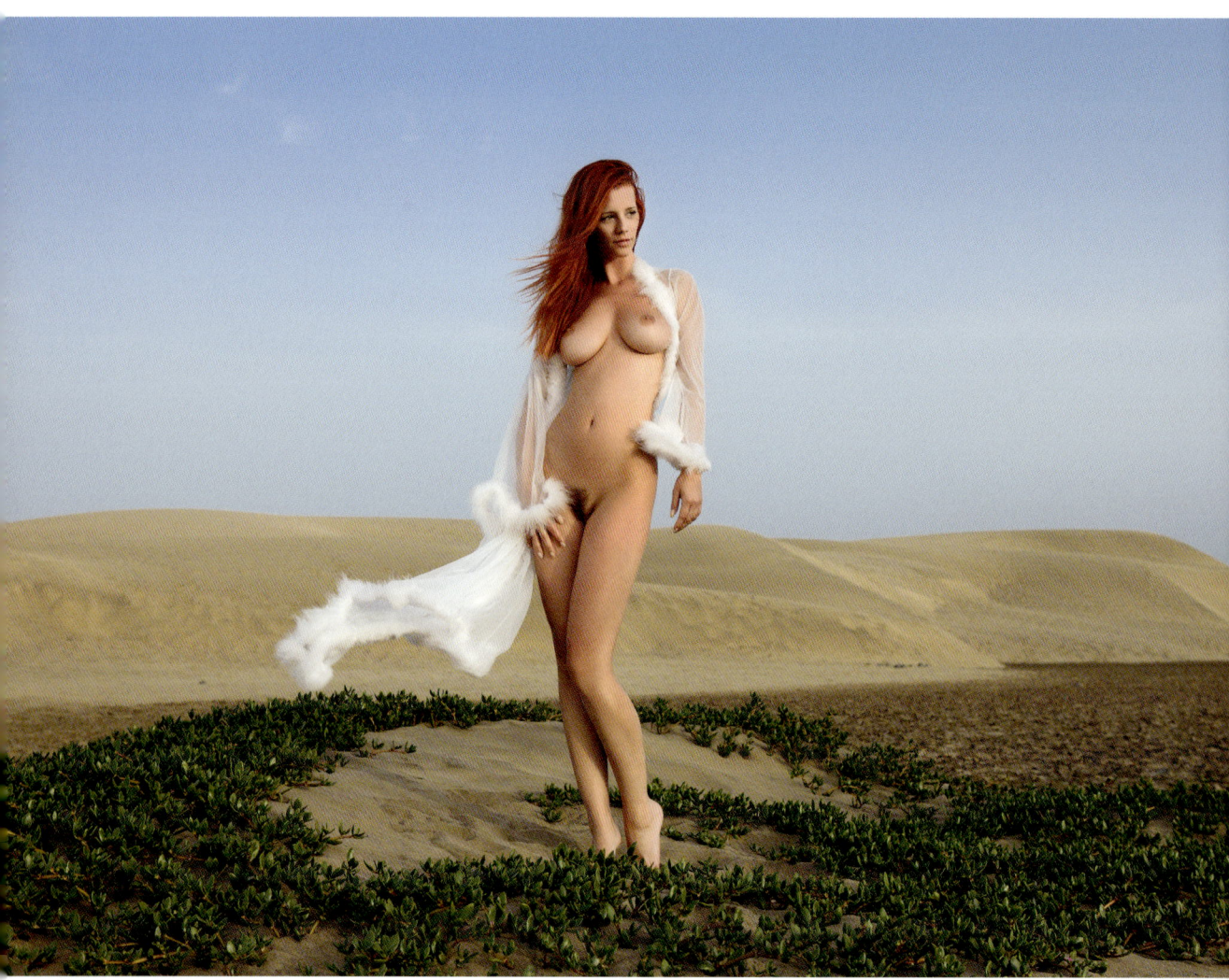

ARIEL DUNAS DE MASPALOMAS

186

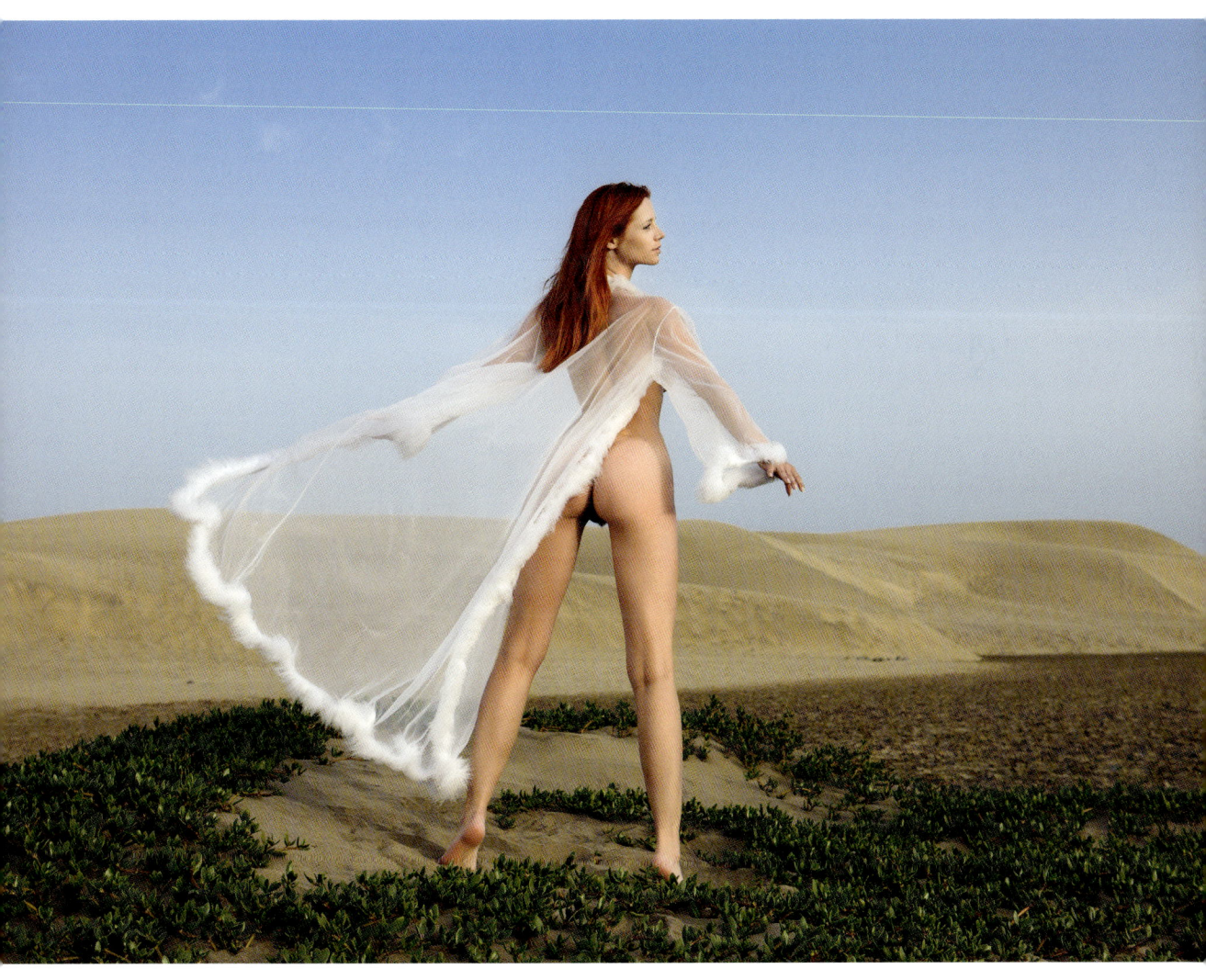

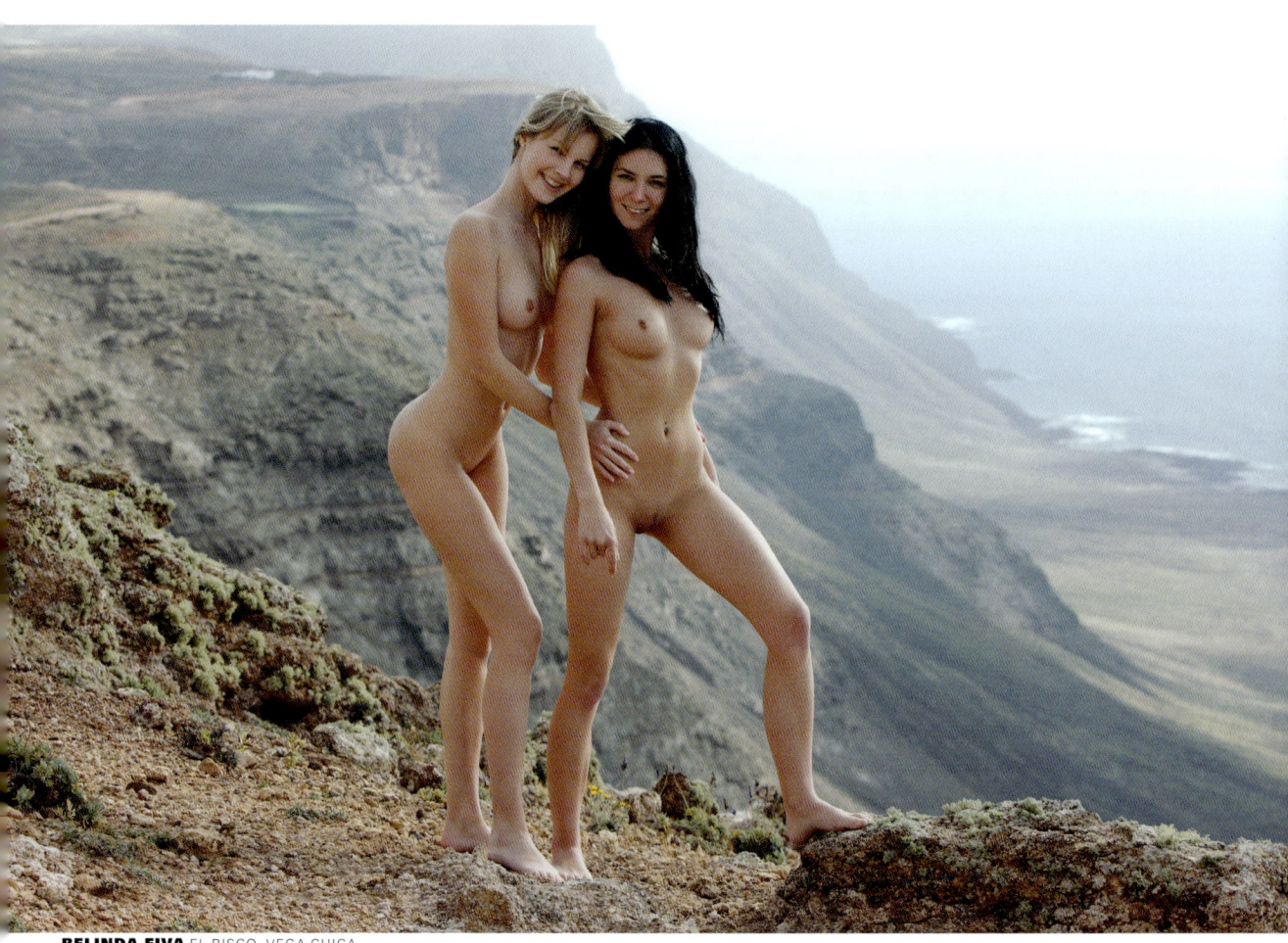

BELINDA FIVA EL RISCO, VEGA CHICA

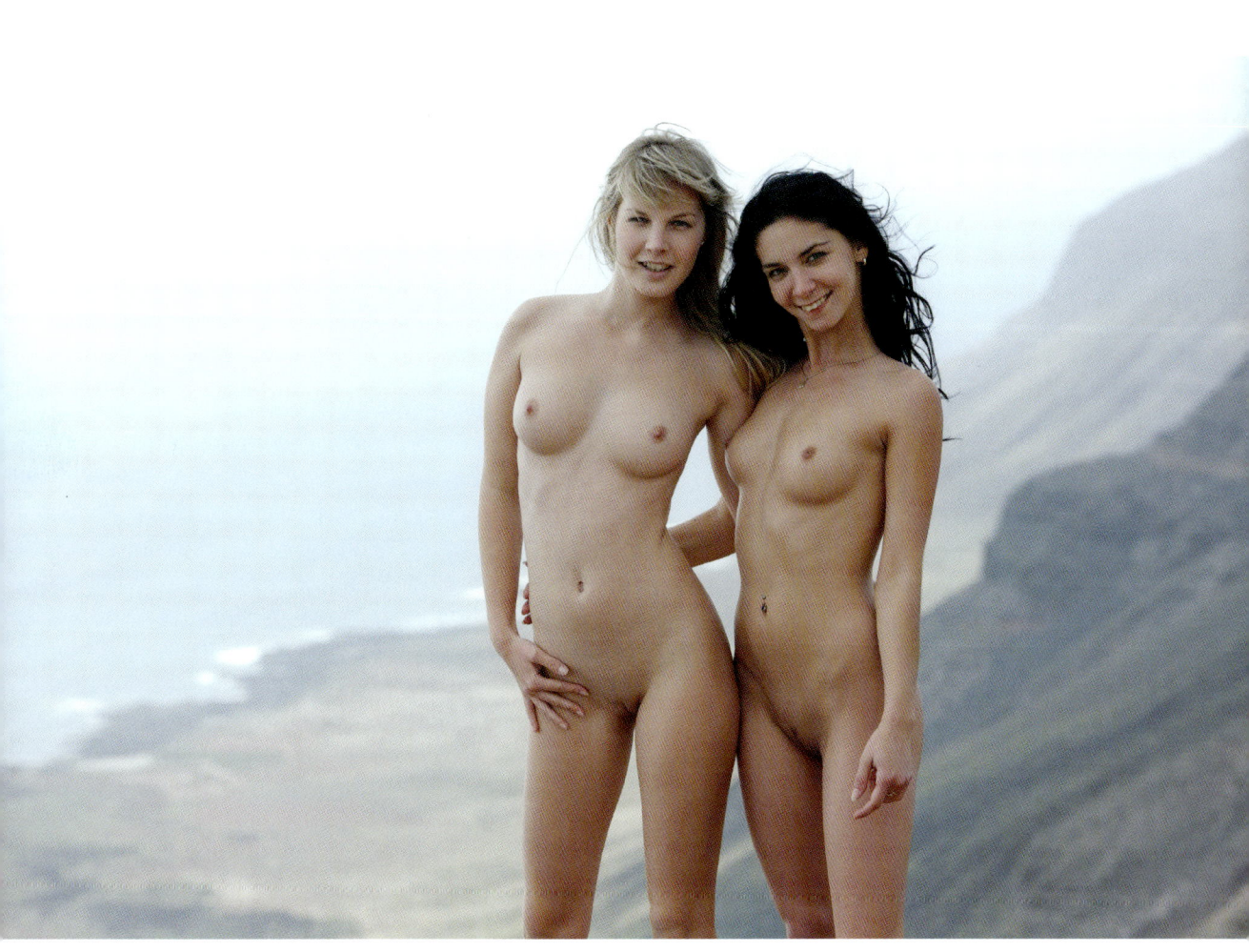

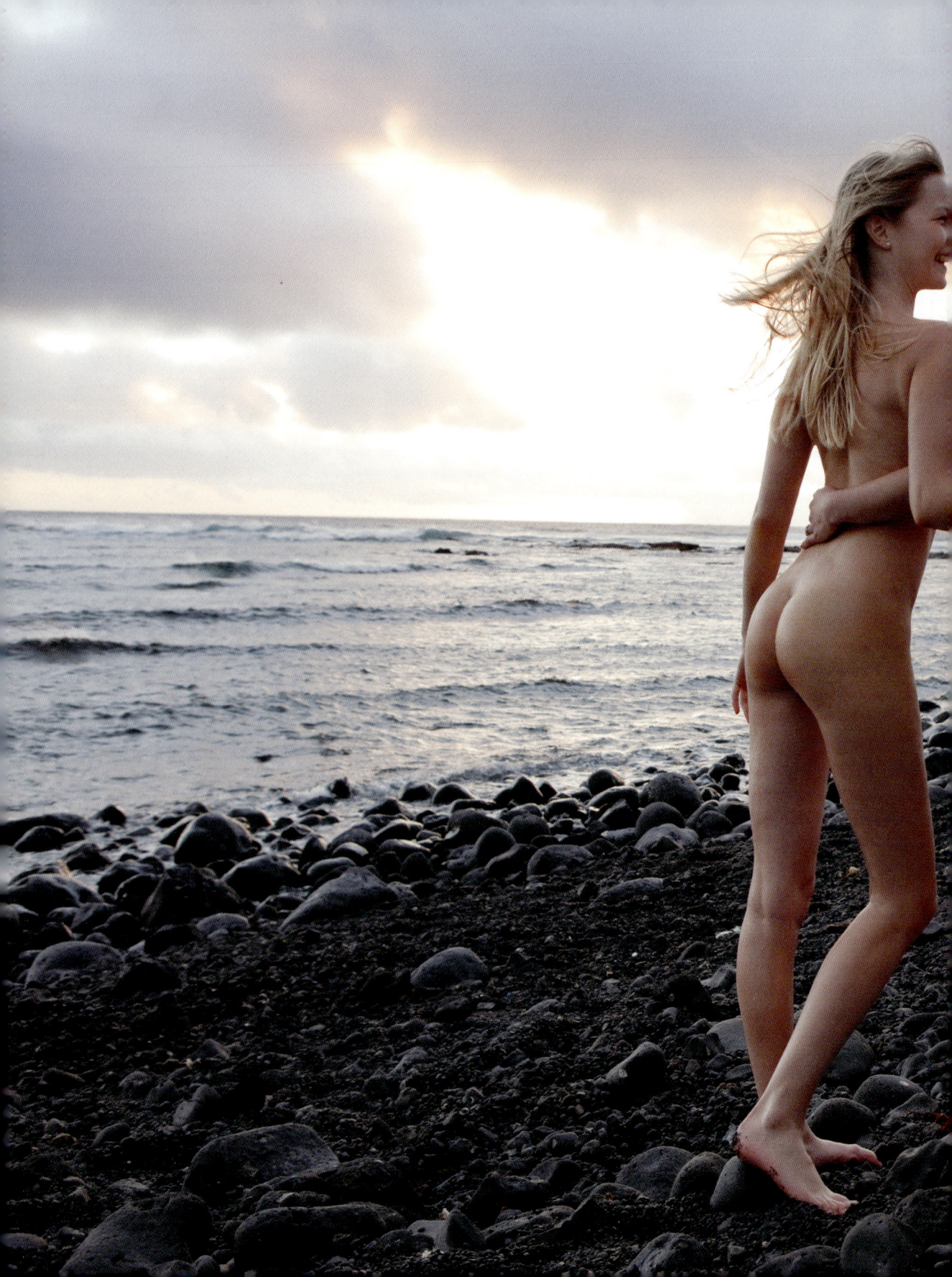